The Dawn of the Cheap Press in Victorian Britain

The Dawn of the Cheap Press in Victorian Britain

The End of the 'Taxes on Knowledge', 1849–1869

Martin Hewitt

Bloomsbury Academic
An imprint of Bloomsbury Publishing Plc

B L O O M S B U R Y
LONDON · NEW DELHI · NEW YORK · SYDNEY

Bloomsbury Academic
An imprint of Bloomsbury Publishing Plc

50 Bedford Square
London
WC1B 3DP
UK

1385 Broadway
New York
NY 10018
USA

www.bloomsbury.com

BLOOMSBURY and the Diana logo are trademarks of Bloomsbury Publishing Plc

First published 2014
Paperback edition first published 2015

British Library Cataloguing-in-Publication Data
A catalogue record for this book is available from the British Library.

ISBN: HB: 978-1-4725-1154-6
PB: 978-1-4742-4332-2
ePDF: 978-1-4725-1456-1
ePUB: 978-1-4725-1305-2

Library of Congress Cataloging-in-Publication Data
A catalog record for this book is available from the Library of Congress.

Typeset by Newgen Knowledge Works (P) Ltd., Chennai, India
Printed and bound by CPI Group (UK) Ltd, Croydon, CR0 4YY

MIX
Paper from
responsible sources
FSC® C013604

Contents

List of Figures

List of Tables

Acknowledgements

I am immensely grateful for the advice and encouragement I have received from Joanne Shattock, Tony Taylor, Laurel Brake, Robert Hall, Simon Morgan, Rohan McWilliam and many colleagues, librarians and archivists. In particular, the project would have been immeasurably more difficult and the finished work considerably weaker, were it not for the generosity of Professor Tony Howe in making available to me a full electronic file of the transcripts he and his team had prepared of the Cobden correspondence, and for commenting on a draft of the final text. I'm also grateful to Sian Nicholas and the organizers of the 'Perception, Reception: The History of the Media in Society' conference at Aberystwyth University, 4–6 July 2012, and Simon Morgan (Leeds Metropolitan University) for giving me the opportunity to air early versions of material from Chapters 6 and 8.

I have been fortunate to benefit from the support and assistance provided by a number of institutions, libraries and archives. The Humanities and Social Sciences Research Institute at Manchester Metropolitan University provided generous support for much of the early archival research for the project, even though by that time I had already made the decision to move to the University of Huddersfield. The award of a Curran Fellowship from the Research Society for Victorian Periodicals enabled the extension and completion of archival research, including work at the Gladstone Library, the National Library of Scotland and the British Library, and I am indebted to the Fellowship Committee for the faith they placed in the project.

I acknowledge with gratitude the permission of the present Earl of Clarendon to quote from the Clarendon Deposit at the Bodleian Library, Oxford, of the University of Southampton Library to quote from the Palmerston Papers, of the National Trust for permission to quote from the Hughenden manuscripts at the Bodleian Library, of Sir William Gladstone to quote from the Glynne-Gladstone Papers in the Flintshire Record Office, Lord Halifax and the Trustees for permission to quote from the Halifax Papers at the Borthwick Institute for Historical Research, and the permission of News UK to cite material in the Times Archive. I am also grateful to the librarians and archivists at the Flintshire Record Office, the National Library of Scotland, Brotherton Library (University of Leeds), the University of Glasgow, Bodleian Library, University of Oxford, the Northumberland Record Office and Balliol College Archives for responding to requests for copies of material.

Monograph writing is not conducive to normal domestic life, and my thanks above all are to Peter, Thomas and Mary-Clare, for putting up with that most undesirable of family members, an academic with a pressing book deadline.

Abbreviations

APRTOK	Association for the Promotion of the Repeal of the Taxes on Knowledge
BDP	Birmingham Daily Post
BI	Borthwick Institute for Archives, University of York
BL	British Library
BO	Bradford Observer
CM	Caledonian Mercury
Cowen	Cowen Papers, Tyne and Wear Archives Service
CP	Cobden Papers
CpUL	Co-operative Union Library, Hanover House, Manchester
CRO	Chester Record Office
DN	Daily News
GGPGL	Glynne-Gladstone Papers, Gladstone Library, Hawarden
MJRL	Manchester John Rylands Library
MS	Morning Star
NA	National Archives, Kew
NLS	National Library of Scotland
NLW	National Library of Wales
NNLC	National Newspaper League Company
NPPARPD	Newspaper and Periodical Press Association for the Repeal of the Paper Duty
NPSA	National Public Schools Association
NSAC	Newspaper Stamp Abolition Committee
PalPUS	Palmerston Papers, University of Southampton
PFP	Potteries Free Press
TNA	Times Newspapers Limited Archive, News UK and Ireland Limited
TWAS	Tyne and Wear Archives Service, Newcastle
UCL	University College London, Special Collections
WDP	Western Daily Press
WilsonPMA	George Wilson Papers, Manchester Central Library Archives
WSRO	West Sussex Record Office

Prologue: William Woods Mitchell and the *West Sussex Gazette*

In June 1853, William Woods Mitchell, son of a jobbing printer in the small country town of Arundel in West Sussex, launched a monthly penny newspaper, *Mitchell's Monthly Gazette* (which quickly became the *West Sussex Advertiser*, and then from January 1855 the *West Sussex Gazette*). The *Monthly Gazette* was a small advertising sheet produced on a rudimentary hand press capable of printing 200 copies an hour (one side at a time), carrying some local news, the reporting, editing and printing all being undertaken by Mitchell himself. It was the first local paper in the whole of West Sussex, although the district had a population of 140,000, and it was an immediate success. Distributed by a network of agents and hawkers around the small agricultural villages and hamlets of the county, many of which it was said were receiving a supply of newspapers for the first time, it quickly established a thinly scattered but extensive readership not just among the rural elite, but also among farmers and farm labourers. Encouraged by the obvious demand for the paper, by October Mitchell had launched a second title, the *South Coast Journal*, with a separate subscriber list, which appeared in the middle of each month, in effect creating a fortnightly newspaper.

It wasn't long before Mitchell's enterprise came to the attention of Joseph Timm, Solicitor to the Inland Revenue at Somerset House on the Strand. The Inland Revenue administered a range of statutes dating back to the early eighteenth century which regulated the publication of newspapers in Britain, and which were known popularly as the 'taxes on knowledge'. Although one of these, the duty on newspaper advertisements, had been repealed the previous Spring, an event which had no doubt done much to spur Mitchell into action, the surviving legislation required, in brief, that all newspapers published more frequently than at monthly intervals were printed on paper on which a penny duty ('the stamp') had been paid, that publishers register their papers and enter bonds to guarantee against their publishing sedition and libels, and that in order to guard against attempts to circumvent legislation about monthly publication, monthly periodicals could only be issued during the few days around the start of each calendar month.

Mitchell had been careful from the outset to abide by these constraints. He had, not without gritting his teeth at the inconsistency of the law, abandoned plans for a weekly *Railway Guide and Market Prices*, and in order to send a few of his papers stamped through the post had complied with the registration provisions, although there was 'nothing . . . more humiliating and disagreeable'.[1] He had carefully reassured himself that a monthly paper, even if it carried news, was not liable to the stamp. He was therefore astonished when, at the end of October 1853, Timm informed him that the Inland Revenue was taking legal proceedings against him for breaking the law which prevented mid-monthly publication, and intended to fine him a 'mitigated penalty' of £5.[2] Mitchell protested, noting that his two papers were quite distinct, that he had kept the Revenue informed of his plans throughout, and also that 'I had hoped that these little sheets would not have been recognized as newspapers, liable, under any circumstance of publication, to stamp duties . . . They contained no political articles or other elaborate reports, &c., which dignify a newspaper'. He also pointed out that given the exemption that was at that point being granted to several successful weekly papers, including the literary weekly *The Athenaeum*, it was doubly unreasonable for the Revenue to proceed against him. Timm, however, was implacable, and faced with the full penalties of the law, Mitchell submitted, and from mid-November 1853 issued his fortnightly papers stamped for 2d.

The effect was catastrophic. As many novice newspaper proprietors had found previously, the increased cost, although apparently insignificant, in practice dissuaded most potential purchasers. Sales of the paper collapsed: in one group of four villages with just over 1,000 inhabitants where he had previously sold 40 copies, the sale dropped immediately to 3. Fired with his sense of the injustice of the situation, Mitchell lost no time in communicating his experiences to Richard Cobden, who as well being a prominent radical MP, and one of the leading figures in the campaigns against the taxes on knowledge, was also a native of West Sussex, and had recently returned to live at Midhurst, a few miles from Arundel.[3] Cobden shared Mitchell's outrage; but he also recognized the powerful propaganda offered by his experiences. Pressing Mitchell for 'any similar proofs of the direct way in which the penny stamp operates to prevent the diffusion of knowledge among the poor', he reassured him that 'So long as I continue in public life I will never cease to agitate for the removal of this stamp, & so far as Mr Bright, & myself, & a few others are concerned, we will make the refusal to repeal it a *causus belli* with any & every government'.[4] He circulated Bright and Collet alerting them to the case: 'The whole rank and file of his readers in some villages were swept away by this shot from the Inland Revenue Office'.[5]

Encouraged by Cobden and his radical ally John Bright, Mitchell threw himself into the campaign against the taxes on knowledge. He kept up a regular correspondence with Cobden, and participated in deputations and meetings. Most significantly, he printed the details of his case as *The Newspaper Stamp and Its Anomalies Practically Considered: A Letter Addressed to the Rt Hon. the Chancellor of the Exchequer* (1854), which he circulated not just to William Gladstone, the Chancellor of the Exchequer, and other leading politicians from both sides of the House, but also to prominent newspaper editors and proprietors.[6] His indignation and frustration at the irrationality of a regime which appeared at odds with so much of the professed aspirations of the ruling elites of whatever faction, shone through his summary of his experiences. 'Had the press been free, and you had asked me how to stop the growing intelligence of the people, I could not have devised a more ingenious plan than to have the red tax of one penny upon it.'[7] He pointed out the inconsistency of stamping socially improving news, but allowing lewd penny dreadfuls to circulate unstamped, and the heavy burden of the 1d on a cheap paper which amounted to a 100 per cent tax. He warned that it was futile to expect the established newspaper proprietors who 'enjoy[ed] a snug unopposed monopoly' to campaign against the stamp: they will 'not zealously ask for repeal any more than the farmers asked for free trade in corn.'[8]

Mitchell's pamphlet hit home. Gladstone and Edward Stanley, son of the Conservative leader Lord Derby, conceded the force of his arguments, while noting the fiscal pressures which might delay an early removal.[9] Several thousands were printed by the Association for Promoting the Repeal of the Taxes on Knowledge (APRTOK) and Mitchell's experiences were taken up by the leaders of the Association. In May 1854 Bright made considerable capital out of his experiences in a long speech to the Commons on the necessity of reform of the stamp legislation.[10] True to Mitchell's warnings, W. E. Baxter, the proprietor of the *Sussex Express*, whom Mitchell had attacked publicly for his refusal to publish an advertisement for the *Gazette*, attempted to undermine his claims in *A Letter to Lord Stanley by "A Country Newspaper Proprietor"*, only to be demolished by a second pamphlet: 'When ... men are obliged to descend to such mean unprincipled deception to make good their case', Mitchell wrote, 'it shows how clearly bad, how rotten, and how utterly devoid of argument to be supported by facts, is the case they advocate.'[11]

Despite the opposition he met from other local newspaper proprietors, and the difficulty of selling at 2d, Mitchell's paper struggled forward. Under the compulsory stamp, the paper was, even allowing for those which would in any case have been sent by post, paying a tax of £2.14.6, per 1,000 copies.[12] Recognizing the vital importance of advertising revenue for the profitability of a mid-Victorian paper, Mitchell ensured the support of local advertisers by guaranteeing a distribution (initially of at least a 1,000, but soon of 3,000–4,000), which he achieved by gratuitous distribution, to different addresses each issue.[13] Having started as an eight-page octavo sheet (10½ × 6 inches), in March 1854 Mitchell was able to convert the *Advertiser* into a weekly, and progressively enlarge its size. The stamp continued, however, to severely restrict the paper's sales, keeping the loss from the purchase price alone at several pounds per issue. In a letter to George Cornewall Lewis around this time, Mitchell noted that on a circulation of 5,500, paper costs were £11.7.8d stamping a further £22.17.4, leaving him a surplus of 2½ d on every 16 copies. Indeed, in the Spring of 1855, with encouragement from C. D. Collet, the secretary of APRTOK, Mitchell was again considering a scheme to evade the tax by publishing four papers with different titles (e.g. the *Arundel Monthly Advertiser*, the *Arundel Monthly Times*, the *Arundel Monthly Chronicle*).[14]

The repeal of the stamp duty in August 1855 finally released the most important shackle on the *Gazette*. By 1856 its circulation had already increased to a weekly average of 4,419, and thereafter increased steadily, extending widely across an area from Brighton and Lewes in the east to Portsmouth to the west.[15] Mitchell sustained a lively radicalism which continued to impress Cobden.[16] He told a correspondent in 1858, with some slight exaggeration, that in 'West Sussex returning 8 members of parliament, not a newspaper was published previously to the repeal of the Compulsory stamp – Now [January 1858], we have a penny newspaper (West Sussex Gazette) circulating 8,200 copies and penetrating into every village of the district.'[17] By 1861, the year when the paper duty, the last of the 'taxes on knowledge' was removed, circulation had reached a weekly average of 14,370, and by 1869 this had increased to just under 24,000.[18] At this point, it was calculated that had the stamp and paper duty still been in force they would have produced a tax burden on this circulation of £7,977 per annum. The paper was printed by two powerful steam-driven 'two-feeder' presses in large premises in the centre of Arundel.

The success of the *Gazette* made Mitchell an important figure in Arundel. By 1869 he had already served twice as mayor, and by the time of his death in 1880 he had been elected 6 times. He was a magistrate and a paternalistic employer, whose offices included a reading room and library, and a large recreation room for his employees, fitted with a stage for amateur plays performed entirely by the paper's staff. The *Gazette* continued to advocate advanced Cobdenite Liberalism, providing, for example, a platform for local advocacy of the land tenure reforms championed by Cobden and Bright in the mid-1860s.[19] Size and circulation apart, there was not a great deal to distinguish the *Gazette* of 1870 from the *Advertiser* of 1853: the 'Our Weekly Gossip' column, with its general commentary on local affairs 'in a lively and easy manner' reflected the journalistic changes beginning to be noticeable by this point, but otherwise, as a contemporary account noted, 'The entire paper is conducted on the *multum in parvo* principle, the various items of news are packed in the smallest possible compass, so as to give space for all events, however apparently trifling . . . [and] reporters and correspondents are stationed wherever needed. In fact, the paper is a model of completeness in every respect.' By 1880 the paper was selling as many as 40,000 copies weekly, making it the largest weekly in the country published in a town of fewer than 200,000 inhabitants, as well as generating a profit of between £4,000 and £5,000 a year.[20]

In 1872 Mitchell indulged himself by writing to some of his old fellow-campaigners and others detailing the transformation of the press he had himself experienced. John Bright was happy to join in celebrating their joint achievements. 'I think the great revolution of opinion on many public questions which is now being witnessed in this country', he responded, 'is owing mainly to the freedom of the newspaper press. It is silently working a change of the most important and, I hope, of a most beneficial character . . . All that we foretold in our agitation for a free Press has come to pass.'[21] Even erstwhile opponents were moved to acknowledge that they had been proved wrong. 'I did not anticipate such a result', confessed the newsagent W. H. Smith, 'but as the cheaper Press before the abolition of the Stamp was more or less discreditable, I entertained some little fear that we should be flooded with immoral and seditious publications. I was wrong, and there can be no doubt that the tone of the Press generally is very much higher now that it was some twenty years ago.'[22] By this point Mitchell had become a symbol of the transformation of the press in mid-Victorian Britain. As the *Printers' Register* proclaimed in March 1870 'When the history of the Penny Press is written, there are few names that will stand out more honourably for indomitable energy and steady perseverance, than that of the proprietor of the *West Sussex Gazette* – WILLIAM WOODS MITCHELL.'

This volume is a contribution to that history. Other names are more prominent, but Mitchell's story effectively encapsulates its main contours. The following pages seek to offer a study of the mid-Victorian campaigns against the taxes on knowledge, and the impact of their repeal on the history of the British press.

1

Setting the Scene

The repeal of taxes on knowledge marked an important moment in the history of the press in Britain. Lucy Brown has described the removal of the stamp duty in 1855 as one of the 'few . . . turning-points around which a chronological history [of newspapers] can be shaped'.[1] Joel Wiener, seizing on the slightly later repeal of the paper duty has similarly described its removal as 'a landmark in the history of journalism, comparable, in its effects, to the termination of press censorship in 1695'.[2] Historians of the political press, the religious press and of the press in Wales, Scotland and Ireland have highlighted the transformative effects of their removal.[3] From a broader perspective, historians of mid-Victorian labour and politics have seen the final removal of the taxes on newspapers as 'amongst the most important legislative initiatives' of Britain's political stabilization in the 1850s.[4]

Yet for all this, the arguments, the campaigns and the consequences of repeal in the 1850s and early 1860s remain largely invisible, even though they were one of the relatively few triumphs of Victorian extra-parliamentary pressure. In the press histories of the later nineteenth century, the campaigns were largely passed over in silence. Modern histories have scarcely done better.[5] The repeal of the taxes appears marginal to studies of the Manchester school,[6] can barely claim a mention in the standard histories of Victorian pressure from without,[7] and even in studies of radicalism or popular liberalism in the mid-Victorian years the subject is given short shrift.[8] Only in the history of secularist radicalism has its history been given any great attention.[9] Where historians have been moved to an assessment, they have tended to be dismissive. For Patricia Hollis, in comparison to the struggles of the 1830s, the later agitation was merely 'one of those many causes, like temperance, foreign refugees, the health of towns, the ballot, corn laws, and land reform which co-opted working men under liberal banners'.[10] For Miles Taylor, perhaps the most perceptive of more recent commentators, the APRTOK was a slightly stranded compromise between old chartists wanting to see the agitation as 'a gladiatorial battle between a censorious state and a virtuous people' and financial reformers who saw it as 'a more pragmatic issue of fiscal administration'.[11]

Inattention has encouraged imprecision and error. The basic chronology of the repeal is frequently truncated or telescoped. The critical legislation is misattributed. Distinctions between the various campaigning groups involved are often ignored, frequently making identification impossible. Indeed APRTOK, the central body in the mid-century campaigns against the taxes, must have strong claim to be the most variously misnamed association in Victorian Britain, being rendered in more than a dozen alternative ways by contemporaries and later accounts. Even the Association's own officers were guilty.[12] Such sloppiness would be less significant were it not that APRTOK was only one of several societies and groups which campaigned against the taxes, and the imprecision can make it difficult to distinguish one from another. In 1861 the APRTOK *Gazette* had to correct a Mr Hennessey (MP) who had sought to claim status as vice-president of the Association while suggesting that its inability to raise funds demonstrated lack of popular support for it, by pointing out that APRTOK did not have vice-presidents, and suggesting he was probably a member of the Newspaper Society Committee, some of the debts of whose Birmingham branch he had tried to pass off as APRTOK's.[13] So when the recent *Dictionary of Nineteenth Century Journalism* (2009), references the 'Association for the Repeal of the Stamp Tax', it is impossible to tell whether it means APRTOK, the Newspaper Stamp Abolition Committee, the London Committee for Obtaining the Repeal of the Duty on Advertisements, which after 1853 was reconstituted as the 'Newspaper Press Association for Obtaining the Repeal of the Paper Duty', the (distinct) Association for the Abolition of the Duty on Paper (AADP), or another hitherto unidentified body to be added to the list.[14]

Perhaps in part because of these confusions, accounts of the final repeal of the taxes on knowledge have tended to follow closely an interpretation propagated most clearly in the writings of media historian James Curran. In a number of more or less self-referential texts, stretching back at least as far as 1978,[15] Curran has presented the campaigns as designed to extend capitalist control of the newspaper industry and promote the effective socialization of the working classes. 'The driving force behind the campaign was a group of liberal industrialist MPs who saw in the repeal of press taxation a means of propagating the principles of free trade and competitive capitalism', encouraging the provincial press and undermining the *Times*.[16] Curran acknowledges that 'the campaign against press taxes was conducted with remarkable skill and tenacity', but he presents the movement as essentially a front for the free trade capitalism of the Manchester Radicals.[17] For him, although the 'posturing as a working-class organisation was never entirely shed', 'unlike the repeal lobby of the 1830s, [APRTOK's] links with the radical working class movement were tenuous'.[18] Curran suggests that the reform campaign conflated ideals of freedom and social control, truth and indoctrination, and operated in a mental framework of a 'tacit model of society which admitted no conflict of class interest, only a conflict between ignorance and enlightenment and between the individual and the state'.[19]

Curran's work has been enormously influential and widely cited, but it is not entirely satisfactory. Partly this is because it rests on a narrow range of source materials, most particularly the history of the movement published in 1899 by Collet Dobson Collet, secretary of APRTOK, and the parliamentary proceedings by which it was effected. Partly because it too readily interprets at face value the rhetorical performances of the Association's leaders, ignoring the complicated processes of hesitation, negotiation and persuasion which brought the political elites to their support of repeal, and places too much store on the undoubted moderation of the parliamentary leadership at the expense of the more complicated and unruly tendencies of activists, supporters and fellow travellers.

In the absence of detailed historical study it is understandable that historians should have been thrown back to such sources, and in particular to the two-volume *History of the Taxes on Knowledge: their origin and repeal*, written by Collet at the end of his life.[20] Based on a substantial archive of APRTOK's correspondence and publications,[21] Collet's book has become the standard reference. It offers an indispensible account of the campaigns, recording activities not elsewhere visible and gives a full and reasonably unvarnished picture of the relationship between Collet and the Manchester radicals. It does, however, have its limitations. The focus is overwhelmingly on the activities of the close-knit group of campaigners around Collet and Cobden. Little effort is made to detail the wider support for the campaign, or to consider the context of the reform in the political agendas of the movement's leaders. The case against the taxes tends to be taken as axiomatic, and the opposition as entirely petty and self-interested. Most notably, Collet downplays the role played by hostility to the *Times*, a motivation visible in the private correspondence of Cobden and Bright which at least in part supports the argument of the official history of *The Times* that the movement was 'a political move directed by the motive of "stopping" *The Times*'.[22] Aspects of the campaign in which APRTOK itself took little part, most notably the 'Constitutional Defence' agitation of 1860 and 1861 (see Chapter 5) are unduly ignored. And of course, without access to the private papers of members of the mid-Victorian cabinets, Collet was left accounting for the movement's progress almost entirely in terms of the strength of the case against the taxes, rather than the tactical calculations of the politicians.

The reason for the neglect which has left Collet's interpretation so largely unchallenged is obvious enough. The campaigns of the 1850s can appear rather anodyne in comparison with the drama of the 1830s 'war of the unstamped press', when a dramatic resistance was sustained against the 4d newspaper stamp regime then in force.[23] Championed by radical MPs in the late 1820s, this struggle drew strength from the successful pressure for parliamentary reform, and from working-class frustration at the limits of political change that the Reform Act of 1832 provided. Between 1830 and 1836 radicals throughout the country published and circulated unstamped papers sold at 1d or 2d in clear defiance of the law. Most significant was the *Poor Man's Guardian*, published from October 1831, by Henry Hetherington, who at the same time founded the National Union of the Working Classes. The *Poor Man's Guardian* sold across the country and its example encouraged the appearance of several hundred unstamped titles between 1830 and 1836.

These papers offered a direct challenge to state control of the press, which had been tightened in the wake of the 'Peterloo' meeting in 1819. They challenged the political system which supported this regulation, arguing forcibly for the power of the working classes to effect change through combination and confrontation. They presented the conflicts of the 1830s as a struggle of labour against capital, workers against aristocrats, 'millocrats' and 'shopocrats', tapping into powerful cultures of plebeian radicalism to create a genuinely popular campaign of resistance to the state. The 'socialist patina' as Patricia Hollis argues in one of two detailed studies of the movement, might have been thin, but it was nonetheless threatening, and as the law ground into action it was met with political meetings, petitions, subscriptions and letters of protest to the unstamped and stamped papers.

The Whig government determined to suppress the unstamped newspapers. Its printers were tracked down and their presses confiscated. Especially employed runners seized stocks of unstamped papers. Particular efforts were made to block up the supply by prosecuting newspaper sellers. The government's use of informants was at best unscrupulous and in many cases illegal. Hollis notes that between 1830 and 1836 at least 1130 cases of selling unstamped papers were considered by London magistrates, and by 1836 almost 800 people had been imprisoned. Repression only fuelled the campaign. Many vendors went back to prison time and again. Publishers produced dummy parcels over which they wrestled with runners at the front of their premises while the actual papers were smuggled out of the rear. An Association of Working Men to Procure a Cheap and Honest Press was formed, and several hundred pounds was subscribed to the Victim Fund for those imprisoned. By 1836 the combined sale of the *Poor Man's Guardian* and the *Weekly Police Gazette* exceeded that of the *Times*, and the owners of the stamped press started to threaten to evade the stamp duty themselves.

The stamp on pamphlets was repealed in 1834. In June 1836 Thomas Spring Rice, the Chancellor of the Exchequer, introduced a measure to amend the press legislation and bring the challenge of the unstamped papers to an end, confessing in the House of Commons that although he 'had resorted to all means afforded by the existing law . . . it was altogether ineffectual to the purpose of putting an end to the unstamped papers'.[24] The measures proposed were a skilful attempt to appease moderate radicalism but retain and in some respects strengthen controls on the popular press. The newspaper stamp was slashed from 4d to 1d per copy. At the same time, penalties for being in possession of an unstamped paper were increased, the government's powers to confiscate printing presses were strengthened, and the securities required by newspaper proprietors were augmented. The definition of a newspaper was extended so that it could be taken to include tracts and pamphlets produced periodically. Working class radicalism was outraged at the 'Gagging' clauses, but the moderate radicals were unwilling to resist, and radical energies were soon diverted into Chartism.[25]

The taxes on knowledge

The legislation of the 1830s essentially added a further layer of legislation onto the various existing acts for the regulation of the press. The 1836 Stamp Act (6&7 Will IV, c.76), sat on top of the provisions of 60 Geo III c.9, and 1 Will IV c.73. These acts constructed a system of registration and sureties, which required printers of newspapers to enter into recognizances against publication of blasphemous or seditious libel, and against damages for private libels, while increasing securities to £400 in London, Edinburgh and Dublin, and £300 elsewhere. They regulated a system of taxation which comprised in total four 'taxes on knowledge'. The least significant of these was a 10% ad valorem duty on the importation of foreign books. Around mid-century this raised about £8,000 a year, not least because the difficulty of distinguishing between the different categories of books led to extensive evasion.[26] It was almost entirely marginal to the campaigns of the 1850s, treated as 'a mere adjunct to the Paper Duty'.[27] The other three, the advertisement duty, the newspaper stamp and the excise on paper became the focus of the 'taxes on knowledge' campaigns of the period 1849–61.

Revision of the advertising duty anticipated the other adjustments of the 1830s. In 1833 the duty, which had reached 3/6 per advertisement, was reduced to 1s 6d and this was the level at which it was levied throughout the 1830s and 1840s. By 1851 the duty was raising £175,000 annually.[28] Newspaper proprietors provided copies of each issue to the stamp authorities, who then counted the number of advertisements and calculated the duty owed. Attempts to circumvent the duty were tightly controlled. Adverts for groups were charged as if each individual had published their own advertisement: so a dozen bakers issuing a brief announcement that they would not give New Year gratuities to servants could be charged as 12 separate advertisements. Reviews of books could not refer to price without attracting duty.[29] As a result, newspaper proprietors and the Revenue waged a constant war of attrition as to what should and should not be defined as an advertisement, especially from the mid-1840s when attempts to prevent advertising material being passed off as news were enforced with greater vigour.

The duty tended to concentrate the local press into a single dominant title engrossing most of the local advertising, especially in rural districts. In London too, it had been estimated in 1834 that as much as 60% of the capital's advertisements were published in *The Times*.[30] It encouraged substantial weekly publication, rather than smaller more frequent issues, because this retained maximum currency for expensive advertisements. The potential imprecision of the division between news and announcements that might be considered promotional and thus advertisements complicated newspapers' reporting. 'Dozens of paragraphs of common interest have every day to be clipped and pared, lest some circumstance of detail bring them within the sweep of the Act', complained James Greig, proprietor of the *Scottish Press*, in 1853.[31]

The newspaper stamp, like the advertisement duty initially a mere ½d, had by 1815 been raised to 4d per paper, and extended to any periodical publication appearing more frequently than 26 days which contained any 'Public News,

Intelligence or Occurrences, or any Remarks or Observances thereon' (60 Geo III, c.9). There was a statutory limit of 1,530 square inches to the total size of newspapers. If editions exceeded this, as *The Times* often did, then they needed to publish a 'supplement' which attracted its own stamp. The stamp carried with it the privilege of unlimited transmission and retransmission through the post free of additional charge. In 1851 the newspaper stamp was yielding £397,000, more than twice the advertising duty.[32]

Newspapers had to be printed on paper already stamped, and with the exception of *The Times* which acquired the privilege of stamping its own paper, this involved the transmission of paper once bought from manufacturers or agents to one of the stamping offices, after which they would be sent on for printing (Figure 1.1). Paper was stamped on behalf of a specific title and was not supposed to be transferrable between newspapers, although this did no doubt happen, and was one of the reasons why the official statistics of stamps are notoriously unreliable as an indication of circulation. Because the cost of the stamp had to be paid 'up front' in the price of the paper, the stamp greatly increased the working capital required to publish large-circulation papers.[33] This provided some protection against the commencement of new newspapers; the restraint appears at times to have been minimal, but it was enough to offer some prospect of protection to newspaper proprietors.

Figure 1.1 '*Illustrated London News* being delivered to Somerset House for Stamping', *Illustrated London News*, 1842 [Mary Evans Ref 10104613]

The excise duty on paper was by far the most complicated and widely applied of the 'taxes on knowledge', not only because in addition to periodicals, pamphlets and books, it covered a great variety of other paper-based products, but also because of the various customs duties on paper and its raw materials that existed alongside the duty.[34] Although substantial reductions were effected in import duties in 1825, and on the Excise duty in 1837 (to £14 14s per ton, or a little more than 1½d per lb) as part of the response to the war of the unstamped press, significant burdens remained. The duty was increased by a further 5% in 1840. Paper duties amounted to about a fifth of the selling price of most printing papers, although opponents claimed they could be as much as 40% of the price of the cheapest papers.[35] There was some modest further progress under Peel in the 1840s, with the reduction of the paper import duty in 1842 and the freeing of rags, which remained the main raw material for paper, from duties in 1845. Even so in 1851 the paper duty yielded £929,000, or nearly two-thirds of the total amount the 'taxes on knowledge' contributed to the Treasury.[36]

The impact of the excise, because it imposed a series of annoying obligations on the paper manufacturers, was more than just a question of cost. Premises had to be registered before any manufacturing commenced (penalty £200); every machine, vat or press had to be numbered (penalty £20); excise officers had to be admitted on demand at any time (one recollection suggested that it was common for an excise officer to be present at all times);[37] every ream or half ream had to be wrapped and labelled separately (penalty £50); satisfactory scales and weights had to be provided (penalty £100); weighed paper had to be kept separate for six hours after weighing (penalty £50); all paper despatched had to be recorded (penalty £200), and notice given before paper was moved from one part of the mill to another (penalty £50); manufacturers could not open a stationers within 1 mile of their mill (penalty £200).[38]

As a result, the burdens of the excise regime were considerable. Additional staff were required for weighing and reweighing. The heavy cost of duty on spoiled paper forced manufacturers into expensive attempts at reforming. It was hard to process paper (e.g. in respect of the finish) for purchasers; once it was processed and the duty paid, it could not be returned to the mill for further processing.[39] Manufacturers found themselves charged with all sorts of offences, even when it was clear that mistakes had favoured the Excise. It was suggested that the excise inhibited the development of alternative raw materials or products. 'We never seem at liberty to introduce anything new, owing to the superintendence continually of the Excise Officer' remarked one manufacturer.[40] (Notwithstanding, the 1850s were marked by various attempted innovations in paper manufacture. In 1853 the Royal Society of Arts was presented with a scheme for manufacture from cane sugar waste and dung from cows who had been fed flax straw, which they were able to macerate into a state fit for use in paper manufacture.[41])

The excise duty appears to have exerted a steady pressure on the paper industry through the early Victorian years. From 1838 to 1856 the number of paper mills in the United Kingdom contracted markedly: from 525 to 393 (a 27% reduction), in the United Kingdom, and even more severely in Ireland, where the reduction was nearer to 50%.[42] Britain was gradually squeezed out of overseas markets. By 1858 substantial sales in Montevideo and Buenos Aires had been superseded by the French and Belgians. Newspaper publishers were also variously inconvenienced. Paper was thoroughly dried out in the production process, so as to minimize the excise charge, and then had to be wetted again before printing, which was said to cost one of the London dailies virtually as much as the burden of the duty itself.[43] Manufacturers who relied on wholesale houses to sell their paper could find themselves at their mercy if pressed for excise payments. Collet suggested in 1853 that the wholesale stationers 'have all the *poor* manufacturers under their control, as the latter, having only six weeks' credit for the duty, are always in want of ready money', and could drive down the price by waiting until the due date before buying.[44] Potential delays in the delivery of stamped paper – which might take almost a week from order to receipt – made it advisable to keep larger stocks on hand to be able to meet incidental demand.

The precise effect the excise regime had on the price of paper is not entirely clear. Newspaper publishers readily complained about price rises. In 1851 John Cassell, a large publisher of popular periodicals, claimed inflationary pressure on the price of paper was caused in part by the paper duty.[45] Ironically the spike of new periodicals stimulated by the repeal of the advertising duty in 1853 put further pressure on the price of paper.[46] In 1854 an 'extreme and most embarrassing scarcity of paper' was reported.[47] Particularly for publishers of cheap books and serials, the price of paper accounted for a high proportion of the costs. Fyfe notes that in the first quarter of 1850 the Religious Tract Society's printing bill was just over £3,000, but in the same period it paid almost £5,500 for paper to its principal supplier.[48] In 1854 the Scottish publisher Robert Chambers remarked to Alexander Ireland, proprietor of the *Manchester Examiner and Times* that 'the increase of the price of paper was 'as much as £750 a year out of our profits – a sad contrast to our hope of getting the duty off. This and the doubling of income tax make me groan a good deal.'[49] At the same time, records for the *Glasgow Herald* show it paid 8½d per lb in 1845, with a modest decrease to 7d in 1855 and 6½d in 1860.[50]

After 1836 the paper duty perhaps directly added only a farthing to the cost of a newspaper, although newspaper proprietors tended to render the burden into a total annual cost (£30 pa even for a small local weekly such as the *King's Cross Mirror* in 1860).[51] It was estimated in 1853 that with a weekly circulation of provincial papers of about 330,000 per week, the total burden of the paper duty was around £250 per week. For individual papers the cost was variously rendered as between a quarter and a third of revenue.[52] In 1855 W. and R. Chambers claimed to have used 378,000 lbs of paper, costing £12,780 11s 3d, which included excise duty of £2482 18s.[53] In 1857–8 it cost the Stirling Tract Enterprise £2,000 in paper duty costs on the 130,000 copies of the *British Messenger* it printed and circulated.[54] Taken together the burden of the three taxes was of course magnified. In 1847 the *Liverpool Mercury* calculated its total bill at £5,246.8s.5d,[55] while in 1851 *The Times* paid £66,000 in stamps, at least £17,600 on paper duty, and £24,000 on advertising duty.[56]

The press in the later 1840s

It is not easy to get a clear picture of the evolution of the press under the revised tax regime after 1836. Nineteenth-century histories of the press tended to content themselves with a title by title approach. More recent accounts discuss the politics of the press, but generally sidestep any direct consideration of the evolution of the newspaper industry itself. Even so, while much work remains to be done, certain aspects of this history are clear enough.

As regards the metropolitan press, the regime encouraged the dominance of the *Times* over the other London dailies. Between 1837 and 1851, while the circulation of the *Times* increased from just over 3M to nearly 12M, the combined circulation of the other 12 metropolitan dailies declined from 10.2M to 8.7M.[57] Over these years sales of the *Morning Chronicle* fell by half, and the *Standard* by nearly two-thirds. By the mid-50s the sale of the evening *Standard* had fallen as low as 700 copies a day.[58] In 1846 the *Daily News*, at 3d undercutting the established dailies, sold over 3.5M and briefly threatened to challenge *The Times*, but it was unable to sustain this price and at 5d its circulation was more than halved.

The development of the railway network enabled the London dailies to reach their provincial readers with increasing rapidity, whether by post or by direct carriage which was more and more the preference of *The Times*; by the later 1840s almost all of its provincial sales were being distributed directly via wholesale newsagents and the railway companies. Improved communications also encouraged dynamism in the London weeklies. Apart from the success of the *Illustrated London News*, established in 1842 and selling 60,000 copies a week within a year, and nearly 100,000 by 1851, the 1840s saw the successful establishment of a number of special interest papers, such as *The Builder* (1842) and the *Musical Times* (1844), and a suite of religious weeklies, including the *Nonconformist* (1841) and the *Wesleyan* (1844). Otherwise, the main area of dynamism was in the new working-class Sunday papers. After the brief flourishing of the Chartist *Northern Star*, whose sales touched perhaps 50,000 per week in 1839, its collapse in circulation (to 7,000 per week by 1844),[59] left the field to a number of popular Sunday weeklies, *Lloyd's Weekly News* (1842), the *News of the World* (1843), and *Reynolds's Weekly Newspaper* (1850). Traditionally seen as constructing a readership out of a diet of crime, scandal and sensationalism, these papers offered a less hard-edged and economically sophisticated version of the unstamped press of the 1830s, and were themselves one stage towards the penny fiction periodicals, most notably the *London Journal*, which also gained very large sales in the later 1840s.[60]

The London press continued to be heavily politicized, with papers conducted for ulterior political motives, or sustained by considerable political subsidy. Stephen Koss, and more recently David Brown and Laurence Fenton, have demonstrated the oblique but powerful interconnections of the political elite and the metropolitan newspapers.[61] Editorial direction was amenable to purchase, as in the funding provided by the Anti-Corn Law League for surveys of social conditions in the *Morning Chronicle* in 1849. Even *The Times*, which could stand above such requirements, was heavily embroiled in the informal networks of information and gossip through which the political elite attempted to shape the discussion and dissemination of news. The fine line of appropriate intervention which the political elite walked was illuminated by the difficulties Lord Clarendon got into as Lord-Lieutenant of Ireland in early 1850s over his direct subsidization of the Dublin *World* newspaper.[62]

The Victorian press historians dismissed the pre-1855 provincial press as a paltry affair without scale, editorial influence or originality.[63] It was true that for most papers existence was a hand-to-mouth affair. Traditionally provincial papers had been operated on a shoestring staff, often with an editor or editor-proprietor conducting operations as Mitchell had done almost single-handedly.[64] Describing his time in Plymouth in the mid-1850s Harry Bussey recalled he 'was practically the entire "staff" of the *Mail*, a paper published once a week. Here, in addition to sub-editorial and reporting duties, I had to write reviews of books, long theatrical notices and occasional leaderettes, as well as to read all the proofs.'[65] Only a small number of titles achieved both influence and solvency. The *Manchester Guardian* and the *Leeds Mercury* could both claim circulations of around 9,000 in 1845; and by 1854 it was said the *Guardian* was making an annual profit of £12,000.[66] A larger number of papers reached circulations of 3,000–4,000, some based around the market of other growing provincial centres, such as the *Sheffield Telegraph*, others which served an extensive country region; but in 1850 2,500 could be taken as a representative circulation for a provincial weekly, and in a town the size of Nottingham, 2,000 was an excellent sale.[67] In many cases local competition diluted readership among a number of titles. The stamp returns of 1851 suggested the *Bristol Mercury*'s average weekly circulation was 5,100, and the *Bristol Mirror*'s a further 2,600.[68] Whatever the circulations of individual papers, a town like Leicester could not be said to be bereft of newspapers, boasting 4 local papers with a combined circulation of 6,000, supplemented by an estimated 6,000 penny magazines, 4,000 religious periodicals, numerous other provincial papers circulating in the town, and the London papers.[69]

At these levels of market penetration, it was difficult for smaller towns to support local papers of their own, and for even larger towns to sustain profitably more than one title. This left many substantial towns without a local press. And it produced a politically unbalanced press. In many new urban centres it proved especially difficult to maintain a Conservative print.[70] For a while in the late 1840s, the *Bolton Chronicle* was the only Conservative title in the whole of the Salford hundred, a broad swathe of south and east Lancashire with a population of over three quarters of a million.[71]

In the larger towns and cities, the press displayed some dynamism. Shades of political difference were often the driver, as in Manchester where the Whig-radical *Guardian* and conservative *Courier* were challenged first by the radical *Times* and when that paper's politics came under suspicion, by the Anti-Corn Law League-aligned *Examiner*. Elsewhere, a good deal of inertia is evident. Outside London, only Glasgow and Dublin were able to sustain a daily paper (*North British Mail, Freeman's Journal, Saunders's Newsletter*). There were no provincial daily papers before 1855. In Belfast, Glasgow and Edinburgh there were a number of twice- and thrice-weekly papers, and a handful of other towns in both Ireland and Scotland had publications which appeared twice weekly.[72] In England only the *Manchester Guardian* appeared more than once a week.

Otherwise, in the larger towns where several titles competed, by occupying different publication days they were able to offer some sort of coverage across the week. Thus the four weekly Birmingham papers in 1847 appeared on Monday, Thursday and Saturday.[73]

Table 1.1 Newspaper prices, 1847

	England	Wales	Scotland	Ireland	Overall
<3d	1%	0%	4%	0%	1%
3d	9%	0%	7%	3%	7%
3½d	1%	12%	3%	0%	1%
4d	10%	25%	12%	18%	12%
4½d	44%	68%	69%	21%	45%
5d	30%	12%	4%	45%	27%
>5d	5%	0%	1%	26%	9%

Source: *Mitchell's Newspaper Directory* (1847).

In England and Wales the norm in the towns of the North and Midlands became 4½d, with 5d remaining widespread in the south, especially for the county papers. Irish papers tended to be on average more expensive, Scottish more concentrated at 4½d (Table 1.1). In the later 1840s a number of new titles attempted to sell at 3d (e.g. the *Fleetwood Chronicle* (1845–), the *Cornwall Weekly Times* (1847–), the *Lincolnshire Advertiser* (1847–50).[74] At Liverpool, fierce competition meant that by 1847 no fewer than four local newspapers were selling at 3d. One, the *Liverpool Journal*, reducing its price to 3d in 1846 to meet the competition of the *Liverpool Weekly News*, was able to triple its circulation to 8,000, and on occasion even more.[75]

This and the parallel experience of the *Daily News* demonstrated the reservoirs of demand for newspapers which the higher price required by the taxes on knowledge generally kept dormant. As historians of the press have long emphasized, the circulation figures for early Victorian newspapers cannot be taken as giving a clear indication of readership. The retransmission privileges afforded by the stamp meant that papers frequently circulated to two or even more separate readers. Although it remained technically illegal, it was common for papers to be hired out by the hour.[76] It is likely that the great bulk of most of the London dailies and a considerable proportion of the weekly press were sold to newsrooms of various sorts, where the middle classes mostly consumed their news, before the papers were then sold on (with purchasers generally buying the right to day-old papers quarter by the quarter). Plebeian radicalism had a rich tradition of the communal reading of the working-class press in pub, club room and political association.

Opponents of the repeal of the stamp constructed a picture of a rich mutualism, and the repeal as 'to force every man to have a newspaper of his own, or none at all'.[77] But equally telling was the fragmented and fractured circulation of news which resulted. Even of Ewell, not much further out of London than Dulwich, it could be said in 1851 that 'with regard to immediate news we live as remote here, as if we had been in the wilds of Yorkshire. Every now and then we see a Times newspaper two or three days old, and that is all'.[78] As it happens, the wilds of Yorkshire weren't necessarily cut off from the news,[79] but in the provinces, distance from the extending railway network could easily translate into delay.[80]

The Provincial Newspaper Society, established in 1836 in the wake of the stamp duty reduction as a mouthpiece for the provincial proprietors, and with a membership of around 110–30 during the 1840s, acted as some sort of collective management of such competitive pressures as did exist in the newspaper market. Throughout the 1840s the Society actively discouraged the cheapening of the provincial press, passing resolutions affirming the impossibility of publishing an ordinary-sized newspaper at 3d.[81] In Liverpool M. J. Whitty of the *Liverpool Journal* came under pressure from fellow proprietors for 'ruining the profession' after reducing his price to 3d, and eventually succumbed, increasing his price to 3½d and then 4d.[82]

In this context the level of newspaper taxation operated as a very considerable obstacle to profitability. It was possible to make money in the provincial press, but many papers were kept afloat by political support, whether of the sort of loan requested from Joseph Sturge by E. F. Collins of the *Hull Advertiser* in 1854, or the direct hand-outs provided by Disraeli to the *Bucks Herald*.[83] The precise extent to the profitability of the provincial press is impossible to ascertain, and estimates were likely to be coloured by partisanship, but the judgement of APRTOK was that on the eve of the repeal of the penny stamp in 1855, only a third of the 600 newspapers then published were able to break even purely on subscribers and advertisers.[84]

The Foundations of the Mid-Victorian Campaigns

Resentment of the taxes on knowledge persisted throughout the Chartist period. The ferocity of the government's response to the unstamped campaigns of the 1830s remained fresh. Radical periodicals offered consistent support for complete repeal, although Chartist support was complicated by the uneasy relationship of its leader Feargus O'Connor with veterans of the stamp wars such as William Lovett and Hetherington, who advocated a 'knowledge chartism' too gradualist and receptive to cross-class initiatives for O'Connor.[1] As a result, despite featuring in debates over national education, the taxes remained marginal to both working-class and middle-class radicalism until the late 1840s.[2]

By 1848 circumstances were changing. The repeal of the Corn Laws in 1846 and the removal of the duty on glass in 1846 offered both encouragement and precedent. The decision to abandon *Chambers' Miscellany* at the end of 1847 drew attention to the difficulty of making cheap publications pay.[3] Moves to remove French newspaper taxes during the 1848 revolution provided inspiration to British radicals.[4] As Chartism fragmented, Henry Vincent's People's League, Joseph Hume's 'General Reform' plan, and in particular the People's Charter Union (PCU) invoked the repeal of the 'taxes on knowledge' as a basis for cross-class alliance.[5] The PCU obtained some modest metropolitan support, but does not seem to have obtained much of a national following, despite publishing the short-lived *Cause of the People* (May–July 1848).[6] It did, however, draw together a group of veterans of the wars of the unstamped who retained a strong interest in the restrictions on the press, and in June, frustrated by coverage in the metropolitan press, launched a renewed campaign against the taxes on knowledge.[7]

During 1848, opposition spread across the political spectrum, from radicals such as James Silk Buckingham to conservative papers such as the *Liverpool Mail* and the *Morning Post*.[8] There were reports of discussions in government circles about reducing the stamp duty on newspapers to a farthing, and the advertisement duty to 6d.[9] As pressure for retrenchment and tax cuts grew, the three taxes on knowledge became part of a long list of indirect taxes from which relief was needed.[10] When Richard Cobden included the repeal of the advertising duty and the paper duties in his radical 'National Budget' at a meeting of the Liverpool Financial Reform Association in December 1848, the PCU redoubled its campaign. In January 1849 it issued an address calling for 'untaxed knowledge', and urging Cobden to incorporate the abolition of the newspaper stamp into his 'Budget'. Looking to create a post-Chartist reform movement which aimed at fiscal rather than franchise reform, Cobden – who had only omitted the stamp to balance his figures[11] – was sufficiently encouraging to prompt the PCU to print and circulate 1,000 copies of its address, and then, on 7 March 1849, to reform itself into the Newspaper Stamp Abolition Committee (NSAC).[12]

Despite its name, the NSAC aimed at repeal of all taxes and restrictions on newspapers. In its address of June 1849 the Committee called on reformers 'to clear the way for free discussion of the people's rights and the people's grievances, by demanding the exemption of the press from all taxation, and its emancipation from all control except that exercised by a court of law.'[13] The core of its active membership was a group of prominent metropolitan radicals, including James Watson and Richard Moore, veterans of the unstamped campaigns of the 1830s, along with G. J. Holyoake and Collet, who formed the backbone of the campaigns against the taxes on knowledge for the next 20 years. Holyoake's primary interest was secularism, but both in the columns of his journal the *Reasoner*, and the *Leader*, he was the most active journalistic voice of the movement. Watson was a printer and publisher, imprisoned on several occasions in the 1820s and 1830s, who continued to publish many late-Chartist, republican and secularist periodicals, including Holyoake's *Reasoner*.[14] Moore, a wood-turner, married to one of Watson's nieces, a member of the Chartist National Convention in 1839, became chair of NSAC, retaining this role and his close day-to-day involvement when it was absorbed into APRTOK in 1851.[15]

Most important of all was J. Dobson Collet, or Collet Dobson Collet as he began to style himself sometime in 1849/50, who served as secretary of the PCU, the NSAC and then APRTOK, serving through to the final disbanding of the Association in 1870. Collet remains a rather obscure figure who preferred to work in the background.[16] A 'noticeable individual with bald forehead, golden hinder locks, and a seeming absence of eye-brows',[17] he was by profession an operatic baritone and teacher of singing and a longstanding member of the Unitarian South Place Chapel, where he was musical director.[18] Collet also occasionally earned a little money as a lecturer and journalist, and between 1855 and the 1870s he was editor of the *Free Press*,[19] an organ of the anti-Russian movement led by David Urquhart, although it is clear that this work, as likewise his work for APRTOK, was at best irregularly remunerated.[20] Collet was stubborn, methodical and conscientious, unwavering in pursuit of the causes he prosecuted. In 1855 he was described by one opponent as 'one of the most self-sufficient men in England, who always speaks as though he thought (as I have little doubt he does) "I am Sir Oracle". . .'.[21] For colleagues his was a public 'life of sacrifice' in which he 'ha[d] given to his country everything that he had to give'.[22]

The NSAC worked hard to create a national agitation. Addresses were circulated and lectures given.[23] Francis Mowatt (MP for Falmouth) presented a petition in the Commons in July 1849 and gave notice of a motion to repeal early in the next session.[24] The support was obtained of leading radicals, including Francis Place, who agreed to act as Treasurer, Thomas Cooper and G. J. Harney, who both advocated the cause in their journals. Attempts were made to set up local associations, out of which emerged, at least briefly, a 'Birmingham Association for the Abolition of Taxes on Knowledge', and something similar in Liverpool.[25] By February 1850 the NSAC claimed a network of local secretaries in 8 London boroughs and 25 towns across Britain and Ireland, as well as support from interested trades, including the London Compositors' Society.[26] In the winter of 1849–50, the campaigns also obtained the approval of O'Connor, and of Chartist conventions in England and Scotland.[27] For all this, the NSAC remained a fringe movement, rooted in the metropolitan radical clubs and their associated periodicals. At the end of May 1849, months after the formation of the NSAC, the *Nonconformist* was still calling for a central committee to organize the emerging campaign against the newspaper taxes.[28] In April 1850, Francis Place criticized the Committee's willingness to accumulate debts, and the offices where monies could be contributed. 'Anyone who might be disposed to assist us would scarcely go to any one of the places named', he warned.[29]

The case against the taxes on knowledge which the activities of the NSAC promulgated is illuminated by a series of articles Harney contributed to the *Northern Star* and the *Democratic Review* between January and May 1850. Harney presented the repeal of the taxes on knowledge as necessary to remove the drag of an uneducated people on progress towards reform. Fiscal restrictions gagged the press as effectively as continental censorship,[30] weighing 'with crushing effect' on cheap publications, and were maintained not for their revenue but 'because they perpetuate the existence of a monopolist press – the corrupt instrument and venal slave of Wealth and Privilege'. What is striking is the way Harney deployed the taxes on knowledge in the service of ultra-radical rhetoric: 'labour and instruction are *primary rights* – rights which cannot be withheld from any man without the withholders being guilty of high treason against Humanity . . . If the starvation of thousands and the ignorance of millions is the price we are to pay for our "glorious institutions", then, I say, *perish those institutions*'.[31] These arguments were taken up in countless articles, letters and editorials, if often in a more moderate register.[32] The dominance of *The Times* attracted particular hostility. A *Westminster Review* article warned against 'an overwhelming newspaper power' wielded by one or two 'mammoth journals'.[33] It was suggested that the 'monopoly . . . [had] degraded journalism into a mere trading enterprise', an occupation for hacks that left the 'filthy and disgusting rubbish retailed to the people, almost literally by the yard' without effective competition.[34]

The newspaper taxes drew criticism from across the political spectrum.[35] However, from the outset, suspicion of the broad rhetoric of 'taxes on knowledge' was widespread. Even generally sympathetic papers such as the *Caledonian Mercury* accepted 'some truth' in the 'taxes on knowledge' label, but 'also some exaggeration'.[36] From the outset John Bright, the Rochdale radical who became one of the movement's leading parliamentary spokesmen, had recognized that 'the newspapers [would] not go warmly for it, being doubtful of the consequences'.[37] Even he was probably surprised at the range of opposition that emerged from periodicals such as the *Christian Socialist*.[38] For many, the sticking point was the penny stamp. Responding to an initial approach by the NSAC, J. A. Roebuck, one of the leading Radical anti-stamp campaigners of the 1830s, had argued that the penny stamp was as much a support for the free circulation of knowledge as a tax on knowledge.[39]

Stamp duty

By 1854 even the traditionally radical *Weekly Dispatch* was defending the stamp. The hostility of the *Dispatch* was in large part the product of a suspicion that the reforming rhetoric of the taxes on knowledge campaigners masked the self-interest of the Manchester School: a desire for a press that would offer more support to the Manchester radicals and their measures.[40] There was some truth in this, as James Curran has recognized. The parliamentary leadership of the campaign was provided by a small group of Anti-Corn Law League veterans, led by the Manchester MPs John Bright and Thomas Milner Gibson, and Richard Cobden, Manchester manufacturer and MP from 1847 for the West Riding. But the natural constituency of support was much wider. In the Commons they were supported, by and large, by the unruly and unpredictable group which made up the Parliamentary Radical party, including Joseph Hume, William Coningham, Herbert Ingram, editor of the *Illustrated London News*, and A. S. Ayrton, MP for Tower Hamlets. The support offered to the NSAC by the *Daily News* during 1849 and 1850 was entirely consistent with middle-class radical attacks on excessive taxation and the call for retrenchment and the removal of fiscal burdens.[41] The removal of the taxes on knowledge served several agendas, the social elevation of the working classes, reform of parliament, and international peace. Repeal also offered progress towards educational reform at a time when other avenues were blocked by fierce religious in-fighting. As Cobden told his friend William Hargreaves, 'The difficulties in the way of setting up any system of education in this country seem to be so great that I am inclined to think the best thing we can do is to pull down all impediments to the diffusion of knowledge, foremost amongst which are the newspaper stamp, the paper duty, & the advertisement tax.'[42]

All this said, the Manchester radicals did tend to become more and more preoccupied with the stamp duty in particular as a barrier to the reconfiguration of a newspaper industry which they felt was increasingly reactionary, unprincipled and bellicose. Cobden in particular, convinced that radical politics required effective advocacy from the daily press, developed a deep-seated antipathy to *The Times* and became disillusioned with the nominally radical *Daily News*.[43] He was aware of the potential of repeal to alter the geographical balance of the provincial press, reduce the influence of the 'Cockney' newspapers and strengthen local journalism.[44] But his real target was the metropolitan dailies. As he told John Cassell in December 1850, 'The *people* have no daily press & never will have until there be here, as there are in America, *penny* newspapers.'[45] The lesson was clear: 'If the cursed stamp was abolished we could have a daily paper speaking our views.'[46]

The attack on the stamp had natural radical appeal, drawing direct links to the successful war of the unstamped of the 1830s.[47] Advocates argued that by raising the price of newspapers the stamp duty 'not only prevents the poor from expressing their opinions, but makes it impossible for men of intelligence to devote their capital to the enlightenment of the working classes', and by increasing the required capital and reducing competition it 'puts the public at the mercy of a few individuals who are but too often incompetent, mercenary and unprincipled'.[48] The stamp duty, as the NSAC pointed out in memorial to the Chancellor, could not even be defended on revenue grounds, given that the proceeds of just over £350,000 in 1849 were more than matched by the £374,000 cost of the transmission of papers.[49] Cases like those of Mitchell in Sussex were used to demonstrate that the increase in the price of newspapers even from 1d to 2d arising from the stamp created an insurmountable obstacle to circulation in rural districts.[50] While opponents ridiculed claims that taking a penny off the cost of London papers costing 4d or 5d would pave the way for metropolitan penny dailies, supporters believed that because the reduction in price would greatly increase the demand, scope existed for the creation of penny papers whose profit on each copy was tiny, but which were able to break even through very large sales.

In the provinces a number of radical papers aligned themselves wholeheartedly with the campaign, including the *Manchester Examiner and Times* (in which John Bright had an interest), the *Glasgow Sentinel*, owned by ex-Owenite Alexander Gardner, the *Newcastle Courant*, the *Liverpool Journal*, and the *Norfolk News*. Apart from a commitment to advanced liberalism, the support of these papers was underpinned by a recognition of the financial penalties exacted by the taxes, and the potential benefits of the increased market a reduction in price might bring. In 1847 the *Manchester Times* was paying in combination £1,700 per year under the taxes on knowledge regime; a telling contrast, it noted to the fact that a Canon of the Collegiate Church in Manchester was paid £1,200 to address his audience.[51]

However, these papers remained a small minority. Supporters of the stamp delighted in pointing out that there was no call from the provincial press for the repeal of the stamp.[52] Milner Gibson attempted to defend the press: 'for people to desire their own taxation for their own benefit seems, on the face of it, a monstrous thing . . . I don't believe', he told a Manchester audience in 1851, 'that opinion to be shared by the great majority of the liberal established press of this country'.[53] The Manchester radicals looked askance at the prospect of a liberal press seeking shelter from the pressures of the market; for them and their allies in the press it was only proper that 'those newspapers which so strenuously advocated free trade in corn, should be made to feel the effects of free trade in newspapers'.[54] The Provincial Newspaper Society took a different line. Although the records of the Society have not survived, there is sufficient contemporary report for it to be clear that it consistently recorded substantial majorities in favour of retaining the stamp. In the autumn of 1851 the vote was 38–7.[55] Lucy Brown has described such votes as 'striking figures to come from a newspaper press which was predominantly Liberal in its sympathies'.[56] In fact the Society was marked by a 'conservative spirit' in the 1850s. The 'newspaper proprietors . . . afraid of opening the door to more newspapers', preferred that the stamp and the securities system be continued,[57] and scoffed at those so bold as to advocate reform.[58] It was suggested that most of the Glasgow papers were not even prepared to print letters from correspondents in favour of repeal.[59]

Recognizing the difficulties of a straightforward anti-competitive argument, the dangers of repeal of the stamp were embodied in various proxies: the disruptive force of dilution of demand, the threat of piracy from new cheap prints, a likely degeneration in the standard of journalism and of the status and respectability of journalists. Provincial proprietors talked of 'a swarm of sheets and broadsides' offering little more than 'police reports in easy sentences', usurping the free circulation of 'material for thought, in carefully written newspapers passing many times through the post'.[60] Supporters of repeal countered that the maintenance of the stamp itself favoured the spread of demoralizing unstamped publications, against which the Inland Revenue was unwilling to act,[61] but opponents were insistent that 'Abolish [the stamp] *in toto* and you open the floodgates of national demoralization, turn the societies of small towns into hotbeds of strife; for not a parliamentary election, a municipal election, nay, an election of a parish constable but would be the occasion of starting a contentious newspaper – petty in power, small in extent, and short of life. But powerful enough, large enough, long lived enough to sow the seeds of bitter and prolific envy, hatred, malice, and all uncharitableness.'[62]

A series of forthright defences of the positive benefits of the stamp were also constructed. The most ubiquitous of these was that it was a reasonable payment for the transmission of newspapers post-free.[63] This was a significant boon, given that after 1849 the weight limit for the penny letter post was half an ounce. (Collet recalled how in sending out circulars, he had to 'make our printer plough their edges, and we used to dry them in the oven' in order to keep their weight below half an ounce.[64]) The cost of the carriage of newspapers by the Post Office fuelled proprietors' fear that the removal of the universal stamp would spell the end of their attractive postal rate.[65] This was a particularly important for the 'county town' papers, those which were sustained by a circulation spread across a considerable rural hinterland, not well served by railways, and more heavily reliant on postal transmission. W. E. Baxter argued not only that the 4,000 circulation his *Sussex Express* achieved from Lewes (total population 10,000) was based on his ability to despatch all but 200 papers to subscribers across an extensive region by post, but that as many as two-thirds would find their way into the post to a second reader within two days.[66]

The privilege of retransmission was said to bring vital benefits. Because the stamp was paid by the original purchaser, its removal, so the argument went, would make papers cheaper for the wealthy, but more expensive for the rest.[67] Unlimited retransmission was presented as a crucial mechanism of the 'diffusion' of information and understanding, a means whereby 'the particular details of knowledge born out of the experience of each place should be conveyed to other places' and 'a healthy action of the public mind is secured'.[68] The 'grand civilising function' of the stamp was its 'plac[ing] town and country on an equality'.[69] 'Many a reader by the country fireside, and many an old man in the cottage of his retirement, where he is not forgotten by his town friends, would sadly grieve at the abolition of the penny stamp, which so quietly and regularly brings them those "heralds of a noisy world".'[70] Newspapers collected personal testimonies of multiple transmissions through three, four, even five hands.[71] Defenders of the stamp romanticized the working men who banded together to get a paper cheaper than a penny each, and the social solidarities encouraged by coffee houses and newsrooms, where for a penny anyone could read the main London or provincial papers over a cup of coffee.

Of course, complete removal of the press's postal privileges, which would have been a serious blow to many provincial papers, was never really suggested. Beyond this, the flaw in this argument was easily identified. If the postal privileges were so valuable, it would be straightforward, as Cobden frequently pointed out, to enact that all existing newspapers have the option to retain the existing tax with all its privileges and restrictions.[72] The *Freeman's Journal* did rather give the game away by conceding in one of its last ditch defences that 'In practice, no man who buys an unstamped paper will put his hand into his pocket and pay another penny for transmitting it gratuitously to a friend.'[73]

Baxter also argued that the proliferation of local journals, in diluting the demand for advertisements in their locality, would destroy the viability of the respectable county press by depriving it of advertising revenue, destroying the many conveniences to commerce and government that came from the ability to reach the whole population of a county with a single advertisement.[74] It was also suggested that the demand for newspapers could not be seen as a function of price, noting that increasing the price of the *Sussex Express* from 5d to 6d had enabled him, because of the greater space he provided and the additional reporting staff he could take on, to increase his circulation.[75]

Advertisement duty

If press opinion rallied to support of the stamp, the advertisement duty was an entirely different matter. The reliance on advertisements for their profitability made the advertising duty a potentially crippling constraint for almost all early-Victorian newspapers.[76] And given that unlike the other two taxes on knowledge it was not imposed at source, the regular demand for payment of the duty could produce acute financial pressure for cash-strapped owners.[77] The significance of the duty should not be underestimated. If the average circulation of a provincial weekly in the early 1850s was somewhere under 1,000, then a 4½d sheet would have generated weekly sales revenue (after 1d stamp and 1½d allowed to agents), of only about £8.[78] A newspaper with only a modest circulation could generate two or three times as much from adverts.[79] In 1849 the editor of the *Bucks Herald* estimated his weekly income as £4 from subscriptions and £13 from advertising; but in fact his balance sheet for 1848–9 revealed that in the third quarter, on subscriptions of £50, his advertising income was £211.[80]

Attempts by the Inland Revenue from 1848 to 1851to extend the coverage of the duty to book reviews, notifications of runners for horse races, or the lists of arrivals and departures at hotels, threw into doubt the distinction between news and advertisement, and brought renewed calls for the repeal of the advertisement tax.[81] Hardly surprising then that within two months of its formation the NSAC had been joined by a London Committee for Obtaining the Repeal of the Advertisement Duty, founded by John Francis, editor of the *Athenaeum*, with the support of a number of editors and proprietors, including John Cassell, at that time publishing the *Standard of Freedom*, Edward Miall of the *Nonconformist*, and Herbert Ingram of the *Illustrated London News*.[82] The Committee obtained support across the London daily and weekly press, although noticeably not *The Times*, and a small number of provincial papers.[83] It sustained a desultory agitation. Circulars and petitions were distributed to encourage the provincial press to come out in favour of repeal.[84]

The repeal of the advertising duty was widely supported by the press, both metropolitan and provincial, even those who were anxious to distance themselves from 'spurious' arguments about 'taxes on knowledge'.[85] The taxing of all newspaper adverts but not advertisement in books, or via placards, hoardings, on vans and omnibuses, was generally resented, as was the extent to which the tax tended to concentration of advertising in the hands of *The Times*.[86] It was a regime which was said to allow the commercial classes to circumvent the tax while leaving the poor, especially those seeking employment, to bear the full weight of the duty.[87] Harney described the advertisement duty as 'unjust and injurious', punishing the poor for their poverty.[88] The relatively small sums raised by the advertising duty also allowed advocates to argue that repeal offered governments the prospect of cheap popularity,[89] even that the revenue would gain from the general impetus given to newspapers.[90]

The advertising duty had few champions. There were one or two proprietors, for whom even this was a reform too far, bringing dangerous risks of new titles and additional competition.[91] Andrew Moody of the *Glasgow Mercantile Advertiser* warned that if the duty was abolished entirely 'public journals will [eventually] altogether escape the control of and cognizance of the Government'.[92] The *Scotsman* observed that the duty did at least prevent unscrupulous newspaper puffers from filling their columns with sham or gratis adverts in an attempt to gull the public into thinking that advertisers thought it worthwhile advertising there.[93] A minority of proprietors shared Baxter's view that the repeal alone would have little or no impact on the price of advertisements, because papers were already publishing as many adverts as they had space for, and there was a tendency for the unstamped penny magazines to ignore the one tax on knowledge that did not apply to them.[94] Some supporters of the broader campaign against the taxes on knowledge expressed concern that repeal of the advertisement duty might be granted simply as a means of forestalling the more needed reforms.[95] But it was only *The Times,* a special case because of the extent to which its huge circulation had enabled it to build a dominant position in the provision of newspaper advertising, which was consistently vocal in opposing repeal.

The advertising duty was a particular bane for the publishers and sellers of cheap books and periodicals. In 1852 John Chapman suggested that perhaps as much as a third of the advertising duty was paid by publishers, and that the cost of advertising meant 'the virtual suppression of pamphlets and low-priced books'. Chapman pointed up the irony of the government spending a few hundred pounds a year on literary pensions, but grinding many thousands of pounds from the literary world via the advertising duty.[96] Yet there seems to have been relatively little active support from the publishing or bookselling trades. Instead, Charles Knight's *The Struggles of a Book against Excessive Taxation,* published early in 1850, concentrated on the excise duty on paper.[97] Knight publicized the cases of the *Penny Magazine* which he claimed was forced to cease publication in 1845, despite a weekly sale of 25,000, and of his *Penny Cyclopedia* series, which had required payment across its full run of £16,500, and was by Knight's calculations also forced to pay around £10,000 in higher prices because of reduced competition in paper manufacturing.

Paper duties

By the time Knight's pamphlet was published an association of the abolition of the paper duty (the AADP) was already in existence.[98] The AADP was primarily a campaign of the paper manufacturers led by Peter Borthwick, manufacturer and proprietor of the *Morning Post*, and Thomas B. Crompton, one of the largest manufacturers in the north of England.[99] In the face of competition from cheaper foreign paper there were moves to organize the paper makers in early 1849 in Scotland,[100] and in late 1849 the AADP was formally instituted in London. Borthwick initially co-operated with the newspaper proprietors, but subsequently he and Crompton attempted to establish a discrete campaign in favour of the repeal of the paper duty. In January 1850 a deputation to the Chancellor of the Exchequer, Sir Charles Wood, elicited optimistic noises about the possibility of the repeal of the paper duties in the next budget,[101] but a year later Borthwick was still 'devoting a most inconvenient portion of my time to the repeal of the tax on paper'.[102]

The AADP attracted broad support from the paper industry, including large producers such as John Mellor (Morton), Benjamin Mellor (Hunslet), Jeremiah Garnett (Otley Mills) and Thomas Wrigley (Bury), one of the largest paper manufacturers in the country and supplier of many northern newspapers.[103] The papermakers were actively supported by a number of the large publishing houses, in particular the Chambers brothers and Charles Knight,[104] and also periodical proprietors, such as George Stiff of the *London Journal* and Samuel Carter Hall of the *Art Journal*, as well as printers such as James Figgins and Thomas De la Rue.[105] Significantly the Manchester radicals and NSAC party seem to have held entirely aloof. Cobden was clear that the campaign against the paper duties should be subordinated to the more readily achievable targets of the stamp and advertising duties, and of the radicals only Joseph Hume offered any public endorsement.[106]

Between 1848 and 1851 the paper manufacturers produced a number of widely cited statements of the case against the paper duties; including James Baldwin, *A Letter Addressed to the Right Hon. Lord John Russell Showing the Evil*

Effects and Injustice of the Excise Laws (1848),[107] *The Excise Duty on Paper: Letter to the Right Hon. Lord John Russell, M.P., from a Paper-maker* (1850), *A Claim for the Repeal of the Paper Duty* (1850),[108] and Crompton's own *Excise Duty on Paper, Considered as Affecting the Employment of the Poor, the Grievances of the Manufacturer, and the Injury to the Consumer* (1851).[109] These pamphlets and the platform speeches with which they were associated offered a consistent case, which focused on the burdens of the industry, resonating with more general attacks from free traders and economical reformers, for whom the paper duty took its place among the excise duties as perhaps the most odious.[110] Great play was made of the burden of the tax in comparison to the lack of value of the raw material from which paper was made, and of the innumerable petty restrictions of the excise regime. Manufacturers claimed that it could cost £100 per week to meet the record-keeping demands of the excise, and that the temptation to fraud was almost irresistible for poorly paid excise officers and hard-pressed paper makers, leaving the honest manufacturer to be ruined by the dishonest.[111] Litanies were recited of manufacturers who were either limping on making very small returns on their capital, or had been forced out of business. The increased facilities for the production of paper which repeal would bring were promised to stimulate economic activity and increase employment. Extravagant claims were made of 40,000 more jobs in London alone, as well as improved employment in rural districts.[112]

The case of the paper makers was amplified by the extent to which paper was a raw material for other trades. One example was the Birmingham button manufacturers, who often generated significant waste paper; another was publishers and the book trade. It was accepted that the duty had no appreciable impact on higher priced books, but on cheap books and pamphlets the surcharge was considerable.[113] As well as *The Struggles of a Book against Excessive Taxation* (1850), Charles Knight also published *The Case of the Authors as Regards the Paper Duties* (1851) in which he explored the disincentives to producing high-quality publications for the working classes inherent in the paper duty: not just the high proportion of paper costs, but also the additional burden of covering unsold stock and the increased capitalization required for the very large print runs needed to make penny titles remunerative. Knight calculated that during the previous 20 years he had spent £80,000 on copyright and literary labour, but almost £50,000 on the paper duty. Without the duty, he argued, 'there would have been a reserved capital' for employing 'the best literary labour'.

The newspaper interest reiterated Knight's line, acknowledging that the paper duties contributed only marginally to the cost of each individual newspaper, but arguing that this margin might still be crucial. Even the poorest country prints, it was suggested, would gain £80–100 by the removal of the paper duty; for larger provincial papers it might be as much as £1,000; in both cases potentially turning a struggling surplus into an adequate profit.[114] By presenting the paper duties as a vital obstacle to a cheap press, supporters of the taxes on knowledge campaign were able to point to broad cultural consequences. For the *Standard of Freedom*, 'by denying the struggling workman the healthful recreation of a cheap press, it has driven him to idleness, or the sensual excitements of dissipation'.[115] Conversely, for opponents of the cheap press the paper duty was less a tax on knowledge than 'a tax on delusion – a tax on folly – a tax on fiction', as Thomas Olver told the electors of East Cornwall in 1852.[116]

Even here the newspaper industry was divided. Sceptics (such as *The Times*) doubted that removal would allow greater remuneration to authors when 'there would still remain the same inducement as now to cut down all the costs to the lowest possible scale'.[117] The danger, as the *Caledonian Mercury* remarked, was that the arguments against the paper duties 'may be very true in the abstract', but not did entirely demonstrate that 'the hardship is so great as regards the community to secure a preference from the Chancellor of the Exchequer'.[118] In 1853 more than half a small sample questioned by the Society of Arts denied that the duty kept up the price of newspapers, except for the very few titles with large circulations. For the proprietor of the *Devonport Independent*, 'the duty of such a circulation as 1,000 a week, averages only 35*l*. per annum; too small a sum to make much improvement in the talent employed'. Even Collet conceded that there was unlikely to be a significant impact, when 'the whole amount on stamped newspapers is only about 50,000*l*'.[119]

The campaigns of 1850–1

By the Spring of 1850, with three separate national organizations attacking the taxes on knowledge, hopes were high: *Tait's Edinburgh Magazine* urged that 'a million signatures' could bring repeal before the end of the session.[120] Although the Liverpool Financial and Parliamentary Reform Association declined any formal connection with the NSAC, thinking the matter 'better dealt with in an efficient and striking manner by a society formed for the special purpose',[121] the taxes on knowledge platform had become part of middle-class radical rhetoric.[122] In the autumn of 1849 the report of the Select Committee on Public Libraries had condemned the taxes. Behind the scenes the parliamentary leadership was being put in the hands of Thomas Milner Gibson, who was pressing parliamentary radicals to keep the question in the public eye, and canvassing support from prominent literary figures.[123] Charles Dickens declined on the basis that he was 'not at all clear of the effect of the removal of the stamp duty from newspapers . . . but I am disposed to think that the tax increases their respectability – that they have a fair return for it in the postage arrangements – and that if it were taken off, we might be deluged with a flood of piratical, ignorant and blackguard papers, something like that black deluge of Printer's Ink which blights America.'[124] Even so, petitions flowed in from Boards of Guardians, town councils, as well as workers groups and mechanics' institutes.[125] Pressure on the Inland Revenue intensified. On 11th March an NSAC deputation to the Prime Minister, Russell, accused Keogh and the stamp office of operating an arbitrary discretion, allowing three indecent publications dealing in libels (one of which was eventually put down by a private prosecution) while proceeding against respectable papers.[126] At Milner Gibson's instigation a parliamentary return was obtained which showed 51 newspapers which stamped only part of their impression, and the NSAC encouraged a number of editors, including Thornton Hunt of the *Leader* and Charles Bray of the *Coventry Herald* to apply for similar privileges.[127]

Growing prosperity and the prospect of a £1.5M surplus in the 1850 budget encouraged campaigners to hope for concessions.[128] In fact, discussions in government circles indicated more interest taxes on soap than knowledge.[129] Sir Charles Wood, Chancellor of the Exchequer, was anxious to try to balance the remission of taxes to ensure that all interests felt as though they had gained something, but Russell demurred: 'Let us consider which taxes by their purpose do most public injury, and the remission of which will do most public good'; a sop to Cobden, or to any other interest, he told Wood, 'shall only incur a just contempt'.[130] By repealing the 'Taxes upon Knowledge', the *Daily News* remarked, 'Ministers had it in their power to place themselves at the head of the united liberals of England', but to the incredulity of the liberal press, the budget ultimately proposed using half the surplus to reduce the national debt, and the rest to remove the tax on bricks and make minor adjustments to the stamp regulations.[131]

The political crosscurrents through which campaigners had to navigate were starkly illuminated by the manoeuvrings occasioned by Milner Gibson's parliamentary motions in favour of repeal of the taxes on knowledge in April 1850. Encouraged by Borthwick, Disraeli announced his intention to vote for repeal, and faced with the prospect of defeating the Whig government with Tory support the parliamentary Radicals were thrown into disarray. 'The moment I announced my intention to support, they (the Radicals) fled the House in confusion or voted with the Government', Disraeli remarked to a correspondent.[132] With Wood and Russell making a vigorous defence on the grounds of financial necessity the motion was defeated by 190–89, to the frustration of the NSAC, many of the 133 Liberals in the majority having previously committed themselves to supporting repeal.[133] A subsequent motion from Hume in favour of repeal of advertisement duty was defeated even more heavily (208–39).

A number of papers, including the *Leader* to which Holyoake contributed regularly,[134] sustained agitation of the question through 1850 and there was some optimism in the autumn that the year's campaign had convinced the government of the necessity of repeal, or at least a substantial reduction in the taxes.[135] At the end of 1850 Crompton's pamphlet, *Excise Duty on Paper* had laid the groundwork for meetings of papermakers in Edinburgh, Leeds, Manchester and Dublin.[136] There was a particularly active agitation in Ireland: tracts were printed and circulated, and at a large public meeting at the end of January several thousand signatures were collected for a petition.[137] In England, a national delegate meeting was held in London at the end of January,[138] and by mid-March 235 petitions signed by 39,537 people had been presented.[139] Crompton pressed for a return of all the paper mills at work in the United Kingdom with a view to exposing the number working fraudulently. It was suggested that in places like Birmingham, where Baldwin piloted a resolution through the Town Council, emphasis had shifted from the repeal of all the knowledge taxes to the paper duties 'as a matter of trade'.[140]

However, tensions were also beginning to appear. In many respects the distinctions between the various associations had always been vague. Each association had tended to draw on the arguments of the others, and here had been a considerable overlap of membership. The letterpress printers of Dublin, firmly committed to the repeal of all the taxes on knowledge, nevertheless subscribed to the Dublin association for the repeal of paper duty.[141] Thornton Hunt, who actively collaborated with the NSAC, was also to one of the Newspaper Committee's deputation to Lord John Russell in March 1851,[142] and when the paper manufacturers met the Chancellor the same month some members of the delegation made it clear that although they pressed for the repeal of the paper duty, they did not do so to the exclusion of the other taxes on knowledge.[143]

There was friction, however, between the radicalism of the NSAC, which remained determined 'to resist all attempts to separate the Paper Duty from the smaller Taxes on Knowledge',[144] and the conservative instincts of some of the paper manufacturers, especially Crompton, who was keen to distance himself entirely from the broader agenda. 'The advertisement duty and the penny stamp on newspapers we have no wish to disturb', he told Disraeli in April 1850.[145] These tensions surfaced publicly at the meeting of the AADP at the London Tavern in early January 1851 which saw the mustering of a strong NSAC contingent and a successful amendment from Holyoake and Collet (ultimately supported by Gibson) to extend an original motion which included only the paper duty, to include the other taxes on knowledge.[146] Crompton was not pleased, and at a meeting in Yorkshire later in the month he made his disapproval clear, indicating he would break up the association rather than have it associated with the broader campaign.[147]

Whatever the reason, the separate agitation for the paper duties seems to have receded rapidly from this point. In March a meeting of Irish MPs sought to keep the campaign alive,[148] but by the end of the year the *Daily News* was noting the tendency of some paper makers to shelter from competition behind the excise regime.[149] Over the ensuing 12 months the Paper Duties society was mothballed, and opinion in the trade seems to have shifted through 180 degrees.[150] In a similar fashion, the March 1851 deputation to Russell also seems to have marked the high water mark of the London Committee for the Repeal of the Advertising Duty.[151] Although support in sections of the press is still visible thereafter, 1851 saw signs of a hardening of attitudes even to campaigners against the advertisement duty.[152]

At the same time, there are signs that concerns were also growing in some quarters as to the efficacy of the NSAC, and the crudeness of some of its tactics.[153] It was suggested that the movement was ineffectively organized, local secretaries were left very much to their own devices, and no true reflection of the force of public opinion had been mobilized.[154] The Manchester radicals were frustrated at the lack of popular agitation. 'The working classes themselves', Cobden told the Bradford Freehold Land Society in January 1851, 'have been particularly silent on this question'.[155] Efforts by Collet to strengthen ties with the National Charter Association in early 1851 may not have been entirely welcome to Cobden and his allies.[156] Faced with the threat of a sectional campaign for the repeal of the paper duties on the one hand, and an ineffectual and perhaps also overly radicalized campaign against the stamp on the other, a decision was taken to reconstitute the agitation and assert a measure of middle-class control. at a meeting on the 13th February 1851 at Fendall's Hotel in London, a strong contingent of parliamentary radicals, led by Cobden, Bright and Thomas Milner Gibson, passed a series of resolutions agreeing to establish an Association for the Promotion of the Repeal of the Taxes on Knowledge.[157]

The Association for the Promotion of the Repeal of the Taxes on Knowledge as a Pressure Group

Alan Lee has described the history of APRTOK as a 'textbook example of the way in which a mid-Victorian pressure group worked'.[1] Yet the Association has also been portrayed as a sectional lobby masquerading as a popular agitation, 'an affair between semi-literary MPs, booksellers, newspaper proprietors, and paper manufacturers' as the *Scottish Review* put it in October 1861.[2] The actual history of the Association is more complicated than either extreme. Although APRTOK needs to be understood as a pressure group, thought of itself as such, and employed all the orthodox tools of the type, its activities and their success are explicable only by recognizing the extent to which it was both distinct and innovative, as much about interest group lobbying and engineering change by exploiting the internal contradictions of the taxes on knowledge regime as a constitutional vehicle of extra-parliamentary pressure.

Organization and control

The transition to APRTOK was choreographed to encourage the appearance of continuity with the NSAC. Milner Gibson was installed as President, but Place remained as Treasurer (with J. A. Novello, the music publisher, charged with the active work as sub-Treasurer), Collet stayed as Secretary, and Richard Moore as Chairman, and all members of the NSAC committee were invited to join the new committee.[3] But it was clear that this was a take-over; the published committee was transformed by the addition of a mass of middle-class radicals, including Cobden, Bright, G. H. Lewes George Dawson, Charles Gilpin and Edward Miall, and the NSAC 'dissolved itself after handing over its books and papers to the Association'.[4] The new directing hand was soon revealed. After the Association's first public meeting on the 5th March in St Martin's Hall, London, Cobden was quick to warn Collet for introducing 'a little too much extraneous matter'.[5]

The controlling instincts of the Manchester radicals are clearly visible in the patchy records of the Association. When Collet visited Manchester to agitate the question in the summer of 1851, Bright along with George Wilson and Henry Rawson, the local leaders of the Anti-Corn Law League faction, met him initially and 'had the question over with him' before he returned a few weeks later to meet 20 or 30 handpicked potential supporters.[6] Cobden expected to see proofs of all important communications and circulars (even if this didn't always happen),[7] and operated as a fairly constant break on the combativeness of Collet and the committee. 'You are sometimes a little too plainspoken for your clients' he warned towards the end of 1853, 'probably from your not always bearing in mind that the "Association" does not always consist of the millions who will be benefited by the repeal of the Taxes on Knowledge, but of a few men who, having themselves the advantage of seeing a daily newspaper, would wish every man in the kingdom to enjoy the same privilege.'[8]

In practice, the organizational structure and active operations of the Association were allowed to carry on very much as before. With no minute book surviving before 1857 it is difficult to obtain a clear picture of the daily operations of the Association. Collet recorded that the 'Committee met regularly once a week', a total of 473 times over the full 1849–61 period, with Moore present 390 and presiding 355 of times, and it seems clear that even in the early days the bulk of the new Committee were at best corresponding members.[9] There is no evidence that Cobden attended committee meetings. Nor was he generally in regular contact with Collet, who clearly had a good deal of freedom for manoeuvre.[10] For Cobden, of course, the taxes on knowledge were one of a range of issues on which he was campaigning, and not one which had especially prominent status, except when something reignited his frustrations with the press. His instincts were to encourage the multiplication of societies agitating for reforms of all sorts, and his attention was intermittent.[11] Gibson, despite his office, only appeared from time to time, though he corresponded regularly with Collet in the later 1850s.[12] Bright, despite his prominent advocacy, had almost nothing to do with the Association directly, clearly assuming a set of parallel but separate activities in which 'We shall keep the question alive in Parl[iamen]t if you & others will do the same out of it', as he told Collet in 1853.[13] All three were fairly regular attenders at the AGM, at least until 1855. Otherwise, for much of the 1850s the link appears to have been maintained most directly via the activity of Novello, who kept the active committee in funds, and signed many of the Association's official communications, although by no means all, and by 1858 it is noticeable that even his name drops away.

There is no evidence of any attempt to develop programmatic statements of strategy, and certainly nothing that was enforced on Collet and the NSAC activists.[14] Nor, apart from nominal presence of a 'Finance Committee', was there any attempt to construct a more articulated organizational structure. In comparison to the Liberation Society, with its executive and strategy committees, APRTOK was essentially uninstitutionalized. Although there are occasional instances of the middle-class leadership taking the initiative (as in November 1851 when, while Collet was attending the National Charter Association and trying to argue for a platform agitation, Gibson, Place and Novello issued an address 'To the Friends of Constitutional Government throughout the Kingdom'),[15] the surviving records suggest that despite the 'new start', the middle-class radicals, according to Collet, 'left in the old hands the executive management'.[16]

This loose structure left considerable autonomy in the hands of Collet as secretary. The secretary was often the linchpin of mid-Victorian extra-parliamentary pressure groups. Cobden described his ideal as 'a clever tactician, & with earnest feelings, & of untiring energy', who would 'do the work for us'.[17] With the exception of the final couple of words, Collet fit the bill. He was active in metropolitan radical circles, on the Friends of Italy committee in 1851, for example, and on the committee of the Shilling Fund for European Freedom in 1853.[18] He was well connected with figures such as Watson and Holyoake, and the freethought groups and publications with which they were associated, as well as 'complete suffrage' radicals such as Robert Le Blond, Thornton Hunt and John Epps. He was, on the other hand, always a bit of a loose cannon, and this tendency was ever more apparent as he came under the influence of the maverick Russophobe David Urquhart. Cobden's exasperation at Collet's intervention in the City election of June 1854 – 'Are you mad to put out that advertisement about the City Election? How are we to get money for the Association in the face of such acts of folly?', speaks clearly to Collet's freedom of manoeuvre, and the potential limits on it.[19]

Alongside Collet the key role was played by Thomas Milner Gibson, who from the outset established himself as the leader of the movement in Parliament.[20] In the histories of mid-Victorian radicalism, Gibson, MP for Manchester from 1841 to 1857 and for Ashton from 1857–68, has been largely overshadowed by Cobden and Bright. An MP who began life representing Ipswich in the Conservative interest, he was an unlikely leader for the Association. His radicalism as the *Pall Mall Gazette* put it in 1865 was always held as an enlightened theory rather than the intense faith of Cobden and Bright, more a matter of commerce than politics, pragmatics rather than rights. Nevertheless he was an effective parliamentary speaker, and an even more skilful parliamentary tactician and draftsman, renowned for framing motions around which potentially opposing interests could compromise. Despite his 'clubbable' manners and easy-going character, over time the Manchester radicals accepted him as one of their own.[21] Gibson had been marshalling support before being installed as chairman of APRTOK, and thereafter his almost annual motions and speeches in favour of repeal became the parliamentary voice of the movement. The fragmentary nature of Gibson's surviving correspondence makes it difficult to ascertain how close his involvement with the month by month activities of the Association were, although it is suggestive that in the later 1850s, when Cobden and Bright's always limited involvement seems to have dwindled away entirely, Gibson corresponded regularly with Collet on APRTOK business, and attended the occasional committee meeting in person.[22]

The lack of formal central structures was replicated by the Association's local organization. Part of the NSAC's initial platform had been the establishment of local 'Free Knowledge Associations', although few seem actually to have appeared.[23] Little changed after the formation of APRTOK. The central committee seem to have made only very limited efforts to develop provincial organization.[24] Collet undertook a couple of lecture tours in the autumn of 1852 and winter 1853–4,[25] but these were more attempts at propaganda than at organization-building. An APRTOK handbill of May 1852 indicated an intention to organize district societies in London 'and elsewhere', to 'give the agitation a more popular character',[26] and a number of local associations were formed, though it is not clear how closely these were ever tied to the central committee.[27] Holyoake helped form an 'Anti Tax on Knowledge Committee' in May,[28] and a Finsbury Knowledge Tax Repeal Association was formed at the start of September,[29] and around this new associations were formed in Bradford, Leeds, Wakefield, Newcastle, Manchester, Liverpool, Sunderland, Halifax and Huddersfield.[30] These local committees remained 'entirely independent' of the central committee, and probably had only a fleeting existence.[31] There was some frustration among working-class radicals at the dissonance between Cobden's rhetoric of popular activism, and the lack of support from the central Association.[32] The problem was of course that in the absence of a continuous agitation there was little to keep them active.

By and large the Association satisfied itself with district secretaries, who generally worked without local associations. At the end of 1853, the APRTOK *Gazette* was able to list 77 towns with district secretaries, including 5 London districts, (only a fraction of the at least 223 local anti-corn law associations which have been identified).[33] They organized occasional meetings, circulated petitions and collected signatures and subscriptions.[34] Their links with the London committee are almost entirely invisible, although William Bowman, who was listed as the Carlisle secretary in the first NSAC *Annual Report* in 1849 wrote in January 1853 that he had been 'in constant correspondence for nearly three years' with Collet.[35] At Manchester, which with the help of Bright and the *Manchester Examiner and Times* sustained perhaps the most vibrant local presence, the secretary for most of the period was Dr John Watts, ex-Owenite lecturer turned Cobdenite educationalist. Watts circulated APRTOK materials around liberal circles in Manchester, and corresponded regularly with the central committee until the close of its active operations.[36]

Like many local supporters, Watts was also an active supporter of the campaign for unsectarian state-funded education. Speaking at Accrington in February 1852, on behalf of the National Public Schools Association (NPSA) he successfully proposed a motion in favour of the repeal of the taxes on knowledge, and was confronted at a subsequent meeting by two rival groups, one placarding for 'voluntary and unsectarian education and no state interference, and repeal of the taxes on knowledge', and the other for 'a national and real unsectarian education, and repeal of the taxes on knowledge'.[37] Similar alignments were visible elsewhere. At Diss in June 1851, F. R. Young was announced as local secretary for APRTOK and the NPSA.[38] The alignments were not identical. Alexander Henry, president of the NPSA, voted against the repeal of the taxes on knowledge in April 1850.[39] But for most supporters the congruence was clear: as Cobden told Joseph Sturge, 'We raise double as much in taxes upon newspapers, advertisements, & paper, as we vote annually for the education of the people – Is not this very like political hypocrisy?'[40]

The lack of any real institutionalization of local support helps explain the extent to which the Association never quite acquired a stable public profile in these years. It is noticeable that Cobden and other parliamentary leaders were more than happy to work with, indeed to actively encourage, a range of alternative groups and campaigns. After the repeal of the advertising duty in 1853, the newspaper proprietors were encouraged to form a 'Newspaper Proprietors

League'.[41] APRTOK also encouraged the Association of the Newspaper and Periodical Press for the Repeal of the Paper Duties, of which Milner Gibson served as president, along with John Cassell, a long-time supporter of APRTOK, as chairman.[42] For Collet and working-class supporters there were likewise various ancillary organizations and spin-offs which imply a certain lack of sympathy for the Association, but support for the agenda, such as the Working Men's Free Press Union formed at the National Hall, Holborn, in March 1853.[43]

This fluidity of allegiance and the subscription (rather than membership) model which the Association adopted, complicate the task of assessing its support. Funding was a perennial challenge. The impoverished state of the NSAC had caused some uncomfortable exchanges between the committee and Francis Place as Treasurer.[44] Its most systematic effort at fundraising was the 'Thousand Sixpences' campaign which Holyoake ran in the *Reasoner*.[45] Collet also worked hard to cultivate the support of the typographical unions.[46] But neither this nor personal canvas for more substantial subscriptions seems to have been terribly successful. The Committee raised less than £60 from January 1850 to February 1851 including £10 from the *Reasoner* fund.[47] No doubt this lack of financial leverage contributed to the willingness of the Committee to subsume itself into APRTOK.

After 1851 the Association largely followed Cobden's repeated counsel that it should 'abandon all idea of getting money in small subscriptions',[48] and look for funding from a relatively narrow circle of 'givers' who supported the radical agendas in which he was involved. Collet's occasional attempts to develop a popular financial base by appealing for 6d subscriptions from working men were emphatically scotched.[49] Initially the formation of APRTOK did generate fresh contributions, but soon the old problems returned.[50] The Association was rarely solvent, and for much of its life relied on lines of credit advanced by Novello.[51] Collet used his occasional lecturing tours to raise funds from supporters, but this was not his forte.[52] He also suggested a campaign to raise a day's saving of advertisement duty from the newspapers who had benefitted from its abolition,[53] but financial support from the press was limited. At times the Association employed a London collector, and considered employing one in Manchester 'that something could be collected in small sums'.[54] During 1852–3 its income of just under £390 fell far short of an expenditure of over £660. Determined efforts by Cobden and Gibson enabled the Association briefly to meet current expenditure and reduce the debt by £100, but thereafter the Association tended to lurch from one financial crisis to another.[55]

The Association's difficulties in maintaining solvency offered an easy target for opponents. Its limited subscriptions were seized upon as evidence that 'an association, mustering by hook or by crook, a revenue of eleven pounds a month, has been allowed to dictate to the Government of this country'.[56] Despite the dangers of accusations of self-interest, much of APRTOK's effort was directed towards the mobilization of specific interest groups, advertisers,[57] booksellers, publishers and paper manufacturers.[58] These efforts were only ever partially successful. Novello (particularly well placed to hold out to provincial editors the lure of regular adverts for his productions) was able to generate some press support for the campaign against the advertisement duty.[59] APRTOK exploited the arguments of the Chambers brothers to draw in some publishers, but although it was possible to garner support from many of the London publishing houses for petitions, most of the more active or financially generous supporters, such as Novello, Cassell or the Chambers brothers themselves, had some newspaper or periodical interest.[60] Bookselling in the 1850s was characterized by fierce protective practices focused on attempts at price maintenance and it proved impossible to achieve any sustained mobilization behind the campaign. In similar fashion, in 1858 Collet complained that despite the benefits the envelope manufacturers had obtained from the Association's efforts, 'yet the munificent sum of 5s. was all that was ever got'.[61]

Yet it would be a mistake to assume that the movement was incapable of drawing on broad popular support. The record of the petitioning campaigns against the taxes on knowledge in the 1850s tells a very different tale.

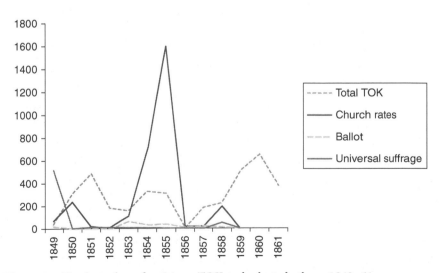

Figure 3.1 Total number of petitions, TOK and selected others, 1849–61

Historians have tended to dismiss petitioning as unimportant by the mid-Victorian period, a hollow hangover from an earlier era of extra parliamentary politics.[62] There is no doubt that the tightening of the procedural rules of Parliament in the 1830s made petitions less effective as a means of raising a topic for discussion in the Commons, and by 1848 there was little confidence left among middle-class radicals in the ability of petitions of themselves to effect change.[63] On the other hand, petitioning activity provided encouragement to the timid politician, and it was clearly taken seriously at the margins of the Victorian game of public opinion.[64] In the context of an agitation which was unusually gendered for the mid-Victorian period, petitions also explicitly allowed a voice to women as well as men.[65] The usefulness of petitioning was one conviction shared by Cobden and the working-class radicals, and so unsurprisingly, petitioning, a central plank of the NSAC,[66] was carried forward into APRTOK, where Collet continued to act as a clearing house for petitions, receiving them from the provinces and finding MPs to present them.[67]

Petitions against the taxes on knowledge were kept up at an impressive level throughout the 1850s (see Figure 3.1).[68] The neglected records of petitioning provided by the *Select Committee on Public Petitions* do provide important data on all the petitions presented to the House of Commons in this period. Interpretation of the data is not easy, but from just under 50 in 1849, the number of petitions for the various components of the taxes on knowledge campaigns reached nearly 500 in 1851, and with the exception of 1852, every year from 1850–5 saw at least 300 petitions presented. After a brief lull in the wake of the repeal of the newspaper stamp in 1855, activity gathered pace again, and in 1859 and 1860 there were over 500 petitions presented. These were very significant numbers in a period in which the campaign for the ballot only once registered over 50 petitions, and impressively consistent when compared with the petitions against church rates, which peaked at nearly 1600 in 1855, but averaged only around 220 across the decade, notwithstanding the considerable resources nonconformist chapels provided for the generation of petitions.

The record of petitioning offers a picture of the support that was mobilized during the 1850s. The petitioners for 1852 demonstrate the diverse base of support for the campaigns. They range from general groups of inhabitants, for example of Carlisle, public meetings, resolutions of associations, or of groups of employees associated with publishing.[69] At this stage about half of the petitions represented various forms of general opinion, and half represented special interest groups. It is clear that the campaign was drawing on the organizational resources of rational recreation.[70] In the North East, for example, J. B. Blackett,

MP for Newcastle, induced the organizing secretary of the Northern Union of Mechanics' Institutes to co-ordinate petitioning activity by the institutes.[71] Pressure was also channelled through groups of interested trades, especially bookbinders, letterpress printers and compositors. In 1855 there was a clear shift in the pattern of support. In the face of significant mobilization of opposition from the proprietors and editors of the newspaper press, the lead in pressing for repeal was taken by groups of workers, especially letterpress printers and newsvendors.[72] Although these were mostly workplace groups rather than unions or collective organizations, APRTOK did obtain some financial support from union organizations in the printing trades.[73] By 1860 the newspaper press had become the most significant support, generally represented as proprietors and workers; related trades remain significant, but it is noticeable that the campaign had once again broadened out to include rational recreation institutions (see Table 3.1).

Table 3.1 Petitions against taxes on knowledge, 1852–60 (first 100)

	1852	1855†	1860‡
General inhabitants	30	17	3
Localities	10	3	
Meetings	10	1	
Rational recreation	17	3	25
Workers groups (related)	25	33	34
Workers groups (unrelated)	1	1	
Newspaper proprietors, etc.	2	35	38
Individuals/misc	5	7	

†In favour of Newspaper, Postage and Stamp Duties Bill.

‡In favour of repeal of paper duties.

Report of the Select Committee on Public Petitions (1852, 1855, 1860).

The recent study of Anti-Corn Law petitions suggests that when League co-ordination ceased the number fell to zero. In contrast, these petitions were not exclusively generated by APRTOK campaigns of course: in the early 1850s and in 1859–61 the other campaigning associations were also instrumental, but they do speak both of an autonomous culture of opposition to the taxes, and of the efficacy of Collet's correspondence networks and continued encouragement in mobilizing support.[74]

The bulk of the Association's support was in consequence delivered from the more natural constituency of radical liberal circles spanning the divide between Anti-Corn Law Leaguers and Chartists of the 1840s. This would certainly encompass the activists such as Thomas Edward Bowkett and John Passmore Edwards in London.[75] In Birmingham, supporters included William B. Smith (1821–95), active Oddfellow, member of the Birmingham Political Union, leading figure in the Freehold Land Society, proprietor of both the *Birmingham Mercury* and the *Wolverhampton Herald*.[76] In Manchester, the circular convening the local association was signed in addition to Watts by J. R. Cooper, ex-Chartist, George Wilson, chair of the League Council and director of the remaining League machine, along with a phalanx of leading middle-class radicals. The December 1853 subscription list for Manchester also included a number of petit-bourgois liberals, including, and others prominent in the city's institutions of rational recreation, including the secretary of the Lancashire and Cheshire Union of Mechanics' Institutes, the Secretary of the National Public Schools Association, and a director and vice-president of the Manchester Mechanics' Institute.[77]

Pressure group politics

APRTOK's loose central organization and uninterest in developing membership or branch structures, coupled with its efforts to sustain a strong petitioning presence partly reflect limitations of commitment, finance and political leverage, but fully make sense only once we recognize that almost from the outset it constituted itself differently to the conventional pressure group model, and that it sought to exert its pressure in novel ways. The average size of petitions during this period (less than 20 signatories per petition) provides one indication of the character of this agitation: designed not to intimidate with numbers but to influence through insistence.[78]

This is not to deny that in some respects APRTOK exploited a range of modes and mechanisms conventionalized by the successful extra-parliamentary pressure groups of the first half of the century, not least the Anti-Slavery and Anti-Corn Law movements in which many of APRTOK's supporters had been active. The Association demonstrated the full repertoire of pressure politics: as we have seen branch associations and petitions; ostensible party-political neutrality; electoral pressure through pledges from parliamentary candidates, and holding MPs to account through their voting record; the propaganda machinery of speeches, lectures, pamphlets, tracts, handbills and periodicals; deputations to ministers; parliamentary interventions and motions.

But this work was intermittent at best, and generally not sustained. Initially the NSAC had been conceived in the established conception of a pressure group. As the *Newcastle Guardian* put it in August 1849: 'It seems to have become a principle with our "governing families" to move only in obedience to pressure from without . . . If they ask for agitation, let them have it . . .'[79] The difficulty was that the parliamentary leaders of the movement were firmly opposed to anything that might smack of rabble rousing. Opponents of the movement sought to present its spokesmen as 'agitators' with all that connoted for conservative opinion.[80] But Cobden had a longstanding concern that public meetings were vulnerable to hijacking by more radical elements,[81] and tended to vacillate between regretting the lack of movement from the people, (which he seemed to think could be 'spontaneous')[82] and warnings against anything that gave any whiff of agitation: 'we comprise steady, sober middle-class reformers – free trade, temperance, education, peace advocates – who will stand by you year to year, . . . provided you handle them judiciously, and do not place them in a position in which they think they are committed to a *tone* of agitation which does not represent their feelings', he lectured Collet.[83]

Collet never acted the role of a lecturing-agent, and the parliamentary leadership were reluctant to be dragged into the treadmill of platform performance. Cobden wearily spoke in November 1853 of being 'persecuted to attend meetings of every kind . . . – Peace, Ballot, Education, Taxes on Knowledge, Juvenile Delinquency, & Mechanics Institutions without number . . .'[84] The Association's AGMs which in the early 1850s attracted large crowds to some of London's high profile venues were gradually allowed to dwindle into fairly low-key affairs.[85] The Association printed and circulated handbills and from 1853 used its *Gazette* to articulate its message to subscribers and the press, but the *Gazette* was a unprepossessing sheet, and bears no comparison with the periodicals associated with other pressure groups (Figure 3.2).

The Association's electoral pressure was again a matter largely of going through the motions. However, with an occasional exception, like the Marylebone by-election in August 1854, in which the Executive Committee issued an address to electors asking them to pledge Sir Benjamin Hall, APRTOK made no real attempt to pledge candidates, or threaten abstentions. The question was most prominent during the 1852 election.[86] At Southwark, Apsley Pellatt, as a paper manufacturer, was particularly forthright in condemnation of the paper duty,[87] and the committee engaged in active opposition to his opponent.[88] By and large, though, things were left to local initiative, of which there was often a great deal. At Boston in 1852, the newly formed Taxation and Representation

Figure 3.2 'A meeting for the repeal of the taxes on knowledge', *Illustrated London News*, 1851 [Mary Evans Ref 10104600]

Society held a meeting of non-electors which loudly cheered calls for the repeal of the taxes on knowledge, and at non-electors meetings in Manchester, the record of Gibson and Bright on the taxes was identified as one of the reasons they deserved popular support.[89] In 1857 the committee contented itself with an address,[90] and in 1859 APRTOK again urged voters to extract pledges on the taxes on knowledge from candidates, and at Grimsby, radicals questioned candidates on their attitude to the paper duties and their willingness to abolish 'all the restrictions on newspapers'.[91]

Perhaps this was part of a gradual drift to an alternative model of rational reform, a liberation 'not by a mob revolution – but by full discussion both within and without the walls of Parliament', as the *Sun* put it in November 1852.[92] Although there is no hard-and-fast line of demarcation, it perhaps makes sense to think of APRTOK less as a pressure group and more as a lobbying organization. It sought first to win the argument about the impolicy of the taxes, second to promote them to a position of priority, and third to make the difficulties of repealing them seem less of an evil than those of maintaining them. The weapons were often those familiar from earlier pressure groups. What marked the Association's campaigns was the extent to which they were moulded into an effective strategic whole, in which parliamentary pin pricks, pressure on the Inland Revenue and publicity for its failings were combined to undermine the will to resist of the government and its organs.

Led by Milner Gibson, a small band of sympathizers kept up a steady drip, drip of parliamentary interrogation, keeping the question before the public, and politicians face to face with the compromises and complexities of the legislation. Every opportunity was taken to organize deputations, to construct and embody a sense of public opinion, to provide an opportunity to ensure the justifications for repeal were properly and fully understood, and to draw members of the government into the obscure complexities of the legislation.[93] A great deal of work was done through informal 'behind-the-scenes lobbying', in which Bright was especially assiduous, and the extensive correspondence networks of the Manchester radicals were used to maintain a steady pressure of ideas and arguments.[94]

So far, so conventional. Where APRTOK broke new ground was in the leverage which it sought to generate for use on such occasions, its shift after 1852 into an attritional stance which aimed not primarily to win the intellectual battle, or to even to worry the political classes with a fear of popular alienation and unrest, but rather to wear down the will of government and officials, by bringing the law and the institutions that implemented it, particularly the Inland Revenue, into disrepute, so that, as Cobden put it, 'both the lawyers and the ministers . . . will be tired of the subject and give up the tax for the sake of peace and quiet'.[95] Whereas the campaigners of the 1830s had attempted to use mass imprisonment to undermine the moral credibility of the government, APRTOK strategy involved drawing out the inconsistencies and illogicalities of the legislation and its implementation to undermine the state's claim to competence and fairness, at the very point at which the construction of the liberal or neutral state was being conceived as fundamental to strategies of social and political stabilization.[96]

In these tactics the Association had been presented with two advantages: a statutory regime which was complicated, contradictory and placed inordinate reliance on the interpretation of officials, and an executive arm of the state which was unequal to the task entrusted to it. The responsible body was the Board of Commissioners of Inland Revenue which had been created by the consolidation of the Boards of Excise and of Stamps and Taxes by the Inland Revenue Board Act (1849).[97] Based at Somerset House on the Strand, the Inland Revenue Commissioners were responsible for all the internal taxation of the Victorian state, direct and indirect. It was a difficult portfolio, and its management was far from efficient for much of the early 1850s, not helped by the long illness of the Board's chairman, John Wood, in the 18 months prior to his death in October 1856.[98]

The Inland Revenue was charged with implementing the interlocking legislation which regulated newspapers described in Chapter 1. Unfortunately, as was often the case, the accretion of successive statutes had served to create various inconsistencies, uncertainties and anomalies. There existed an almost limitless supply of questions with which it was possible to engage the Revenue, embroiling it in clarifications that might themselves create further confusion. Because the legislation left the Board responsible also for initiating any legal proceedings to be brought against those who transgressed the law, it and its officials, in particular Thomas Keogh, Secretary to the Commissioners of the Inland Revenue, and Joseph Timm, Solicitor to the Revenue, were left doubly exposed.[99]

The weapons of this campaign were the letter and the memorial. Collet, aided especially by associates such as Holyoake, kept up a stream of questions and observations. Individuals affected by the duties, newspaper proprietors, publishers, paper makers, manufacturers of envelopes or writing paper, were encouraged to engage in correspondence of their own, with a view to luring the Revenue into error or to pushing its officials into decisions or judgements that they would find hard to justify, or which would 'solve' one problem only at the expense of creating an anomaly elsewhere. As Collet noted in *Taxes* the resources of the Association in these struggles were two-fold: it could seek for exemptions and relaxations of the regulations, especially where it appeared that these were already being granted in some cases, and if and when these were refused, could then press for prosecution of those who appeared to be flouting the regulations and principles thereof as espoused in that refusal.[100] The campaign's munitions were ridicule, irony and gentle sarcasm.

Milner Gibson in particular proved himself a master of this kind of strategy, balancing the constructive appeal to Parliament for repeal, with an orchestrated campaign of oblique vilification of the statutory system and the institutions and individuals forced to operate it. 'No-one', remarked Charles Cowan, 'could have had greater satisfaction than Mr Milner Gibson in teasing or worrying the Excise at this time, by bringing repeated demands for drawback or remission of duty, founded upon their previous concessions, in showing the absurdity of as well as the injustice of the duty and of the laws passed to maintain it.'[101] Cobden was initially sceptical. In 1851 while urging Collet to exploit the contradictory decisions of the Board, he expressed 'doubt [at] the policy of . . . acrimonious attack'.[102] In the autumn of 1853 he told Collet that 'I never had much faith in that kind of tactics'.[103] But by 1854 he was apparently won over to the strategy. 'We must make a push now, and by dint of *persecution* I hope both the lawyers and ministers, to say nothing of John Wood & Co., will be tired of the subject, and give up the tax for the sake of peace and quietness'.[104]

Having pulled the parliamentary leaders along in this strategy, Collet, Moore and Holyoake went further, adding two further prongs to the attack: deliberate albeit temporary defiance of the law designed to probe and push the limits of the appetite of those responsible for active enforcement of the regulations, and – most controversially – active pressure for its full implementation, on the basis that it was only by systematic enforcement that the insufficiency of the legislation could be fully exposed.[105]

In respect to legal defiance, Collet's instincts were cautious. He recognized that the reforms of the 1830s had largely undercut the basis for a sustained campaign of illegality along the lines of the 1830s. Instances like the case of John Lennox, who defied the stamp regime by publishing his *Greenock News Clout* on cloth rather than paper, suggested the difficulties of this approach.[106] 'I don't pretend to be very squeamish about breaking such iniquitous laws as the newspaper laws' he remarked in January 1852, 'but it is always worth while to think twice before breaking any law, and in the present instance I think more can be effected by acting within the pale of the law than by going beyond it.'[107] Gradually, though, the Revenue's struggles to sustain the stamp regime without being drawn into unpopular and unprofitable prosecutions of papers such as the *Athenaeum*, which at times clearly involved adjusting statute and interpretation to the accommodation of illegal practices brought him to the conclusion that 'The principle acted on by the Government is, that a law can be repealed only in consequence of its systematic violation by the people.'[108]

Given Collet's initial wariness about placing himself in jeopardy by illegality, 'there was only one part', as he put it looking back, 'which it was in our power to perform. This was to demand the enforcement of the law, which was expressed in terms which no one could accept without bidding adieu to common sense and common humanity.'[109] In the case of the *Norwich Reformer* (see below), having failed to persuade the *Reformer*'s Norwich publishers to present a complaint against *Punch*, Collet had arranged for one to be prepared at the Association's offices and signed by its porter.[110] Doubts were expressed: it 'was, to some of us, new, and even revolting' Collet conceded, and he was instructed by a resolution of the committee not to 'take cognizance of any information' against existing publications.[111] True to what became well-established form, Collet refused to be restricted, and 'in his private capacity, engaged friends outside the Committee to send in complaints'. Newspapers were circulated with 'warnings' to printers and newspaper proprietors about the way in which the legislation was administered.[112] Thereafter the tactic gradually became an accepted part of the Association's arsenal, not least for its ability to simultaneously embarrass the Revenue and the putative 'law breaker'. Entirely typical was the warning the Association gave the Lord Mayor of London in 1854 – naturally in a widely publicized letter – that in placarding Crimean war news on more than one day per month, and on unstamped paper, he was breaking the stamp laws. 'Do not, my Lord, drive Mr Timm to desperation', pleaded the letter ironically, 'by making him feel it to be his duty bootlessly to threaten the Lord Mayor of London with a prosecution for defrauding the revenue.'[113]

Challenges such as this crystallized the chaos of compromise and confusion that characterized the implementation of the law, and also the unwillingness, and probably incapacity of the Inland Revenue to justify the discriminations it made, and displayed the Revenue as a cruel bully, as Place, Watson and Collet put it, 'trampling on the poor and letting the rich break the law with impunity'.[114] They could be publicized, either by the independent publication of chains of correspondence, which was a feature of the Association's own publicity, especially the *Gazette*, or – and even more effectively – in official returns of correspondence, such as those of the Inland Revenue presented to Parliament in 1854 and 1858. This tactic had been used in the 1830s, but was brought to further ironic refinement in the 1850s by the ability of opponents to use requests for parliamentary returns of correspondence to put the state into the position of publicizing its own shortcomings. Revenue officials were well aware of the traps that they were being lured into. But even though they attempted to forestall exchanges which were purely designed to embroil the Board in 'useless discussion', as Timm put it to Holyoake, it was difficult to avoid without opening themselves to the accusation of indifference and indeterminancy.[115]

What is a newspaper?

All these elements came together in the pressure commenced by the NSAC and continued by APRTOK for clarification of which, and under what terms, publications could be said to fall under the aegis of the newspaper stamp legislation; or, as it was often formulated, the 'what is a newspaper?' question.

The statutory position was unclear. The initial eighteenth-century legislation had sought to address 'public news, intelligence, or occurrences, printed in any part of the United Kingdom, to be dispersed and made public';

by 60 Geo III c.9 this coverage was extended to 'remarks and observations thereon, and published periodically, or in parts, or numbers, at intervals not exceeding 26 days'. This left a number of uncertainties: first that no attempt was made to define exactly what 'news' was; second that it was not clear if the 26-day frequency limit applied only to comment on news, or was designed to cover also news itself. There were also complications about whether the legislation covered monthly publications. The general assumption had been that it did, but unfortunately 6 &7 Will. 4, c.76, offered three apparently distinct but in fact overlapping definitions.[116]

By the later 1840s a practice had grown up, without any explicit legal sanction, that where periodicals catered only for a specific single class of news, these 'class papers', were deemed by the Inland Revenue not to be newspapers under the acts, and so were not required to be stamped. This status was made doubly anomalous by the willingness of the Revenue to allow these and other periodicals, such as Charles Dickens's *Household Words*, to register as newspapers so that they could stamp part of their issue to take advantage of the 1d postal transmission. The problem was not only lack of definitiveness, but the incapacity of any of the potential arbiters of the distinctions to offer any sort of clear criteria: as was reported in a number of papers in 1851 (very likely extracted from an APRTOK circular) 'The Board of the Inland Revenue does not know; its solicitor does not know; its secretary does not know; the Barons of the Exchequer do not know.'[117]

Yet during 1850 the Revenue brought pressure to bear on a number of unstamped periodicals for publishing news, including the *Norwich Reformer*, a modest unstamped radical monthly which was effectively suppressed because it included a 'record of progress' column which the Revenue insisted brought it under the stamp regulations, while refusing to explain why numerous other monthlies and weeklies, including the *Athenaeum* which provided a great deal more news remained unmolested, and were in some instances even allowed to stamp part of their impression, so as to take advantage of the postal privileges, but print the rest unstamped.[118] In the autumn, the *Wakefield Examiner* was prosecuted for printing separately on unstamped paper accounts of a local court case which was attracting considerable attention.[119] The editor's defence was that this was a widespread practice and it would be invidious for him to be singled out for punishment, but his protest at the Revenue's 'token' £10 fine was met with a stern demand to pay, or face the full penalty of £20 per sheet.

Milner Gibson and the NSAC took up these cases. A flyer, '"Liberty of the Press" as interpreted by the government' which printed the correspondence over the case was circulated.[120] In both cases, the vulnerability of the Revenue to accusations of double standards was all too clear, as the NSAC pointed out when it memorialized the Board the following month, noting that not only were numerous publications registered as newspapers and yet permitted to print part of their impression on unstamped paper, but also that because many were being allowed to publish news on the unstamped paper.[121] A number of newspaper editors/proprietors, were encouraged to write to the Board seeking the privilege of publishing part of their impression without stamps. As it became clear from correspondence subsequently published in the *Daily News*, the Board had put itself in a position of operating a double standard; in some cases acquiescing in the practice of partial stamping, but in other cases arguing that by dint of registration a newspaper became liable to stamp all its issues. In the face of the interrogation of the fully stamped papers, the Board could only shelter behind the assertion that it had 'no power whatever to grant to the publisher of any newspaper permission to publish a portion of the copies thereof without the stamps to which they are liable'.[122] In similar fashion, when the NSAC memorialized the Postmaster General in November 1850, the response was that 'his lordship has no power to judge of or determine the questions named therein'.[123]

In January 1851 C. J. Bunting, editor of the now defunct *Norwich Reformer*, wrote to the Board asking in the light of the publication, without intervention, of Charles Dickens's *Household Narrative*, whether 'the privilege of inserting articles containing news has been conceded by the Board to monthly periodicals', the response was a bald statement that 'no such concession has been made'. This was a golden opportunity for campaigners: at best a crude evasion by the Inland Revenue, and an obvious unfairness, at worst a clear falsehood, in that in practice '[a] *direct infringement of the law* upon the part of a literary giant is *tolerated*, whilst mere pigmies are regarded as fair game for the exercise of its powers', as Bunting put it.[124] In April 1851 S. G. Bucknall, proprietor and editor of the *Stroud Free Press* prodded the Board into action by deliberately printing a single copy on unstamped paper and then sending it to them asking if there would be a penalty for publishing. Having engineered the prosecution, Bucknall was then able (as perhaps had been the intention all along) to make capital out of it in evidence before the Select Committee on Newspaper Stamps later that summer.[125] Reluctantly – 'with a groan and a grimace' on the part of the Inland Revenue, as the *Daily News* observed[126] – a case was commenced against the *Narrative*, but allowed to get bogged down in the courts. While the case stalled, the periodical remained free to continue its publishing arrangements unmolested, a tolerance which contrasted strongly, as APRTOK pointed out, with the summary treatment of less prominent journals. Seeing an opening, Collet canvassed for newspaper proprietors publishing unstamped publications willing to publish news and try their right in court, or indeed to publish an unstamped paper.[127]

Whig politicians were perfectly aware of the difficulty this arrangement placed them in. 'This distinction may be politic', George Cornewall Lewis, who became Chancellor of the Exchequer in 1855, told Sir Charles Wood privately in October 1851, 'but it is quite arbitrary – it is unsanctioned by law – it is made by the mere authority of the government, & although the news published by the Athenaeum, or the Builder, or the Law Journal, may not interest the public at large, it is news to all intents and purposes.'[128] Eventually, in December 1851 the verdict of the courts was that *Household Words* was not subject to stamp because it wanted one of the defining qualities identified under 60 Geo III c.9, namely that it was printed at greater intervals than 26 days (i.e. that the defining terms under the act were cumulative, not alternative, and lack of any one provided exemption).[129] Collet noted that the result probably delayed the overall success of the campaign, in that 'The public would not have allowed Charles Dickens to suffer under laws professedly enacted to prevent blasphemy and sedition.'[130] But elsewhere there was rejoicing. The question of repeal had become academic, noted the *Leader*, 'only get enough judgements on them, and you soon reduce them to mincemeat. This Newspaper Stamp Act, for instances – it is evident that in five or six bouts a few Judges could knock it to pieces.'[131]

The government commenced proceedings to reverse the judgement. Milner Gibson countered with a petition of protest and a call for a committee to inquiry into the conduct of the Stamp Office.[132] At the same time the Association attempted to put pressure on Sir Frederick Thesiger, who had become Attorney-General in February, to prosecute papers breaking the law with the tacit acceptance of the Inland Revenue, but he refused to act without instruction. The Association pointed out the arbitrary nature of a law whose scope could only be ascertained by inviting prosecution: 'So long as the officers of the Crown can go into Court without risk of personal loss, while the defendant is exposed to heavy losses . . . the Excise is only another name for the Inquisition.'[133]

For a while the Association cast around for an opportunity to try the implications of the *Household Narrative* case.[134] There were calls for the establishment of an unstamped daily to advocate abolition, but Collet pointed out that the capital involved would be beyond the reaches of the Association, and too vulnerable to vigorous prosecution from the Revenue. Collet tried unsuccessfully to generate interest in the collection of a £1,000 guarantee fund for the publication of four ostensibly separate unstamped monthly newspapers as a way of circumventing the law.[135] However, the Association did persuade Frank Hay Grant, a writer for the *Reasoner*, to publish the *Stoke-upon-Trent Narrative of Current Events*, with a view to finally overthrowing the partially applied regulation that a monthly publication must appear at the beginning of the month.[136] The first issue of 14 February 1852 was drawn directly to the attention of the Inland Revenue, which warned Grant that his paper was illegal, but on being told he would continue to publish until convicted, shied away from legal action, pleading 'want of instruction'. The *Narrative* was discontinued after 12 months on the grounds that this principle had been established by its non-prosecution, although as the case of W. W. Mitchell illustrates, the Revenue had continued to proceed against other papers, which were published alternately at fortnightly intervals, in a more obvious attempt to subvert the stamp legislation.[137] Although legislation which excluded publications appearing at periods of more than 26 days from the operation of the stamp duties, was lost when the Derby government fell in December 1852, the Inland Revenue stopped pursuing monthly newspapers as being liable to the newspaper stamp.[138]

Encouraged by the reluctance of the Revenue to proceed against the *Stoke Narrative,* Collet's next scheme was the *Potteries Free Press* (PFP), an unstamped penny weekly published in Hanley, with the masthead 'Under the Protection of the Association for Promoting the Repeal of the Taxes on Knowledge', as an even more direct challenge to the Inland Revenue.[139] Milner Gibson was horrified, demanding an urgent meeting, and Collet agreed both to keep the paper visibly distinct from the Association and to give it up as soon as it was determined in court that it required a stamp.[140] In the meantime, he took great delight in needling the Stamp Office, confessing disappointment in its fourth issue, 'that the lynx-eyed guardians of the Inland Revenue have not deigned, as yet, to take notice of our proceedings'.[141] Sidestepping Collet's challenge, the Revenue initially proceeded not against him, but against one of the paper's newsvendors, who was convicted for selling an unstamped newspaper.[142]

The PFP was eventually suppressed in April 1853 after 10 or 11 issues.[143] Collet was left, despite donations of nearly £40, with a debt on the paper of over £27,[144] but it had stimulated the publication of other unstamped papers, including James Watson's *Political Examiner*, and stiffened the resolve of journals such as the *Racing Times*, which claimed exemption as a 'class publication' and faced down threats to prosecute it.[145] In March 1853 the Attorney General conceded that proceedings against the *Racing Times* had been withdrawn, but refused to be drawn on whether this had been because the paper could not be distinguished from the *Builder*, the *Athenaeum* and others.[146] '[T]he B[oar]d of Inland Revenue from what I hear', Milner Gibson told Holyoake, 'begins to show decided symptoms of "punishment".[147] The opportunities opened up were not lost on Cobden, who urged the establishment of an unstamped weekly addressing emigration, with a view to testing 'how far the stamp office would allow the exemption of *class publications* to go'.[148]

Eventually, the Newspaper Stamp Duties Bill of August 1853 repealed the third clause of 60 Geo III, c.2, excluding monthly papers from the remit of the act, but it created further uncertainties as to whether a monthly, now not subject to the requirement of the stamp, was thus by definition not a newspaper and could thereby be refused a voluntarily part-stamped issue. The Act also left it unclear whether the first clause covered a paper which published *any* news, or only one whose *primary* aim was to publish news (and as the Association's address to Gladstone of December 1853 detailed, there were difficulties in either case).[149] In February 1854 Milner Gibson told an APRTOK soiree that the 1853 Act did 'nothing more than . . . exempt the interesting *Household Narrative* of Mr Charles Dickens from any further prosecution'.[150]

The continued uncertainties the Revenue faced were illustrated by the case of Henry Shaw and the Dublin *Commercial Journal and Family Herald*. In a bid to avoid some of the stamp duty, in addition to his regular stamped paper Shaw had published a parallel unstamped edition, which purported to include only adverts and literary matter, but not the news and comment thereon which would bring it under the terms of the act.[151] Several attempts were made to proceed against Shaw, without decisive success, and by September 1853 there were renewed complaints. When the case was eventually heard at the Court of Exchequer before a special jury, it found for Shaw, apparently swayed by suggestions that the 1853 repeal did materially alter the definition of a newspaper liable to stamp because it repealed that part of 6&7 Wm IV that declared any paper containing 'any public News, intelligence or occurrences or any remarks or observations thereon' to be a newspaper, by removing the first any and the words 'or any remarks or observations thereon'. If the verdict could not be overturned, the Board noted, it would be impossible to maintain the stamp duty.[152]

From August 1853 to the repeal of the newspaper stamp in 1855, the Association kept up its guerrilla warfare against the Revenue. In February 1854 Keogh was upbraided for informing the *North Oxfordshire Monthly Times* and the *Wrexham Monthly Advertiser* that they could not publish on both stamped and unstamped paper, despite this being the widespread practice of London periodicals, and apparently in direct contradiction both to the 1853 act, and his evidence to the 1851 Select Committee on the Newspaper Stamp.[153] Collet and Holyoake had some fun with their 'does blank paper count for nothing?' question, which sought to lure the Treasury into clarifying how the proportion of advertisements in a newspaper – one of the criteria for coming under the stamp requirements – should be calculated.[154] Holyoake published a weekly *Fleet Street Advertiser*, half advertisements and half blank sheets, sending copies to the Inland Revenue, and members of the government.[155] Holyoake, indeed, was particularly adept at this game. During 1854 he also engaged in a long correspondence with the Treasury and the Post Office, seeking either permission to stamp without having to falsely swear that the *Reasoner* was a newspaper (denied by Inland Revenue) or to allow *Reasoner* to pass for penny postage stamp (denied by Post Office).[156] Holyoake initiated an indictment of the proprietors of the *Clerical Journal*, over their registration of the paper for the purposes of part-stamping its issue, accusing them of perjury and conspiracy to defraud the Post Office. The *Journal's* proprietors were driven to petition for revision of the law in order to defend themselves from 'the same vexatious proceedings by any person having any malignity towards them'.[157] In the summer of 1854 the Association made capital from a parliamentary return which identified 136 publications registered as newspapers but part unstamped (the real figure, it suggested on the basis of Mitchell's *Newspaper Directory* might have been as many as 200). It obtained legal advice that these periodicals were making a fraudulent declaration and were guilty of a criminal misdemeanour.[158] At the same time it was observed that many were also over the 2oz weight limit applied to part-stamped periodicals.

This pressure was brought to a head in May 1854 when Milner Gibson, despite initial opposition from the government, successfully obtained the agreement of the Commons to a motion that 'the Laws in reference to the Periodical Press and Newspaper Stamp are ill-defined and unequally enforced' and demand the early attention of the House.[159] Even *The Times* was prepared to concede that the newspaper laws were 'ill-defined and unequally enforced . . . . so capricious as to escape all ordinary powers of understanding', and was forced back onto the visibly pragmatic argument that this was inevitable, because the alternative – imposition in all cases – was unwarrantable.[160] In June 1854 Cobden found John Wood 'terribly out of temper with the Attorney General & abused him soundly for having thrown the Inland Revenue Board over in his speech on Gibson's motion. He said that . . . in future he should never act without his *written* opinion.'[161] Internally, the Treasury recognized the awkwardness of its position, a minute suggesting in August that it would be useful to have clarification of some of the 'practical difficulties in the administration of the present law', and was inadvisable to engage in a defence against 'the vague and unjust charges of a general character made against [the] Board'.[162]

After 1855: Harrying the Excise

After the repeal of the newspaper stamp the Association was briefly in abeyance, but once it had resumed active operations in 1857 the successful formula was applied to the excise duty on paper. The *Gazette* was relaunched, deputations resumed and the committee reactivated its extended correspondence network. The Association also had the advantage of consistent support from the *Morning Star*, the penny daily started in March 1856 by Cobden and Bright to advocate Manchester School views (see Chapter 7). Holyoake was one of its stable of editorial writers, and contributed to the paper's strong support for the repeal of the paper duties.[163] Although Cobden and Bright's attention after 1856 was largely engrossed by the *Star* or diverted by domestic afflictions, Milner Gibson retained his interest and commitment, and while he was out of Parliament after his defeat in the 1857 general election, A. S. Ayrton, the radical MP for Tower Hamlets, kept up the pressure of parliamentary questioning.

The success of its 'what is a newspaper' stratagem encouraged the Association to a reprise around the question of what defined 'paper' for the purposes of the duty. Capital was made of the case of Florentine buttons, which were made of material which if kept in sheets would be liable, but if cut into shapes was not, unless it were then covered with white paper, when it would again attract duty.[164] The Association took up the case of Captain Barry whose patent for 'artificial parchment' made out of the parings of animal skins attempted to circumvent the duty. Barry was prosecuted by the Inland Revenue, and was forced to give up the manufacture because of the cost of the extended legal proceedings, which dragged on into 1859 when the Court of Exchequer found in favour of the Attorney-General.[165] As APRTOK was quick to point out, if 'paper' could be made out of animal, and not merely vegetable, matter, then how could a distinction be made between paper and all sorts of products, for example roofing felt which had long competed with paper, but was exempted on the grounds, it had been thought, that it was primarily manufactured from animal produce.[166] The Revenue was also harried on the question of 'half-stuff', an intermediate stage between rags and paper, which was exempted from duty by the Paper-makers Act (2&3 Vict c.23), but had later apparently been redefined as paper by the Inland Revenue once the manufacturers began preparing it in sheets for ease of transportation, preventing domestic manufacture, while the same product was freely imported without being taxed as paper. Once again, as the press observed, the excise was 'breaking down by the inability to define what the article intended to be taxed really is. The Board of Excise has one rule for defining paper, and the Board of Customs has another'.[167]

As the range of papers on the market increased and their uses became more diverse, and the claims for exemptions and drawbacks multiplied, the administration of the tax became more and more complex. The Association's successes were trumpeted as small victories, but then used as levers either to prise further reductions or to lift further stones of inequality. A year-long campaign by John Scott, a London envelope maker, succeeded in the face of initial refusal in persuading the Inland Revenue to offer a drawback on waste paper to all envelope manufacturers.[168] This achieved, the Association tried the analogous case of writing paper, and of wall-paper hangings, and when the Revenue refused, further arbitrary anomalies were created.[169] In the end, Collet noted, the Treasury 'took refuge in an embarrassed silence'.[170]

The justification offered for allowing a drawback on cards used in Jacquard weaving, that it was analogous to the paper used in pressing woollen stuffs, which had traditionally also been allowed a drawback, was held up to scrutiny. The problem was, as an APRTOK deputation told Lord Derby in April 1858, placing bounds on the principle of 'analogy'; on that basis, the exemption allowed to books at the Universities in Greek and Latin on the basis that they were purely educational, should be extended to all schoolbooks. And likewise, if exemptions were allowed on certain forms of papier maché on the grounds that it is widely used and 'one of which the applications are likely to become so numerous and so valuable', where might this line be drawn? The Association seized gleefully on passages in the *Second Report of the Board of the Inland Revenue*, which appeared in May 1858 and which appeared to blame envelope manufacturers for not having noticed since 1850 the advantages of combining this with paper making, and which justified the drawback on the principle that 'paper which does not go into consumption is, if practicable, fairly entitled to exemption or drawback.[171]

It also publicized the more dysfunctional elements of the excise system. In 1859, William Scholefield obtained a return of the proceeds of the excise duty on pasteboard which demonstrated that the operation generated almost no revenue because in nearly all cases the addition of paste to manufacture the pasteboard led to a reduction in weight. 'An Excise duty that brings in no revenue', the *Morning Star* remarked, 'is an abomination'.[172]

As before 1855, the committee at turns asked for relief, and then for more rigorous imposition, encouraging one manufacturer to seek relief for writing paper through an extension of the drawback, another to ask for the application of the paper duty to scaleboard and felt, in light of the Barry decision.[173] As before the pressure had its effect in wearing down the resolve of the authorities. Little appetite was shown on either side of the Commons to resist Milner Gibson's motion in June 1858 that 'it is the opinion of this House that the maintenance of the Excise on Paper as a permanent source of revenue would be impolitic', Disraeli as Chancellor and Lord John Russell from the opposition benches both concurring in debate, and the motion being agreed without a division. Although this was just a general declaration and the critical question remained as it always had been, the ability of the government finances to bear the loss of revenue that repeal would occasion, this sort of admission, coupled with continued pressure on the administration of the duty continued to sap the will of the Inland Revenue. In its 1859 *Report* the Revenue conceded that the longstanding expectation of abolition, combined with pressure for exceptions had created considerable 'embarrassment'.[174] Charles Cowan later recalled that he 'expressed [his] surprise one day to the chairman that these demands for drawback . . . His answer was, "You know, Mr Cowan, that the duty cannot be maintained long, and we are obliged to comply with these demands just to keep the people quiet"'.[175]

In January 1860 APRTOK committee produced a brief for Gladstone on the impolicy of the paper duties, in which under the head of 14 general propositions it was able to detail 50 specific anomalies and difficulties in the legislation.[176] In proposing the repeal of the paper duties in February 1860, Gladstone, reported that of the 15 arguments presented by 'the agitators for its repeal', 13 had been accepted by the Inland Revenue, and that in particular, the difficulty of defining paper was placing the Revenue in the same ridiculous position it was in before the repeal of the stamp duty of being unable to define what a newspaper was.[177] The Paper duty, as the 1860 report of the Inland Revenue baldly confessed, was 'rapidly becoming untenable'.[178]

Conclusion

There is no doubt that the constant pressure gradually wore down the resistance of the tax authorities, and the government. They kept a brave face, and stuck to their guns, but they increasingly felt their position to be indefensible. '[T]he Stamp Office assumes the power of making a publication a newspaper and not a newspaper at the same time. If a class periodical is a newspaper, it ought to pay a stamp on its entire impression; if it is not a newspaper, a stamp of one penny ought not to free it through the post office', Cornewall Lewis confessed to Sir Charles Wood. 'It seems to me that if this rule is attacked, there will be great difficulty in supporting it on *legal* grounds.'[179] Eventually, even while governments continued to resist repeal, Milner Gibson's parliamentary pressure told in the form of resolutions which condemned the taxes in principle, and in various attempts, both legislative and administrative, to adjust the operations of the regime. This success did not determine either the timing or the nature of the process of repeal: these remained dependent on exigencies of politics, finance (and often foreign affairs). But they did create the necessary predispositions in ruling circles in favour of removal as soon as that was a matter of practical politics, and they created the appearance of a policy determined by exhausted expediency, that, in the case of the repeal of the stamp, the law was to be adapted to the hitherto illegal practice of those papers who had chosen to stamp part of their imprint in order to take advantage of the rights of postal transmission. Despite rejecting all the substantive arguments brought forward by opponents, 'they acknowledge that they have been coerced, concussed and bothered into' repeal, as the *Stirling Observer* put it, 'that the legal is to succumb to the illegal, the regular to the irregular, solely because the law officers of the crown are not wise enough, nor bold enough, nor sufficiently energetic, to carry out the law at present in existence.'[180]

4

Repealing the Advertising and
Stamp Duties, 1851–5

The APRTOK campaigns of the early 1850s sapped the will of leaders
across the political spectrum to retain the newspaper taxes in the
longer term. Success in obtaining repeal, however, remained a matter of
fiscal arithmetic and political calculation. In this, the strong identification of
the campaign with Manchester School radicalism was a double-edged sword,
with one edge a great deal sharper than the other. In the political flux of
the early 1850s both Whigs and Liberals inclined to see their natural allies
in the Peelite grouping which combined commitment to Free Trade with
conservative instincts. Despite its role in achieving free trade, antipathy to
the Manchester School leaders within Liberal governmental circles was fierce.
Whigs like Grey were indignant at Cobden and Bright's extra-parliamentary
activities.[1] The legacy of the Peelite financial reforms of the 1840s was a
number of uncertainties. Peel's resort to income tax as a peacetime expedient
aroused mixed responses. Radicals feared income tax as a mechanism for
supporting extravagant expenditure, especially on war, but also recognized
its ability to offer a substitute for revenue from indirect taxes and so underpin
further removals of customs and excise duties, but there was no consistent
Radical position, beyond general desire for reduced expenditure. While
there was an inclination towards direct over indirect taxation, in general
income tax was accepted at best reluctantly, and only as an expedient means
of removing indirect taxes.[2] The campaigns came to be seen as 'a test of [the
radicals'] utter inefficacy', their inability 'to sink that surprising individuality
which is their characteristic, and to organise themselves into a party'.[3]

During the budget debates of 1851, fiscal discussions were still dominated
by concerns to address the needs of the counties and so cement the victory of

free trade. At the same time, as Woods told Russell in January 1851, military expenditure was 'at a discount', and parliamentary sentiment was 'all on the economical tack'.[4] In February 1851 it was reported by the *Morning Advertiser* that the government intended to reduce the paper and advertisement duties by two-thirds, but there was little evidence in the government's private correspondence of any great attention to the newspaper question.[5] In the event, despite pressure from the Radicals for the use of surpluses generated by income tax to abolish further duties, and some pressure from Russell to try to conciliate rural opinion by reducing the burden on agricultural rates, the strongest voice in the cabinet for popular tax reductions was Wood's, and he focused on the abolition of the window tax and reductions in timber and coffee duties, on the basis that the government was unlikely to conciliate the rural interest, and 'if not, we ought to combine the greatest possible strength in all other quarters'.[6] The Manchester Radicals were again frustrated, but the problems faced by APRTOK are nicely illustrated by the stance of the historian George Grote, one of the Association's backers, who commiserated with Wood over the criticism he had received for 'a budget both honest and founded on right principles'. No matter that the reductions were not quite what he might have chosen, 'No Chancellor of the Exchequer can be fairly tried by such a standard', he remarked, 'There is so much of what is comparative between different items all of them evil, that great diversity of opinion cannot be avoided.'[7]

Parliamentary politics and repeal of the advertising duty

Pressure on Russell in early 1851 did manage to secure a Select Committee on the Newspaper Stamp, with Milner Gibson as chair, and Cobden leading the questioning.[8] Proceedings were carefully orchestrated by the radical majority on the committee, which heard from 22 witnesses in all. Five were officials of the Inland Revenue (including Timm and Keogh). Most of the rest provided a procession of opponents of the stamp, including the Manchester bookseller Abel Heywood, Bunting of the *Norwich Reformer* and Bucknall of the *Stroud Free Press*. The case for the taxes was left to Mowbray Morris of *The Times* and Alexander Russel of the *Scotsman* (who claimed that it had not been the intention to call him as a witness),[9] with support from W. H. Smith, the newsagent. Russel described his experience as 'a wrangling struggle against being forced into answering unfair questions by the enemy'.[10] Frederick Knight Hunt of the *Daily News*, despite that paper's previous support for the Association, was only willing to support full repeal if associated with an effective protection of copyright. Despite opposition from a minority of members led by Henry Rich, Milner Gibson's determination to produce a strong recommendation in favour of repeal narrowly prevailed,[11] and the verdict of the *Report* was unequivocal: the stamp should be abolished and replaced by postage for printed matter at 1d for under 2 oz; and brief copyright protection should be provided for original publishers of intelligence.[12]

By the end of the Committee Milner Gibson was talking optimistically of support from Gladstone and the government for the repeal of the advertising duty.[13] The Committee's recommendations were announced on 26 July, and printed *in extenso* in the *Daily News* and some provincial papers, but in general the press response was far from enthusiastic.[14] There were exceptions, including the *Nonconformist* which welcomed all of the Committee's findings,[15] but even the generally sympathetic *Caledonian Mercury* described the characterization of the stamp as a 'tax' as 'the egregious error that runs through the report'.[16] Collet was forced to take up cudgels in series of letters on the Select Committee and its evidence in the *Daily News*.[17] The formal publication of the *Report* in mid-September allowed for further press discussion, but there was little sense that the Committee had created a firm basis for immediate government action and was quickly all but forgotten.[18]

In any case, Disraeli's 1852 budgets were again formulated against a backdrop of calls for increased military expenditure, which the death of Wellington seemed to encourage.[19] 'If the public will allow themselves to be humbugged by such a device as that of the *French invasion*', Cobden lamented, 'they must pay for their folly'.[20] By the time Disraeli introduced his provisional budget in April, Milner Gibson had obtained a further commitment from the Chancellor that any reluctance to remove the impositions was purely financial. For all this it was clear that the political leverage available to push for repeal was limited. The Conservatives had other priorities, and divisions within the Whig-Liberals remained deep. Lord John Russell was prepared to envisage the ultimate removal of the paper and advertising duties, 'but certainly not the stamp duty on newspapers, with any good will', and certainly not with any enthusiasm.[21] Even this frightened the Whigs. George Grey confided to Wood in August 1852 that from what he could infer from Russell's correspondence, 'if he had to make [a budget] I wd not like it at all', arguing adamantly that with free trade safe, the Whigs should have nothing more to do with 'Cobden and Co'.[22] Such sentiment was hardened by the furore created during the 1852 election by Joseph Hume's response to

Collet's suggestion that the co-operation of Russell be sought for APRTOK's election activities. 'I consider Lord John as *not sincere* as a Reformer, both *civil* and *religious*'; 'We shall certainly succeed, but it will be against both the *Whigs* and Tories', Hume told Collet in a letter which was widely published in the press, to furious responses from Whigs and Peelites alike.[23]

Unresolved questions of the Tories' willingness to accept the free trade settlement of the later 1840s continued to preoccupy Cobden and the Radicals, to the exclusion of almost all else, a little interest in the question of education, and general concerns for peace and retrenchment apart.[24] There was some anxiety to construct an effective pressure in favour of radical tax policy, but an acute awareness that it was 'a complicated question', and Disraeli would 'so mystify the matter as to leave nothing very tangible for us to contend with'.[25] The only prospect of removal of the taxes on knowledge seemed to be if it could be presented as fiscally productive, and there is evidence that the government was considering a scheme for a sliding scale which reduced duty to 6d on the smallest classified advertisements, but also imposed duties up to 2/6 for adverts longer than 20 lines in the hope it might produce an overall increase in revenue.[26]

In the aftermath of the election there was some talk of the Derby government offering a series of popular reforms in order to secure the support of the new parliament, including a repeal of the paper duties ('with a view to the relief of the shopkeepers, as well as the printing and publishing interests').[27] In fact it was the abolition of the advertisement duty which was initially included in Disraeli's draft budget, before fears of increased government expenditure caused it to be dropped.[28] In the end, despite the obligatory deputation to Lord Derby, the budget of December 1852 offered nothing on taxes on knowledge, beyond an attempt to adjust the stamp law in the light of the *Household Narrative* case.[29] There is some evidence of popular disappointment at this lack of action,[30] Grey was concerned that Disraeli had 'skilfully enough thrown out baits to many different sets of noisy people'; but in Liverpool, Robertson Gladstone was more concerned with the possible replacement Chancellor: hoping to be spared Wood: 'Anything but him! – a block of wood, worked with wires, will have more sympathy with the views and feelings of the people than he has.'[31]

The defeat of the budget and subsequent resignation of Derby and Disraeli and formation of the Aberdeen government, in which Gladstone and not Wood became Chancellor, appeared to provide the association with an opportunity. Cobden's refusal to join the government without a formal cabinet commitment to the taxes on knowledge and the ballot[32] did not force them into the coalition's programme, but the proceedings of the Tory administration appeared finally to have laid the spectre of a protectionist revival to rest, and the power of the Peelites seemed greatly augmented.[33] Virtually the entire new administration had abstained from Milner Gibson's previous parliamentary motion. There seemed for the first time a realistic possibility that the repeal might be imminent.[34] Collet, energized by the prospects of pushing against a half-open door, mounted a whistle stop tour of the constituencies where ministerial by-elections were being held.[35] Emboldened perhaps by the greater visibility of the APRTOK campaign, and the indications of political favour, it is possible to see a greater sense of press support.[36] During a deputation of the London and provincial press to the Chancellor in March, Smith of the *Daily News* reported that the *News*, the *Herald* and the *Chronicle* supported a reduction to 6d, and would pay £700 to £800 more duty.[37] Opponents of reform shifted from defence of the duties per se and towards an argument that other taxes, especially the income tax, but also duties such as the tea duties, or the cost of international postage, were much more objectionable.[38] In turn opponents of the taxes developed new fiscal arguments, the cost of collection and the absurdity of three taxes essentially on the same commodity, which impeded the revenue-raising potential of the other two.[39]

The 1853 budget has long been recognized as the cornerstone of a Gladstonian approach to finance which formed the fiscal basis for the relative stability of both state and economy in the mid-Victorian years, by establishing workable compromises between the competing demands for the remission of direct or indirect taxation, and for reform of the income tax itself, and in doing so providing the mechanism for completing progress towards free trade in the context of unrelenting pressure for increased expenditure.[40] If in retrospect Gladstone's measures appear as the careful working out of clearly established principles, closer attention demonstrates the degree to which they were constructed out of ad hoc adjustments and hastily concocted expedients, in which the overall logic of fiscal balance appeared to play second fiddle to immediate demands of politics as well as purse; his 1853 correspondence reveals Gladstone, faced by Whig anxieties about the income tax, desperately casting around for various expedients, including the possibility of replacing income tax through the extension of succession tax to real property.[41]

Pressed both to remove the supplement stamp and abolish entirely the advertisement duty, Gladstone, unconvinced that the public finances could spare both, explored various means of increasing the yield of the advertising duty, while seeking the opinion of the trade as to whether they would prefer total abolition of the advertising duty, or reduction to 6d along with the removal of the supplement stamp.[42] The proprietors of the larger provincial papers, such as W. E. Baxter, were for a reduction in the duty combined with the removal of stamp on supplements, which would allow them expand the space for advertisements as far as the increased demand required.[43] The smaller provincial papers and those concerned about the already dominant position of *The Times* were more cautious, fearing that the main result of the removal of the supplement stamp would be a huge increase – perhaps as much as £40,000 in one estimate – in *The Times*'s profits, without any great benefit to those for whom pressure on space was less.[44] Gladstone was apparently swayed by Baxter's reasoning, circulating his letter to the Cabinet, and highlighting its conclusion that 'abolition of the advertisement duty, without a reduction to the stamp on supplements, would not bring the advertiser the benefits sought'.[45]

The pressure on this element of Gladstone's planning was intensified by the outcome of Milner Gibson's annual motion in favour of repeal of the taxes on knowledge introduced on 14 April, days before the Chancellor's budget statement. Quoting correspondence with Edward Baines in which Baines noted that on average each advert prompted 8 letters, but that as many as 200 could be received, Milner Gibson sought to shift the grounds of debate by arguing that the entire removal of the advertisement tax would be more than compensated for by an increase in revenue from the mail.[46] Despite Radical anxieties at engineering a defeat of the Liberal government with Conservative votes, the resolution in favour of the repeal of the advertising duty passed.[47] '[T]he hostility of the House was strongly marked', James Graham noted to the prime minister, Lord Aberdeen, 'while the support, which we received, was lukewarm'.[48] William Ewart, a longstanding opponent, wrote apologetically to Gladstone, excusing himself on the basis that he had always voted against the taxes, and felt obliged as a matter of honour to uphold his position.[49] The cabinet response was to treat the defeat as a matter of Radical hostility, ignore the substantive resolution, and continue attempts at reworking the budget which largely focused on the income tax measures.[50]

The budget itself, presented the following week used the re-imposition of income tax for seven years and its extension to Ireland to abolish or lower duties on some 300 items, including paper, despite protests from the paper makers that restrictions on the export of rags imposed by continental governments gave European manufacturers an advantage over British manufacturers.[51] Russell described it as 'large, honest and framed for duration',[52] but the decision to follow Baxter's line and reduce the advertising duty from 1/6 to 6d while taking the stamp off supplements containing only advertisements split the parliamentary radicals. Joseph Hume was reported to have observed that the budget was 'a great and comprehensive scheme', and that 'we mustn't split hairs, we must take it, as a whole'.[53] But Bright described the advertisement duty proposal as 'a shabby proposition', and the *Leeds Times* dismissed it as 'about as absurd a crotchet as ever entered into the head of a financial projector'.[54] Bright, Cobden, Ewart and others had a 'long conversation' with Gladstone at the Reform Club, in which they 'puzzled him a great deal', but from which they hoped Gladstone would see that his adjustment would bring only very narrow benefits.[55] In early May Bright was optimistic about 'get[ting] all the advertisement duty off', while conceding 'Gladstone is puzzled about the whole question of the press'.[56] At the same time Cobden sought to rouse provincial newspaper proprietors to further exertion, warning Joseph Woodhead of the *Huddersfield Examiner* that the effect of Gladstone's proposal would be merely to line the pockets of the owners of *The Times,* and potentially 'to create a *Times* in every County – a Leviathan which will swallow up all readers & advertisers'.[57]

It is significant that discussions in government circles made no reference to the wider APRTOK campaign. Apart from a deputation led by Milner Gibson on 22 April, at which point it seems that Gladstone might have been shifting his position to removing the stamp on supplements publishing news as well, active pressure at this point came almost entirely from the press itself. Gladstone was subjected to a deluge of letters and memorials against his proposal.[58] The provincial press remained quite sharply divided along grounds of narrow self-interest. Some newspaper proprietors welcomed the existing statutory limitation on the size of stamped papers and supplements as a form of protection – given that the standard size was adequate to their needs and prevented competitors from growing larger, and sought quite explicitly on this basis to argue against not just an unstamped advertising supplement, but any unstamped supplement.[59] For the same reasons, led by John D Cook, editor of the *Morning Chronicle* and one of Gladstone's regular correspondents, a number of metropolitan newspaper proprietors petitioned against the remission of the stamp on supplements, which they argued would 'be to confer on *The Times* a monopoly of the worst description, to the serious injury of every other Morning Metropolitan Journal'.[60]

At the end of April a number of provincial newspaper proprietors met in Manchester and endorsed the removal of duty from all supplements.[61] This view was supported by the Provincial Newspaper Society at its annual meeting in early May, where it was resolved that the remission of the supplement stamp on sheets containing entirely advertisements would be 'entirely inoperative as regards provincial newspapers, and altogether unsatisfactory'.[62] The meeting agreed (after long debate, and without an overwhelming majority) in favour of priority to the removal of the supplement stamp, also approving Gladstone's proposed reduction to 6d, while deliberately avoiding any attempt to resolve the differences of opinion that existed over the question of a complete repeal.[63] In early May a deputation had a series of meetings with influential MPs such as Palmerston, Gladstone and Disraeli.[64] Baxter laboured to dismiss expressions of provincial sentiment, such as the outcome of the Yorkshire proprietors' meeting, as 'representative of "third class" papers – with very little circulation and of recent establishment', simply too small to have experienced the want of room for adverts experienced by the larger more established papers.[65] Even so, the pressure for full repeal of the advertising duty and the other taxes, not least because of the annoyance of any imposition, remained considerable.[66]

Gladstone's compromise was rejected in the Commons on 1 July 1853, after a speech in which he had attempted to justify the retention of the 6d as fundamental to the balance between direct and indirect taxation. In a curious manoeuvre, the direct motion from Milner Gibson to remove the final 6d was defeated 109–99, but later after many MPs had left the chamber, a resolution to replace the 6d with 0d was passed.[67] Initially, though, there was a period of uncertainty. Bright told Wilson on 5 July that 'Gladstone is very shabby about the advertisement duty – even now it is not certain that he will yield & he and his are greatly angry at our beating him on Friday'.[68] Bright laboured hard to persuade the government to accept the verdict of the House, and from Sheffield Isaac Ironside urged Gladstone to abandon his 'pertinacity in resisting the abolition of the advertizement duty'.[69] On 20 July Gladstone confirmed he would. The Newspaper Stamp Duties Bill which received royal assent, on 4 August 1853 and came into immediate effect enabled papers to issue four-page supplements of adverts or news, without additional duty, with (to the frustration of *The Times*) a 1/2d duty on larger supplements.[70] In effect a permanent increase in the size of newspapers from 8 to 12 pages had been allowed, and the trade in newspaper advertisements effectively thrown open.

The Crimean War and the stamp duty

In the initial euphoria of this unexpected triumph over the advertising duties, there was optimism that victory presaged the rapid repeal of the stamp and paper duties.[71] Cobden welcomed it as 'the key to the whole question of the taxes on the press – The rest will follow'.[72] As early as April, Milner Gibson had told Holyoake 'We must make up our minds to "strike while the iron is hot" and worry them out of the stamp'.[73] Meanwhile, there was some uncertainty as to the best way forward. For Cobden it was now purely a matter of finances; in response to Collet's suggestion that 'we ought to strain every nerve to get the paper duty off this year', he advised that Collet 'don't injure [his] nerves in any such unnecessary labour. If Gladstone have the surplus to bear it, he will take off the paper duty as a financial measure recommended by sound policy with which he will be glad to associate his name'.[74] The case of William Woods Mitchell and the *West Sussex Advertiser* (see Prologue) which came to Cobden's attention in the autumn of 1853 reignited his anger but also seemed to provide further incontrovertible evidence of the impolicy of the stamp. 'Is it not enough to make one's blood boil over', Cobden wrote to Bright in November 1853, 'to think that the hypocrites at head quarters who uphold this tax pretend it to be favourable to education? . . . As respects this stamp, I hope you are prepared to give all your energies to it – Pile up your indignation against Lord John, if he persists in his mouthing phrases about education & still upholds the stamp.'[75] Bright was active behind the scenes, cornering Cardwell in December 1853 and priming him on the evils of the stamp act.[76]

This impetus was soon dented by the threat of war in the Crimea. Cobden became increasingly pessimistic; as he told R. W. Smiles, secretary of the NPSA, after the war had broken out, 'War must be, I fear, accepted as a substitute for every social and political reform'.[77] At an APRTOK soiree to celebrate the repeal of the advertisement duty in February 1854 speakers protested at Cobden's suggestion that it could not be expected that old taxes would be removed while new ones were being imposed.[78] But many of the Association's subscribers were of Cobden's mind. Renewing his 10/- subscription in May 1854, Herbert Spencer wrote that he was unwilling to increase the amount as requested given that this was no time for a determined effort in the cause.[79] There was little direct pressure on the Chancellor before or after the 1854 budget, despite the near doubling of income tax and an increase of other excise duties. Cobden felt that given the imperative to increase taxes, Gladstone had done as well as could be expected.[80]

At the same time, another result of the Crimean War was to deepen hostility to *The Times* in government circles, and to strengthen the feeling that the public life was being conducted against the backdrop of a hostile and increasingly overweening press. The processes of press management which had served in earlier periods seemed no longer operable.[81]

J. W. Croker had commented to Brougham in July that circumstances had 'developed the powers of the press to an enormous influence – an influence the greater because it has become so subtle that we breathe it as we breathe the air . . . [public opinion] was of old the queen of the world; she has now become its tyrant, and the newspapers her ministers.'[82] The *Times*'s increasingly outspoken broadsides at the Aberdeen government and some of its members,[83] pushed ministers to the conclusion that its influence was too great.[84] It appeared to many that to end *The Times*'s competitive advantage would be to strike a real blow against the tyranny of the press.[85] '[I]f England is ever to be England again', observed Russell plaintively, 'this vile tyranny of the Times must be cut off.'[86] It may be that Tory hostility also contributed. Cobden had told William Mitchell in April 1854 that 'there is such a bitter feeling of hostility amongst the old Tory party against the *Times*, & such a hopelessness of contending against its power, that many of them would go for the repeal of the stamp duty to spite it, even if they "cut off their own nose" at the same time'.[87]

Initially, the government's rejection of further action during the 1854 parliamentary session to clarify the law on newspapers brought fresh opportunity.[88] The APRTOK leadership recognized that its widespread toleration of unstamped 'class' papers left the Revenue vulnerable to provocations in similar vein. Cobden recommended 'the starting of a good many unstamped papers for special objects . . . The more of them the better – for as the Inland Revenue Board will not be able to prosecute, the regular *stamped* newspapers will by & by begin to call out for the removal of the stamp, to put *them* on a fair footing'.[89] The apparently inexhaustible demand for war news presented a particularly potent opportunity for commencing cheap papers under the 'class newspaper' definition. There already existed a weekly paper, *Holt's Army and Navy Gazette*, devoted to war news, which had been launched in February, and by the end of September unstamped war sheets were multiplying. At the start of October Collet convened a meeting of provincial unstamped publishers in Manchester to explore the most effective way of working round the law as amended in 1853.[90] At the same time, encouraged by Collet, J. W. Finlay, editor of *Edinburgh Guardian* brought out a daily *War Telegraph* in Edinburgh, quickly followed by the *War Express* and *War Telegraph* in Manchester.[91] The *War Telegraph*, which aligned itself explicitly with APRTOK, was reputed to have achieved a daily average circulation of 20,000 within a fortnight of being established and at its peak was circulating an enormous 35,000.[92] Within a few weeks there were seven unstamped war papers in publication, and a campaign of defiance was underway with faint but unmistakeable echoes of the 1830s.[93] The Inland Revenue considered prosecution, but given the active assessment of the whole question that had been forced on the government, proceedings were delayed.[94]

As Cobden had predicted, fears from the stamped weeklies at the threat to their readership led to a rush of letters to the Chancellor and the Inland Revenue, and eventually a 'shower of writs'. For some, it was one anomaly too many: in the absence of a stamp law which was 'a reality, not a mockery', and which could protect the fair trader, 'the sooner equality is produced by allowing all to exist on the same footing the better', remarked the *Glasgow Citizen*, hitherto a staunch advocate of the newspaper stamp.[95] In early November a meeting of Scottish newspaper proprietors instructed a deputation to Gladstone urging the effective implementation of the stamp laws.[96] The Manchester papers banded together to indicate that any further tolerance of unstamped titles would force them also to publish on unstamped paper, and agreed to indemnify each other against any penalties. Belatedly the Revenue initiated prosecutions of Finlay and two others. On 17 November Keogh issued a general circular announcing the government's intention to enforce the stamp laws, followed on the 28th with a circular which explicitly named *Holt's Army and Navy Despatch*, and two other titles, threatening the paper's suppliers, printers and vendors with the full rigours of seizure of goods and chattels permitted by the legislation.[97] Collet led a counter-deputation to the Chancellor including representatives of the war papers urging a stay in government activity, without avail.[98] The Chancellor and Attorney General admitted the difficulties of the case, but offered no guarantees.[99]

After 39 issues Finlay bowed to pressure and replaced the *War Telegraph* with the stamped *Northern Telegraph*.[100] The *Army and Navy Dispatch* was taken over by Holyoake in December 1854, with the intention of publishing it unstamped weekly via the transparent device of marginal changes to name each week (*Collet's War Chronicle* one week, *Moore's War Chronicle* the next).[101] Further threats of prosecution led Holyoake to resort instead to a two-page unstamped halfpenny *War Fly Sheet* which he issued as a supplement to the weekly *Empire*. This was continued to 22 June 1855 despite a series of summons to the Exchequer Court, and threats of fines of over £600,000.[102] Recurring to a familiar theme, in the Commons on 22 December Bright drew attention to Revenue pressure on the proprietor of a Nottingham paper for publishing a sheet containing an article on the taxes on knowledge, and the lack of parity in treatment of the posting of telegraphic news in London clubs.[103]

By the start of 1855 it was clear that the provisions of the stamp law were being flouted ever more widely, to the outrage of the established titles.[104] In Manchester there were further discussions about the possibility of the *Manchester Examiner and Times*, which had already moved to daily publication in an attempt to combat the competition of the war sheets, defying the stamp legislation.[105] Radicals such as William Sharman Crawford threw their weight behind the war press campaign.[106] Supporters of repeal such as Ireland and Co in Manchester muddied the waters by forwarding complaints to the Inland Revenue.[107] Within months new titles were appearing in confident anticipation of the imminent abandonment of the newspaper stamp legislation. A government whose authority had been severely compromised by the fiasco in the Crimea was ill-placed to confront defiance of laws which had already been brought into disrepute. In the country discussions of possible new ventures proceeded on the assumption that the stamp was 'virtually repealed'.[108] April 1855 saw the launching of the daily 'democratic' *Glasgow Times*, the *Glasgow Daily News* (which initially sought to defend itself by changes of title), and the *Northern Daily Express* (Darlington).

The events of 1855 were bittersweet for the anti-knowledge tax campaigners. In February, Gladstone's bill to repeal the newspaper stamp and the newspaper security system (also allowing any printed matter to be transmitted for a penny per 4oz, and formally sanctioning the partial stamping of a newspaper in order to qualify for re-transmission via post for seven days) was passed by the House of Commons.[109] Gladstone's intention, as he put it later was 'completely to set free the press' from taxation which restricted 'the handling of public events and news of all kinds, and to apply to this subject the principles of free commerce which have been extended with such efficacy to the general mercantile transactions of the country'.[110] Unfortunately the Aberdeen coalition collapsed just as the bill was introduced, and Gladstone was replaced by Sir George Cornewall Lewis, a longstanding upholder of the stamp regime (see Figure 4.1).

A period of anxiety for supporters of repeal followed: there was confidence that Lewis's intentions were good, but the parliamentary world was in turmoil, and he was not seen as the strongest figure.[111] There was talk of opposition to the securities legislation repeal from Campbell in the House of Lords, and Cobden could not shake off a fear that 'The present tone of the press against the aristocracy must be calculated to frighten those in power at the prospect of "opening the floodgates & letting in a deluge of unstamped newspapers" as it is called.'[112] The language of portions of the press was apocalyptic enough. The *Field* predicted that the repeal of the stamp and securities system 'will reduce the

Figure 4.1 'W. E. Gladstone presents his budget to the Commons', 1860 [Mary Evans Ref 10001009]

circulation of the *Times* by one half, and annihilate the *Daily News*, the *Morning Chronicle* and the *Herald*. The *Post* may survive because it appeals to a small and wealthy section . . . The evening papers have not a chance of life', and the major provincial titles, including the *Leeds Mercury* and the *Scotsman*, 'will be annihilated, or must descend to rivalry with the cheap journals'.[113] 'A cheap press can exist only by a great circulation, and must look *downward* for that to the classes *below* the present newspaper buyers', the *Field* continued, and 'if they write for a lower class, they must write *down* to the lower tastes; . . . they must flatter their passions and prejudices'; this 'is the fearful experiment which the madness of our rulers is about try in an old country'.

The established press mounted a vocal opposition to the details of Gladstone's measure. *The Times* was outraged at the 4oz limit which would force it to pay an extra ½d stamp.[114] 'I believe that the Gov[ernmen]t and the Post Office have but one object in view at the present moment, & that is how to prevent us delivering the slightest benefit from the alteration in the stamp law', John Walter, the owner of *The Times* told Arthur Dasent.[115] At one point Delane, the editor, contemplated the establishment of a collaboration of the

London press to transport and deliver printed matter independently of the Post Office, believing it could be done for ½d per paper.[116] The notion that the measure was first and foremost designed to strike at the political pre-eminence of *The Times* gained a certain currency. Some provincial newspaper proprietors, recognizing how much they relied on London papers, *The Times* in particular, for their foreign intelligence, were afraid that the Bill might in turn force it into damaging efforts to protect its 'copyright'.[117]

The deep divisions within the press were once more brought into sharp relief. Newspaper proprietors across the country met to pass resolutions and submit petitions opposing repeal, advocating, if needs must, the introduction of a halfpenny stamp instead.[118] The Provincial Newspaper Society printed Russel's *Edinburgh Review* article and sent it to every MP,[119] and a printed circular was issued, arguing that there was no great call for reform except among 'persons whose avowed object is the diffusion of opinions adverse to religion and subversive of the rights of property', suggesting that it would 'widen the divisions between the various ranks of society, by producing a class of newspapers addressed only to the lower orders, and ministering to their worst passions and propensities', and that the proposed general permission for the transmission of printed matter at 4oz for 1d 'would encourage the circulation of mischievous, immoral and infidel publications, eight or more of which might be sent for one penny through the length and breadth of the land'.[120] At the same time, the minority of the press in favour of repeal rallied in support and condemnation of *The Times*'s clarification of its position.[121]

Cornewall Lewis's announcement on the 19th March that he intended to rework Gladstone's measure was clearly seen by supporters of repeal as a 'repudiation'.[122] Ultimately, more concerned with risk of unpopularity associated with plans to borrow £16M and increase taxation by £5M just at the point at which peace was in the offing,[123] Lewis seems to have bowed to the significant opposition to plans to wipe out the securities system, and *The Times*'s specific protest at Gladstone's postal proposals, while recognizing that the retention of any stamp would leave the Revenue open to exactly the same sorts of pressures that the APRTOK campaign had been able to apply to the compulsory penny stamp.[124]

The compromise was not universally popular. The *Civil Service Gazette* wrote darkly of communications from several usual supporters of the ministry 'intimat[ing] that the pressure of local opinion from their respective constituencies [would] compel them to vote against the Government on the question'.[125] In fact, there was some feeling even on the Conservative benches that the repeal would bring political advantages (of the sort Cobden hoped for, for the radicals). Hence Bulwer Lytton spoke and voted against an attempt to postpone the second reading of the bill, telling Disraeli that 'a penny journal containing moderate Conservative opinions ... would do more to popularize Conservatism, than half the party speeches we make in the House'.[126] *The Times* kept up its pressure for a complete abolition of the weight limit on penny transmission through the press.[127] Between the second and third readings a deputation of Yorkshire newspaper proprietors waited on the Chancellor pressing the case for a ½d postal rate.[128] It was suggested that the printing of a part-stamped edition would create considerable (even insuperable) inconvenience.[129] The Provincial Newspaper Society met in London under the presidency of Baxter, and endorsed the halfpenny rate, appointing a deputation to the Chancellor including Baxter, Baines (*Leeds Mercury*), Hobson (*Leeds Times*), Austin (*Maidstone Journal*), Johnson (*Worcester Journal*), Johnson Gedge (*Bury Post*).[130] Interestingly the *Manchester Guardian*'s London Letter urged support, noting that the current regime merely created space for the undesirable penny fiction of the *London Review* type and advocating the creation of space for competition from the news.[131] Ultimately the call for a halfpenny postal rate was rejected, largely, its proponents suggested, because the Post Office authorities were concerned at the pressure on the system that was likely to be created by the increased volume of newspapers which would have resulted.[132]

Tellingly, the Association appears to have taken no real part in the political lobbying which immediately preceded repeal (although Holyoake and Truelove attempted to oppose calls for a rejection of the act at a meeting of London Newsvendors).[133] There was a sense that the Association's campaigns had succeeded. Speaking at APRTOK AGM on 21st February 1855 in Exeter Hall, Bright spoke as if 'our battle is won, and there is not much to say about the question'.[134] There was little parliamentary controversy.[135] By and large it seems that supporters and opponents had all accepted that in its general terms the bill would pass. Apart from discussions about postal rates, only the issue of copyright generated any heat. The problem of how to secure the protection of the intellectual property of matter published in newspapers had long been a thorny one. The difficulty of distinguishing what might be claimed as copyright and what was fact or information in public domain was considerable, and this had allowed the practice of extensive cutting and pasting from one newspaper to another. This was especially a concern for *The Times*, whose news gathering machinery was the most extensive, and whose reports were systematically copied by the London and provincial weeklies. In 1852 Brougham had suggested to Cobden that the dangers of piracy might make it politic to retain the stamp on daily papers, removing it only from weekly papers.[136] Peter Burke's *The*

Copyright Law and the Press (1855), argued that copyright legislation was not in a position to deal with the repeal of the stamp, that if the current toleration of piracy continued, provincial weeklies would be able to supersede metropolitan dailies and 'cheap reprints, say at a penny each, of the leading contents of the morning papers will appear even at an hour after publication of the originals'.[137] As Lewis's bill was being debated, *The Times* pressed for protection from the new penny papers that were expected to mushroom. 'The moment *The Times* or the *Morning Herald* arrives on the banks of the Mersey or the Clyde, all its precious news, its costly reports, and priceless correspondence from the seat of war, will be seized upon by the *Manchester Pickpocket*, the *Bury Appropriator*, the *Birmingham Plunderer*, the *Liverpool Thief*, the *Glasgow Burglar*, the *Paisley Pilferer* or the *Edinburgh Pirate* . . .'.[138] The anti-democratic instincts of this rhetoric were obvious to all.[139]

In Committee, Cornewall Lewis briefly intimated his intention to grant newspaper proprietors 'a copyright in every original article, letter, paragraph, communication' and other composition, with penalties for any republication within the first 24 hours.[140] Such a provision was hardly likely to gain widespread support, doing nothing for the provincial weeklies.[141] Despite endorsement in the debate on the third reading on 30th April, from speakers including W. J. Fox, who argued that the stamp legislation did ensure that newspapers possessed 'a certain amount of capital and intelligence' along with 'a certain degree of talent displayed in its management, but, without [a copyright clause] all would be pulled down to one common level', it was ultimately accepted that there is no workable way of imposing copyright in news.[142] Instead, revision of the bill was confined to two minor additional clauses: one that periodical publications must be posted within 15 days of publication; the second making the Postmaster General responsible for any decisions about whether any printed paper was entitled to privileges of postage.[143] A subsequent attempt to enable a newspaper weighing 6d to be carried through the post was defeated without a vote and in May the bill was approved 138 to 60, progressing quickly through the Lords, with only token opposition from Lord Monteagle.

The Paper Duties, 1858–61

APRTOK remained effectively in abeyance for the 18 months after the passing of the repeal of the newspaper stamp. Cobden and Bright were struggling with the establishment of the *Morning Star* (see Chapter 7), and Collet was throwing himself into re-launching the Urquhartite *Free Press*.[1] After a false start in March 1856 activity recommenced in November 1856.[2] A suggestion that the Association for the Repeal of the Paper Duty might hand over its funds to APRTOK was unsurprisingly ignored.[3] But adverts were placed in the press asking for information from papermakers about the anomalies and injustices of the paper excise, and a circular to the press achieved some notice.[4] In December representatives of the English and Scottish cheap newspapers met in Manchester to consider the best means of furthering the campaign.[5]

The initial signs were not encouraging. By August 1856, despite signs of improved trade, Cornewall Lewis was predicting a final quarter budget deficit of £3m.[6] Supporters recognized that little was likely without 'a really formidable agitation'.[7] The committee, accepting, apathy in parliament, continued to claim 'out of doors a good deal of intelligent disquiet at this mischievous tax', but there was little sign of any active pressure.[8] An APRTOK deputation to Cornewall Lewis in February 1857 pointed out rather plaintively that repeal had been often promised, but met the same old mixture of reluctance and incomprehension, and the sixth AGM in St Martin's Hall later that month reinforced the sense of a campaign that had yet to acquire any fresh momentum.[9] Faced with vocal pressure on the income tax, the 1857 budget concentrated on its reduction from 16d to 7d, and a diminution of tea and sugar duties.[10]

Prospects were not improved by the general election of March/April 1857 which swept away almost the whole parliamentary leadership of the agitation; Derby exulted that 'The Peelites and Manchester men are obliterated'.[11] Cobden was defeated and in no to hurry to find a new seat, disheartened by the 'sort of Palmerston putrescence' which had resulted.[12] Milner Gibson retreated from London politics, 'privately much [crushed] for the Manchester defeat, and [feeling] very much like a fish out of water'.[13] Elsewhere, W. J. Fox, A. H. Layard, Sir Joshua Walmsley, and a number of metropolitan supporters of the taxes on knowledge campaigns were rejected.[14] Ayrton, almost the lone surviving parliamentary spokesman, perhaps unsurprisingly was unwilling to press the paper duties on the attention of the House.[15]

Step by step, however, a parliamentary leadership for the agitation was reconstituted. Bright was elected for Birmingham in August 1857, and Milner Gibson for Ashton in November. But Cobden resisted all approaches, and despite his enthusiasm for the development of the cheap press, remained strangely detached from the campaign as it re-emerged in 1858.[16] Meanwhile provincial radicalism remained divided and demoralized. Visiting Manchester in November, Joseph Cowen, the Newcastle radical, observed 'a complete disunion of parties', the old leaders 'in sullen discontent', their opponents 'indifferent to Reform measures'.[17] Certainly, such impetus as there was in the reform movement seemed to be centred around Cowen's Northern Reform Union, which had minimal contact with the Manchester School leadership, and whose supporters were inclined to ambivalence about the taxes on newspapers.[18]

It was only with the disintegration of 'popular Palmerstonianism' in the wake of the Orsini affair and the proposed Aliens Act that there were signs of renewed enthusiasm for platform advocacy, and stirrings of parliamentary probing.[19] Gladstone was pressed by supporters like George Wilson, although he could not be stirred into optimism. 'My sentiments about [the paper duty] . . . are as they were', Gladstone told Wilson, 'but. . . . the immediate prospects of finance have undergone a sad change since they were [settled]'.[20] Despite encouraging noises from Derby to a deputation from APRTOK in April 1858,[21] Disraeli's 1858 budget was forced to focus on a deficit of £3.5M, and offered 'A Gladstonian budget without Gladstone'.[22] In June, however, Milner Gibson obtained Commons agreement that 'the maintenance of the excise duty on paper, as a permanent source of revenue, would be impolitic'. Supporters celebrated the 'doom' of the paper duties and even the more sanguine were convinced that abolition was now only a matter of time.[23] By July the talk was of private assurances coming from the Derby ministry that the duties would be abolished in the next budget.[24]

In the wake of Gibson's success, the Association sought to try to mobilize the newspaper interest. Now that the divisive issue of the stamp no longer pertained, there was hope of 'strong and united action, [and] no petty rivalries or jealousies'.[25] Unfortunately, and no doubt to the great frustration of Collet and the active APRTOK committee, the outcome of the meeting of the London press, was not an accession of support, but the decision to create a distinct group, a 'Newspaper and Periodical Press Association for the Repeal of the Paper Duty' (NPPARPD), with Milner Gibson as president, Cassell as chairman, John Francis as treasurer and Henry Vizetelly, proprietor of the *Illustrated Times*, as secretary.[26] In the autumn of 1858 NPPARPD formed auxiliaries in Dublin and Edinburgh, and was active in Bristol and Birmingham.[27] The Dublin auxiliary pressed repeal on Irish members of parliament at Dublin Castle,[28] and instigated a petitioning campaign which attracted broad support from the Irish press, as well as from the Irish business classes.[29] The National Association for the Promotion of Social Science conference in Liverpool resolved 'that the continuance of the paper duty is a great obstacle to the progress of education, and ought to be abolished forthwith'.

Not all newspapers were convinced. There was still a suspicion of 'cheap literature' and its evils, and sneering doubts as to the benefits of 'the multiplication of penny prophets in print'.[30] Noticeably in 1858 and 1859 there are signs that, with the exception of the peculiar position of the metropolitan penny dailies, the previous economic divisions within the press were slowly making way for more straightforwardly political ones. For the hardline Tory press, the pressure was always, as the *Magnet* termed it in 1859, an 'impudent agitation'.[31] Similarly Conservative titles expressed doubts of any great public benefit: 'paper is cheaper than ever it was, the poorest man in the country can readily obtain his sheet whenever he wants it', the *Leeds Intelligencer* argued; 'there is a revenue to be raised; and it must be raised, or ought to be, in the manner least oppressive to the general public'.[32]

The attitude of the paper manufacturers was also shifting. The consensus of the years around 1850 had fractured. No doubt there remained considerable resentment within the trade at the 'harsh and dictatorial tone often assumed by the Excise officers at the paper mills'.[33] James Baldwin of Birmingham, and J. H. Rawlins of Wrexham, longstanding opponents of the excise, and the West Riding Paper Makers Association, participated in APRTOK deputations between 1857 and 1859.[34] In Birmingham, from the outset a strong supporter of the agitation, considerable play was made of the commercial burden associated with the quantities of paper used in packing and manufacture.[35] Noticeably, though, responses to attempts by the Liverpool Chamber of Commerce and the NPPARPD to mobilize the chambers of commerce were mixed.[36]

During 1858 public activity was dominated by the NPPARPD, completely eclipsing APRTOK, although the committee was continuing to work behind the scenes.[37] The *Era* talked about an 'unbounded activity . . . circulars innumerable, published pamphlets without end', suggesting that the NPPARPD had 'canvassed districts with the utmost pertinacity, and sent out deputations whose name is Legion'.[38] The NPPARPD cultivated the printing trades unions and associations, and encouraged an active circulation for subscriptions among printers, journalists and publishers.[39] It published *The Tax upon Paper – the Case Stated for Its Immediate Repeal* (1858), providing a broad conspectus of the history of the newspaper taxes, the arguments advanced by Baldwin and others against them, and also the anomalies of the excise as displayed by the APRTOK campaign.[40] John Cassell gave lectures in a number of English cities, although without great success. Despite hopes that the working classes would 'flock . . . in their thousands' to hear Cassell at the Birmingham Town Hall, and send a message to the Chancellor, the attendance was only modest.[41] In February there was talk of a further public meeting in Scotland, but the committee seems to decide instead for private lobbying of the trade.[42] In truth, the manufacturing interest was divided and radicals were too preoccupied with parliamentary reform to give too much attention to the paper duty.

Optimism that the state of the finances would by 1859 have removed the only remaining obstacle to repeal was dashed by the revelation in January 1859 that the national finances were less healthy than had been thought, followed quickly by the announcement of an increase in the Naval Estimates of £961,810,[43] though Milner Gibson sought to argue that the previous vote bound the government, if it needed the revenue, to find a less objectionable mode of raising it.[44] Attempts by the NPPARPD to frame the question as more a social than a financial one left Derby unconvinced. It would seem that Disraeli's plans for his 1859 budget did at one point include repeal of the paper duties, but once again the exigencies of the revenue intervened.[45]

However the Conservatives' defeat in the 1859 general election paved the way for a Palmerston cabinet which not only included Gladstone as Chancellor of the Exchequer but also Milner Gibson as President of the Board of Trade, an appointment which prompted his immediate resignation as President of APRTOK and of NPPARPD (where he was replaced by William Ewart). It was widely accepted that Gladstone would seek economy of expenditure and further removal of excise duties,[46] and the *Standard*, perhaps mischievously, noted that with Milner Gibson in the cabinet the repeal of the paper duties was assured.[47]

In fact there was little likelihood of a natural Cabinet majority for repeal. The initial proceedings of the government were not reassuring. A provisional budget in July met a sharp rise in defence expenditure and a projected deficit of £5M with a ramping up of income tax from 5d to 9d. In the country, the radicals were outraged at further 'spoilation and robbery'.[48] But some breathing space was provided for Gladstone to begin wrestling with military spending and reductions in taxation.[49] As so often before, the status of the income tax was at the heart of the problem. Gladstone was still inclined to see the income tax as a temporary war measure, and in this context the prospect of sacrificing the paper duty revenue was likely to be distant.[50] The unexpected success of Cobden's secret negotiations with the French over a comprehensive free trade treaty also brought its own problems. Anticipating a contentious reception for the treaty, even Bright wondered in October 1859 whether it might not make more sense to concentrate on the customs duties, and postpone the attack on paper.[51] The press campaign, though, continued unabated. There was a widespread assumption that the duties would be removed, reflected in planning for new newspapers and extended publication of existing titles by early 1860.[52] The NPPARPD meet in December to organize a large deputation to Gladstone, and the petitioning campaign once more wound into action.[53] The 'taxes on knowledge' theme was somewhat buried by this stage, although Radicals continued to press the need for repeal to 'bring a newspaper to every man's door'.[54]

From the outset discussions over the budget were tense, with Gladstone fighting hard to rein in plans for large borrowing to fund fresh naval fortifications. From outside the government Bright pressed hard for repeal 'as a great relief to industry and a great act of justice to an important trade', and a way of getting press support for the government's broader financial scheme.[55] Inside Gladstone, armed with the arguments provided by APRTOK's 'Evils of the Excise on Paper' memorandum and supplementary information provided via Ayrton, was privately conceiving a bold reconstruction of the excise system.[56] Gladstone's commitment was not immediately apparent. On the 2nd February Monteagle, the former Whig Chancellor of the Exchequer, told Clarendon that 'Gladstone was audacious enough for many things, but he would bet me any money that he had not dared to think of *that* [i.e. repeal of the paper duty]'.[57] In the face of the cabinet majority Gladstone was forced reluctantly to concede increased levels of military expenditure,[58] but was able to forestall Palmerston's attempts to deal with the budget piecemeal, and separately from the French treaty.[59]

1860 budget

Framed as an epochal budget, not least because of the lapsing of the 'long annuities', but also because Cobden's commercial treaty with France necessitated 'a new and unusual course' (as well as a loss of £646,000 to the revenue), Gladstone's 1860 budget was fiercely anticipated. People queued all day for seats in the Strangers' Gallery, and the House was full to bursting.[60] In the end the verdict was unanimous that Gladstone had surpassed even himself. It was a speech of 'extraordinary brilliancy . . . I doubt if Gladstone's achievement was ever surpassed on a similar occasion', commented the radical MP Sir John Trelawny.[61] Forced to admit that the predictions of the 1853 budget had been overturned by increases in government expenditure, Gladstone proposed to remove 46 articles from the tariff (leaving only 44, including sugar and tea, which he intended to remove in 1861), and to repeal the paper duties, making up the deficiency in part by various new charges and stamp duties, but primarily via an income tax of 10d in the pound for incomes over £150, and 7d in the £ for those from £100–150. At the same time Gladstone proposed the abolition of the impressed stamp on newspapers to be replaced by a combined book/newspaper postal scale, including a new 1½d scale for 6oz.[62]

Ominously, in the Commons the announcement of repeal was met with 'comparative indifference'.[63] To begin with supporters were optimistic. Cobden considered the budget 'a very clever one – The Paper duties will catch all the "Press", & the wine duties all the rich people, whilst the prospect of a trade with France, at last, will insure the support of the manufacturing & trading world'.[64] Commercial interests were divided but generally supportive.[65] Prompted by Bright, a number of meetings were held in February to rally support for the budget and Cobden's Commercial Treaty.[66] 'Friday last was a day ever to be remembered by the whole civilized world. The entire habitable globe will be beautified by it', gushed J. R. Jeffery, prominent Liverpool radical.[67] But doubts were quickly voiced as to whether the budget would pass.[68] The 10d in the £ income tax rate was hard to stomach. Gladstone's haste unnerved many moderate Liberals, while among the Whigs resentment festered at what seemed a sordid bargain for the support of Manchester school radicalism.[69] For Robert Cecil, more fundamentally, the budget involved a dangerous 'transfer of taxes from one class of the community to another'. He was concerned that 'Once admitted that a direct tax may be laid on for the purpose of taking off an indirect tax . . . there is no reason that the process should not be repeated *ad infinitum*'.[70]

By the end of February, it was clear that there would be a strenuous resistance. The Conservative press attacked the wasteful frittering away of opportunities on French knick-knacks, and warned of the disadvantages of the measure for the independent provincial press against the 'monopolists of the cheap press'.[71] The paper-makers met in London in February, frightened at the prospect of free competition from French paper-makers and worried about continued controls on the export of rags;[72] manifestoes were issued in England, Scotland and Ireland.[73] By the end of February, Cobden was reporting 'receiving many letters . . . protesting against the duty being removed from paper'.[74] In mid-March *The Times* published a long memorandum from 'The Association of Paper Manufacturers'.[75] John Evans, chair of the Paper Makers' Association, had a meeting with Gladstone but found him 'determined to have his own way and . . . positive some new material will be discovered'.[76] The papermakers received some support from Henry Bohn, the publisher, who argued against the measure largely on the grounds of the loss of the drawback on exports of books.[77]

Initially *The Times* had not directly opposed repeal, describing the duties as 'a serious, sometimes ruinous burden upon trade'.[78] 'The Times dont like either Treaty or Budget but it wont commit itself till it sees how the Country is disposed to take them' commented Stanley wryly.[79] But once the paper's attention had turned to the problems of the paper manufacturers, with whom it had strong connections,[80] aided by a series of forceful letters from Thomas Wrigley, a substantial papermaker from Bury who had been prominent in the campaign for the repeal of the paper duties in the late 1840s, *The Times* offered a sustained assault on Gladstone's policy, primarily his refusal to adjust the import duty on paper to take into account the widespread control of exports of rags in Europe, coupled with a steadily more visible rejection of the policy of giving priority to removal of the paper duties.[81]

Bright's reaction was predictable. The *Times*'s policy, he told Cobden, 'has been base beyond all its former doings in that line, and it is now selling everything honourable in the country, in the hope of destroying Gladstone . . . It is a fearful curse to have a paper with so much power, and guided by a principle so selfish and so Satanic.' The stance of *The Times* Bright understood, but not 'the stupid folly of the Daily News, and other high price papers [which] cannot live long even at their present price – for the *Times* swallows them all up – but they have not the sense to see that with cheap Paper, and *their Papers cheap*, they would have a great advantage over the new Cheap Press – their old names and connexion would give them.'[82]

APRTOK and the NPPARPD did what they could to generate popular pressure in support of the budget. Friends and correspondents were urged again to write to MPs and get up local petitions. NPPARPD memorialized all MPs in mid-February, and held public meetings.[83] The provincial press had focused initially on unhappiness with the proposed postal reforms, but the notice of a motion to retain the paper duty by Sir William Miles brought hastily convened meetings of the Midland Counties Newspaper Proprietors and the London and country press at the end of February and strong resolutions to oppose Miles by all means.[84]At the start of March the *Morning Star* warned of 'strenuous efforts' against the budget 'by treacherous friends' as well as enemies.[85] But there was little sign of mass involvement. It was difficult to sustain popular interest as the campaign became embroiled in issues like the fate of the import duty on foreign paper.[86] The petitioning campaign of the 1860 session demonstrated the effective mobilization of special interests but little popular enthusiasm. Collet and Moore were active feeding the press campaign; Holyoake, with frequent commissions from the *Morning Star*, was a regular visitor at Collet's.[87] Otherwise, the APRTOK committee focused on meeting the particular claims of the paper-makers, producing two circulars, *The Rags Delusion* and *The Rag Scarecrow*.[88]

Parliament remained the crucial theatre of conflict. The bill for the repeal of the paper duties battled its way through the Commons in March 1860, in what Gladstone described as 'the severest Parliamentary struggle in which I have ever been engaged'.[89] Initially supporters were confident that he could carry Parliament in the face of the 'utter disorganisation of the Tory party', but it quickly became apparent that his problems were as much with his own party.[90] There was little enthusiasm for repeal among the Whigs. Cornewall Lewis described it privately as 'reckless and hazardous and intended merely to discharge the bad political debts of the government',[91] and Palmerston became increasingly obstructive (see Figure 5.1).[92] At the crucial cabinet meeting of 12th April only Milner Gibson supported Gladstone. While not blocking repeal directly, Palmerston made sure the lack cabinet support was clearly communicated to the opposition benches via the Queen, and through the same channel Derby reassured Palmerston that he would not seek to defeat the government if Gladstone was baulked and resigned.[93] The bill only narrowly passed its third reading on the 9th May.[94] Only a sense that the government had gone too far to retreat kept the measure alive.[95]

In the country, the radicals detected treachery. J. R. Jeffery denounced Palmerston's failure to stand up to Disraeli, and the conduct of Cornewall Lewis, 'sneak[ing] away into the side gallery during the debate'.[96] There were

Figure 5.1 'A Derby course incident', *Punch*, 26 May 1860

also warnings that opinion against repeal was 'gaining strength' in places like Liverpool.[97] Gladstone abandoned the proposal to remove the impressed stamp for newspapers,[98] but on the 10th of May Monteagle gave motion in the Lords that he would move the bill be read that day six months hence. There was anxiety, especially in Whig circles, about damage to the standing of the House of Lords, that the rejection would generate a radical upsurge, but Derby remained convinced that resistance would enhance the Lords' prestige.[99] As one radical remarked, 'The Lords appear to have thought that it is only a Manchester question, and as nobody likes the Manchester School they were safe in giving them a kick.'[100] Support and petitions were organized in the metropolitan debating clubs.[101] APRTOK issued an address 'To the electors of the United Kingdom' noting the unconstitutional nature of the Lords efforts, 'an act of usurpation'.[102] A last ditch effort was made on the 19th, when a deputation from a demonstration at St Martin's Hall, on 15th May, which featured many of APRTOK stalwarts, including Collet, Holyoake, Novello, Passmore Edwards and Washington Wilks and other metropolitan radicals, met an obdurate Derby to press the case for repeal.[103] The Association secured Lord Wensleydale to present a long petition rehearsing the Association's case to Lords,[104] but 'Lord Derby gave one of his most eloquent and powerful speeches, perfectly smashing Gladstone and his policy, and his Budget and his treaty!'[105]

Constitutional defence

Robert Cecil was delighted; the Lords had realized that they had 'a living power, wielded freely by themselves and recognized instinctively by the people'.[106] The Whigs rejoiced in private. 'The debate and division were not so much for the retention of the paper duties as a protest ag[ain]st a reckless, dangerous powerful demagogue making democratic capital for himself out of the revenue', Clarendon told Brougham.[107] Russell was confused, Milner Gibson 'savage'.[108] Palmerston sought to diffuse pressure for an immediate challenge to the Lords' vote by appointing a committee to inquire into precedents for the Lords' action (including Gladstone, Bright and Russell).[109] At the same time, he adopted an increasingly uncompromising stance, at the start of June tersely precluding any possibility of a compensatory reduction of any other tax to balance out the retention of the paper duties.[110] Gladstone was left exploring the possibility of proposing the temporary suspension of the paper duties.[111] Meanwhile there was fury in radical circles. The *Morning Star* claimed receipt of protest letters too numerous to read, never mind print.[112] 'I propose we abolish the "House of Incurables"', wrote Cowen's lieutenant R. B. Reed to Holyoake, 'London ought to be thoroughly agitated upon the question of privilege, Lords Derby and Monteagle ought to be mobbed at once. Tar and feathers will be cheaply enough bought at London.'[113]

Collet's *Taxes* skimmed over the constitutional agitation of 1860–1, as indeed has modern scholarship.[114] But within days, an extra-parliamentary agitation more widespread and vehement than anything since 1848 had sprung into life. In the cabinet Milner Gibson and Gladstone once again found nominal sympathizers like Russell unable to summon any resolve for resistance to the Lords. Cobden was less ambivalent; writing from Paris he presented the case as one of a determination of the Commons deriving from a decade of petitions, discussions, committees and press commentary arising out of the APRTOK campaign, being overturned by a rash act of the Lords.[115] Ayrton was anxious that any agitation should confine itself to consideration of the case for repeal itself, the Commons having 'ample power to assert its own privileges without the aid of any public meeting'.[116] Out of doors, although Collet and the APRTOK group were alive to the danger that the agitation against the Lords would generate unhelpful hostility, and open up a much wider reform agenda in which the paper duties would be lost sight of.[117] Uncertainty as to the most appropriate or effective line to take was visible in the variety of alternative petitions which APRTOK was circulating by the end of May.[118] There was also, despite a preliminary meeting to discuss the possibility of joint action with the provincial press, little appetite for agitation from the NPPARPD.[119]

Although APRTOK continued to issue circulars to MPs favourable to the cause encouraging their resistance,[120] leadership of the agitation against the 'coup d'etat' of the Lords was quickly constituted under the banner of the Constitutional Defence Committee, meeting for the first time at Fendall's Hotel, one of APRTOK's old haunts, on 25th May 1860. Cobden's long-time associate William Hargreaves was elected Treasurer.[121] A parallel central committee was established in Manchester, where Wilson and Ireland were both active.[122] By mid-June London was flooded with 'blood red placards' containing an 'inflammatory appeal'; handbills were circulating by the thousand.[123] A network of local associations was established in the capital, and by the end of June associations were in existence in Manchester, Rochdale, Newcastle and Kidderminster.[124] In Yarmouth a meeting for reform with protests against the Lords' conduct was initiated by a newly formed working men's association.[125] A Bradford Working Men's Financial and Parliamentary Reform Association held an open air meeting.[126] In July the Manchester Association claimed correspondence with 304 locales, petitions from 149 places, and had an agent organizing meetings and petitions;[127] 121 petitions and 43,179 signatures reached Parliament within three weeks.[128]

Collet himself does not appear to have taken any public role in this agitation, though Holyoake and a number of APRTOK members did.[129] The confrontation resonated with enduring traditions of anti-aristocratic radicalism, and drew support from a wide constituency. Although it is not clear how far they subscribed to the crude anti-aristocratic rhetoric the London committee were resorting to by the end of June,[130] it is notable that this included figures like Henry Vincent, R. W. Smiles and Frederick W. Chesson, all of whose mainstream nonconformist radical credentials were impeccable.[131] Even so, the underlying context of the paper duties crisis was often lost sight of in the 'constitutional defence' cry.[132] There was talk of a movement to stop the supplies until the rights of the Commons over taxation were vindicated.[133]

Unfortunately, these efforts provided as much evidence of the feebleness of support as of popular pressure. At Birmingham, impatience and windy civil war rhetoric were clearly prompted by a lack of vigour in the local prosecution of the campaign.[134] An open air meeting in Liverpool on 9th July was marked by disorderly opposition during which the chairman, Lawrence Heyworth, was knocked from the lorry serving as a platform, injuring his hand.[135] Subsequent meetings of the Liverpool Reform Association were very poorly attended, with even stalwarts of the Financial Reform Association like Robertson Gladstone demonstrating suspicion despite 'a burglary in the broad face of daylight'.[136] At Manchester the central committee eschewed the platform for a personal canvas of parliament, along with a deputation to Palmerston, who promised the government's best endeavours to defeat the opposition in the Lords, but refused to be drawn on its course of action if it were defeated.[137] In mid-July the Bristol Liberals formed a local auxiliary of the Constitutional Defence Society, but decided that it was not expedient to appeal to the public at that time.[138]

Mobilizing solid support proved difficult. 'People are terribly apathetic and awfully stingy in providing funds' confessed one radical.[139] The volunteer movement attracted widespread enthusiasm and provided a platform from which to disparage Gladstone's proposals.[140] Opponents of the duties were confident that there was no real appetite to take on the Lords. The penny newspapers 'may bluster', Clarendon told Brougham, 'but wages are too high and the country too prosperous for a row at this moment'.[141] Even Granville, convinced that 'the paper duty has been too much knocked about ever to become a reliable source of revenue', accepted that it was 'clear that H of C will not allow repeal even if the Cabinet acted as one man, . . . The weighty part of the press is against the repeal – the feeling in the country is one of apathy if not hostility'.[142] Despite almost nightly meetings in London, newspaper coverage of the agitation was largely confined to the *Star* and the *Daily Telegraph*. Hargreaves muttered about a conspiracy of silence.[143] Cobden could not understand how the cheaper press for whom the repeal of the paper duties was a pressing commercial necessity, should continue to be so easily swayed by anti-French sentiment, telling Lawson of the *Daily Telegraph* that 'if he hounds on the government in his newspaper to waste money on fortifications & armaments, he cannot have the tax removed from his raw material'.[144]

The delay caused by the deliberations of the Committee of Precedents took the wind out of the agitation. Inevitably the report was inconclusive, identifying a series of instances in which the Lords had indeed rejected bills with financial implications, but also noting the long-established principle that the Lords should not meddle in financial bills. Proposals from both Gladstone and Bright that the report should assert that none of the precedents had amounted to the Lords interfering in judgements about taxation were rejected. Both sides claimed vindication.[145] For the liberal press, the intrusion of the Lords was without constitutional justification.[146] Toulmin Smith was enraged that the 'so-called "search for precedents" has been a monstrous FRAUD'.[147] There was especial anger that the Lords' rejection of the Paper Duty Repeal Bill was itself listed as one of the precedents.[148] But by the time of the report was debated in early July, the costs of the country's commitments in China had become clear, and any remaining justification of the abolition of the paper duties seemed to have disappeared, enabling Palmerston to assert the abstract rights of the Commons, while in practice accepting the Lords' intervention.[149] Gladstone's bluff had been called and he was left to submit in humiliating fashion.[150]

Up to this point there had been hope in radical circles that the Commons might debate itself into a determination to resist, and the efforts of the London CDC (Constitutional Defence Committee) leadership had focused on this end.[151] A well-attended national conference of the CDC called Palmerston's proposed inaction 'an act of treason against the constitution', pronouncing that no government deserved the support of the Liberal party 'that is not prepared to vindicate the privileges of the Commons and to secure the rights of the people'.[152] Calls for were made that the paper manufacturers refuse to pay duty from the 15th August, and it was suggested that the Commons could petition the Crown not to collect the tax,[153] but what the radicals couldn't engineer was the dissolution that would have given them a chance to mobilize the electorate around the threat to its prerogatives. G. H. Whalley, MP for Peterborough, was reported to have offered the CDC a £500 subscription to a fund to support individual MPs willing to resign and precipitate an election, but predictably nothing came of this.[154]

Deprived of external leverage, the constitutional defence movement was thrown back on parliamentary activity. There was still the possibility that the government would make repeal a question of confidence, and capitalize on the general unwillingness within the Commons to countenance another dissolution so soon after the elections of 1857 and 1859.[155] It was 'absolutely essential', Gladstone urged Palmerston on the 1st July, not merely to rely on declaratory resolutions, but to seek remedy. 'Difficulty', he admitted, 'surrounds us on all hands . . . but . . . I see no way of ultimate hope or safety, except some plan of action founded on the principle that the Lords are not to tax the people without their consent'.[156] The Speaker's advice was taken on reintroducing the paper duties during the current session, but the Liberals were generally anxious to avoid a further heavy defeat which might only strengthen the Lords' position, and Gladstone again found himself overwhelmingly defeated in cabinet

Figure 5.2 'The paper cap', *Punch*, 2 June 1860

(Figure 5.2).[157] At this point Bright appears to have made the decision that there was nothing to be gained by breaking up the government, but every prospect of repeal in 1861 if the ministry held together.[158]

There was bitter disappointment when this determination became clear. Even relatively sympathetic accounts acknowledged that Gladstone had lost a good deal of his Parliamentary standing.[159] Gladstone and Milner Gibson of course were constrained by their place in government, and partly for this reason seem to have attracted less opprobrium.[160] Radical prints consoled themselves with the suggestion that it was all part of a long-term agreement: 'that [Gladstone] will retain office in order to enjoy the pleasure of repealing the duty next April as part of a scheme of finance which their Lordships cannot choose but adopt.'[161] Bright's role, however, came in for severe criticism. Out of doors there was considerable unhappiness at the part Bright had played in abandoning resistance to the government at the last moment.[162] Considerable anger was prompted by the suspicion that Free Trade, in the guise of the French Treaty, had been favoured over the political rights of the people.[163] Even in the House itself the radicals were asking why Bright was not leading them.[164] Henry Slack of the London CDC spoke of 'the shameful conduct of the Liberals in the House of Commons, for which Mr Bright and his friends are to a large extent responsible'.[165]

The success of James White at the Brighton by-election in which his support of the constitutional defence movement figured prominently might have provided momentum,[166] but the CDC leadership were sapped by lack of consensus over strategy. Outlandish schemes were floated to create a martyr to the Lords' intervention by inducing the prosecution of a papermaker for refusal to pay the excise duty.[167] A CDC conference in London heard calls for independent members of the House to attempt to prevent the passing of supplies, before resolving to put matters in the hands of Gladstone.[168] But Gladstone declined to meet the deputation, instead receiving five representatives privately, persuading them that there had been little more that could have been done.[169] In desperation, a small deputation of MPs met Lord Derby to urge the Lords not to reject the paper duties, a move roundly attacked by *Reynolds's News* as 'as great a breach of constitutional usage as the rejection of the bill itself'.[170] In the country it was clear that the popular agitation was running out of steam. In Liverpool a meeting of the Reform Association called to protest against the Lords' action was abandoned in the face of an organized opposition.[171] Hargreaves accepted that there was 'an entire absence of interest in all public questions', and a political culture marked by a 'general tone . . . of selfish expenditure'.[172]

Tensions between the Manchester School radicals and the constitutional defence activists widened into open breach in early August when Henry Brookes resigned as secretary of the London CDC, publishing a bitter tirade against Bright, arguing that the movement had been 'betrayed, and virtually abandoned' by 'a small section of the executive committee . . . comprising the proprietors, the editors, writers, contributors and partisans of the *Star*', which he suggested had its roots in an overriding concern to ensure Cobden's commercial treaty passed safely through the House.[173] Brookes suggested from the outset that the close identification with the Manchester School gave the movement 'a rude, impulsive and reckless vigour', but also alienated many potential supporters, and that ultimately Bright seemed to have worked assiduously to 'paralyse' opposition in the Commons. The charges were refuted at the meeting of General Committee on the 16th, which endorsed the conduct of the executive, but it was clear that the movement was rapidly running out of steam.[174] In early August fewer than 40 turned out at Bodmin to hear Whitehurst, a member of the London committee, speak on 'Taxation by the Lords'.[175] Of the London papers, only the *Star* was willing to try to keep up some semblance of active interest.[176] The *Wells Journal* exulted at the humiliation of the editors of the cheap papers: 'they have brought their full batteries into play, they have been defeated by the representatives of the nation, and . . . the public are well content that they should be defeated.'[177]

Adjustment of the import duty

Attention switched to the customs adjustments required by the French treaty, and the paper manufacturers' resistance to the equalization of the import duty with the excise duty which had formed a bass line to the budget controversies throughout 1860. 'Turn which way we will', the *Birmingham Post* noted, the paper question 'stares us in the face, mixed up in some way or other with the consideration of every question of importance'.[178] There were two problems. First the export restrictions placed on French rags, which it was argued gave French papermakers an unfair advantage, and second the appropriate mode of adjusting import duties on foreign paper so as to balance the excise burdens on domestic manufactures. Through Spring 1860 Palmerston wriggled hard to avoid pushing reform of the import duties through, while Gladstone pressed Cobden without success for French concessions on rag exports, conscious despite reassurances from Milner Gibson that Thomas Wrigley, the papermakers' leader, had confessed a sufficiency of rags, that there would be 'a strong and perhaps formidable movement . . . to limit the free entry of paper goods to the produce of those countries which allow the export of rags'.[179] There was some sympathy for the manufacturers, who argued that the adjustment of 1853 had explicitly introduced a penny supplement to the import duty to take into account the additional burdens that the excise regime placed on British manufacturers, and to remove that differential would amount to a 'bounty on the introduction of French paper'.[180] The continuation of excise surveillance was again presented as creating burdens of collection, fraud, complicated drawbacks, far in excess of the nominal duty. Once again, the *Times* opened its columns to several widely noticed letters from Thomas Wrigley which made the papermakers' case.[181] Gladstone's solution was to impose an import duty of 16s. per cwt, on the basis that it covered the excise duty which was effectively 14s. 9d. per cwt, and gave an extra allowance of 1s. 3d. for the additional burdens of the excise system. Even supporters of repeal of the paper duties such as C. E. Rawlins objected, arguing that the burdens of the excise regime far exceed its nominal weight.[182]

Although there was gossip in London in July of plans to resort to a penny import duty on French paper to keep the papermakers happy, when Gladstone reluctantly agreed to meet the papermakers they found him 'obstinate as a mule'.[183] At the start of August there was further conflict in cabinet as, to Gladstone's extreme annoyance, Palmerston sought to take advantage of an offer from the French Council of Ministers to delay the application of the Treaty to paper for a year.[184] This offer, Palmerston told the cabinet on the 3rd August, 'intirely cut the ground from under us', arguing that the removal of the duty could now be defended neither by the requirements of the treaty nor by general free trade arguments.[185] The prospect of Gladstone's resignation, and perhaps the resignation of the government itself, if defeated on the customs duties on paper, once again reared its head, and ultimately compromise was again achieved.[186] Gladstone was pressed into conceding on the fortifications, in return for acceptance of the customs duties, the necessity of which Palmerston publicly endorsed at a meeting of supporters of the ministry at Downing Street.[187] By 266 to 233 the equalization of the import duty on paper to the excise duty passed the Commons on the 6th August.

The misguided attempts of the Conservatives to make 'a great party affair of the very small question' thought Gladstone, 'enabled us to wind up with a triumph'.[188] Nonetheless, the end of session left him exhausted and despondent.[189] But thereafter the tension subsided. The tariff settlement, it was felt, 'pushe[d] the whole question a stage forward, and renders the total abolition of the paper-duty inevitable'.[190] Political attention turned to the diplomacy of the French treaty, which Cobden and others were adjusting item by item in Paris.[191] 'Gladstone is settling down to his work in harness, as if he had not kicked over the traces and nearly upset the coach', commented Graham, 'and Bright, after much bluster, has barked without biting, and is content to have Gibson in the Cabinet, and

Cobden at Paris, without an attempt to bring the Lords into subjection.'[192] Milner Gibson, who was wrestling agreements on the French treaty out of a reluctant Foreign Office and an uncooperative Palmerston, confessed to Bright that he 'had not an idea at present how the question will now look in connection with the financial aspect of the country', although by the end of the year the ending of hostilities in China was a source of 'glee'.[193] For all his private concern at the 'pitiable position' Gladstone and Milner Gibson had been left in, Bright's plight was scarcely better.[194] After a final parliamentary sally in August, and a public letter of 16 August to the Northern Reform Union which seemed to promise a more general agitation for retrenchment and parliamentary reform, Bright took flight to Sutherland, unwilling to sustain an out-of-doors agitation.[195]

The budget of 1861

As the new parliamentary session approached, the metropolitan radicals made plans to resume their agitation, but without much optimism.[196] There was renewed talk of a disintegration of the administration, and a Palmerston–Derby coalition. Old Whigs like Ellice intrigued against repeal,[197] while *The Times* and much of the established metropolitan press continued to push the need for greater military spending – in part as a dodge to sustain the paper duty, the *Daily Telegraph* suggested.[198] Before Christmas tensions in the cabinet had already resurfaced; Disraeli's informant reported the 'disturbance': 'Gladstone wishes to pursue his democratic system and begin at once with repeal of paper duties. Lewis, Wood, G. Grey (the three baronets) moving heaven and earth against him'.[199] Bright remained pessimistic, anxious, with the help of correspondence from Cobden, to stiffen the sinews of Milner Gibson and Gladstone for the Cabinet discussions to come.[200]

Nonetheless, the fiscal battle was rejoined in early 1861 in a more propitious situation for opponents of the paper duties, not least because the end of the China war had reduced pressure on expenditure. But the debates in Cabinet quickly resolved into a familiar pattern. Once again the political will to press for reduced expenditure proved to be at best diffuse, with even friendly voices like Charles Paget succumbing to the lure of naval expansion.[201] Palmerston worked assiduously to oppose what he saw as Gladstone's desire for 'large reductions in army and navy'.[202] In February he urged serious consideration of the demands of the naval lords for increased naval expenditure to meet France's threat to British naval supremacy, identifying the repeal of the paper duties as the first priority if budget plans were to be adjusted.[203] Gladstone was horrified at attempts to revise the estimates within three weeks of cabinet decision and announcement to Parliament, and confessed himself unable to formulate a budget until after the end of the financial year on the 31st March.[204]

In the country there was considerable excitement and anxiety through to the spring of 1861, as supporters of repeal waited to see if the implicit promise of 1860 was to be redeemed.[205] The advanced Liberals attempted to keep up pressure for retrenchment, but it proved difficult to sustain an agitation.[206] The attention of the London ultra-radicals, including Holyoake, Wilks, Passmore Edwards and Slack, tended to be distracted by the more general franchise agitation, at least until Russell's predictable abandonment of his measure in early February. APRTOK's core of supporters was unmoved. Wilkie Collins told Collet that 'I cannot honestly say that I think the repeal of the Paper Duty is, in any sense, one of the urgent public wants of the present time.'[207] The Association's AGM took place in the modest surroundings of the Whittington Club.[208] With Milner Gibson in government and Cobden more interested in broader commercial policy, APRTOK was rather marginalized, and the committee contented itself with reiterating, rather wearily, the arguments that had been advanced in 1859 and 1860, leaving supporters in the localities to counter efforts to generate the appearance of a popular agitation for the better claims of tea and sugar.[209] At the same time, the papermakers continued to press their case, and after a deputation met Palmerston in mid-March, were suggesting that the Prime Minister had promised them that the duties would survive at least another year.[210]

In the face of tight financial calculations, Gladstone seized on Milner Gibson's suggestion that he could save £665,000 in the first year and so balance the books by delaying the implementation of the paper duty repeal to the autumn.[211] Notwithstanding, by April, once again, he and Gibson found themselves the only supporters of repeal in the Cabinet, once again obliquely threatening resignation.[212] During the fierce discussion in the cabinet Palmerston lost his temper for the only time Gladstone could recall.[213] But moderate voices urged that 'the repetition of what occurred last session, would probably lead to discredit and defeat in the House of Commons and probably further [fatal] resistance from the Lords.'[214] Reluctantly on the 13th April, Palmerston and the Cabinet acquiesced, with the *quid pro quo* of a reduction of 1d on the income tax, and on the basis that in the light of the events of 1860 they were more or less committed to supporting repeal.[215]

There remained the task of piloting the measure through Parliament. In early May Gladstone was being warned that 'the Paper Duty is to be opposed *in every possible way*.[216] Moderate Liberals were unenthusiastic. Cornewall Lewis was told by one of his correspondents, Richard Potter, that the budget was 'very unpalatable' and 'in the judgement of most commercial men a very unsound one'.[217] Northcote reported that 'Disraeli is in the highest spirits because the battle is to be fought by tactics and not by brute force, and he thinks he is going to display great powers of generalship', but the Lords were not inclined to resist a second time.[218] Gladstone also cleverly brought forward all his financial measures in one bill as a way of avoiding them being picked off individually. Derby and Disraeli worked hard to dragoon opposition votes, attempting to persuade one of the Whig opponents of the duty repeal to move the rejection, on the basis that there was more chance of Whigs supporting the motion, without success. In the end seems that 20 potential opponents did not support Disraeli, largely because they feared the likely dissolution, and in the crucial division on the paper duties on 30th May, the measure squeezed through 296 to 281.[219]

It is not always possible to discern a meaningful role in the budget politics of 1860 and 1861 for newspapers; debates in government circles resolve quickly into disputes over taxation and expenditure, and the internal dissensions of Liberalism under the Palmerstonian ascendancy, just as extra-Parliamentary pressure coalesced around the question of the prerogatives of Houses of Lords and Commons. But newspaper politics were never far beneath the surface. Palmerston defended his policy '[b]ecause I imagine Bright, who is our real Budget maker or Chancellor of the Exchequer' was bent on either repealing paper duties 'to carry on his Penny Papers without loss or else to turn out the present Government'.[220] Although, as the *Birmingham Daily Post* pointed out, the newspaper trade, and especially the cheap newspaper trade, made up only a small fraction of the total consumption of paper, it was often around the implications for the press that the newspaper debate over the paper duties revolved.[221] For Henry Bohn, the publisher who had broken ranks and opposed repeal in 1860, 'the whole controversy has been mainly engendered by the red-republican disciples of [the Manchester] school . . . Down with "taxes on knowledge" was the first insidious cry, and for a time drew after it many unsuspecting philanthropists, . . . but by degrees it has transpired that the real taxes were not on knowledge at all, but on packing and low-class printing papers, in which Manchester and Birmingham, and their representatives have a preponderating interest'.[222]

Underpinning the debates of 1860–1 remained two diametrically opposed views of the trajectory of the press. The Cobdenite view expressed by the *Morning Star* but apparently widely shared within radical circles, of the continued importance of further challenging the monopoly of the *Times* and the established 'dear' London press,[223] and the Whig-Tory view expressed by the *Saturday Review*, that the development of competition among the penny press must progressively lower its tone, and that while the promise was of great educational benefits, 'What we are actually likely to get is a succession of journals like . . . *The Divorce News and Police Reporter*.'[224] For the metropolitan radicals of the North London Political Union, the Lords' rejection of the paper duties showed that they 'desired to fetter the poor man's press and keep political knowledge from him'.[225] Radical orators conjured a newspaper 'conspiracy' against those who spoke out plainly on the 'political condition of the country' identifying journals which 'were bribed by the Government to assist in stifling public opinion'.[226] 'The object of the Manchester School in advocating the repeal of the paper duty', suggested the *Dublin University Magazine*, 'is, that the British press shall be democratized by a multiplication of cheap penny newspapers, which shall dilute and weaken the political power now exercised by influential organs. . . . . [Bright] will have the British press Americanised, rather than Frenchified, so that every village may give birth a penny journal that shall report the dictates of Manchester, but not have intelligence enough to examine them, or independence enough to comment upon them'.[227]

Conclusion

As it happens, the impact of 1861 on the price and supply of paper was undramatic. None of the dire predictions of the papermakers came to fruition, notwithstanding the additional effect of the Lancashire Cotton Famine on the supply of cotton mill waste, an important raw material for paper. Instead, 1861 marked a peak in rag prices, which proceeded to fall steadily for the next two decades.[228] In any case, from 1861, alternative sources of paper finally began to offer a realistic alternative. Although wood pulp was not widely used before the 1880s, Edward Lloyd, of *Lloyd's Weekly Newspaper* established his own esparto estate in Algeria and began using it to produce paper at his own mill in 1861.[229] It was suggested that newsprint prices declined by 20% in the immediate aftermath of repeal, notwithstanding fears for the drying up of the supply of cotton (and other grades of paper even more: trade paper halved in price),[230] and fell steadily in the 1860s, from a price of around 6½d 1860, newsprint had fallen (including loss of 1½d tax) to 4d by 1870.[231] This did not stop the cheap press being printed on paper of the poorest quality, 'little better than tissue, . . . or alas as brittle as glass', as the *Era* put it in 1862.[232]

The Cheap Press

Cobden was convinced that the repeal of the stamp duty would trigger 'a complete revolution in newspapers'.[1] When the paper duties were finally repealed in October 1861 there was similar talk of 'a great and singular revolution. . . . A tumultuous scramble . . . The wildest competition'.[2] By and large, this is what historians of the press have seen, although accounts of the consequences of the reforms of 1855 and 1861 have tended to portray this as a gradual process lasting 20 or 30 years. To be sure, not everything changed in 1855 or in 1861. In looking at the newspaper press of the 1850s in Britain, Miles Taylor acknowledges the greater volatility of the market, the increased competition, especially between the old press and the new, but downplays these features to explore the heavy wastage rate of new papers, especially in the years before 1865 in the provinces, and in those towns which had an established press in 1855.[3] In Scotland, Robert Cowan suggests, although repeal 'rapidly induced changes in price, circulation and frequency of circulation, the crop of new papers was smaller than is commonly supposed or was then anticipated'.[4] In Northern Ireland it has been pointed out that the total size of the Belfast press varied little from 1850–1900, and the spread of the provincial press, though steady and eventually significant, was slow.[5]

There were significant elements of stability in the newspaper history of the later 1850s and 1860s. There was remarkable persistence of the main titles, both of metropolitan dailies and weeklies and in the provincial press. Only 15 of the Irish papers extant in 1850 failed to survive until 1890.[6] The press, and especially the metropolitan press, continued to be strongly implicated in political subsidy.[7] There was also surprisingly little change in the style and layout of the press. The number of illustrated prints slowly increased, but even they had little effect on typography and layout. Forms of journalism and genres of newspaper writing also changed little: there was no move to a 'new journalism' in the 1850s, and even the new London titles offered largely the same balance of content, local, district, national and foreign. Journalism was still passive, and reportage of the spoken word, in parliament or on the platform, continued to dominate. Even so, the changes which are visible in the wake of repeal are significant. Perhaps not always in the way contemporaries had expected or predicted, and certainly not simply as a result of the removal of the newspaper stamp, but for all that what occurred was an upheaval which leaves little scope for arguments which emphasize continuity.

Much of the existing discussion of the impact of 1855 and 1861 attends primarily to the creation of new titles and the expansion in the number of papers published. Across Britain, there was a post-repeal surge. Aled Jones notes that while 1830–55 had seen 415 new newspapers established, the six years from 1855–61 saw a further 492, including as many as 130 in the 12 months after repeal alone, and by 1861 137 papers in 123 towns where previously there had been no newspaper at all.[8] In Wales the number of papers, especially new denominational weeklies, grew rapidly after 1855, and the first daily in Wales, the *Cambrian Daily Leader*, was launched in 1861.[9] The overall picture is visible from the data provided by *Mitchell's Press Directory* from 1846. Mitchells was not a fully comprehensive listing, and provided an (almost) annual snapshot derived at varying points in the year. Nevertheless, the total number of newspaper titles listed does show the shift from a fairly level trend from the mid-1840s to the mid-1850s, to a steady and sustained, if not dramatic, increase from the mid-1850s for at least a decade (Figure 6.1).

The experience of the London press only loosely reflects the overall picture: there was relatively little change in the list of 'national' dailies. *The Times, Daily News, Morning Post, Morning Advertiser, Morning Herald,* (and evening papers such as the *Globe*) for the most part continued very much as before. 'Your opinion as to the failure of the new law corroborates what I have heard from many other newspaper proprietors', Mowbray Morris of *The Times* wrote to J. T. Pitt of *Saunders' Newsletter*, 'The Times has profited on this, as it has on every previous occasion, when a blow has been aimed against its prosperity. I trust that your books record a similar favourable verdict.'[10] Although several of the morning papers struggled as they had before 1855 with small circulations, the first of the front rank dailies to disappear after 1855 was the *Morning Chronicle* and that was not until 1862. Nor was there any obvious challenge to the established Sunday weeklies. Initially the only major challengers were the *Daily Telegraph*, launched in the summer of 1855, initially as a 2d daily, the *Saturday*

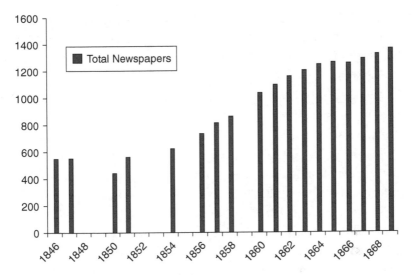

Figure 6.1 Total newspapers

Review, first issued in November 1855 and the *Illustrated Weekly Times* launched to compete with the *Illustrated London News* in June 1855.[11] Otherwise, as the promoters of the *Morning Star* found, it proved harder to shake up the London press than many of the supporters of repeal would have liked (see Chapter 6). The impact of the removal of the stamp was felt predominantly in the dramatic rise of local titles in the metropolitan districts, papers such as the *St Pancras Gazette* and the *Shoreditch Observer*. From the mid-1850s to the early 1860s these contributed disproportionately to the average of about 10 newspapers a year being commenced in London; it was suggested in 1859 that at one point 14 of these 'parochial journals' had been published in the borough of Finsbury alone.[12] By this point these were being joined by the first phase of newspaper publication in outer London, papers such as the *Bromley Record* (1858) and the *Barnet Press* (1859).[13]

Outside London it was a very different story. Here the frenzy occasioned by the repeal of the stamp duty was obvious and immediate, especially in the cities and larger towns. Whereas in small towns like Doncaster already served by two titles, it could be reported that repeal had no noticeable effect, in places like Manchester, Liverpool, Glasgow, the race to publish new titles had begun before the official removal of the duty, with a number of papers appearing in unstamped form in anticipation of repeal, and intensified in the immediate aftermath of repeal.[14] At Manchester five new daily titles were launched, followed by several weeklies. At Sheffield, the four existing titles were joined by the *Sheffield Iris* (relaunched), and two new daily papers, the *Sheffield Daily Telegraph* and the *Morning's News* (½d). Samuel Harrison, proprietor of the weekly *Sheffield Times* expanded to publish an evening *Sheffield Daily News* (from December 1856) and a (morning daily) *Sheffield Times* (from June 1858).[15] Smaller county towns were not far behind. At Cheltenham four cheap papers were launched almost simultaneously in 1855.

In centres of population which had struggled before 1855 to sustain a local presence, it had been one of Cobden and Bright's central aims to facilitate the creation of new titles. Here there is plenty of evidence of success. By the end of 1855 there were papers in 33 towns which had previously had none.[16] In the Midlands it was suggested that 11 towns had acquired their first paper by 1860, including Glossop (2), Mansfield, Newark, Retford, Gainsborough, Hinckley, Loughborough and Peterborough.[17] In Scotland, Airdrie, Annan, Ardrossan, Blairgowrie, Crieff, Fraserburgh, Haddington, Hamilton, Hawick, Invergordon, Jedburgh, Kirkwall, Moffat, Peterhead, Portsoy, Rothesay and Selkirk were all able to support a paper for the first time.[18]

Care is needed in interpreting this spread. After 1855 a thriving business emerged in the part-printing of papers in London, with a space (at times relatively small) being left for filling with local news so that the sheet could be badged as a local issue, along the lines of the *Teesdale Mercury* (1855–).[19] In 1862 the *Critic* suggested that there might be as many as 350 titles of this or a similar sort in existence, indicating that one publisher alone was providing sheets for 200 distinct papers,[20] and there were estimates that as many as half the papers established in towns previously without by the end of 1855 might have been of this model.[21]

Although it provides welcome opportunities for quantification in an area where this is usually very difficult, it is important not to become fixated with the question of new newspapers. The surge of new titles appearing after 1855 was only part of the transformation being wrought, and it contributed less to the fundamental reconstitution of the British press than other changes in the nature of the press, as respects in particular frequency, price and size.

Of greater significance was the rise of the daily press, especially in the provinces, which was only partly a matter of new titles. This had been a crucial part of Cobden's motivation.[22] The numbers of new dailies, especially once the dust settled, might have been small, but the effect was revolutionary. In the larger cities the initial rush of new foundations predominantly comprised daily papers, and in some places they were quickly joined, and often largely superseded, by established titles converting themselves into dailies. At Manchester in 1855 no fewer than five daily titles were soon in existence, including the established *Manchester Examiner and Times* which had promptly converted to daily publication, and the *Manchester Guardian* which quickly followed suit. Within weeks the *Examiner and Times* was selling 15,000 copies and that limited only by printing capacity. 'What a shove we have given the slow coaches on the newspaper road!', its part-owner Bright rejoiced.[23] Liverpool claimed not only the *Northern Daily Times* established in 1853 (and surviving to 1862), the *Liverpool Daily Post* (June 1855) and the *Liverpool Mercury* (1858), but also a number of short-lived titles (*Events* (1855), *Liverpool Daily Mail* (1857), *Liverpool Morning News* (1859)). 'The recent changes in the law', John Hamilton, editor of the struggling weekly *Empire*, remarked to Gladstone in September 1855, already 'induce people to prefer news and politics daily'.[24]

Between 1855 and 1860 approximately 28 provincial dailies were established in England (Table 6.1). Just over half of these had failed by the end of 1860, most lasting just a few months. The *Glasgow Daily News*, one of the earliest foundations, had folded by the end of 1855, the copyright, goodwill and printing materials sold for £200.[25] Some managed to obtain circulations that were large in comparison to pre-1855 standards, but not enough for solvency at the reduced prices. The *Birmingham Daily Press*, which was established just before repeal in 1855, managed to build a circulation of 8,000, but was unable to maintain it and ceased publication in August 1858, leaving the field to the *Birmingham Daily Post*, which was able to build a stable financial base.[26] Within five years of repeal, where previously in effect there had been no provincial dailies, enduring titles had come into existence in Manchester (2), Liverpool (2), Birmingham, Bristol, Newcastle (2), Sheffield, Plymouth and

Table 6.1 Total Number of Daily Papers in Britain, 1846–70

	1846	1856	1863	1867	1870
London	14	15	21	25	18
Provinces		7	25	36	71
Wales			1	1	2
Scotland	2	7	9	14	11
Ireland		6	14	13	14
Total	16	35	70	89	116

Source: Mitchell's Newspaper Directory

Nottingham.[27] Outside the major cities it was harder to sustain the shift to a daily press. At Nottingham, several cheap daily papers failed after a short-lived struggle; the most long-lived, *The Express*, a daily halfpenny sheet, survived until May 1856 on its original diet of war news, but then folded, its editor accepting that conversion into a general newspaper was unlikely to pay.[28] The city did not have a successful daily until the *Nottingham Daily Press* was established at the start of 1860.[29] There was a further little surge of new dailies associated with the repeal of the paper duty. The *Scotsman* moved to a daily in 1860, and a daily *Western Morning News* was launched at Plymouth at the start of 1860. The *Dundee Advertiser* converted to daily publication (alongside its semi-weekly issue). At Nottingham, the *Nottinghamshire Guardian* announced that it was finally ready to become the *Nottingham Daily Guardian*.[30] The *Leeds Mercury* moved to daily publication from October 1861, and the *Cambrian Daily News* (Swansea) was launched. Things moved more slowly elsewhere. Many of the long-established moderate Liberal papers were slow to react, so that in Norwich the *Norfolk News* did not begin a daily issue, the *Eastern Daily News*, until the end of the 1860s; Northampton did not acquire an established daily paper until 1878.[31] In Belfast only the *Belfast Daily Mercury* went to daily publication before 1868 when it was followed by the *Belfast Northern Whig*.[32]

Although the position of *The Times* was pretty much unassailable, the new provincial dailies presented a significant challenge to the existing metropolitan morning papers. Towns and cities came under pressure from what might be described as the 'inundation' of cheap papers in which those of the provinces were often most in evidence.[33] In Preston for example, Andrew Hobbs has shown that 'as soon as the provincial daily newspaper was invented in 1855, it became more popular than its London rival in most reading places'.[34] A major part of the advantage of the provincial dailies was that they were available from early morning, whereas the London papers did not arrive until later.[35] Chester experienced considerable penetration by the Liverpool and Manchester dailies in the later 1850s, precluding not just a local daily, but also reducing the space for any additional weekly challenger.[36] The sales records of a W. H. Smith stall in Bradford for 1868 show penetration of the local market by the *Times* and the penny dailies, but also that the Manchester press was able to more than hold its own: the *Manchester Examiner* sold nearly twice as many on average as the *Times* and three times as many as the *Manchester Guardian*.[37]

In London, where new titles were less numerous, the disruptive force of 1855 was seen in the challenge of cheapness. Until the appearance of the *Morning*

Star (see Chapter 7) the *Daily Telegraph* was alone in the field. Its reduction in price to a penny in the autumn of 1855 was borne of desperation, but it was successful.[38] By the summer of 1856 the talk was of several new metropolitan penny dailies, and even of the proprietors of the *Times* investing £250,000 in a *Penny Times*.[39] Initially both the *Telegraph* and *Morning Star* were four-page single-sheet papers and were in some senses competing after June 1857 with the *Standard,* which having converted from an evening to a morning paper, offered eight pages for 2d. By December 1857 the *Standard* was estimated to have a circulation of 100,000, and in February 1858 it converted to a penny double sheet, becoming the first penny daily to match the size of *The Times*.[40] A few titles were even cheaper: although the halfpenny press was really a feature of evening papers from the late 1860s onwards, in 1858 commentators were suggesting that there were already a number of halfpenny papers; one a district paper in London claiming privately a circulation of 10,500.[41]

The removal of the stamp took a penny off the price of papers not being transmitted through the post, which for most provincial weeklies and metropolitan dailies involved a reduction to 4d or 3d. However, the new provincial dailies generally appeared as penny or 2d papers, often driving established titles to offer for 2d or 3d what they had previously sold at 5d. At Manchester the *Manchester Examiner and Times* stole a march on the *Manchester Guardian*, which converted into a 2d daily, by positioning itself as a penny daily. 'The Examiner . . . beats the Guardian hollow', noted Bright, and 'it is in fact the only great organ now in the Manchester district'.[42] Its average daily circulation (not including the separate *Manchester Weekly Times*) increased from 18,150 in 1856, to 22,224 in 1857, 26,096 in 1858 and 32,310 in 1859.[43] In the summer of 1857 it claimed a circulation 'threefold greater than the circulation of all the other daily and weekly Manchester newspapers together, and more than double that of all the newspapers published throughout the entire county of Lancaster' (exclusive of Liverpool).[44] Eventually, in October 1857 the *Guardian* reduced its price to a penny. The pressure was less intense on the established weeklies. But they too found themselves challenged by new penny titles, and also the cheap weekly editions of provincial dailies. The repackaging of the Saturday issue of the *Manchester Examiner and Times* as the *Manchester Weekly Times* allowed the paper to develop a significant regional circulation amongst, it was claimed, 'the better class of tradespeople, mechanics, etc'.[45]

In London there was spate of price reductions associated with the removal of the paper excise at the start of October 1861, including 1d off *The Times*, the

Athenaeum, *Lloyds Weekly Newspaper*, while those papers already at 1d, like the *Penny Newsman* attempted to counter by increasing their size. September 1861 even saw the brief appearance of the *Farthing News*, 'a most sorry affair, but from its novelty a great number were sold'.[46] This further pressure on price helped to flush out some of the weaker survivals of the pre-1855 regime. The *Morning Chronicle*, for example, responded to the initial readings of the paper duties bill in 1860 by announcing a reduction in price to 2d and stuck by this, despite the subsequent delay.[47] But the reduction could not reverse its decline, and it folded in March 1862, bankrupting George Stiff, who also owned the *Weekly Times* and the *London Journal*.[48] The *Lancaster Gazette*, while describing repeal as 'one of the most wanton acts of folly ever perpetrated by a British minister' reduced its price to 2d unstamped (or 2½d with supplement).[49] At the start of 1862 the *Hertford Mercury* reduced to 3d (4d stamped) proclaiming this rather plaintively as a limit for a county paper with an appropriate staff.[50]

By the spring of 1856 there were signs, as the London correspondent of the *Luton Times* put it, that 'the dear press all over the country is feeling the pressure of its cheaper rivals. I could write down the name of about twenty or thirty provincial papers that *ought* to die'.[51] The growth in newspaper circulation was, in London especially, overwhelmingly accounted for by the growth of the cheap press. It was estimated in December 1857 that the London penny press were issuing 100,000 copies daily.[52] *Morning Star* estimates attributed all bar 20,000 of the increase in sales of British dailies from 70,000–330,000 to the growth of the cheap press.[53] Within London there were substantial shifts in circulation. Most of the established London dailies which sought to retain their prices net of the removal of the stamp had suffered substantial reductions in sales. 'I hear at the railways wherever I inquire that the old high-priced press is going down before the competition of the pennies', noted Cobden in November 1856, '& that even the Times has passed its zenith', although the paper continued to retain most of its circulation.[54] The *Morning Herald* struggled and was sold by its proprietor.[55] The reputation and circulation of the *Morning Chronicle* plummeted under the ownership of Sergeant Glover.[56] The repeal of the paper duties offered no more obvious challenge than had the previous reforms to *The Times*, which won back some of its lost circulation between 1862 and 1867. In 1863 it was suggested that daily circulation was around 66,000, and the issue containing coverage of the marriage of the Prince of Wales topped 110,000.[57]

By 1861 the penny London dailies, the *Telegraph*, *Standard* and *Star* dominated the national trade.[58] The circulation of the working-class weeklies had also considerably increased. Similar continuities are visible in the metropolitan evening papers before the appearance of the *Pall Mall Gazette* in 1865, where the *Globe* was able to stutter along as a 6d paper until 1866, before finally being forced into priced reductions. As a 2d weekly, *Lloyd's Newspaper* increased circulation from 97,000 in June 1855 to 170,000 in September 1861, and thence to 412,080 in 1865.[59] *Reynolds's News* increased its circulation from 50,000 to 150,000 by 1861.[60] The potential for growth was visible in the recovery of the *Weekly Dispatch*, by 1869 a 2d weekly circulating around 70,000 copies.[61] The 'low class' periodicals were augmented by the launch in 1864 of the *Illustrated Police News*, crudely illustrated with woodcuts, alongside the range of other penny dreadful serials.[62] Price reductions also facilitated the spread of cheap 'class' papers, such as the *Grocer's Journal* advertising 8 pages for 1d,[63] the *Clerical Journal* reduced its price from 8d to 3d and moved from fortnightly to weekly publication, and the *Church Times* established in 1863 as 8-page-penny weekly.[64]

In the provinces amidst the ruins of many failed ventures, a few dailies thrived and a new crop of cheap weeklies slowly emerged. The *Manchester Examiner and Times* claimed that in five years the cheap daily press had obtained a daily circulation of 85,000 to compare with a total of 23,000 for all the older dear daily press.[65] The *Leeds Times* boasted unprecedented advance in the year after repeal.[66] The *Bury Times* sold less than a thousand copies of its first impressions in July 1855, but by 1858 attained an average circulation of 6,700. Of the new papers established in towns previously without a local press, (and where there was by definition less local competition), prices varied. Of the 27 identified as having been started by the end of 1855, 7 were penny papers, 8 cost 1½d, 15 2d, 2 cost 3d and 2 went as high as 3½d.[67] In Ireland, only the *Belfast Morning Post* and the *Lurgan Gazette* were selling at a penny in 1857, but by 1864 had been joined by 12 further titles.[68]

By 1859 the cheap press had already almost achieved equality in terms of numbers of titles in England and Wales at least (Figure 6.2). This was the result both of new cheap papers, and of reductions in prices of the existing titles. Figures for the Midland Counties computed by the *Leicester Journal* suggested that of 78 papers only 14 were 'full-priced' journals, 9 had 'an intermediate price' and 55 were cheap, including 21 journals dating to before 1855.[69] In Lancashire and Yorkshire only 12 of the 175 papers were 'full price'. Only Ireland diverged markedly from the pattern with 63 full-priced and only 34 cheap (Table 6.2).[70]

The eventual repeal of the paper duties in 1861 accelerated and generalized reductions in price. The *Hereford Times*, anticipating the change, had converted

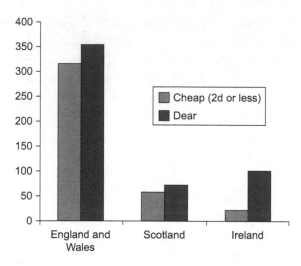

Figure 6.2 Balance of cheap/dear press, 1859

from a 5d weekly to a 2½d twice-weekly as early as January 1860.[71] The *Bristol Mercury*, which launched its cheap title, the *Bristol Daily Post* in January 1860, followed it up by reducing the price of its issue from 4d to 2½d (3½d stamped, or 3d in country districts served by the paper's own carriers).[72] In Dublin by February 1861 the *Evening Mail*, the *Evening Post*, the *Evening Packet* and *Saunders' News-Letter* all reduced in price and enlarged, and *Daily Express* also enlarged to a double sheet.[73] The *Leicestershire Mercury* talked of 'a flood of journals in the Metropolis, many as low a price as half a penny', brought about by anticipation of repeal.[74] By 1863 it was said that there was a substantial body of papers which had reduced to a penny waiting for the frenzy of competition to

Table 6.2 Newspaper prices, 1860

	England (not London)	Wales	Scotland	Ireland	Overall
½d	2	0	5	0	7
1d	175	7	31	8	221
1½d	72	1	10	5	88
2d	72	6	22	13	113
2½-3d	74	4	23	31	132
3½-4½ d	125	7	37	48	217
>5d	7	0	5	12	24

Source: *Mitchell's Newspaper Directory* (1860).

die down, so that they could claw back some of the reduction, 'a slight advance' promising to 'remove newspaper publishing from the category of gambling to that [of] honest enterprise'.[75] This was wishful thinking. In the opening address to *Y Tyst Cymreig* in June 1867, William Rees noted that 'We in the Newspapers now live under the domination of the penny'.[76] Although there remained some localities where understandings between proprietors had enabled prices to be kept at 1½d or even 2d, by 1869 penny titles made up around 60% of the press, and 1869–70 brought a further rush in London, sparked by the *Daily News*'s successful reduction to a penny: by the end of 1870, the *Globe* and the *Sun*, had followed suit. Similar pressures were visible in the provinces. Hence the establishment of the *Brighton Daily News* as a penny paper in November 1868 had within six months prompted five of the Brighton weekly papers to reduce their prices from 3d or 2d down to 1d (Table 6.3).[77]

The flood of new titles in the provinces, the downward pressure on price and the spread of the daily news together created a competitive vortex. Lamentations from proprietors and editors over the savagery of the new market litter the press in the years after 1855. The established press, in particular, saw only internecine strife and insolvency.[78] The *Montrose Telegraph* suspended publication in November 1855 blaming the 'mad competition' among cheap newspapers.[79] In the spring of 1856, the *Scotsman* wrote scathingly of the 'starving newspapers' of Edinburgh, which represented 'nothing but the spites, and stupidities, and mismanagement of a few foolish and disappointed speculators'.[80] The struggle for survival was cut-throat. The *Leicester Weekly Express*, which folded at the end of 1856, described the process by which it was squeezed out by its main rival. 'A week or two's start, and the oldest journal in the town came in very close to

Table 6.3 Newspaper prices, 1869

	England	Wales	Scotland	Ireland	Overall
½d	12	0	5	0	17
1d	471	27	68	35	601
1½d	77	4	14	2	97
2d	115	11	18	26	170
2½–3d	67	1	21	32	121
3½–4½ d	25	6	1	23	55
>5d	2	1	2	5	10

Source: *Mitchell's Newspaper Directory* (1869).

us. A few weeks more and a stupendous "enlargement" was announced and "no increase in price". Another brief interval, and an "enlargement" "on the other hand" breaks forth, offering still further advantageous terms.'[81]

In a rapidly changing landscape, there was little reliable evidence as to the best way forward. Particularly in the provinces, it was difficult to identify an effective strategy in the flux of market conditions. Newspaper owners vacillated between meeting the competition head on or retreating behind defensive positions. Experimentation was widespread. The *Leeds Intelligencer* moved to biweekly publication in 1855, but then in March 1856 reverted to a weekly issue, but with a 4-page supplement, the supplement itself being abandoned in January 1859 in favour of a larger format 8-sheet paper.[82] In the summer of 1857 Baxter's *Sussex Express* announced that it was converting back to an all-stamped edition.[83] The combined pressures of frequency and price often forced titles into alterations which offered little opportunity for real added value or profit. The *Kilmarnock Journal* converted from a 4 ½d weekly to a 1½d thrice-weekly, but not surprisingly quickly perished.

The old gentlemanly understandings between rival editors which had persisted before 1855 despite political differences and editorial mud-slinging quickly perished. In moving to 2d in 1858, the *Glasgow Herald* had taken care to enter into private agreements with its leading rival that they would both continue to publish at 2d, only on the day to find that its contemporary had announced a reduction to 1d, which it was then forced to match.[84] The launching of cheap titles with the deliberate aim of choking off competition appears to have been almost routine. At Sheffield it was said that an attempt was made to organize a combine of the weekly proprietors to produce a cheap daily to kill off the newly established *Daily Telegraph*, and when this failed, the proprietor of the *Independent* brought out the *Morning's News* at ½d with the same intent.[85] The *Northern Whig* concluded in 1861 that 'newspaper rivalry has degenerated into the lowest form of trickery . . . emulating the tricks of pig-jobbers'.[86]

At Liverpool there were accusations of an attempt to sell penny papers at a loss purely to ruin the existing titles.[87] Indeed Liverpool gained a reputation for the fierceness of its newspaper competition, driven entirely by price, and sense that papers could not afford to be undercut by rivals.[88] The *Northern Daily Times* had initially reduced to 2d in June 1855, but was forced to reduce again to 1d when the *Liverpool Daily Post* opted for 1d (it later returned to 1½d). The *Liverpool Journal* attempted to charge 3d (for its 12 pages plus 4-page supplement), but when its main competitor, the *Liverpool Mercury* reduced to 2½d the *Journal* was forced to follow suit.[89] In February, after several months of advertising its sale,

Thomas Baines, owner of the *Liverpool Times* for more than 25 years, 'unwilling to become further involved in the ruinous competition which now characterises Liverpool newspaper affairs' abandoned publication.[90] The *Liverpool Standard*, a Conservative and 'low church' paper, of which it was said £20,000 had been spent in its establishment, was put up for auction in January 1856, partly on account of a decline in both circulation and advertising revenue, but without a bidder.[91] By May 1856 the *Mercury* was selling Monday and Wednesday issues at 1d as well as a large double-sheet Friday edition for 2d, apparently in an attempt to force out the *Liverpool Journal* and the *Liverpool Daily Post*.[92]

The career of Samuel Robinson provides an example of the pressures on profits and the expedients to which they could drive owners. Although he had fiercely opposed the repeal of the stamp duty, Robinson subsequently launched the *Fifeshire News*, a penny newspaper apparently designed to strangle the *Fifeshire Express* launched at the same time, which it succeeded in doing within six months, though not without losses of £200. The *News* quickly attained a circulation of 10,000, but in attempting to extend its market into neighbouring counties Robinson fell foul of agents who did not pay their debts. He also lost considerable sums in a short-lived attempt to publish the *Perth Constitutional*, and later the *Kirkcaldy Independent* which he established in 1859 but could not make pay. Robinson offered such favourable rates to newsvendors as an inducement to push his papers that he could barely cover his paper costs, and he also inflated the returns of stamped circulation by sending a stamped copy of the paper to each advertiser. His financial problems were compounded by a number of costly libel cases, including one against the *Mercantile Advertiser* which cost him not only 106 guineas in damages, but a further £400 in costs. Even as his business was collapsing Robinson was paying £60 for stereotyping apparatus, designed to enable him to use stereotyped columns to extend his stable of papers. Having forged some bills, he was arrested in flight in London, and was sentenced to five years penal servitude.[93]

Outside the larger towns and cities competitive pressures were generally less severe, though the removal of the stamp significantly increased the number of places where sustained local competition existed. There may have been some market segmentation, providing protection for conventional weeklies, especially in rural districts, where the extent of circulation and breadth of news coverage perhaps counted for more than immediacy, and where papers were able to console themselves that their larger and better class of circulation, weekly currency and greater potential for onward transmission to friends and relations, all made them more attractive to readers and advertisers.[94] On this basis some provincial weeklies carved out a role for themselves alongside the dailies. The *Bradford Observer* was confident that 'The public must have the news of the world every day; but the public is content to have its own parochial or borough news once a week.'[95] The *Newcastle Guardian*, which had stuck with its weekly edition, claimed that the cultures of newspaper reading continued to operate in ways favourable to a 'full-sized, first-class weekly journal, containing the news of the week carefully digested and well-arranged, with editorial comments on all topics of leading interest'; 'Those who have leisure for perusing a daily paper', it argued, 'frequent news-rooms and other places of public resort where they find the *Times* and other metropolitan journals open for perusal. It is impossible that the barren and fragmentary details – necessarily such – furnished by a penny print can satisfy those who have been accustomed to better fare.'[96] There may have been a little wish fulfilment here, but significantly by 1858 cheap papers were taking up the argument that the postal regime provided unfair obstacles to the circulation of cheap papers via post into the rural districts, urging a uniform farthing per ounce postage rate.[97]

The forces of competition rapidly reconstituted the economics of newspaper production. Newspaper finances had always been precarious, but the repeal of the stamp increased the stakes substantially. It was reported that over the course of the four years of the life of the *Dublin Daily Press*, the proprietors accumulated debts of over £30,000 pounds, itself dwarfed by the £60,000 the *Sydney Daily Empire* supposedly swallowed up in a couple of years.[98] The combined pressures of price, size, frequency and the squeeze on advertising were compounded by the difficulties faced by new papers, especially national papers, in getting to market.

Formally, entry barriers can hardly be said to have increased in these years. The proliferation of titles indicates the reverse. The statutory requirement that newspapers register and provide sureties against libel was enforced intermittently at best (see Chapter 8). In 1856 Collet suggested that he could launch a new London weekly paper, the *Free Press*, for £6 per week, plus £30 additional start-up expenses, (not including editorial costs or any charge for his own editorial management).[99] For a London daily paper, the costs could still be considerable.[100] Even with their lamentable circulation the cost in 1857 of the *Standard, Morning Herald* and *St James' Chronicle*, goodwill, machinery, etc., was £16,500.[101] But opportunities, especially in the provinces, were often much less costly. The assets, including printing materials etc., of the *Derbyshire Times* in 1855 were valued at £552.[102] At the extremities, it was possible, for example, to buy the copyright of the *St Pancras Gazette*, together with press and type, for £50.[103] Not that even that investment was necessary; specialist printers could offer a full newspaper printing service of 2,000 copies for prices around £12 per edition.[104] As a result, one feature of the newspaper landscape after 1855 was the possibility of avowedly short-term publications at a very cheap price, such as the daily halfpenny *Manchester Election Chronicle* published during the 1857 election.

At the same time, the capitalization of the metropolitan and major provincial dailies grew significantly under the pressure of investment in the machinery required to produce the rapidly expanding print runs. In 1854 it was possible to establish a provincial weekly with a capital of £4,000 (although not easy to make a profit at this level).[105] In the course of discussions within Lord John Russell's connections in 1855 it was suggested that £25,000 would be needed either to relaunch an existing London daily, or establish a new one.[106] Disraeli had been advised that at least £10,000 would be needed to launch his weekly venture, the *Press*; initially he raised only about £6,000, and it is clear that thereafter he had at times to go cap in hand to wealthy backers of the Conservative party for further subsidies.[107] The precariousness of the business meant that the cost of borrowing, especially for new titles, was ruinously high.[108] One response to this was the use of limited liability companies. The most high profile of these was the ill-fated National Newspaper League Company associated with the *Dial* newspaper (see Chapter 7). But limited liability newspaper promotion was generally a failure in this period. The Law Newspaper Company Ltd, launched with a capital of £6,000 to publish the *Solicitor's Journal and Reporter*, failed in 1861.[109] 'A constitutional monarchy, with a wise ministry, is the only form of government under which a newspaper can flourish', one observer commented.[110]

Shrinking margins on newspaper sales made advertising all the more significant. The *Leeds Times* indicated that even at a price of 3d, in 'an indifferent advertising district', breakeven circulation was 8,000.[111] It was suggested that the advertising published by the penny press was often unpaid or very heavily discounted (or simply unwanted repeats), published to disguise weakness, 'a mere decoy to tempt unwary advertisers'.[112] Competition for advertising intensified. Advertisers to one title were pestered by other papers, seeking to capture their business.[113] Advertisers recognized that they were in a strong position. The editor of the short-lived *Gloucestershire Times*, a three-halfpenny paper, complained that advertisers sought to get him to agree to free insertions as a six-month 'trial'.[114] One of the successes of the London local press was its ability to tap into a demand for local advertisement. The *Clerkenwell News*, for example, was dominated by advertising (which made up 16 of its 24 large columns).[115] The cheaper press often struggled to generate sufficient advertising revenue. Even as sales were expanding rapidly in 1856, the *Manchester Examiner and Times* found it difficult to increase advertising revenue.[116] At the same time, advertising grew markedly in the popular weeklies, especially the more moderate *Lloyd's*, after 1855.[117]

Opponents of repeal had predicted a cheap press driven by the inexorable imperatives of cost-cutting to pare their investment in production to the level at which they could survive only by shameless piracy. In fact, the pressure of daily production and the competition for readers operated in the reverse direction, increasing the premium on the scope of newsgathering, the quality of the editorial matter and the force of the journalism. Within five years of repeal, despite the pressures for economy, the London press and the more successful provincial papers were developing into specialized operations. In 1858 the *Standard* had a staff of 12 parliamentary reporters.[118] At the *Glasgow Herald*, Alexander Sinclair recalled the great increase in pressure within the editorial department caused by the shift to daily from tri-weekly publication, and the resulting substantial increase in staffing,[119] The *Newcastle Chronicle* could promise four reporters and the contribution of the editor to report a meeting of the Northern Reform Union in February 1859.[120]

Provincial journalism remained a small-scale affair. T. Wemyss Reid remembered the offices of the *Northern Daily Express* in the later 1850s as consisting 'simply of two rooms and two cellars in a house', one room for compositors, one doubling as the counting house and place where papers were sold and adverts taken in by day, and the editorial office for editor, sub-editor and reporters, in the evening.[121] The proprietors of the weekly *Norfolk Herald* hired John Proudfoot in 1858 'on the distinct understanding that, for a salary of 28s per week, he was to do anything and everything he was asked to', his jobs including editor, sub-editor, reporter and also assistance with the printing.[122] Anthony Hewitson was earning 28/- as a reporter on the *Preston Chronicle* in 1858, and had risen to manager at £2.6s for the *Preston Herald* in 1861. But this income continued to be supplemented by freelance contributions to as many as 20 other papers while he worked as a reporter for the *Preston Guardian* in the 1860s.[123]

One sign of the development of the press was its altered status. Prior to the mid-1850s the press, and the provincial press especially, was barely respectable. As Wemyss Reid put it with affected exaggeration, 'The ordinary reporter on a country paper was generally illiterate, was too often intemperate, and was invariably ill-paid.'[124] George Edge's nominal salary, as editor of the *Derbyshire Times* was £120, though this was a precarious existence, and Edge was almost two quarters in arrears on the failure of the paper in January 1855.[125] The contrast with the 1859 picture of Beresford Hope, of reporting as 'a gentleman's calling', requiring a sound grasp of history, politics, classical languages, as well as of a general 'literary capacity', is striking.[126] It was symptomatic that John Walters of *The Times* and Edward Baines of the *Leeds Mercury* should feature as two of the exemplary biographies in *Small Beginnings; or the Way to Get On*, published in 1860. Certainly by this point it is possible to see a new public prominence for journalists; not only in modest anniversaries and farewell dinners, but also in more substantial public testimonials, such as that afforded Russel, editor of the *Scotsman*, in 1860 headed by Macaulay, which amounted to £1,600.[127]

For the new daily press increasing circulations and the foreshortened timelines of publication, inexorably demanded costly investment in printing machinery which could place considerable strain on the finances of papers, as the case of the *Morning Star* illustrates (see Chapter 7). For new cheap evening papers in particular, sufficient printing capacity to cope with the short printing window was paramount.[128] In the early 1850s, of the London dailies only the *Times* and the *Advertiser* had to print more than 3,500 copies each day, and few of the provincial papers circulated more. By 1860 a paper such as the *Caledonian Mercury* was printing 7,000 copies an hour. New rotary Hoe presses were deployed by *Lloyd's Weekly News* in 1856.[129] *The Times* followed in 1857, the *Standard* in 1858. By July 1858 the *Manchester Examiner and Times* was investing £4,000 in new presses in order to produce 15,000 impressions an hour.[130] But adoption was slow. It was suggested in February 1861 that only 14 Hoe machines had been sold in Britain, and Hoe was granted a five-year extension of his patent on the grounds that he had not yet been able to enjoy any significant profit from it.[131] By 1864 *The Times* was printing on two ten-cylinder Hoe machines, but was still using its 1848 Applegath machine to print its supplement or advertising sheet.[132] In the provinces the key shift was still from manual to steam presses, as in the adoption of steam at the start of 1856 by the *North and South Shields Gazette*, *Sheffield Daily Telegraph*, and in the following year by the *Wrexham Advertiser* and *Falkirk Herald*.[133] The *Hereford Times* announced in January 1861 that to support its shift to twice-weekly production it was bringing into use a four-feeder machine and a second steam engine, allowing it to print 5,000 copies an hour (Figure 6.3).[134]

Figure 6.3 '*Daily Telegraph* ten-feeder printing machine', *Illustrated London News*, 7 April 1860

Getting to market

As production runs increased and reliance on annual subscription and postal delivery declined, so distribution networks became more extended and complex, and gaining a secure footing in the market place all the more important. After 1855, *Chambers' Journal* noted that the unwillingness of the government to embrace the American model of a halfpenny postage had effectively driven newspaper distribution to the railway companies: one new daily journal in the West of England, it noted as early as August 1855, stamped only 400 of its 14,000 edition.[135] By 1858 the distribution of the Glasgow press was almost entirely via rail and steamer.[136] In 1855 the London and North Western, and Midland and Northern Railway companies had taken on newspaper parcel carriage at 3 farthings per pound weight.[137] The shift encouraged the spread of the wholesale newsagents who gathered together various titles into single parcels for dispatch to local agents across the country. *The Times* remained an exception, despite the fact that the post-1855 regime involved a postal charge of 1½d; indeed it was noted in October 1856 that over 5,000 copies daily were passing through the post cut down so that they came in under the 4oz limit for a penny stamp.[138] At the same time, outside the main urban centres, there is evidence that a division remained between the penny press serving towns and such of the rural hinterland as could be reached easily by rail, and titles which continued to issue substantial numbers of stamped papers for postal distribution to the rest of the hinterland. In Carlisle during the year to 30 June 1863, while the *Carlisle Examiner* and the *Carlisle Express* issued no stamped editions at all, the *Carlisle Patriot* circulated 35,000 a year, and the *Carlisle Journal* 98,000.[139]

Margins were squeezed as papers jostled for the attention of agents and newsvendors. The pressures were perhaps even more obvious after 1861 when further price reductions created an organized campaign from newsagents for a greater allowance, but they were a feature of the business from 1855. Newsagents, both wholesale and retail, were unenthusiastic about promoting the new penny titles, given the limited trade allowance they received. Papers had to offer generous discounts to newsagents and street sellers. These might have been as substantial for the penny press as 10 for 6d.[140] Especially before 1861, when paper costs were artificially inflated, this pushed profit on each copy down to fractions of a penny. Increasing casual sales and falling prices put further pressure on the distribution chain. As prices fell, newsvendors pressed for an increased allowance to compensate. In 1861 most penny papers had already been charging no more than 18d for a quire (24) sheets, occasionally less (the *Penny Newsman* allowed 28 for 1s 6d), but margins were especially tight when returns were not allowed on newspapers – those taken needed to be paid for and sold.[141] (One exception was the working class *People's Paper*, which had allowed returns it would seem in 1853.) In the aftermath of the repeal of the paper duty and its attendant price reductions, London publishers attempted to cut the commission to 1½d per dozen, forcing many provincial newsagents to charge a halfpenny more than the cover price.[142] Newsagents like W. H. Smith sought to use their dominance of the supply chain to maintain commission rates. In Newcastle, Joseph Cowen refused to bow to pressure, and Smith's subsequent attempt to exclude his *Newcastle Chronicle* from the station news stalls, prompted a vigorous campaign in his columns against 'News-agent despotism', and active measures to combat the exclusion, including the parking of travelling vans opposite all the local railway stations.[143] In the larger cities papers organized their own newsboys brigades, although there was controversy in Glasgow in 1868 over the proposed creation of a news-boy brigade, which was vigorously opposed by the newsagents.[144]

Newsvendors' shops spread throughout working-class districts in the larger urban centres, supplementing grocers, barbers, confectioners and others who sold papers.[145] In 1865 the village of Little Gonnerby in Lincolnshire was served by a 'newsvendors shop' which shared its premises with a baker and grocer, indicating its trade by a card in the window offering to execute any orders for newspapers.[146] But there was also a surprising longevity of postal distribution and the voluntary stamp. In 1868–9 *The Times* was issued with 2,089,950 stamps, the *Standard* 652,224 (and another 923,124 for the *Evening Standard*); in Scotland the *North British Advertiser* took 673,000; and the stamp was still important for some county papers: the *Sussex Agricultural Express* took 335,500 stamps, the *Midland Counties Herald* 266,000 and in Ireland likewise, many of the papers relied significantly on stamped copies.[147]

Profit and loss

The arithmetic of newspaper accounting was not for the faint-hearted. Even a relatively successful London penny paper like *Bell's News* required a circulation of c.50,000 just to pay expenses, given that the basic cost per copy would probably amount to three-and-a-half farthings (7/8 of a penny), and at a gross profit of about a tenth of a penny per paper, a sale of this magnitude would yield only £20 to include payments to editors and printers, and allowances for depreciation.[148] In the provinces the scale was smaller, but the pressures just as acute. A letter published in early 1857 purporting to be from the editor of a defunct penny weekly confessed to being unable to make a profit on a circulation of 5,000, even when saving on reporting costs by 'cutting out the greater portion of the news from the county papers, and rewriting it'; even with a circulation double that it would have been difficult to obtain sufficient advertising revenue, the letter continued: the paper, because of its exclusively working-class readership, 'can only obtain the inferior class of advertisements . . . at a miserably low scale'.[149] These statements were ridiculed by *Luton Times*'s London correspondent who asserted that 'I could produce undoubted testimony – personal, black-and-white, day-book and ledger testimony – in proof of the fact that many a cheap newspaper now flourishes and pays very fair profits on considerably less sale than this. One gentleman, I am informed, is making 500*l.* a year profit on the sale of a penny paper which averages very little more than 5,000 per week.'[150] The truth was that there was no universal formula: profitability depended on economy of production, the extent of competition and on the nature of the market. Country papers with substantial districts and hence greater potential for advertising revenue could thrive on smaller circulations; hence the *Hereford Times* claimed circulation of 5,000–6,000 at start of 1861, which it presented as large for a paper in its circumstances, and the basis for shifting to twice-weekly publication.[151]

Profit had always been in elusive in the newspaper industry. Stephen Koss's work records in detail the tribulations and the subsidization of the London dailies, most of which relied on some form of subsidy during the early and mid-Victorian decades.[152] Nor were prospects much better for the weeklies: the well-known dependence of Disraeli's *Press* was almost certainly mirrored by the experience of other general weeklies.[153] Competition after 1855 only intensified these challenges. For several years it may be that the *Daily Telegraph* was the only London penny daily making a profit. The *Standard's* approach to Disraeli in 1862 provides a profit and loss statement which suggests that it had never been profitable since its conversion to a penny.[154] Although not public knowledge, the *Caledonian Mercury* was said to have lost £1,760 in the first year of cheap newspapers.[155] In April 1862 the paper was acquired by its editor, James Robie, funded by loans from several leading Whigs, including Duncan McLaren, Bright's brother-in-law, and was supported by further loans in subsequent years, before failing amidst acrimonious public disputes over the basis on which these loans had been provided in 1867.[156] Provincial papers also often limped on, without prospect of commercial solvency, in the hope of political subsidy or patronage. In the spring of 1856 the *Wolverhampton Journal* had a paid readership of only about 500, and was losing from £5 to £10 a week, but was kept up while the proprietor touted it to parties who he thought might invest, including one of the candidates for the mayoralty.[157] Despite the hopes of many proprietors, the repeal of the paper duty in 1861 did not bring relief, not least because of the further downward pressure on prices that came with it. *Lloyd's Weekly*, which had been making £12,000 a year net profit before repeal was losing £500 per week in the aftermath, and one weekly journal proprietor indicated that having reduced his price from 2d to 1d sales would have to increase from 120,000 to 400,000 to maintain profits.[158] Predictably, there were further casualties. Henry Lea, proprietor of the *Halfpenny Miscellany* was declared bankrupt in April 1862 with liabilities of £14,600 against assets of only £1,900.[159] Although the removal of the paper duty brought a £7,000 increase in the profits of the *London Journal*, the fortunes of George Stiff its proprietor were dragged down by the *Weekly Times* because its reduction in price to 1d brought even greater losses.[160]

It wasn't impossible to make a profit. In the 1850s the *Birmingham Journal* was reputed to be one of the most lucrative of the provincial papers, netting its proprietors £5,000 pa.[161] It was said of James Wilson that by 1858 the *Economist* (admittedly at 8d per copy in 1860 hardly a representative of the 'cheap press') was worth £3,000 pa to him, and was helping to support lavish establishments in London and outside Bath.[162] As the decade progressed, indications that the newspaper industry was becoming more profitable began to multiply.[163] Through the 1860s the *Manchester Guardian* was making an average annual profit of £16,000.[164] In 1869 it was suggested that the profits of the *Morning Advertiser*, despite its limited sale, were £14,000 a year.[165] The *Western Morning News* was converted to a limited liability company in 1866 generating significant profits for shareholders and for employees via a profit-sharing scheme.[166]

Even so, the rate of attrition, for new titles and for old, was high throughout the period.[167] Between 1855 and 1861, many new titles lasted only days or weeks. It was claimed (but also disputed) in December 1859 that of the 411 penny papers established since the repeal of the Stamp Act, 372 had failed.[168] Examples certainly abounded. Two of the new Manchester titles, the *Manchester Halfpenny Express* and the *Manchester Penny Express* did not survive to the end of July 1855.[169] The *Newcastle Courier* managed only four weeks, the *Bristol Guardian* only 11 issues. A number of papers like the Sheffield *Morning's News* struggled on while the Crimea continued to create demand for daily information, disappearing once the campaign ground to a winter halt.[170] The weekly *Bristol Telegraph* managed 56 issues, but folded at the end of June 1856, blaming the ending of the Crimean war, the lack of political feeling among the masses and the superiority of the cheap London papers.[171] Of the new Cheltenham papers, the longest surviving was the *Cheltenham Mercury*, which struggled on to July 1858.

Between 1859 and early 1863, 11 Edinburgh newspapers ceased publication.[172] Some of these were post-1855 titles, but some were more longstanding. Repeal also caught out a number of more established titles whose shift to more frequent publication in response to the change proved disastrous. *The Belfast Commercial Chronicle*, established in 1805, converted to daily publication in 1855, but was forced to cease publication by early September. Other established papers simply failed to weather the competitive storm. The (Glasgow) *Constitutional* collapsed before the end of 1855.[173] The *Yorkshireman* folded in October 1858 after nearly 25 years publication, in the face of its failure to produce an adequate return on its capital.[174] None of this amounts to a case for downplaying the changes wrought by 1855. This was the thrust of much contemporary rhetoric, which sought to discern in the statistics of newspaper failure evidence for the 'failure' of repeal. In fact, of course, the level of turnover of titles was itself an index of the significance of 1855.

Levels of failure remained high through the 1860s: the *Newspaper Press* recorded 87 bankruptcies in the four years 1867–70.[175] In part this was generated by the continued propensity to politically motivated foundations, many of which did not have the necessary commercial logic. The *Western Counties Daily Herald* established in Plymouth in 1868 to advocate the Conservative interest lasted just three months; the *Western Daily Standard*, launched on the same basis in 1869, did not last much longer. The working-class press remained at best on the margins of commercial viability. In 1866 the editor of the *Commonwealth* was seeking contributions of the order of £500 from several supporters in order 'to make a last and determined effort to keep up' the paper.[176] The *Beehive* struggled along, making a surplus of just over £15 on a turnover of £1,459 in the second half of 1866.[177]

Nevertheless, in the provinces by 1865 the upheavals ushered in by 1855 and 1861 had largely passed and a new stability was emerging. The spread of titles into new towns continued, but at a reduced pace, alongside a consolidation into fewer titles in larger towns and cities (in 1864 it was suggested that over the previous 10 years some 11 weekly newspapers had expired in Edinburgh, and perhaps double that number in Glasgow; at Dundee five or six newspaper offices had been reduced to two).[178] In the agricultural districts, some of the old county presses such as the *Hereford Times* carried on very much as before, although the pressure of the daily press was considerable.[179]

Defenders of the taxes on knowledge like W. E. Baxter found their gloomy predictions confounded. By 1867 Baxter had a stable of 24 titles and was reputed to own more newspapers than anyone else in the country.[180] One development of the 1860s was the spread of chains of provincial papers. Some of these were merely retitled 'local' versions of the same imprint, as in the stable of 15 titles parasitical on the *Dorset County Express* in the 1860s, or the series of titles associated with Alexander Mackie and the *Warrington Guardian*. Others were actual chains, including the strings of Baxter and of George Bacon.[181] As circulations expanded so papers grew in size. Although this process is extremely difficult to describe with precision, incidental material abounds. Hence, at the start of 1868 the *Manchester Guardian*, *Examiner* and *Courier* all announced enlargement to 8-page sheets on 4 days.[182]

Newspaper failure was just the tip of the iceberg. The challenges of increased competition brought pressures which operated across all aspects of newspaper production. Considerable churn of ownership is also visible. The Edinburgh *Daily Express* which survived from 1855 to 1859 before being merged into the *Caledonian Mercury* went through a series of proprietors. Its first owner, C. D. Young, engineer, iron founder and contractor started it as a pre-repeal penny paper, but sold it sometime after to a party whose bills of purchase were discounted by Young's bankers, but who also could not make it pay, later selling it to a third group who sought to make it a party organ, before it was eventually acquired by the *Caledonian Mercury*.[183] Nor were weeklies immune. Competing with the established *Wrexham Advertiser*, between 1855 and 1863 the *Wrexham Telegraph* went through four owners, five editors and probably six printing offices.[184]

The impact on circulation was not always easy to discern. Although they had never been an entirely reliable guide to circulation, before 1855 the stamp returns provided some indication of the overall circulation of newspapers and the progress of individual titles. By 1861 the *Scotsman* was reporting that only about 400 of its circulation of 11,000 were being stamped for sending through post (with others being sent in parcels of three under book postage rates).[185] With the compulsory stamp gone, we are driven back to reliance on partial data which can be used to provide some sort of index, the always suspect self-professions of individual papers, and the occasional indication provided by the records of individual titles. No doubt there were large increases, but their pattern and timing is masked by volatility of sales, and are all but impossible to describe reliably. The circulation of the London dailies in particular was seasonal, falling off markedly outside the Parliamentary session, and after 1855 the tendency for dramatic news events to see large spikes in demand was amplified. In 1862 the *Northern Press*, a Liverpool title whose normal circulation averaged around 3,000, sold nearly 10,000 copies of an edition issued with a portrait of Major O'Reilly, the recently elected MP for Longford.[186] News of a sensational murder would produce a sizeable increase in demand: in Inverness in 1862 news of a murder in Glasgow left the 'newsvendors . . . literally besieged, and', it was reported, 'many, very many, had to go away empty handed', while in 1866 the day after the London Hyde Park Riots, demand for the cheaper titles was nearly three times their normal circulation, and 'some of the small newsvendors in the suburbs were running to and from the publishing offices during the entire day'.[187] News of the assassination of Lincoln in 1865, created such a surge in demand that by mid-afternoon, despite the printing of a third edition, copies of

The Times were being sold for 2/6, and evening papers selling at two and three times their cover price.[188]

All this makes establishing a precise picture of newspaper circulation impossible. But we need have no doubt that numbers increased very substantially, and from the mid-1850s, and not just from the 1860s, as has been suggested by Brown. It is significant given the widespread evidence of shift in the transportation of newspapers from post to rail that in 1860 Post Office statistics indicated that 71M newspapers had been transmitted through the press, a figure which had altered little from 1857.[189] It was suggested by the *Star* in 1860 that in 1855 the whole circulation of the British daily press amounted to about 70,000 issues, of which the *Times* accounted for about 50,000; but that by July 1860 although the circulation of the *Times* had largely stagnated, the total circulation of the daily press had increased to about 330,000.[190] Through the 1860s the *Standard* and the *Daily Telegraph* obtained ever larger sales, but struggled to convert them into profit. Daily sales of the *Telegraph* increased from about 140,000 at the end of 1861 to close to 200,000 by 1869; *Standard*'s circulation from 30–46,000 in 1860 to 160–170,000 in 1874.[191] The oldest of the parochial papers, the *Clerkenwell News,* claimed a circulation of 14,000 in 1858.

Similarly, it was suggested that within two years of repeal the aggregate circulation of the Birmingham press had increased from around 15,000 to between 30,000 and 40,000.[192] By 1864 it was estimated that Birmingham's two daily and four weekly newspapers were circulating around 250,000 copies weekly.[193] The circulation of Mitchell's *West Sussex Gazette*, having nearly tripled from 1856–61, continued more steady growth, nearly doubling again across the 1860s. Such figures need to be treated with some little caution. There is repeated evidence that newspapers shamelessly inflated even their 'guaranteed' circulation figures provided to newspaper directories. In 1856 for example, a court case involving the *Wolverhampton Journal* heard evidence that although the paper's circulation was little more than 500 bought, and another 500 distributed free, the *Journal*'s entry in *Mitchell's Newspaper Directory* indicated a guaranteed circulation of 2,000 weekly.[194]

Consumption

Disruptive pressures within the newspaper industry were mirrored (and also fuelled) by the transformation in the cultures of newspaper consumption encouraged by the removal of the stamp duty. 'People will not now have to buy the day before yesterday's *Times*, or borrow from a public house an old *Advertiser*', as the *Daily Telegraph* put it in October 1855.[195]

It is important not to over-exaggerate here. Papers had always been bought over the counter of local agents and booksellers, and although traditionally a significant proportion of the circulation of both national and provincial papers had been distributed through the Post Office, this had clearly been changing, at least for the London dailies, well before 1855. From 1848 the rapid development of the railway network was paralleled by the rapid expansion of W. H. Smith's station bookstall trade.[196] On the eve of repeal of the stamp duty almost all the non-metropolitan sale of *The Times* was being transmitted by W. H. Smith, who paid a £4,000 premium to receive the earliest copies of the paper. After 1855 aided by what appeared to be a steadily dwindling enthusiasm at the Post Office for the labour involved in distributing large numbers of papers, the newsagents, led by Smith nationally, engrossed a steadily greater share of the trade.[197]

For the cheap press in particular, the focus of selling moved rapidly into the streets, with hawkers of the new penny dailies at the forefront.[198] As early as July 1855 the *Daily Telegraph* attempted to exploit a corps of 500 ragged school boys, with glazed hats with printed advertisement for the paper, paid at a farthing per copy sold.[199] Bold placards with bolder headlines were used to sell papers: 'Palmerston cut up', 'The Roebuck and Morley Sham', etc.[200] This was not, as Wiener has recently suggested, merely a feature of the penny papers. By the mid-1860s the competition of the newspaper placard had spread across the full range of the press, from penny sheets to the clubland titles.[201] Omnibuses were used extensively to advertise titles.[202] The cheap press was hawked on the streets by newsboys who 'pushe[d] and puff[ed], and bawl[ed] and declaim[ed] incessantly'.[203] Metropolitan omnibuses were assailed at their stops by the rival cries of the penny papers, all stressing price and size.[204] The launch of *Fun* in 1861, 'was heralded by a mob of newsboys who blocked up Fleet Street . . . and clamorously forced the new-born . . . on the unhappy pedestrian'.[205] Similar recourses were visible in the provinces. A paper like the *Sheffield Times* employed a miscellaneous range of occasional and part-time sellers, artisans who sold papers to trade shops, oddjobbers who mixed posting bills with some street selling, often selling several times more than the wholesale newsagents, some of whom could themselves supply 30–40 sub-agents.[206]

Opponents were not slow to associate the phenomenon with a degeneration in newspaper readership: 'bawling newsmongers . . . chanting the murderer's achievements in doggerel verse and in ear-splitting tones . . .'[207] At Exeter in 1860 magistrates intervened to confiscate boards advertising the *Western Morning News* used by placard boys; and in 1863 further action was promised in response to complaints about 'hand-bell ringing and the pertinacious pushing of penny papers into the faces of honest citizens'.[208] Unsurprisingly, the cheap press stood as defenders of the street newsvendors: in January 1858 the *Morning Star* offered the anecdote of Palmerston, on meeting a newsboy hallooing out a misleading cry about the Indian Mutiny, 'asking the man how he dared to deceive the public so. "My Lord", said the shrewd outsider of literature, "I follow my business as you follow yours".[209] Initially at least it seems these boys were often not employed directly by the newspapers, but were self-employed, taking supplies of papers on the same terms as booksellers.[210] By the mid-1860s it was reported from Dublin that 'We are suffering from an entire change in the Newspaper business under which the Penny papers have almost entirely taken the place, in the country, of the old established and dear papers. The profit derived from the Newspaper business may be said to have disappeared, as the Public buy in the Streets the papers which now take the places of those they obtained through the Newspaper Agent and at the Bookstalls.'[211]

New patterns of selling inevitably created new patterns of readership: both of ownership and location. At Hawick as early as September 1855 it was suggested that 'Newspapers are to be seen everywhere, and everywhere the important events of the day form the prime topics of conversation. Individuals who formerly never thought of looking into a paper . . . who at least never saw the use of purchasing such a thing, now appear to be smitten with a desire for news.'[212] Within five years it was widely accepted that the post-repeal upheaval had 'created a new class of readers', and that 'the circulation of newspapers has undergone not a change, but a revolution. It has not only spread beyond its former limits, but it has created, or absorbed, a wholly new class of readers.'[213] It is not clear if this was new working-class readers or just the spread of middle-class purchasing. It was noted that 'Newspapers are much read by the lads . . . the *Daily Telegraph* is the most popular newspaper with them.'[214] More than this, it was suggested that the very ephemerality of the papers meant that once read they were casually discarded or handed on, so that many would get to be read in the railway carriage, the office or the home, found and read by porters or servants. Opponents of the cheap press were quick to sneer that it catered merely for the half-pay lieutenant, the dissenting shopkeeper and the 'spruce City clerk' perusing 'those "spicey" social leaders which form the great attraction of the *Daily Telegraph*'.[215] On the other hand the Manchester newsagent Abel

Heywood believed that 'the newspaper is the idol of the working man. Every day unfolds to him new action, stirring events mixed up with the grave and the gay, importing to him more extended sources of knowledge and pleasure, which, before the removal of the tax, he was incapable of attaining.'[216]

Where previously four or five had clubbed together to buy a copy of *The Times* each might now buy their own.[217] Newspapers which previously had been read in clubs and reading rooms, or hired at public houses by the hour, could now be purchased, and brought home to be read by men and by women.[218] What this meant for the established patterns of newspaper reading based in communal or associational reading spaces is not entirely clear. Initially the signs did not look good. Speakers at the annual general meeting of the Warwick Athenaeum in 1858 noted the 'baneful' influence of the cheap press on the subscription list.[219] Observers of the empty seats in the newsroom of the Chorlton upon Medlock Mechanics' Institute in Manchester in 1856 attributed the gaps to the cheap press's promotion of home reading.[220]

Railways not only transported newspapers wholesale, they also assumed the role as the most characteristic site of reading. For the *Nonconformist* in 1863 'newspaper reading is, with a very large class, simply a railway occupation'.[221] 'Every train that sweeps out of London, from 8 to 10 o'clock', the *Aberdeen Journal* remarked 'presents one white sheet as it passes you', and all that can be seen is 'compartments filled with newspapers, dotted with people's heads'. It was not just on trains, but on other forms of public transport and public places, 'on board Thames steamboats, and in all the leading thoroughfares and public places', as the *British Quarterly Review* put it in 1859.[222]

One account of circulations in an unnamed county town of about 6,500 inhabitants suggested that in the late 1840s, before the arrival of the railway, no more than 8 or 10 morning papers were sold, including those for the local reading rooms, but with the coming of the railways numbers had increased to 26–30 copies of *The Times*, five or six copies of the other high-priced dailies, and about 80 'penny [daily] papers' ('sold principally to tradesmen and second class firms, where they are read by the mechanics'), with a corresponding increase in the weekly London papers, where previously perhaps as many as 50 copies were circulated (half sold in shops, half by post), now 350–400 copies sold to 'principally mechanics' and 'labourers'.[223]

Although Miles Taylor suggested that 1855 created a landscape favourable to a Conservative press revival, it is hard to dissent from the traditional view that notwithstanding the disappointments of the Manchester School radicals, repeal did, at least in the short term, shift the balance of newspaper politics fairly decisively towards Liberalism. In part this was pre-programmed. The widespread suspicion of the conservative elite of the vulgarizing tendencies of the cheap press inevitably deterred them from attempting to exploit the new opportunities. In part it reflected the spread of newspaper reading to a class likely, at least in the surface, to be attracted to the popular and often diffuse liberalism of the majority of the press. By 1861 the London press comprised 50 Liberal papers, 17 Conservative, 20 independent and 128 neutral.[224] The national picture was even more striking. According to the calculations of *Mitchell's Press Directory* in 1859 scarcely more than a sixth of British papers identified themselves as Conservative. Nearly half proclaimed Liberalism or Radicalism, and although this left a third who were formally neutral, it was generally accepted that many more of these had Liberal leanings than Conservative (Figure 6.4).

Efforts to generate a Conservative challenge were sporadic.[225] The first Conservative penny daily was not established until the *Nottingham Daily Guardian* was launched in 1861, and the pace of change in the Conservative press did not noticeably quicken until the later 1860s under the impetus of J. E. Gorst.[226] In Ireland (and to a lesser extent in Scotland), the cheap press grew in tandem with the spread of nationalism.[227] The repeal of the Stamp Duty was followed by the establishment of a number of nationalist papers. Between 1855 and 1859 William Kenealy, Peter Gill, P. J. Smyth, Martin O'Brennan and Denis Holland founded nationalist titles, the *Tipperary Leader* (1855), *Tipperary Advocate* (1857), *Waterford Citizen* (1859), *Connaught Patriot* (1859), *Galway*

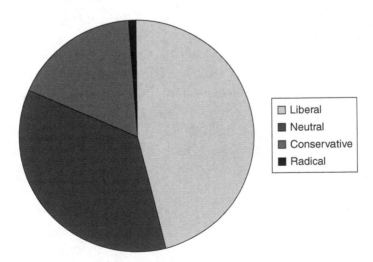

Figure 6.4 Political complexion of the British Press, 1859
Source: *Mitchell's Newspaper Directory* (1859).

American (1862).[228] The relationship was less obvious in Scotland, but included the *Scottish Thistle* (established 1857) by James Bell, owner of the *North Briton*, which became the *Edinburgh Weekly Chronicle* in 1860.[229]

Typographically, the appearance of the mid-Victorian press changed little; even the new penny papers sought to provide a cheaper version of the established press rather than anything radically new in terms of appearance, content or even style. There was a slow breaking down of the large set-pieces of early Victorian journalism, but no more than the 'multum in parvo' style of large numbers of small items and extracts which had long marked the coverage of local news. There was perhaps a greater penchant for sensationalism, and a tendency across the press to give particular attention to scandal, accident or violence.[230] By the early 1870s there was a greater provision of original local literary matter in the provincial press, but feature-writing was still the exception, and even the interview made few inroads in the 1860s.[231] In February 1870 a frank interview with an old and frail Thomas Carlyle which was widely extracted prompted the *Publishers' Circular* to protest that 'metropolitan journals of established reputation' would offer 'such gossip as a serious article of news'.[232]

Changes occurred largely behind the scenes. News gathering became more sophisticated. The more successful provincial dailies expanded their own staff. Attempts by provincial papers such as the *Western Morning News* obtain a foothold in London for news-gathering purposes had by the mid-1860s prompted the formation of the early press agencies, including the Central Press (established 1863), which provided news summaries, accounts of Parliament and London Letters, produced by staff writers.[233] The development of telegraphic services such as Reuters created a greater uniformity of foreign news, and reports of provincial events were often identical across a large part of the London press, having been furnished to all papers by a single source. For the *Lincolnshire Chronicle*, 'in this wholesale monopoly of news supplying engendered by the creating of the penny press, it is easy to perceive the germs of a power which will ultimate place the whole of the newspaper press of the country at the mercy of a few individuals.'[234] Otherwise, standards of reporting evolved slowly. The *Manchester Guardian* news continued to be 'cobbled together in a ramshackle fashion'.[235] Much reliance was still placed on networks of freelance local 'correspondents'. But just as increases in circulation required expansion of the printing operation, for many papers, larger and larger page extents required more extensive journalistic establishments. By 1870 the *Warrington Guardian* was a 12-page sheet of 8 26-inch columns (equivalent of

106 columns of *The Times*) and its sister titles were served by a total staff of 65, including 10 reporters.[236]

During the 1860s Manchester radicals delighted in celebrating the beneficial effects of repeal, the almost universal consensus that the penny press had become a force for improvement, and ironies that it was struggling papers like the *Globe* who now found themselves engaged most systematically in the sort of scissors and paste work which had been predicted of the cheap press.[237] These shifts of scale were reflected in the increasing demands of capitalization. It was reported in the mid-60s that the proprietor of the *Pall Mall Gazette* set aside £60,000 to launch the paper, and had to spend £50,000 before success became likely.[238] By 1872 estimates of the cost of establishing a London daily had reached £100,000.[239] The costs of printing machinery escalated rapidly: even a modest local paper could spend over £40,000 on machinery in the 1870s.[240] They were also registered, as in Mitchell's *Sussex Gazette*, in a transformation of the physical presence of the press, translated from obscure back-rooms into new purpose-built premises prominently position in the centres of towns, as did the *Huddersfield Chronicle* in 1870.[241]

Conclusion

The closer examination of the experience of the press in the years immediately after 1855 which is possible in the age of digitized newspapers presents a picture of wholesale transformation, both of degree and of kind. This was a transformation numbers of titles and geography of publication, but in many senses these were merely epiphenomenal. More fundamentally, 1855 was experienced in intensified competition and instability in the newspaper market; the creation of a new 'cheap press' which was not segmented and separated, but which mirrored the offering of the established press only at a lower price; the appearance of the new provincial dailies and cheap weeklies; pressures of the mass market (production, printing, distribution); and transformation of reading cultures (if not readerships). There was nothing assured or stable about any of these developments up to 1861, but as the 1860s progressed they were slowly consolidated. Pressures at all points were intense and the margins of survival were often tiny. In this sense the presence of the financial burdens still imposed by the paper duty continued to amount to a critical inhibitor on the further development of newspapers, something which contributed to the particularly conflicted character of the campaigns for their removal.

What is not in doubt is the remarkable shift in rhetoric which occurred between the mid-1850s and the early 1860s in the way the cheap press was characterized. True, the 'cheap' slur was never entirely abandoned. It is possible to find it even in publications which one might have expected to champion penny papers, such as *Chambers' Edinburgh Journal*, whose snide 'The Rise and Fall of the *Daily Flambeau*', appeared in June 1862. Yet, paradoxically, the willingness of *Chambers'* to resort to the stereotype is perhaps an indication of its loss of real purchase. Some prejudice remained but the horror had been lost. And in many quarters even contempt had been replaced by grudging acceptance. Even an arch-evangelical like John Cumming could attest in 1859 that 'The newspaper press was another remarkable fact. There were penny London papers that had a respectability, an excellence, a good sense, a talent, and an amount of knowledge and research that perfectly amazed and surprised him in every sense of the word.'[242] Through the advocacy of the *Standard*, steps were taken to absorb the cheap press into the identity of progressive Conservatism.[243] Accounts of the cheap papers increasingly emphasized their parity with the established press in all aspects, save perhaps the quality of the paper they used.[244] The old argument that penny papers would increase the class divide was replaced by the argument that the penny press 'enables all classes of society to glance daily over the same printed page. The peer and the peasant, the rich merchant and the humble working man, become readers of the same journal, and have their thoughts and feelings directed once a day into one channel.'[245]

The *Morning Star*

Introduction

The *Morning Star* and its sister paper the *Evening Star*, launched by Cobden and Bright in the spring of 1856, which assumed the mantle of the archetypical representative of the post-1855 penny press, often given a priority which actually belonged to the *Daily Telegraph*,[1] offers a case study of the challenges and difficulties of the metropolitan cheap press. Its fate would determine the extent to which the hopes the Manchester School radicals entertained of the removal of the taxes on knowledge would be fulfilled, and help illuminate the opportunities and prerequisites of for the cheap press in the years after the repeal of the stamp.

Establishment of the *Morning Star*

The possibility of their own newspaper had long been a goal of Cobden and Bright. There were the sympathetic provincial papers, in particular the *Manchester Examiner and Times*, but a London daily remained vital if the School's principles were to be projected effectively on the national stage. Cobden was convinced that 'if there were no ~~party~~ <stamp>, that a paper pledged to the Peace Conference views, & *free on other questions*, might have a very large circulation. It is only by a *daily* paper that we can really influence public opinion'.[2] During 1854 and 1855 as the metropolitan press fell over itself in apparent pursuit of the most bellicose position, and *The Times*, in particular, seemed determined to feed popular Russophobia and military adventurism, the need for such a paper seemed ever more pressing.

Cast into despondency at the state of progressive politics, the Manchester Radicals remained wedded to their hopes that without the stamp, 'the cheap press may knock to pieces some of the old idols which the people have been in the habit of worshipping, without asking whether they are of gold, brass, or clay'.[3] In the turmoil of the concluding months of the war, various opportunities presented themselves. The *Morning Chronicle* was being touted about at a cost of £5,000 for a controlling interest, before being rescued as a Peelite paper by Gladstone.[4] There were tentative enquiries about acquiring the struggling *Daily Telegraph*, a possibility scotched by Bright, who did not think if it went down to a penny it could survive.[5] Consideration was also briefly given to taking over the *Empire*, a radical London sixpenny weekly, conducted with the support of Cobden, Wilson and other members of the Peace party; but despite the desperate efforts of its editors George Thompson and John Hamilton to raise fresh finance for the paper with a view to converting it into a Radical daily, Cobden and Bright were again unwilling to commit.[6] 'There is no use building on a bad foundation', Bright observed, 'a *new* paper is far better in our case than an old one'.[7] A new title would require greater investment than the APRTOK radicals could afford; but the Quakers of the Peace Society had the resources, and equally troubled by the widespread press support for Britain's involvement in the Crimean war, they had become convinced of the desirability of a penny daily 'representing the opinion of the "Manchester party"'.[8]

Once the stamp was abolished, planning began in earnest. William Haly, an old League acquaintance of Cobden's, had been laying the groundwork, collecting information about the American cheap press.[9] Cobden held discussions at the start of August with Sturge, Henry Richard, the editor of the *Herald of Peace*, and Bright. Bright, enduring his own frustrations with the editorial policy of the *Manchester Examiner and Times*, was enthusiastic.[10] George Wilson and Henry Rawson, already proprietors of the *Manchester Examiner and Times*, agreed to play a key role in managing the new enterprise.[11] The immediate priority was capital. Cobden was only able to afford a nominal amount. Milner Gibson was noncommittal.[12] Bright was willing, and was confident of raising capital among the old League party in Lancashire. But prospects for substantial investment rested on the Sturges and their circle. Converting general support into financial commitment did not prove easy. The economics of the *Daily Telegraph*, whose breakeven point at a penny was reported to be a circulation of 40,000 copies, 'rather chills the ardour of some of our friends', Bright confessed,[13] although a number of League and APRTOK supporters, including E. R. Langworthy and Elkanah Armitage, eventually agreed to invest. Joseph Sturge, who offered £2,000 of his own, which he was prepared to use to finance a shareholding for Wilson, also raised a further £1,450, mostly from his Quaker contacts.[14]

One stumbling block was editorial control. Potential backers sought guarantees, while wanting to remain at arm's length from any direct responsibility for the conduct of the paper. Bright was anxious for some 'security . . . that the paper shall be *permanently honest*', especially in the midst of 'the temptations of the capital', and for measures to ensure 'that it may not be sold, as the Daily News sold us'.[15] There were proposals to invest the contributions from the Peace party in Wilson's name with Cobden and Bright acting as trustees of sorts. Cobden, though happy to see Wilson as one of the paper's 'trustees', was adamant that it needed to be managed and led from London, safe from Manchester interference. Although in December, after several months of canvassing, there was talk of commencing publication with as little as £5,000, eventually it seems that about £9,000 was raised, nominally vested equally in Rawson and Wilson; although for a paper purportedly espousing the views of an important section of Northern businessmen, the financing was arranged in an surprisingly chaotic fashion, and the basis on which money was given, loaned or invested was far from clear even to the principals.[16]

Questions of control were complicated by sensitivities about the paper's overall tenor and specific stance in a number of areas. Cobden and the Manchester Radicals were very keen that the paper should not become a peace paper *tout court*, and for this reason they tended to discount Sturge's suggestions of Henry Richard or E. F. Collins of the *Hull Advertiser* for editor. The question of education presented most difficulties, given the divergent views of the Quakers and the League radicals, but ultimately it seems there was acquiescence in the paper's advocacy of a national education scheme.[17] Discussions over who to appoint as editor rumbled on into February, despite Cobden's determined advocacy of Haly, 'not as a mere desk editor, but as a man having a scheme for establishing a penny paper',[18] but eventually Haly was appointed with Hamilton, formerly of the *Empire*, as sub-editor. The decision was made to simultaneously commence a morning and evening issue in March 1856, on the basis that although a morning journal might have the greater influence, an evening paper would appeal to the working classes and to clerks and others, and could, as Hamilton put it, 'give all the news of the six or seven morning papers, with first class editorial matter, with a digest of the leading articles of the dailies'.[19] Offices were taken just off the Strand, a stone's throw from Somerset House, an irony unlikely to have been lost on any of those involved. The inaugural editorials of 17th March positioned the titles as independent, 'papers for the PEOPLE- not for PARTY', aligned to peace, retrenchment and reform, and against the monopoly of the London press that had kept newspaper prices up since 1836.[20]

Early difficulties

The launch did not go well. Despite the drawn-out planning, practical preparations had been rushed. The paper didn't even have an agreed name until February. Rather belatedly, a press was bought in Paris for £700, along with a reserve machine for £240, and type for under £500, but not enough time was allowed to get all the production arrangements in place.[21] Everything came together in rather a rush. The quality of the early issues was poor. Bright thought 'the sub-editing is bad, the city article is bad, and the *reading* is *bad*', and the editorials 'flunkey-ish'.[22] Sturge was dismayed at the 'grievous want of spirit latent in the leaders', and received numerous complaints about the quality of the leading articles.[23] Bright had not seen any improvement by the end of March 'it can't compare in any one point with the Manchr Examiner', he told Cobden, 'I have only seen two tolerable leaders in it yet . . . The *reading* of the paper is execrable every market paragraph almost is confusion.'[24] Cobden worked hard to rally and reassure. He was soon having second thoughts about Haly, but told Sturge that the *Evening Star* was 'the very best Evening paper I ever saw', and plugged it hard: 'If such a paper can be produced at a profit for 1d, I see no limit to the sale.'[25]

It was, of course, a big 'if', unless substantial sales could be obtained; and distribution posed a challenge. From the outset it seems that the *Star* abandoned the traditional emphasis on subscription sales. Postal distribution was not entirely discounted (Sturge had hopes of promoting the Star in places like Bristol and Bath, where there was not a daily paper), but it was expected that the bulk of sales would initially come in London or via the railway bookstalls.[26] Concerned at Londoners 'instinctive repugnance to such an innovation, & [that] the very cheapness of the article will excite prejudice by being associated with the notion of vulgarity', Cobden had foreseen difficulties arising from the hostility of the existing newsvendors, unenthusiastic about promoting the paper given the limited trade allowance they received.[27] Despite Rawson's optimism that the paper could rely on the demand it would create,[28] it struggled for a foothold at the railway stations, and Sturge noted that 'in large and populous

Figure 7.1 'The newsboy', *Illustrated London News*, 4 January 1862

districts the "Stars" cannot be come by'.[29] Considerable reliance was placed on street sellers (see Figure 7.1). At the launch 'The streets swarm[ed] with lads wearing glittering stars on their breasts or caps, thrusting the paper into every hand I know not with what success.'[30]

Circulation figures disappointed. In mid-March Haly reported that 25,000 had been sold on one day, and more could have been had there been capacity to produce them, and the Rugeley poisoning case temporarily raised sales as high as 50,000 a day; but it seems regular sales were about 17,000 for the two titles combined.[31] Although exact figures were difficult even for Cobden to ascertain, regular sales were still clearly well below what was needed for solvency.[32] Despite reports in May of a daily sale of 27,000,[33] at the end of August 1856 the combined circulation had fallen back to 17,000,[34] and by December to as low as 12,500.[35] Cobden in particular was frustrated. Given the consensus that a circulation of 30,000 would be required to break even,[36] he had wanted advertisers to be guaranteed that figure, even if this involved a large free distribution, in order to get them committed, recognizing that advertising income was always likely to be the key to profitability.[37] Although the early issues had less than three columns of advertisements, within a month they were fully occupying the front page, and advertising income, about £100 a week in early June, had reached £160 a week in August.[38] Cobden remained anxious that the metropolitan circulation on which advertising was most reliant remained inadequate, fearing that the *Star*'s advertisers were inclined to over-estimate its circulation,[39] and by June he was scouting around for 'any *influential* parties to work to procure *advertisements* for the Star'.[40]

The struggling sales made control of costs all the more crucial, but as Hamilton had warned, this proved far from easy. As soon as it could, the *Star* used cheap straw-based paper,[41] and economized on reporting staff, especially parliamentary reporters, but this was not enough. In early April the paper was still losing between £100 and £200 a week.[42] The losses put further strain on the already difficult relationship of Rawson and Haly. Rawson was frightened by the continued growth of expenditure, and had no confidence in Haly's ability to manage production economically.[43] Meanwhile the efficiency of the *Star*'s editorial office was compromised by petty feuds, lack of clarity of roles, and ill-directed attempts at economy. Haly was sacked in early May, but the problems remained.[44] The weakness of the commercial intelligence was a repeated complaint. The parliamentary reporting staff was really too small for the job. Pressure led to silly blunders.[45] In early August there was mortification that an article on 'the Aldershot affray' attracted the ridicule of *Punch*.[46] Cobden and Sturge remained exercised at Rawson's lack of hands on control: '*There is no head.* I defy a concern so full of details, many of them new & requiring to be dealt with at discretion, at a moments notice, to prosper if managed by deputy:- to say nothing of ~~exposing~~ <leaving> a business of pennies & shillings beyond the eye of the owner & master.'[47]

The question of who would replace Haly was left unresolved. Despite his merits, it was not felt that Hamilton offered an alternative. Cobden suggested A. W. Paulton, an experienced journalist who had been writing for the *Star*, hoping that he might invest £1,000, and then in the face of Rawson's opposition, Henry Richard (again suggesting £1,000 be found to give him a stake in the paper).[48] Ultimately the decision was fudged, with Hamilton installed as editor, alongside Richard who would take charge of the leaders.[49] For a while there was some stability, but before long the lack of clarity created fresh dissension.[50] Richard was encouraged to consider himself as joint editor with Hamilton, and Hamilton was soon complaining that although he retained the 'rank, title and dignity of editor', Richard had usurped his position.[51] A reconciliation was effected, but what Richard had described as the 'reign of muddle' continued.[52] Complaints about a leader in February 1857 brought the response from Hamilton that it had been provided by one of the most reliable and fastidious of the paper's writers, and so he 'was less upon my guard'; 'However', he blithely reassured Cobden, 'while we have plenty of letters sent to the office about almost every leader, none have reached us as concerning this one.'[53] Management was lax, and accounting controls were weak.[54] At the end of October Cobden confessed that he did not know if the paper was yet making money, and doubted if Rawson did either.[55]

Rawson's lack of active involvement in day-to-day decisions was really only a side issue to the paper's underlying problem – a chronic shortage of working capital.[56] Hamilton's fear that the initial capital would 'all go like chaff', was all too quickly confirmed.[57] What Bright breezily summed up as 'a question of more capital and good management',[58] actually involved substantial investment to boost the circulation.[59] Within weeks of the papers' launch it was clear that another £5,000 was needed, and over the course of the rest of the decade, the principals had to return, begging bowl in hand, to the Peace Society on several occasions for additional funds.[60] It is impossible from the surviving correspondence to build a precise picture of how this finance was raised, although it is clear that in 1859, for example, further funds were raised; investors were promised no liability, but a reckoning of the value of the paper after three years, and a repayment of their principal in proportion that the value of the capital had increased or decreased.[61] Sturge provided a further injection but was understandably reluctant to meet repeated calls, and it would seem that Bright and Rawson, and other Manchester Radicals, including William Hargreaves and Samuel Morley, also invested.[62]

Although the arrangements of Autumn 1856 created a workable editorial team, problems of leadership, commercial and journalistic, remained. In Spring 1857 Bright contrasted the fortunes of the *Manchester Examiner* which was 'becoming a real property', with the *Star* which 'I think is less carefully managed'; it was '[s]urprising that such a paper at such a price should not sell 50,000 a day – & I think there are men who could do it – but they are not easy to find.'[63] Commenting on the paper's involvement in a potentially financially disastrous libel case in the summer of 1857, Joseph Parkes, to whom Bright had turned for help, fearing some insidious Palmerstonian intrigue at work, commented that '. . . more negligent editorial or Sub-Editorial misjudgement I seldom knew'.[64] By September the paper had been paying its way for several months, with advertising revenue increasing, but even allowing for claims that it had now reached the 30,000 sales figure, it is difficult to see how the paper could really have been generating a stable profit.[65] It was estimated that the expenses of *Star* were approximately £638 per week, which with £25 per day of advertising revenue would put the breakeven point at 26,000; but the indications were that the *Star's* advertising income was routinely only half that, meaning that circulation would need to reach 55,000 or 60,000 before the paper could be commercially successful.[66] Significantly within months Bright was commenting that the paper, 'seem[ed] to stick in the mud . . . more than it ought to'.[67] A weekly edition had been launched in January 1857, quickly absorbing *Bell's News*; but it was not continued beyond the year end.

In fact, the *Star's* immediate concerns were more defensive, as the commercial competition of its penny rivals began to bite. Despite fears that the delays in launching the paper might open the door for other titles, early competition did not really materialize. At the outset, the only opposition at a penny came from the struggling *Daily Telegraph*. The *Telegraph* was enterprising enough to counter the launch of the *Star* by enlarging to 28 columns (with an additional two inches to each column) for three months, thus providing as much as a fourth more reading matter than the *Star*, and enabling it to increase its own sales notwithstanding the new competitor.[68] The *Star's* natural rival for Liberal readers, the *Daily News*, chose to rest at 4d, and also remained inclined to bellicosity in foreign affairs and timidity on domestic issues.[69] The conventional wisdom had been that given the cost of paper under the excise regime, it would be impossible to go beyond four pages for 1d, but in February 1858 the *Standard* did just this, and its offer of 8 pages for 1d very quickly ate into the circulation of the *Star* and the *Telegraph,* forcing the *Telegraph* to expand to a double sheet.[70] Cobden was puzzled how any profit could be made on these terms, but urged a decisive response or 'half the penny papers will kill t'other half in settling down in life'; 'A bold system of advertising a double *Star* would give you the lead again, for the public have not generally committed themselves yet to your rival. But not a moment should be lost in making the change if it be contemplated'.[71] The timing was particularly unfortunate for the *Star* which was in the process of trying to move its operations to Salisbury Square, Fleet Street and install new printing machinery, at a cost of £4,000, a challenge compounded by delays in obtaining the machinery, though in August Bright hoped that the paper would shortly have 'the best premises and machinery in London'.[72] Soon there were indications that the *Star* was being overwhelmed by its rivals; circulation was said to have dropped back to 10,000.[73] Efforts were made to promote the paper outside London, but it remained stymied by the tiny margins it could offer sellers.[74]

For all this there were shreds of encouragement. Although the stock *Star* reader was the 'dissenting shopkeeper' or the artisan radical, within a year or two of launch it had established a sufficient reputation to circulate among public figures.[75] Cobden spoke of a visit to the Bishop of Oxford, his neighbour in Sussex where the *Evening Star* was delivered to the breakfast table, and he, the bishop, Lord Aberdeen, Roundell Palmer and others discussed the progress of the paper.[76] Samuel Warren (lawyer and popular author), and the Conservatives Lord Egmont and Sir John Pakington, were all claimed as readers. At the start of 1858 Cobden was told by Warren that 'all men of the Walpole stamp – men with a conscience – take in the Star – ... I asked Warren what induced such people to take in the Star – He replied it was their faith in its honesty & independence'.[77] Bright was confident in 1859 that 'only the Times has a greater influence of all the London journals'.[78] In Spring 1859 the value of adverts was reported to have doubled in the previous 12 months, and on one particularly good day in April a combined total of 39,000 copies were sold.[79]

By this time there had been yet another editorial reconfiguration. Both Richard and Hamilton had become increasingly prone to ill-health. Hamilton was to continue to deteriorate and die in October 1860. By April 1858 Bright was convinced a new editor would be needed: 'the staff has been too weak for what has been to do lately'.[80] For a while, John Baxter Langley, who had been on the staff since 1855, was apparently acting as, and styling himself, editor, and during this period he seems to have struck a deal with the Chartist Ernest Jones, for the *Star* to absorb Jones's struggling *People's Paper* in return for space for Jones to print Chartist news.[81] Eventually, after an entirely characteristic period of vacillation and delay, the mantle fell on Samuel Lucas, Bright's brother-in-law, and previously chair of the National Public Schools Association, who was taken on as a shareholder and 'active managing partner'.[82] At first Lucas' precise role was ill-defined, but although Richard had understood it to be to manage the commercial side of operations, Lucas was soon assuming full editorial control. In February 1859 he was alienating Holyoake by declining one of his articles on grounds of expense, and by September 1859 was the recipient of Cobden's stream of editorial suggestions.[83] Richard withdrew from any active involvement in the paper, resentful at this displacement, dissatisfied with Lucas' editorial policy, and smarting at the treatment he was receiving.[84]

The *Star* and the *Dial*

You must not blame the Star people for want of liberality. They have a terribly hard task on hand to keep the paper alive', Cobden consoled Richard in August 1860, at which point the *Star* appeared as far away from profit as ever.[85] Circulation continued to struggle. Opponents were suggesting that as much as £300,000 had been sunk into the paper, but once again a new accession of capital was needed.[86] The paper's well-known tribulations compromised not only its own advocacy of the repeal of the paper duties, but also of those associated with it like Bright, whose position was presented as a self-interested attempt to reduce the losses on his investment.[87] For Thomas Wrigley, the papermakers' spokesman, repeal would merely 'gratify the cupidity of a small political party, the leaders of which were interested in a portion of the daily cheap press'.[88] The *Star* drove forward the Constitutional Defence movement in 1860, with Lucas, Alfred H. Dymond (the office manager) and William Hargreaves three of the most active members of the London committee,[89] but gossip among government Whigs, scornful of what they dismissed as the papers' attempts to intimidate them, was that Bright's desperation for the repeal of the paper duties reflected a monthly loss of £500.[90]

Given this, it was hardly surprising that the *Star* proprietors reacted favourably to the suggestion of amalgamation with the *Dial*.[91] The *Dial* was another of the pacifist, liberal responses to the universal hawkishness of the *Times* and London press in 1853–4.[92] A National Newspaper League Company (NNLC) had been established in 1855 to recruit 50,000 shareholders (quickly adjusted to 10,000) and launch a London daily with a broad reformist platform.[93] Despite a four-year campaign of platform proselytization, which reiterated many of the themes animating the taxes on knowledge agitation, the NNLC struggled to raise the necessary funds, and in the face of the growing impatience of its shareholders, in January 1860 it had commenced publishing a 3d weekly, the *Dial*.[94] Amalgamation gave the *Dial* promoters the daily they had promised, and offered the *Star* a welcome accession of capital, while removing the prospect of a rival which might easily have lured away its nonconformist readers.[95] A new company, the London Press Company Ltd was created with eight shareholders, four to represent the 50% shareholding of the *Dial* party and nominally four for the *Star*, (Rawson (749), Wilson (170), William Hargreaves (60), Lucas (200), although in fact Bright owned 420 of Rawson's nominal allocation, and Samuel Morley 100 of those standing in Wilson's name).[96] Lucas was formally appointed editor for seven years, with Rawson in charge of the finances. There was 'no surrender, or change of principle, and no change of *course* in any particular, conceded or demanded' Bright assured Cobden.[97] *The Morning Star and Dial* was first issued on 21 October 1860. The weekly *Dial* was transferred to the new company in April 1862 (at which point the *Dial* was dropped from the title of the daily paper), but was abandoned in June 1864.[98]

The juncture was not a success. The combined *Star and Dial* was not to the liking of many of the NNLC shareholders. There was more coverage of Dissent, sufficient for Matthew Arnold in 1863 to deem the *Star* a 'true reflexion of the rancour of Protestant Dissent in alliance with all the vulgarity, meddlesomeness, and grossness of the British multitude'.[99] One story told of the paper being chosen by Prince Albert as the only daily fit for Royal breakfast table as a result of a decision not to cover a salacious divorce case.[100] But the *Dial*'s supporters had looked for an earnest Christian paper, and found the worldliness and occasional frivolity of the *Star*, its sporting news and theatrical coverage, anathema.[101] The *Dial* directors resented the strenuous resistance to any alteration of the overwhelming 'Manchester School' identity of the paper,[102] but above all, they were indignant at the paper's continued insolvency. Despite widespread recognition in the contemporary press that the *Star* was not a paying concern,[103] the *Dial*'s investment was apparently made 'on the assurance that the paper was more than paying its expenses, [and] that no fresh plant or machinery would be required for many years'.[104] For a while, aided by the removal of the burden of the paper duties, and the addition of the some of the *Dial*'s existing 8,000 subscribers, there was a small profit.[105] But quickly the *Star* fell back into losses of £2,000–£3,000 a year, and it soon became apparent that as much as £5,000 was required for new printing machinery, which would enable it to print 35,000 copies per hour, and 150,000 in time for the normal morning delivery.[106]

There is little evidence that it was able to sell in such numbers. Evidence from the resale values of papers sold by the Alnwick Mechanics' Institute suggests that the *Evening Star* was generally more greatly valued than the *Standard* or the *Daily Telegraph*, but sales stubbornly refused to reflect this, and the although the paper's pro-Northern stance during the American Civil War of the early 1860s attracted radical readers, it was not commercially advantageous.[107] In 1862 the *Star* was accused of currying favour with striking cabmen, in a crude attempt to persuade them to shift their patronage from *Lloyd's Penny Weekly*.[108] Throughout the 1860s Bright reassured his correspondents that the paper was on the verge of prosperity. In 1864 he told

Charles Sturge that 'the circulation does not lessen, but it increases and has improved throughout the year', without offering specifics.[109] But the circulation never achieved the sort of increases needed. Advertising revenue continued lag behind its rivals, and the pressure on costs was fierce.[110] Problems with printing and production continued.[111] In Spring 1864 the enlargement of the *Standard* created concerns that the *Star* would have to follow suit at a further cost of £3,000 a year.[112]

Friction between the original promoters and the *Dial* shareholders sapped the paper's vitality, and after the initial post-amalgamation surge fizzled out, it largely reverted to the pattern of the later 1850s, uneven production values, editorial drift, struggling circulation and stubborn losses, and an increasingly sectional identity.[113] It continued to present itself badly: the paper even thinner and more transparent than the *Standard*, giving 'a dirty & muddled effect owing to the ink on the one side showing itself on the other'.[114] A year later the newsprint was still of insufficient and inconsistent quality and the type in need of replacement; the staff was still too small and the journalists with too much to do.[115] Lucas was intelligent and well-respected, and widely connected within radical circles,[116] but his appointment did not provide the *Star* with the editorial leadership it needed. He was prone to asthmatic episodes, and was often absent from London owing to ill-health. [117] Charles Cooper, who served as sub-editor in the early 1860s, recalled that he generally did not appear in the offices after dinner, and that 'practically the *Morning Star* did not get much editorial supervision in those days'.[118] On Lucas' death in 1865 there were various suggestions for editor. But Bright's preference was Justin McCarthy, who had been in effect standing in for Lucas during his final illness, and ultimately he was appointed (perhaps initially as 'Literary Editor'), with Dymond as business manager'.[119] The transition, which coincided with the sudden death of Cobden, was significant, because, under the leadership of McCarthy, who became a successful politician and literary figure, the *Star*, although no more commercially successful than previously, came as close as it ever did to fashioning a recognizably novel and distinct form of cheap journalism.

The *Morning Star* as a penny paper

For Cobden at least, the *Star* carried with it the reputation of the whole campaign for the repeal of the taxes on knowledge and its claim that the repeal of the stamp duties would enable the creation of a new press.[120] From the outset he harboured expansive ambitions, hoping to see the *Star* as the first of many popular penny papers. By the end of 1856 he was encouraging his correspondents to establish provincial penny papers wherever they saw an opening, following the editorial line of the *Star* and the *Manchester Examiner*.[121] The jewel in the crown would have been a penny paper on Manchester School principles in the West Riding to counter the *Leeds Mercury*,[122] but Cobden envisaged a stable of papers, with the *Star* at its heart, linked by Rawson, who went up in his estimation after his work for Bright and Gibson in 1857, which would 'all play into each others hands, & become a sort of partnership in telegraphic & other news' while taking advantage of their combined purchasing power to beat down paper costs.[123]

The *Morning Star* was the British advance guard of this experiment, but the *New York Times* and *New York Daily Tribune* were its exemplars. Despite the *Daily Telegraph* and later the *Standard*, there was little in the history of the British press to provide a model for the conduct of the new penny press. Cobden had always seen America as pointing the way. The ability of the States to support a number of profitable penny dailies remained the bedrock of his confidence in the eventual success of the *Star*. 'Depend on it', he told Richard in November 1856, 'the penny Press must not only go to New York for its printing machine but also for its model of management' and journalistic style.[124] From New York he learned the need for the paper to avoid long conventional editorials, arguing that the readership of the penny press required brevity; it should like the New York papers 'sparkle with full or short leaders on the living & moving drama of public life', and if long leaders were required they should be mixed in with 'little semi-leaders (shall I call them) on the ~~news~~ <incidents> of the day'.[125]

For all this, it is not clear that the *Star* developed a radically novel journalism. Indeed, Rawson conceded that the paper was 'in effect a copy of the 4d papers'.[126] It probably took the lead in extending to the dailies the particular penchant for melodrama and scandal of the working-class Sunday weeklies, and this became a stand-by of criticism from competitors through the 1860s.[127] Despite the wishes of Sturge and his constituency, the paper did not shy away from coverage of sport and the theatre.[128] Some relatively insignificant concessions were made to the assumed demands of a popular readership for less wordy matter. Literary reviews tended to be brief. Editorials were initially kept to modest size; but this did not last as a perceptible difference with its rivals among the dailies, and by 1861 it had reverted to three long articles.

The papers were not without stylistic dynamism, although it has been suggested that in terms of the spread of American journalism, the *Daily*

Telegraph was the most influential.[129] Even by Cobden's exacting standards there was plenty of good writing,[130] and the *Saturday Review* grudgingly 'acknowledged' that the *Star* 'not unfrequently display[ed] whatever originality is involved in the advocacy of independent crotchets', in exonerating the paper from its general attack on the mediocrity of the penny press in 1859.[131] From 1861 the *Star* published Edmund Yates's 'The Flaneur' column, which had previously appeared in the *Illustrated London News,* which was in effect the pioneering gossip column.[132] In the *Evening Star,* the 'Readings by Starlight' column offered a platform for promising writers, including Archibald Forbes the war correspondent, James Greenwood, and the novelists George Manville Fenn, and Richard Whiteing, who provided pungent cockney commentary in the manner of a costermonger.[133] As editor, McCarthy in particular gathered an impressive roster of contributors, including John Gorrie, a protégé of Duncan McLaren,[134] the novelists William Black[135] and William Hale White, who was parliamentary reporter 1865–6, contributing a column 'Below the Gangway', E. D. J. Wilson who became leader writer for *The Times,* and T. Wemyss Reid, who went on to be one of the most prominent journalists of the late-Victorian period.[136] The *Star* offices and McCarthy's hospitable salon at his home in Kennington Park were a clearing house for progressive views.[137] This was a new journalistic clerisy: when presented to McCarthy, Whiteing confessed 'I felt like the initiate of a priesthood'.[138]

But if there was a *Morning Star* style at all, it was constituted by its outspoken editorial language. Few punches were pulled. The *Star* achieved a reputation for the vigour and force of what McCarthy described as its 'combative pens'.[139] For some this was just 'blaggardism and ultra nonsense'.[140] Delane of the Times despised the *Star's* penchant for what he described as 'attacks on individuals of a calumnious kind'.[141] Even its supporters worried that at times what Sturge described as 'too much of an appearance of personal animus',[142] and Bright a 'tone of complaint and asperity', had 'interfered with its circulation without doing any good to the good cause'.[143] The results of the 1857 election were particularly chastening. '[M]uch as I like to see the humbug [Palmerston] exposed day after day in the Star, it may probably', Cobden conceded, 'do more harm to the Star than to him'.[144] The paper's endorsement could be equally problematic. In 1862 the *Saturday Review* observed that 'Nothing has been so seriously detrimental to Mr Gladstone as the constant panegyrics of the *Star*.'[145]

In effect, the *Star* was distinguished more by its politics than its prose. Bright had envisaged the paper as advocating essentially 'the views which Cobden and I have advocated in and out of Parliament'.[146] Cobden kept up a constant flow of correction and contribution to the editorial staff from Haly through to Lucas and William Hargreaves, along with a stream of his own comments to be inserted anonymously, and clippings from other papers which he felt should be extracted in the *Star*.[147] Sturge and the peace party bridled on occasions, especially over Education, but saw their responsibility as just to persuade, remonstrate and if necessary indicate dissent.[148] Cobden consistently stressed the need for the paper to 'make itself the organ of moral reformers of every rational kind' by, for example, attacking the betting system and those involved in gambling.[149] At the same time, he worked hard to ensure that the *Star* did not 'cease to be a newspaper in the widest sense, & become merely an organ of the peace party to be supported by those who already share [its] opinions'.[150] Instead the *Star* became known as 'Cobden's paper', and after 1857 as Cobden became a more marginal figure in British political life, as the official mouthpiece of the 'Manchester School',[151] and eventually as Bright's 'kept newspaper' as the *Scotsman* put it.[152]

Bright was inclined to protest. 'I do not inspire the *Star*. Its principles and politics were determined on when it started, and it does not require fresh inspiration from day to day', he told Edward Ellice in December 1859.[153] To no avail. At the start of 1861 a [sharp] spoof extract from 'an unpublished volume of Lord Macaulay's History of England', 'The Protectorate of John Bright', was widely circulated, in which the election of Bright as Protector of England was followed by the flight of the Queen to Australia, the assumption by Bright of the title of 'John the First', and his taking possession of the royal palaces, upon which he 'appropriated that part of the Westminster edifice in which the Peers formerly met as offices for the *Morning Star and Dial* newspaper'.[154] But it is likely that despite a widespread belief that he frequently wrote editorials, he did so rarely, accepting that he was an amateur, and 'amateur writing does not answer for a newspaper'.[155] Certainly Bright generally found the paper's editorial line congenial; his correspondence was littered (if less systematically than Cobden's) with commendations and recommendations for material in the paper. He was close to Lucas and his successor McCarthy, who recalled that he dropped in regularly, almost nightly during the struggles over the Reform Bill in 1866.[156] He saw the paper as a necessary corrective to the general press line on all manner of issues, and was capable of suspecting clandestine attempts to undermine the paper from the establishment.[157]

From the outset the *Star*, despite its finances, built up a strong cadre of leader writers and contributors from metropolitan radical circles, including

Holyoake, F. W. Chesson, who had worked with Hamilton on the *Empire*, and was taken on after its final collapse in the summer of 1856,[158] L. A. Chamerovzow of the Anti-Slavery Association, and later Washington Wilks, whose outspoken anti-Palmerstonianism encouraged Cobden to lure him back to London from Carlisle.[159] These were supplemented by writers recruited to meet specific needs, including Henry Mead (author of *the Sepoy Revolt* (1856)) who provided the *Star*'s editorial comment during the Indian Revolt, and Julius Faucher, a German free-trader who contributed articles on continental affairs;[160] along with contributors such as J. E. T. Thorold Rogers, the radical Oxford don who during the early 1860s was encouraged to contribute letters on rural reform.[161] Some, like Henry Merritt, who wrote on art, were shared with the *Manchester Examiner and Times*. In the 1860s especially, its offices were a refuge for the denizens of what McCarthy called the 'Exile-world of London'.[162] The *Dial* connection brought Edmond Beales onto the Board, and during the reform crisis of 1866–7 the *Star* was the mouthpiece of Beales and the Reform League.[163] With this perhaps came a narrowing of the openness of the paper's columns to radical opinion. By 1865 G. J. Holyoake was conscious that his idiosyncratic liberalism might not have ready appeal to Lucas, although 'More than any other journal the *Morning Star* has always reflected the multitudinous opinions of the public.'[164] Lucas, unconvinced, declined the contribution.[165] Nor was the paper close to Gladstone, who unlike his careful cultivation of Thornton Hunt, seems to have limited his connection to the *Star* to occasional corrections of its pronouncements on him.[166] But despite the inevitable vagaries of its editorial line ('I fear that our friends of the Peace party will be horrified – some days – with the *Star*', Hargreaves noted in 1861),[167] the *Star* did largely fulfil its editorial purpose as the mouthpiece of Manchester School radicalism, with close links to Kossuth, Louis Blanc and other European exiles.[168]

In the period between its establishment and the repeal of the paper duties, the *Star* offered consistent support to taxes on knowledge campaigners. During the American Civil War the *Star* gained credibility and readers on the radical left in recognition of its vigorous support of the North, for which it earned from *Punch* the nickname 'the Yankee Journal', and along with the *Daily News* and the *Spectator,* served as a vital counterweight to the anti-Northern stance of *the Times*.[169] Bright drew on his personal knowledge to make significant contributions,[170] seeking to use his contacts with Charles Sumner to try to obtain copies of diplomatic communications between the British and American governments in advance of the other papers.[171]

Copies of the *Star* were passed to Lincoln as representative of pro-Northern sentiment.[172] Its advocacy of the North enabled the *Star* to become the staple reading of radical students like the young T. H. Green.[173] Even then, despite being recognized for its independent foreign coverage, the *Star* was unable to dent the perception abroad that the *Times* remained 'the sole representative of the English press'.[174]

It acquired the status of keen exposer of political abuse, but the accusation of being 'anti-British' could never be entirely shrugged off.[175] It took a leading role in promoting/publicizing the work of the Jamaica Committee in 1866, and its position as 'the unblushing apologist of the Jamaican humanitarians' was identified (along with doctrinaire free trade and peace at any price) as one of the three great questions on which it mistook the opinions of the public.[176] Its sympathetic coverage of Irish topics, even during the Fenian outrages of 1867, and its tendency to a strain of anti-royalism (about which even Cobden was doubtful (he described the *Star*'s campaign against the proposal to make Albert 'King Consort' in 1858 as 'rather of the *Advertiser* school, & savors too much of Cockney clap-trap for my taste'),[177] made it an easy target for critics, as when it appeared after the death of Prince Albert without the traditional black borders. At times, the paper seemed very deliberately to court controversy, with more than one eye on commercial imperatives, as in the furore created in 1864 over an 'interview' procured with Muller, a convict accused of murder, by a *Star* correspondent who tricked his way into the prison where Muller was being held, which inevitably attracted strong condemnation at the potential subversion of the course of justice, all in the interests of titillating readers, for whom the newshops, placarded in large letters, announced the scoop.[178] Likewise in 1865 it was roundly condemned for publishing a fictitious list of holders of Confederate bonds, along with two fiercely condemnatory editorials; not least because it must have known that the list was a hoax.[179]

The end

By 1867 there were already signs that the *Star* might not have a long future. Between 1860 and 1867 the NNLC was able to declare dividends varying from £1 5s to £6 5s per cent; in 1864 revenue of £1,050 was attributed to the *Morning Star.* In 1865 Bright reported that the paper was 'now paying a fair dividend, and its future is promising',[180] though this had not prevented backers like Charles Sturge having to press for the repayment of loans in 1864.[181] The disruption caused by the deaths of Lucas and Cobden, and also the ill-health of Hargreaves, who had become Bright's most active confidant in the first half of the 1860s, had prompted discussions of a further revision of the paper's ownership. Bright initially suggested raising a further £15,000 among friends such as Frederick Pennington with which to buy out the *Dial* shareholding: 'the Paper would then be in hands competent to manage it, and not afraid of any expenditure upon it.'[182] He talked of the potential of a 20–25% dividend, but apparently could not convince the proposed investors.[183]

Once again, under the business management of Dymond, described by Cooper as capable but 'utterly discouraged by his difficulties with the directors', the *Star* lacked leadership.[184] Although McCarthy was close to Bright, there were suggestions that he was never entirely happy on account of the constraints on his editorial freedom.[185] By 1867 whatever surpluses there had been to fund dividends for the NNLC had dried up and its shares (£1 paid up) were being offered for as little as 3/- each.[186] There was talk of amalgamation with the *Daily News*.[187] Rawson had long-harboured ideas of uniting the two papers, maintaining the *Star* as a penny paper, and the *Daily News* at 2d, while economizing on editorial expenses.[188] But nothing was finalized. Around this time the NNLC made an attempt to buy up the other 50% shareholding in the *Star* and Rawson and the other proprietors offered to sell their half for £9,000 or to pay £8,000 for the *Dial's* half.[189] In the spring of 1868 the *Star* proprietors apparently came to an agreement to sell their share to the NNLC, but it became clear by April that the NNLC directors were not able to raise the capital needed to complete the purchase, or had had second thoughts about the valuation.[190] By this time Bright's commitment to the paper, which had been waning since at least 1865, had all but vanished: 'I wish I were well out of it. The trouble it has given me has been great and constant', he told Hargreaves. Ultimately, the *Dial* sold its shareholding with a loss of £9,500, bitter at the 'clandestine doings' of the Manchester School proprietors.[191] A stray reference in Hodder's *Life of Samuel Morley* talks of a meeting on the 20th July 1868 to discuss the affairs of the *Star* and the *Daily News*, at which it was arranged that in September the proprietors of the *Daily News* would take over the *Star*, but the take-over does not seem to have happened.[192]

However, the writing was on the wall. The success of the *Pall Mall Gazette*, established in 1865, and of the *Echo* was cutting heavily into the circulation of the *Evening Star*. The decision of the *Daily News* in June 1868 finally to abandon its efforts to maintain a higher price and reduce to a penny, was a heavy blow, compounded by the *News'* launching at the same time of a penny evening paper, the *Express*, which although only half the size of the evening editions of the *Standard* and the *Star*, further cut into the *Star*'s market.[193] 'In the presence of such a rival', wrote one observer, 'it will be hard for the *Morning Star* to stand, and few will regret [it] absorbed by a prudent, decent and powerful liberal journal.'[194] In 1868 Bright, faced with the prospect of a place in the cabinet in Gladstone's government, sold his shareholding to Rawson on the pretext that it would be incompatible with holding Cabinet office, no doubt relieved to be free of his financial responsibilities.[195] 'If I were as rich as some of my friends', he later told Thorold Rogers, 'I would not have suffered the *Star* to fail – or to want a successor – but I cannot afford to join in newspaper experiments. I have been in two of them & have burned my fingers'.[196]

Bright's withdrawal stimulated dissatisfaction in the other proprietors more concerned with the paper's lack of commercial success, and a further withdrawal of support from Milner Gibson and other Liberal party chiefs.[197] It also prompted McCarthy to give up the editorship and sail for America. John Morley was appointed to replace him, amidst talk of the *Star*'s absorption by another title; by this point the circulation may have fallen as low as 5,000.[198] Although the *Star* improved its writing and apparently its circulation under Morley's editorship,[199] the proprietors were unwilling to fund further losses, and Morley was unhappy.[200] F. W. Chesson, editor of the *Evening Star*, reported that Rawson would have kept going longer, but was unable to raise any further capital in the depressed state of the Lancashire economy; instead he took £3,000 in cash and an interest of £2,000 and a place on the *Daily News* board.[201] Key editorial staff leached away: Edward Russell was appointed editor of the *Liverpool Daily Post* at the start of October 1869. The final issue of the paper appeared on 13 October 1869. Its valedictory statement claimed that its two aims had been 'the advocacy and propagation of political principles which were then counted extreme in their Liberalism' and 'to establish the feasibility of providing journalism of the best sort under what were then the untried conditions of a penny newspaper'. The second, it claimed, had been demonstrated by spread of penny papers 'in London and the provinces',[202] and the first was now best served by amalgamation with the *Daily News*. In all, the attempt was said to have cost £80,000.[203]

There was talk of a monthly paper to be published from the *Star* office, and the plant and machinery were apparently kept intact for several years, with a view to a fresh publication, but nothing eventually emerged.[204] All that was left was the muted farewells of the *Star*'s rivals, which made little fanfare and spoke – implicitly – mostly of irrelevance. All the *Daily Telegraph* could bestir itself to note was that the *Star's* valedictory reference to establishing the penny press was somewhat misleading given its own anticipation by six months (17 September 1855) of the penny price.[205]

By 1869 the *Star* offered little that was distinctive. Its pages were filled with the normal small change of the Victorian press, speeches, lectures, along with a diet of middle-class frauds and swindles, murders (and even supposed murders), fires and railway accidents. Foreign coverage was shrinking. There were a few desultory letters, but nothing which suggested a vibrant dialogue with its readers. The coverage of its traditional radical constituency remained: the ballot, trade unions, land reform debates; it was still flogging the military punishment question, but there were no great editorial agendas. Provincial prints like the *Exeter and Plymouth Gazette* at least gave it the respect of drawing the moral that its collapse demonstrated both the failure of Bright's political principles and the inability of sustaining indefinitely a newspaper on anything other than commercial principles.[206] Only its former staff were more generous. At least, thought Whiteing, 'it had done its work in helping to save England from the blunder of an alliance with the slave power'.[207]

Regulations and Securities: A Free Press?

With the repeal of the paper duties in the 1861 budget all three of the 'taxes on knowledge' against which the campaigns of the 1850s had been directed, had been swept away. The final acts appeared to be played out between the summer of 1861 and 1863 in a series of public testimonials to the leaders of the campaign. By the end of June the NPPARPD was wound up, with tributes to Milner Gibson and Gladstone.[1] A separate subscription later produced a substantial testimonial to John Francis for his work as secretary of the NPPARPD.[2] Milner Gibson was presented with a handsome table centrepiece, and two seven-light candelabra, at a public breakfast at Freemason's Hall, in February 1862.[3] Somewhat belatedly, Milner Gibson, with assistance from Cobden, Holyoake and Thornton Hunt, organized a testimonial for Collet, which in part took the form of making good the outstanding amounts notionally due to him as Secretary.[4] Novello set aside his own claim to £100 owing as treasurer. They had to work hard to drum up support from a public which Cobden accepted had already forgotten the subject.[5] Eventually, at the end of 1864, and in no small part through the instrumentality of Richard Moore, a subscription was handed without fanfare to Collet.[6]

Yet the business of the campaigners was not entirely concluded. Collet made it clear to the readers of the *Morning Star* in July 1861 – at which point he was serving as a witness to a Select Committee on the Export Duty on Rags which was investigating the papermakers' ongoing complaints about continental restrictions on the trade in rags – that although the NPPARPD had been wound up, APRTOK remained in existence.[7] The Association's programme, Collet reminded his readers, had always included the removal of the press registration and security system and this still remained to be achieved.[8] Not until 1869, by which time stalwarts like A. S. Ayrton and Milner

Gibson had once more been pressed into combat with the Inland Revenue, was this remaining objective realized.

This final act was not a glamorous one. In his *History* Collet conceded that the opponents of the taxes on knowledge had not succeeded in arousing any popular hatred against the registration system, 'No proprietor of an important and well-paying newspaper objected on his own account to give security for it, and only in a few small districts would the people be deprived of cheap newspapers by the Security System',[9] and although the eventual removal of the system received some notice in the emerging newspaper trade press, it made little impression in the mainstream press. Yet this coda forms an integral part of the story of campaign against press restrictions in the 1850s and 1860s.

The strengthening of the security and registration regulations had been fundamental to the 1836 settlement, which had 'defined newspapers broadly enough as to include most tracts published periodically, and increased the penalty for mere possession of an unstamped newspaper' and also 'sanctioned the search of private houses and the seizure of materials connected with the publication of illegal papers'.[10] Working-class radicalism had been outraged at the 'Gagging' clauses.[11] The legislation applied only to papers under a certain size (714 square inches) and more significantly, sold for less than 6d per copy; so that more expensive middle-class papers were excluded, but cheaper working-class papers brought within its scope.[12] Moreover, prosecutions could only be initiated by the Attorney General or a Stamp Office official, so that decisions to prosecute often took on a political hue.[13]

Anti-regulation

Hostility to the security system was part of the broad anti-knowledge taxes movement from the outset.[14] But it was marginalized rather in the early years of the campaign, especially once the NSAC had mutated into APRTOK. Explicit mention had to be imposed from the floor at the 1852 annual meeting, although the intervention prompted Milner Gibson's generous acknowledgement that it had always been a part of the association's agenda.[15] As the repeal of the taxes became a realistic prospect, the continuance of the requirement became more obnoxious.[16] The radical platform continued to present controls on the press as part of the repressive state.[17] The registration and sureties question was given prominent billing in the lectures of provincial activists like John Watts in the later 1850s.[18] Reformers were convinced, as Bright put it in 1854, that 'The

stamp was retained with tenacity, not for purposes of revenue, but from a fear
... that cheap publications, containing political news, might be dangerous, and
have a tendency to spread immorality and evil amongst the people', an opinion
encouraged by the suggestion of counsel for the Crown during the Shaw trial
'that the prosecution was taken not so much for the revenue, but on account of
the licentious character of the press'.[19]

The registration clauses conflicted with notions of a free press firmly
entrenched in liberal thought, as a medium of rational debate that lay at the
heart of the efficient functioning of the 'public sphere'.[20] 'The English press is
not free', trumpeted the *Leader* in January 1851, 'it never has been free, and
never will be free if those who wear the chain hug it as an ornament, and boast
of their liberty. The English press is subject to a censorship less visible but not
less efficient than any that exists on the Continent . . . it performs the work
of hindrance warily, unobtrusively and thoroughly'.[21] Opponents attacked the
system as fundamentally opposed to the principles of British justice; binding
them over to keep the law without any indication that they were likely to
break it.[22] For republicans and secularists like Holyoake, legal restrictions on
publication were part of a wider pattern of government censorship which reared
its head again in March 1858, when the prosecution of Edward Truelove for
publishing W. E. Adams's *Tyrannicide: Is It Justifiable?* prompted the formation
of a Press Prosecution Defence Committee (with James Watson as Treasurer
and Charles Bradlaugh, who was emerging as Holyoake's successor as leader
of British secularism, as Secretary).[23] For supporters, the registration legislation
offered a security against irresponsible press attacks, and ensured the general
standing of newspaper editors and proprietors, and provided some defence
against that 'class of literature' which 'render[ed] the masses discontented,
infidel and democratic'.[24] Not so, argued Milner Gibson in his May 1854 speech:
'The inevitable consequence of such a system was, that the cheap literature of
the country, instead of being under the control of men of capital, who were also
men of respectable station and pure moral character, who could direct it for
purposes of public utility, fell into the hands of disreputable persons, whose
productions weakened and demoralized, instead of purifying and enriching the
public mind'.[25]

Prior to 1855 the much greater burden of the stamp and the advertising
duties diverted attention from the requirements for registration and sureties,
a general inattention compounded by the almost entirely haphazard way in
which in the legislation was enforced. It is clear from Parliamentary Returns
that where proprietors had approached the Inland Revenue, its officers had

been attempting to enforce the security regulations.[26] But even at the height of the Chartist threat in the early 1840s, evidence to the 1843 Lords Select Committee suggested that the Stamp Office regime allowed 'men of straw' who were incapable of meeting the costs of libel to be registered as proprietors of papers.[27] Little had changed by the early 1850s. As Sir Richard Bethell, the Solicitor General, indicated in 1854, the desire of successive governments to administer the newspaper laws according to their spirit rather than their letter, from 'the desire not to injure useful and lawful undertakings', inevitably meant that the law was enforced unequally.[28] In any case, Inland Revenue officials had no reliable method of differentiating between registered and unregistered papers.[29] At Wigan, Thomas Wall, the stamp distributor and postmaster, even published his own paper, the *Wigan Observer*, without going through the proper forms of registration.[30]

Most pre-1855 proprietors, of stamped papers at least, were reasonably well-established men of business. Even for them, the system was not without its inconveniences. In its entirety, the registration procedure required as many as 18 different parties, whose attendance often had to be co-ordinated at a single point.[31] Any minor changes of title, or of publishing arrangements, or of proprietorship, technically required a fresh registration and a renewal of all securities, which required the guarantors to present themselves in person to make the necessary declarations at the place at which the newspaper was printed. Although the requisite forms should have been available at local offices of distributors and sub-distributors of stamps, this was not always the case. In those districts without a resident magistrate it could be particularly inconvenient to have to get all guarantors and the magistrate together.[32] And where guarantors gave notice to the Inland Revenue of their withdrawal of guarantee, the Revenue solicitor could chase proprietors for substitutes.[33]

Nor was it always easy for proprietors of small local papers to get people to stand surety to the amount required.[34] In one instance, it took the editor of the *Colne and Nelson Guardian* over four months and numerous applications to potential guarantors before he was able to secure the necessary sureties: 'When I tell the parties that the amount insured for is £300 they look upon it as they will have the money to pay', he noted.[35] In the early 1860s, the publisher of the *Dundalk Express* claimed that in restarting his paper after a period in abeyance as a result of Inland Revenue prosecution, the only way he could obtain the sureties he required was by paying 20% of the money value and promising 20% of his profits.[36]

Even under the stamp duty regime the registration requirements seem only to have been applied to stamped papers; and indeed one of the anxieties expressed in the run-up to repeal in 1855 was that papers which chose to issue an entirely unstamped edition would be able to circumvent the security requirements, which 'were indeed to open the floodgates and offer a premium to a low class of newspapers, . . . which in adverse seasons, commercial depression, and industrial hardship might inflame the multitude, upset constituted authority, and reduce the country to a state of anarchy'.[37] Large sections of the existing press, and not merely those who sought to oppose the repeal of other elements of the taxes on knowledge, rallied round the registration and security regulations.[38]

One of the problems with the system was the scope it allowed for local discretion, which opened up officials to accusations of impartiality and malice. One such instance was furnished by the case of the *Glasgow Free Press*. This was a paper which although apparently operating unregistered since its establishment in 1852, had for some reason in April 1864 come to the attention of Mr Fletcher, the official with oversight of the registration of Scottish papers, who proceeded to vigorously pursue the editor, A. H. Keane, even after – having failed to secure the transfer of ownership so that he could undertake the registration as proprietor – Keane ceased publication of the original title, and relaunched the paper, properly registered, under his own ownership. Keane was fined £50, but had to suffer 'the continued and oppressive prosecutions of a Government Official, who does not scruple to use the influence of his position . . . for the sole purpose of crushing a political antagonist'. Even though a penalty was not exacted, Keane complained that Fletcher continued from February 1864 to April 1865 'to subject me to endless trouble and annoyance of the most aggravating nature', the latest of which was, having changed the place of printing, to be asked for a fresh referee for one of his sureties. All this, Keane complained, while Fletcher 'allowed other papers to go unregistered for years'.[39]

Gladstone's 1855 Newspaper Bill catapulted the registration and security clauses back into the spotlight by not merely proposing the repeal of the newspaper stamp, but also all the provisions which had been created to protect it. Cobden and Bright had given the matter little attention, although some of their correspondents urged them in 1855 to ensure the proposal to remove the requirements – 'the great hindrance to the increase of papers', as John Walter of Newmarket described them – was not quietly abandoned.[40] APRTOK memorialized the Attorney-General in January 1855, pointing out that the laws were unnecessary, unenforceable, and judging by the evidence Timm had given to the Select Committee on Newspaper Stamps in 1851, misunderstood by the very body charged with implementing them.[41]

True to form, a section of the press again leaped to the defence of the system. The *Freeman's Journal* argued that it provided 'an obstacle to the scurrilous writers who abound in every society, and against whose abuse of the freedom of the press the law of libel is directed', and went as far as to suggest that the removal of the security system was the real substance of Gladstone's measures, the repeal of the stamp being merely a smokescreen, part of a general Whig desire 'to have a fag press take the place of independent journalism'.[42] An anti-repeal circular of March 1855, focused largely on the dangers of infidel and democratic publications, arguing that the abolition of the security measures 'would take away all security for the conducting of the newspaper press by persons of known responsibility, and would give practical impunity for abuses of the liberty of the press, dangerous to the peace of society, to private character, and to the press itself'.[43] Even the *Daily News* regarded registration as a surety for the character and respectability of the press, suggesting that it could be made voluntary by allowing postal privileges only to those papers which registered.[44] Then, just at the decisive moment, the Aberdeen government fell, and Gladstone was replaced as Chancellor by Cornewell Lewis, who as we have seen persevered with removal of the stamp duty, but abandoned without fanfare Gladstone's measures to repeal the security provisions.[45]

The legislative volte face, and the Inland Revenue's pre-1855 practice of concentrating on stamped publications, meant that considerable uncertainty prevailed as to the nature of the regulations which pertained after 1855. The APRTOK *Gazette* suggested that without even the revenue motive, it was inconceivable that the Inland Revenue would attempt to enforce the statutes, which had become 'trash'.[46] A number of proprietors were advised that registration was no longer required.[47] Probably most of the new papers which sprang up in the wake of repeal were not registered, and no effort was initially made to enforce the statutes, even where unregistered papers were stamped and copies lodged with local stamp offices. In September 1856 it was conceded that 'some legal doubts have arisen on the subject, and that the question has been referred to the law officers of the Crown, and that in the meantime stamps have been supplied to certain newspaper proprietors pending the determination of the point'.[48]

However, in April 1857, a timing which seemed to coincide suspiciously with the defeat of the APRTOK leadership in the general election of Spring 1857, the Inland Revenue suddenly sprang into action: a circular was issued, reminding unstamped newspapers that the registration provisions of 60 Geo III cap.9 section 8, and 7 William IV cap.76, remained in force and would henceforth be enforced.[49] In fact, the explanation for the timing was probably less sinister. Action appears to have been prompted by an intervention by Humphrey Brown, MP for Tewkesbury, complaining that two unregistered papers, the *Joint Stock Companies Journal* and the *Tewkesbury Weekly Record*, were 'pandering to vicious passions, under an idea of their non-responsibility'.[50] Elements of the established press rather belatedly awoke to the scandal that for two years 'None of the proprietors of the "cheap" press, have complied with the law . . . and under the auspices of the "Society for the Repeal of the Taxes on Knowledge" they bid defiance to the requisition in the act'.[51]

The treatment of the *Leamington Mercury*, which was given a month's grace to sort out its defective registration, shows that the regulations were not applied in an entirely high-handed way.[52] But the new press muttered darkly about the belated decision of government 'that papers are not to be allowed to spring up from the labouring classes, lest they should breathe unwholesome truths which would prove unpalatable to the aristocracy or lords of the land', and to 'harass or crush the cheap press'.[53] Why', asked the *Luton Times*, 'is this absurd system perpetuated? It is an unnecessary harassment of newspaper proprietors, who . . . have no more right to be called on to enter into such a bond, than lecturers or authors'.[54] Suggestions of double-standard were encouraged by the continued reluctance of the Board, doubtful of the response of a jury, to prosecute the *Free Press*, which under Collet's editorship continued to offer provocative defiance.[55]

While the NPPARPD increasingly drove the public campaign against the Paper Duties, the APRTOK committee turned its attention to the campaign against the security regulations, arguing that there was even less call for them now that they no longer protected the revenue. There was little support or enthusiasm from Cobden, Bright or Milner Gibson, and the mantle of parliamentary spokesman for the Association fell on the somewhat unlikely head of A. S. Ayrton. To little sympathy from the leading metropolitan dailies, Ayrton took up the case of *Joint Stock Companies Journal* and the *Tewkesbury Weekly Record*.[56]

In the meantime, Collet circulated publishers of newspapers to see if they had been contacted by the Inland Revenue to instruct them to register their papers and give security against libel, assuring them that APRTOK 'mean to resist this innovation'.[57] A handful sought to co-operate, and the Association raised the question once again of the definition of a newspaper. Copies of the *Free Press* were sent to proprietors being pursued for securities suggesting they ask the Revenue why it had not proceeded against it, just one of a 'host of others' who are allowed to publish without giving security. 'Either the law is good for all, & should be enforced against all, or it should not be enforced at all – There is no middle course', Timm was told.[58] Collet was able to induce James Dare, proprietor of the *Westonian* (Weston-super-Mare) to repeatedly challenge Timm to explain why the *Press* was allowed to remain unregistered and unmolested, while his own paper was pursued.[59] The Association also took up the case of Joseph Heap of the *Bury Times* (the only prosecution brought in this period) highlighting the iniquities of a regulation which was enforced arbitrarily against some publishers but not others. In July 1857, the *Gazette* seized gleefully on Sir Stafford Northcote's parliamentary response that the *Free Press* 'was not considered a newspaper, and therefore no proceedings would be taken against it', as demonstrating that the Chancellor 'substitutes his own caprice for the statute'.[60] Although the *Bury Times* was convicted, the Association professed optimism that the exposure the case had given to the 'preposterous nature of the proceeding' should have 'discouraged the Board of Inland Revenue from enlarging the sphere of their operation'.[61]

The new regime also opened up the Revenue to further accusations of arbitrariness in that 60 Geo III c.9 s.13 covered publishers of pamphlets, although the practice before 1855 had been to enforce it only on stamped publications (i.e. newspapers). Holyoake worried the Revenue with enquiries about whether they intended to extend their new vigour to pamphlets,[62] and an APRTOK address to Derby in April 1858 dwelt on the decision not to enforce the provisions of III Geo 60 on pamphlets, a discrimination 'unfounded in reason as it is in law', and one which in effect left the officers of the Inland Revenue having 'taken upon themselves to dispense with such parts of the [Act] as they did not chose to carry into effect', threatening a renewal of the 'what is a newspaper' question which had so distracted Revenue and governments in the early 1850s.[63] Nor did the irony escape Collet and Moore in December 1859, when an attempt by the Governor of Sierra Leone to supress a hostile newspaper by enforcing harsh security laws was annulled by the British government. 'We are at a loss', they told Sir Hugh Cairns, the Solicitor General, in an open letter, 'why a regulation should be continued in England which is too oppressive for an African colony to endure'.[64]

At the end of March 1859 Moore and Collet obtained an interview with Timm who, at least in their account, was unwilling to offer any real defence of a system which he conceded was not generally enforced, not least because there was no machinery for enforcement, and no obvious purpose.[65] This intervention and a subsequent memorial to Sotheron Estcourt, the Home Secretary in the Derby administration, may have helped convince the government that there was nothing to be gained from opposing Ayrton's bill to repeal the registration system, and they could rely on the regulation as it applied to books and pamphlets, that they should have the name of the printer attached.[66] Cairns's acceptance in Parliament in February 1859 that 'most people would agree as to the utter absence of any necessity for continuing' the sureties,[67] ushered in a frustrating and ultimately fruitless parliamentary campaign pursued by Ayrton and APRTOK over the next three years. In 1859 Ayrton got a bill through the House of Commons for the complete repeal of the securities system, only for it to be blocked belatedly on the basis that the government was reluctant to repeal both securities provision and registration. The offer of consultation and a government sponsored bill in 1860 was rejected by Milner Gibson as unjustifiable temporizing given that Gladstone in 1855 had proposed pretty much what Ayrton was proposing and obtained the broad support of the ministry of the day.[68] In 1860 Ayrton's revised bill, retaining registration, but abolishing securities, passed swiftly through the Commons, encouraging the *Morning Star* to rejoice 'Thus the worthless security system, which clogs a free press, is at an end, for we scarcely suppose the House of Lords will reject the measure.'[69] In fact, not least because of the resolute hostility of Lord Redesdale and Lord Chelmsford (who as Frederic Thesiger had crossed swords with APRTOK in the early 1850s), the Lords did effectively block the legislation for the next three years.[70] In the face of this resistance, the inevitable sense of its relative insignificance in comparison with the triumph of the paper duty struggle, and lack of any sustained attempt at enforcement on behalf of the Revenue, the activity of the remaining APRTOK activists became progressively more half-hearted. A petition was circulated, but did not get as far as being presented to the Commons, and a memorial to Gladstone as Chancellor was prepared, pointing out the anomalies of the system.[71] Thereafter, APRTOK ceased even intermittent operation until called once more to arms in the late 1860s.[72]

The abandonment of Ayrton's efforts left the press subject to a set of regulations that were partially enforced and widely dismissed as outmoded and unnecessary. Historians of the press have given the subject little attention, beyond the suggestion that 'very few cases seem to have been brought under the legislation and the outcry over the prosecution of the *Camden and Kentish Town Gazette* in the late 1860s suggests that it was rarely used'.[73] Certainly many unstamped titles were allowed to proceed unmolested. It was, for example, suggested by the *Newspaper Press* in July 1868 that any attempt at general enforcement would have meant the 'virtual suppression of the local journals throughout the metropolis, which answer a harmless and useful purpose'.[74] The obligations were not generally known, and compliance was often made on the understanding that the process was entirely formal,[75] although this did not mean its requirements were thereby rendered trivial. In submitting to the demands of the Inland Revenue for registration, W. A. Vincent of the *Walsall Guardian* couldn't help adding in a postscript that 'I consider the forms altogether "frivolous and vexatious," and of no earthly use. . . . The Government might as well require every person on attaining manhood to find sureties, or as if in a civilised country like this it is not enough for a man to be responsible for his own acts'.[76] Comparison of the printed Return of registered newspapers in 1865 with *Mitchell's Press Directory* suggested that there were 361 unregistered papers across the country, something more than a quarter of the total.[77]

Prosecution was infrequent. The view within the Revenue at least in 1866 was that local revenue officials did not have the means of determining whether a publication was legally a newspaper, and any general instruction to them to procure copies of all unregistered papers in their district, 'would lead to serious and useless expense'.[78] Even so, many proprietors and editors did find themselves under the sometimes draconian weight of the regulations, egged on by rivals eager to take advantage of any potential defaults. Hence when, in August 1864 it became known that one of the sureties for the *Dundalk Express* had withdrawn, and the other had been pursued by creditors, Patrick Dowdall, proprietor of the *Newry and Dundalk Examiner*, urged action on the Treasury Solicitor, his antagonism no doubt heightened because Gerald McCarthy, the proprietor and editor of the *Express*, had previously been convicted of libel but, not having previously lodged sureties, had escaped liability through bankruptcy. A number of McCarthy's nominees for the provision of sureties were rejected as insufficient, and only after he was jailed for contempt did he finally manage to satisfy the Stamp Office.[79] Similarly, the *St Pancras News and Marylebone Journal* was pursued in 1865 on the information of a rival that it was publishing libellous and scurrilous matter.[80] Where one part of the regulations did not provide leverage, there were always the others. Hence, when a suggestion to the Revenue that the proprietor of the *Grantham Journal and Melton Mowbray Advertiser* had not properly registered was returned in the negative, the accuser suggested that as the place of printing had recently been moved, the proprietor should still be pursued for insufficient registration.[81]

True to form, that portion of the press represented by the Provincial Newspaper Society continued to regard the surety regulations as 'wholesome and needful'.[82] During his period as president of the Society in 1866–7, Joseph Fisher, proprietor of the *Waterford Mail*, attempted to push the Board of the Inland Revenue to take action against the 'constant and persevering disregard of the law by a number of persons publishing unregistered newspapers'.[83] Fisher was at pains to point out that the members of the Society 'do not shirk from fair competition from any quarter' but were committed to the view that publishers of newspapers should have 'shewn their qualifications for that duty by giving the security required by law'. Unsurprisingly, he was not satisfied by the Revenue's passive stance, given that *Mitchell's Newspaper Directory* allowed the Revenue to ascertain easily what papers were being published.[84] In 1867 the Provincial Newspaper Society pressed publishers of the directories to distinguish registered and unregistered papers.[85] Charles Mitchell, of *Mitchell's Press Directory*, refused, but contacted the Revenue to indicate that he was prepared to co-operate with them privately if approached.[86]

As it happens, the retirement of Joseph Timm in 1866 brought some renewal of pressure, not least because his replacement William Melville seemed determined to apply the law more vigorously, partly perhaps because of pressure from the Provincial Newspaper Society, but also no doubt in response to the sense of political crisis and renewed revolutionary threat engendered by the Hyde Park Riots and the activities of the National Reform League.[87] In the autumn of 1866 the Board initiated approaches to unregistered or faultily registered newspapers, with the result, it was claimed, that a large number of newspapers were induced to register.[88] Prosecutions of the *East London Observer*, the *Hornsey Hornet* and the *Owl* renewed the public controversy.[89] It was suggested that the Revenue was searching out changes in publishing arrangements that could warrant a new set of guarantees.[90] Faced with renewed hostility, the Attorney-General offered the extraordinary defences that the Revenue was not acting on the then government's instructions, and also that its principle was that '*They never stir till their attention is called by some of the public* to a breach of the law in certain particulars.'[91] The surviving records of the Revenue show a slow but persistent trickle of cases during 1867 and 1868; the *Yorkshire Chronicle*, for example, was first contacted in March 1868, and sent 7 further communications before the end of July. Thirty-one newspapers were reminded about their failure to comply with statutory requirements in May 1868. Once started, cases were pursued with dogged persistence. The *Folkestone Observer* was pressed over an extended period at the instigation of the Folkestone Town Clerk's Office, initially because of a series of 'scurrilous articles' in the paper, on the basis that the nominated printer on the paper was a journeyman formerly in the editor's employ.[92]

One reason for the greater burdens of the security system during the later 1860s appears to be that, perhaps as late as 1868, there was a move away from the practice of the Inland Revenue deciding whether the securities and bonds offered were sufficient, and a move back to the letter of the law which stipulated that it was the responsibility of the Baron of the Exchequer to take recognizances and magistrates' bonds.[93] For example the *Tiverton Gazette*, as a long-established paper not an obvious candidate for a sudden crackdown, was pursued because on more than one occasion its nominated surety had declined on request. The paper's proprietors protested not so much at the requirement for posting sureties, but rather that this should come from interested parties, telling the Revenue that 'it seems a very hard case that the government should so to speak single out newspaper proprietors and put them to this trouble and inconvenience whilst a very large number are allowed to enjoy their freedom . . . it is nothing more than trammelling the liberties of the press.'[94] Hugh Gilzean Reid, of the *Middlesbrough and Stockton Gazette* was annoyed at the urgency with which he was pursued by the Stamp Office, while no such pressure was placed on his contemporary the *Stockton News* even though it was involved in a libel case, and the *Stockton Guardian* was ignored entirely.[95]

In almost all instances, the pursuit of papers by the Inland Revenue took place without press coverage. Papers subject to pressure from the Revenue were generally unwilling to make a public fuss. In a few cases, though, the determination of the proprietors meant the case came to court. The first to gain widespread attention was the prosecution in July 1868 of the *Camden and Kentish Town Gazette*. The paper had objected to be subject to a requirement that large numbers of metropolitan papers were clearly flouting with impunity. In court, the prosecution argued that virtually all the 200 new papers launched in the previous year had registered. Yet, as the paper noted, an inspection of the Somerset House registers revealed registrations for only two of the six papers then being published in the borough of St Pancras.[96] The paper's legal defence was organized by a re-activated APRTOK, and unsurprisingly took refuge in legal niceties, arguing that the impact of the 1855 Newspaper Stamp Act on the 1836 Act was unclear.[97] But the wider response demonstrated that the security laws could still raise echoes of radical resistance: 'No time should be lost', wrote Fair Play to the paper, 'to show the Government that the newspaper is the people's property and the people's protector; and if others will join in, we will wring this Magna Charta of Press Freedom from the despotic grasp of the Crown'. In Camden, unfortunately, no other joiners were forthcoming.[98]

Nationally, though, things were beginning to stir. The old APRTOK spokesmen, Ayrton and Milner Gibson, had renewed their interest in 1867 in response to the Inland Revenue's new impetus. In May 1867 and June 1868 the pair pressed the government in parliament, calling for the law, if it must be enforced, at least to be enforced in some systematic way, and not merely arbitrarily on the basis of private information motived by malice or pique.[99] Ayrton attacked 'laws which could never have been placed upon the statute book except in the most evil times, when the old Tory party was engaged in desperate struggle to repress the expression of public opinion'.[100] For the first time in a number of years, there were also signs that even the established press, or at least the liberal portion of it, were prepared to voice their support for repeal. The *Daily News* and the *Manchester Guardian* both objected to the renewed attempt at enforcement, the *Guardian* suggesting that the Government was 'rather ashamed of the proceeding, which amounts to the oppressive misuse of a law never intended for this purpose, and which has remained on the statute book through the obstinacy of the House of Lords'.[101]

Meanwhile, a reconvened APRTOK committee was actively supporting a more notorious and less easily intimidated opponent of the registration clauses, Charles Bradlaugh, editor of the secularist *National Reformer*.[102] The Revenue had approached Bradlaugh in April 1868 indicating ('underlined in red ink') that the *National Reformer* must be registered as a newspaper. Bradlaugh refused, arguing that the *National Reformer* was not a newspaper within the meaning of the act, and defying the government to prosecute. In Bradlaugh's case the necessity of finding securities against blasphemy struck at the very core of the paper's identity and purpose. A modest campaign of petitions ensued, and Ayrton, Milner Gibson, Moore and Collet participated in a meeting at the Commons to organize a petition in Bradlaugh's defence,[103] but despite discussion at Cabinet level, the decision was taken to proceed with the prosecution.[104]

The initial court case in June 1868 was abandoned because of objections to serve from some of the special jurymen and it fell to the subsequent Gladstone administration to preside – rather embarrassedly – over the continuing legal proccess, which came back to court in February 1869.[105] At this point the Revenue was still actively pursuing unregistered or faultily registered papers. Twenty-nine provincial papers were sent a circular reminder of their obligations in January 1869, including well-established papers such as the *Wolverhampton Chronicle*, the *Lancaster Guardian* and the *Ipswich Journal*.[106] The proprietor of the *Lynn News and County Press* was advised by Milner Gibson not to comply immediately with the demands of the Revenue, but to wait until the conclusion of the *National Reformer* case.[107] APRTOK commissioned a detailed legal case for Bradlaugh, which offered a series of defences, and argued that the *National Reformer* was not a newspaper because its main objective was not to give the public general intelligence, but to 'carry on a special propaganda of particular views'.[108] In court, Bradlaugh was able once again to illustrate the arbitrariness of the regulations, demonstrating, despite an explicit denial from Hugh Tilsley, Inland Revenue solicitor and author of the standard work on the stamp laws, that the *Sporting Times* was not registered, among other papers including the *Family Herald* and the *London Reader* which the Attorney General acknowledged were unregistered.[109] The court found against Bradlaugh, but gave him leave to appeal.

Perhaps not surprisingly, Bradlaugh's case attracted little sympathy, even among opponents of the registration clauses. Some Conservative titles, indeed, were still quite comfortable that the legislation might be used to suppress particular types of publication. Why had the law not been applied earlier to the *National Reformer,* asked the *Manchester Courier*, given that it has been published for several years and 'had during that time disseminated a vast amount of what we can only consider the worst kind of moral poison'.[110] Perhaps more surprisingly, the case appears to have attracted little support from within radical or labour circles, although the council of the Reform League resolved to petition for repeal of the laws at their meeting on 16 March 1869.[111] As it happens, there was no need for further agitation. When the case came before Court of Exchequer in mid-April, it was clear that the bench was inclined to accept elements of Bradlaugh's defence, and was unwilling to push for the imposition of penalties,[112] an understandable moderation, given that a week before Ayrton, now a member of the government, had introduced a bill to repeal the regulations.[113] The case was adjourned, and quickly abandoned. Ayrton's bill swiftly passed through the Commons and was approved by the Lords on 21 June,[114] along with a bill to enforce the copyright deposit of periodicals in the British Library.[115] The trade journal the *Printers' Register* celebrated that the campaigns against the taxes on knowledge had 'been worthily crowned by the repeal of a number of vexatious restrictions upon newspaper enterprise, in the way of requiring securities and inflicting unreasonable penalties on journalistic transgressions.'[116] Otherwise, reaction in the newspaper world focused primarily on concerns that the removal of registration did not end up depriving newspapers of the rights to their titles.[117]

9

Conclusion

The years 1869 and 1870 do seem to represent the beginning of a new phase in the history of the British press, even if the removal of registration clauses was a temporary victory, compulsory registration of newspapers and their proprietors being reintroduced by the Newspaper Libel and Registration Act (1881).[1] A surge of new local foundations in London in 1869, when in comparison to the previous annual average of around 10, 30 new titles were established, suggests that the removal of the securities restrictions themselves may have had some impact.[2] But there were also broader shifts afoot. The formation of the Press Association (1868) and the nationalization of the telegraph companies paved the way for the rearticulation of news gathering around a number of news agencies working alongside new London offices and expanded rosters of journalists. Once again a war, this time the Franco-Prussian war, provided a fresh stimulus to newspaper demand, and the extension of new technologies.[3] The establishment of joint stock newspaper companies accelerated rapidly after 1870 notwithstanding the difficulties of the economy.[4] By 1870 the newspaper entrepreneur Alexander Mackie's chain of seven linked *Guardians* in Cheshire each had their own office, reporters, local advertisements, while sharing general advertisements, and with the exception of the *Chester Guardian*, all published in Warrington, where Mackie had 'every appliance to secure speed, including iron making-up tables, rolling proof rollers, hoist, damping machines, folding machines and a double-feeding printing machine 'of enormous size', along with 'Mackie's own Type Composing Machine, driven by steam, and setting at the rate of a *Times* column per hour'.[5]

By 1870 the press was also in throes of the shift to the next stage of Victorian pricing – the halfpenny press. By the late 1860s half-pence was a common price for the London district weeklies. The launch of the *Echo*, the first London halfpenny evening paper, itself seemed to mark an important moment, not least because of its immediate success. The pages of the *Printers' Register* in 1869 and 1870 paid frequent testimony to its noticeable success 'judging from the pressure of its advertising columns and the almost irritating persistence with which it turns up everywhere'.[6] The further novelty at this point was the appearance of halfpenny dailies in the provinces, generally evening papers like *Bolton Evening News*, but in some cases morning papers like the *Dundee Courier and Argus* and the *Brighton Daily News*. In June 1869, seven months after its launch, the *Brighton Daily News* could report 'a revolution . . . amongst the [five] weekly journals in Brighton', forced successively to trim their price to 2d and then to 1d.[7] Encouraged by the demand for war news, 1870 saw a surge of new titles or developments of existing papers, including a bulge of new evening papers. As many as 9 evening papers were launched in Lancashire alone in 1870, although only 2 survived more than a year.[8] Circulations leapt forward again, and across the political spectrum; in 1871 the Conservative *Preston Herald* claimed that within a year its circulation had increased three-fold.[9]

The impressed stamp on newspapers required for postal transmission was finally abolished at end of September 1870 as result of Postage Act of 1870, which reduced the rate to ½d, which once more made the post attractive as a means of circulation: Ayherst notes that 10,000 copies of the *Manchester Guardian* were posted on the first day of the new arrangements.[10] The Postmaster General retained the right to make regulations regarding size, weight and wrappings; and also to determine what was, and was not, a newspaper within the meaning of the Act; and indeed, via the Post Office regulations of October 1870 introduced a system of registration with the Post Office.

The final act of the APRTOK committee came in 1870 when it met for the last time at Richard Moore's house in Bloomsbury to frame one last petition in the name of the Association, objecting that despite the removal of the impressed stamp, newspapers were still to be entitled to special postal privileges over other forms of printed material, including pamphlets, on the basis that it would continue to be difficult to define a newspaper, and the regulation would be impossible to police without 'great expense and loss of time' at the 'Post Office'.[11]

The application fell on deaf ears, and the Association quietly faded. Thereafter Collet continued his connection with David Urquhart and the *Free Press*, serving as editor until it ceased publication in 1877. In the 1880s he was still publishing *Diplomatic Fly Sheets* and despairing at the reactionary state.[12] From 1877–83 he was also associated with several veterans of the taxes on knowledge struggles, including Holyoake and John Watts, in the Travelling Tax Abolition Committee, which successfully campaigned against the penny per mile tax levied on railway train journeys.[13] In the 1890s Collet gathered together his records from the 1850s and prepared his two-volume *History*, initially serialized in the *Weekly Times and Echo*, owned by Passmore Edwards, himself a stalwart of the taxes on knowledge campaigns, and then prepared after Collet's death for book publication by Holyoake. Responses to his calls for contributions towards the publication costs from prominent figures in the newspaper industry were mixed: there were contributions from H. S. Harmsworth, the *Daily Telegraph*, *Daily News*, the *Manchester Guardian*; but others declined. 'I am afraid I cannot get up any enthusiasm for Mr Collet's book', George Newnes, the doyen of the new journalism told Holyoake, 'it is a very old story and has often been well told'.[14]

Resonance: Gladstonian liberalism

Newnes was perhaps churlish, but not entirely unfair: the campaign had found its way into the popular narrative of Victorian liberalism, albeit in a form far briefer than Collet's two volumes.[15] It was not just that the struggle against the newspaper taxes had been incorporated as a largely conventional element of the radical programme, in the way visible in John Scott's *The New Magna Charta of the Nations* (1859) where the repeal of the paper duties, was included along with direct national taxation, manhood suffrage, payment of MPs in a typical amalgam of Chartism and middle-class radicalism.[16] But also that during the 1860s and 1870s the division over the paper duties became a litmus test of the values of Liberalism and Conservatism.[17] Throughout the 1860s and 1870s the Radicals made capital out of the picture of the Tory party ranging against the taxes on knowledge and rejoicing at the Lords' rejection of paper repeal in 1860.[18] In Liberal circles, the struggles against the taxes became part of a conventional litany of liberal progress, and conservative obstructionism.[19] So powerful and so successful was this rhetoric that various desperate attempts were made to claim the achievement for Conservatism.[20] The removal of the taxes was celebrated as a democratization of knowledge, opening up the possibilities of political education on which successful liberal politics was predicated. 'With regard to the taxes on knowledge, for example', Robert Mann told a Labour Representation Committee meeting in Birmingham in 1870, 'nobody could have spoken with such effect upon that struggle as men who had themselves to struggle with the difficulties placed by Parliament in the way of acquirement of knowledge. Before the repeal of the newspaper stamp duties he himself had never been able to afford to buy a newspaper. When he wanted to read one he went to a public house, spent twopence or fourpence on beer, according to the state of his exchequer and "took it out" in newspaper reading. No member of the House of Commons could have felt as he did about the "taxes on knowledge" because he had suffered all his lifetime, and had felt he was suffering all his lifetime from want of education.'[21] This sensibility was perhaps particularly powerful for those emerging into adulthood and political activism in the 1850s and 1860s, but it was nonetheless enduring for this. For John Wilson, looking back from as late as 1910, the repeal of the paper duties in 1861 was a watershed moment in which 'the Lords were defeated and the era of cheap books and newspapers ushered in'.[22]

The history of the campaign helped contribute to a general rehabilitation of Cobden, Bright and the Manchester School, as neither Whigs nor middle-class advocates, but disinterested labourers for the benefit of the working classes. However, the beneficiary above all was Gladstone. In the 1860s and 1870s his own self-fashioning celebrated the benefits of the free press, a 'powerful political engine' contributing to an informed and responsible working class,[23] but more tellingly, the successful repeal of the taxes had been a key conduit for his journey from anxious Peelite to populist Liberal, and deserves greater prominence as part of the evolution of Gladstonian Liberalism than has been hitherto given.[24] The 1860 budget, partly because of Gladstone's determination to push through his fiscal reforms in the face of financial pressure and the opposition of the Whigs, marked a significant milestone in the development of the 'People's William'.[25] Listening to him introduce it in the Commons, the Whig Clarendon recognized not just Gladstone as the man of the day, but concluded 'that he is moving towards a Democratic union with Bright'.[26] E. D. Steele has suggested that the defeat of the paper duties in 1860 manifested Palmerston's popular eclipse of Gladstone. But this would seem to overlook the riposte of 1861.[27] If nothing else, Gladstone's responsibility in particular, for precipitating the struggle with the House of Lords over the Paper Duties made him the people's idol for the first time, and helped to overcome the suspicion of large sections of the radical party that had complicated the political realignments of the 1850s.[28] For Holyoake, writing at the time, the budget 'did more by his tone of sincere sympathy for the people to render it popular than even its generous contents. In proposing the repeal of the Paper-duty, the grace of the concession was even greater than the concession itself.' Gladstone, Holyoake suggested, was 'the first Chancellor of the Exchequer who ever gave the people what he might have withheld . . . The grateful tones with which the working class are mentioning Mr Gladstone's name must surely satisfy him that a Minister of State may safely trust the generous and intelligent instincts of the people.'[29]

Although, as Matthew has pointed out, we can discern a coherent thread running through Gladstone's fiscal policy from 1853 to 1861, one which, superficially at least, was manifested in his role in the successive removal of all three of the taxes on knowledge, it is also important to recognize the complexities and uncertainties which lay beneath that trajectory. For almost all the period of the campaigns against the knowledge taxes, Gladstone's political identity remained fluid. The parliamentary radicals struggled to accept him as one of their party, either in spirit or reality. In 1857 an unconvinced Cobden could still question his soundness of questions of international affairs: 'his conscience has not yet taken him in our direction or if so he has failed to follow its dictates.'[30] At a number of points in the 1850s a juncture with the Derbyites seemed a realistic possibility,[31] although Gladstone's former Peelite colleagues were coming to see him as offering a 'fatal gift of eloquence to any Gov[ernmen]t he joins', as Edward Stanley put it in February 1860.[32] As late as August 1860 it was still possible to present him as a Peelite, searching through the customs system to root out the 'last and widely-spread fragments of the shattered bulk of protection, that still lay strewn through our commercial system'.[33]

In the aftermath of the crisis of 1861–2 this was no longer a viable interpretation. The *Daily Telegraph*, with unusual prescience, noted in July 1860 that the conflict would 'set a permanent mark on the character of many an English politician; and it may result sooner than some public men expect, in carrying Mr Gladstone to the head of the Liberal party as its unquestioned leader'.[34] Cobden's mission to France, with which the politics of paper became so entwined, brought Gladstone into closer alignment with him, and into conspiratorial relations with Milner Gibson,[35] in marked contrast to his only very incidental previous correspondence with any of the Manchester Radicals. Despite the tensions it brought, their collaboration transformed Cobden's opinion, just as opinion in the country shifted.[36] At the end of the 1860 Parliamentary session, while describing Gibson as an 'honest radical', Cobden reserved for Gladstone the characterization as 'a democrat of the purest type!'[37]

There was a parallel reassessment in working-class radical circles. 'A new party is wanted and will come, of which your policy will be the programme' wrote one supporter to Gladstone in August 1860.[38] Gladstone's appearance on the platform with Bright and Milner Gibson at Bradford in December

1860 heralded the change,[39] and by 1862 the constant approbation of *the Star* confirmed the transition. For Joseph Cowen, feeding Holyoake with material for an article on Gladstone in 1862, 'A good point too I think could be made of the fact that Mr Gladstone carried the repeal of the Newspaper Stamp, Advertisement Duty and Paper Duty – points for which Radicals have so long and so ably struggled. Hetherington, Watson, Carpenter, Collet and all the other champions of a free press have had their views carried out by the M.P. for the Oxford University'.[40] Here, we should note, one of Gladstone's greatest assets was that he could be seen by radical supporters as not of the Manchester school.[41]

Of course, this cuts against the frequent rendition of contemporaries of his journey as a move from Peelite conservative to Manchester School fellow traveller.[42] Gladstone's position in Palmerston's government made him the lightning rod of hostility from the Conservative press,[43] and in tory invective he was presented as a Manchester radical. For Robert Cecil Gladstone's defeat in 1860 was a Manchester School defeat, 'weak in all but bluster';[44] for Palmerston in 1861 his triumph was a Manchester School triumph. Indeed, by bringing Cecil much more into prominence in the House of Commons,[45] the paper duties crisis helped underpin a projection of Gladstonianism defined in terms of alliance with the Manchester School radicals.[46] In reality, although Gladstone's almost single-handed struggle for retrenchment and excise reform bound him to popular radicalism, what was equally significant about the Paper Duties crisis was the way in which the defeat of July–August 1860 and the subsequent victory of 1861 both elevated Gladstone to unchallenged leadership of the progressive forces in parliament and simultaneously confirmed the suspicion of much of the constituency of popular radicalism that the leaders of the Manchester School could not be relied upon at points of crisis. This alerts us to the danger of reducing the campaigns against the taxes on knowledge of these years to a Manchester School movement.

The campaigns against the taxes on knowledge were always much more than this. In the localities the campaign encompassed a broad interest range in which, although the Manchester leadership no doubt curbed the enthusiasm of some sections of the working classes,[47] anti-Manchester opinion was powerfully represented, from figures like the Sheffield Urquhartite Isaac Ironside[48] to Joseph Cowen's Northern Reform Union, which despite Cowen's eventual alignment with Gladstonian liberalism was in the 1850s characterized by strong anti-Manchester undertones.[49] Throughout, the campaign drew on the powerful rhetorical resources of working-class radicalism. Although the revolutionary edge of Harney's contributions of the early 1850s was not sustained, the agitation continued to reverberate with radical rejections of the mid-Victorian status quo.[50] After its brief dalliance in the early 1850s, 'official' Chartism under Ernest Jones showed little sustained enthusiasm for the call, but even Jones incorporated it into his 1852 and 1859 election campaigns, and the more demotic and eclectic post-Chartist radicalism of *Reynolds' News* was much more unreservedly supportive, despite the paper's strident hostility to the Manchester radicals. Reynolds's own editorial interventions presented the newspaper taxes as 'those fiscal impositions devised by the fertile ingenuity of oligarchic rapacity, for the plunder of the persons and the prostration of the souls of the English people', and the paper was inevitably drawn to the anti-aristocratic overtones of the campaigns of 1860 and 1861.[51] Meanwhile the ex-Chartist Samuel Kydd also presented repeal of the taxes as 'a mighty step towards redeeming the working class from that political and social bondage which, in this enlightened age, is quite intolerable, and indeed becoming impossible'.[52] Although not a powerful strand of later Victorian Chartist memory, the presence of the campaign is visible there as well.[53]

The significance of the Manchester Radicals and their allies as financiers and parliamentary spokesmen cannot, of course, be gainsayed. For all the NSAC survivors would have liked to have been financially independent, their dependence was all but absolute, and if APRTOK wasn't merely a creature of the Manchester politicians, there was an extent to which they were prepared to use it as far as was possible, without embracing its active workers as equals.[54] But although the Manchester School dominated the parliamentary leadership and the sight of the political elite, their control over the ex-Chartist metropolitan radicals who made up the active membership of the committee was at best diffuse and indirect. Attendance at committee meetings was no more than occasional, and direction was largely a matter of trying to deflect activity into more comfortable channels. The readiness with which the parliamentary leadership collaborated with other associations, and in particular the alacrity with which they joined forces with the established press interest in establishing the NPPARPD is suggestive of the lack of control which they felt they could exert over Collet and Holyoake, especially after 1855, when Collet's Urquhartite associations made him ever more politically suspect in conventional political circles. By 1860–1 APRTOK was acting largely independently of the Manchester interest, even to the extent of standing aloof from the activity of the *Morning Star* party in the constitutional defence movement.

How significant this split was depends on our assessment of the role APRTOK actually played in the freeing of newspapers from their tax burdens. It is not easy to get excited about APRTOK's success. Its cause did not involve (except briefly in the early 1860s) any fundamental or charged matter of political division. Almost from the outset the political elite had accepted that the taxes on knowledge were scarcely defensible, except on the grounds of financial necessity. Nevertheless, the tenacity with which repeal was resisted at each stage suggests the strength of underlying reluctance lurking below the reassurances of mid-Victorian Chancellors. Even Gladstone seems to have been brought to repeal not by some long-established determination, but out of the clash of his fiscal instincts with the contingent pressures of the anti-taxes on knowledge campaign. In this respect, as the fulsome tributes of his co-workers testified, a crucial role was played by Milner Gibson's parliamentary manoeuvrings, his subtle framing of resolutions, his marshalling of the evidence of the failings of the state and his sheer persistence in the face of obstruction in the chamber and political pressure outside. This role was not heroic. It was said of his speech in 1850 that it was 'very sensible and well-studied . . ., full of facts, though not particularly fervid',[55] and this might have stood as a fair summary of the political campaign as a whole.

Parliamentary manipulation played the greatest role in the removal of the advertising duty, and in that respect perhaps Cobden was not entirely without justification in claiming that 'Gibson Bright & I have got the graceless public this great boon, by making it a *casus belli* with the Treasury, & by dint of coaxing & threatening they have conceded it at last to make peace in the camp'.[56] But, even in 1853, the weight of the force which the parliamentary leadership brought to bear was derived from the extra-parliamentary work of Collet and the committee – the orchestrated campaigns which drew out the inconsistencies and anomalies of the application of the stamp laws, the challenges of finding stable ground on which to defend the regime, even in theory, and the weary confusions of those charged with tier implementation. The committee, and Collet in particular, proved endlessly inventive in seeking new ways of promulgating their arguments, and illuminating the weaknesses of their opponents. Holyoake's recollections spoke in understandable hyperbole about Collet's 'twenty schemes of action' each meeting, but Collet's secretaryship was characterized by a restless search for new lines on which to draw out the Revenue into exposed positions, and for new modes of engagement once they were exposed.[57] Even at the apparent denouement of the agitation in Spring 1860, the innovation continued. At the start of March the Association announced it would 'open a little museum . . . in the

Library of the House of Commons, a glass case . . . filled with specimens in lucid order, affording an optical and practical demonstration of the groundlessness of the assertion that paper can only be made from rags'.[58]

In this sense the APRTOK campaigners were right to rejoice in the sense of their agency, that it was their 'subtle strategy that worried the Inland Revenue department almost out of its senses, until commissioners and lawyers gave up the enforcement of the laws almost in despair, & became partisans of the movement for its abolition', as Cobden said in giving tribute in 1862 to Collet.[59] Even the relatively unsympathetic *Caledonian Mercury* accepted that the newspaper stamp 'was not abandoned because it was deemed wise that it should be so, but because it was found impossible to retain it. That impossibility was brought about by the Association, or rather than by the Secretary to the Association . . . For years, the Association steadily pursued its policy, gradually widening the breach in the Stamp Act, till at last when the war excitement was turned to account the rampart was nearly blown altogether, and the place being untenable was surrendered at discretion'.[60]

The success of APRTOK in this way helped to open up new forms of extra-parliamentary pressure, modes of positive action which went beyond the potentially empty rhetoric of the platform and the enervated ritual of the petition, which moved, we might say, from the accumulation of moral force in allies to the erosion of morale force in opponents.[61] Looking back in his *History*, it is clear that Collet had no conception of the Association as a machine of agitation, as a vehicle of popular pressure: 'It is true that we preached the faith as widely as we could, and advised our converts to record their numbers in petitions to Parliament, but we reckoned our gains, not by the number of those who had been advertised into the true faith, but by the number of Acts of Parliament of which we had been able to obtain the repeal'.[62] Indeed, it is noticeable that APRTOK was not usually terribly active at the point of parliamentary debate. Its fundamental role was to create a broader sense of impetus, to provide the context within which its parliamentary spokesmen/leadership could operate (both inside and outside of parliament), to provide specific, technical advice and comment at the moment government measures were being framed, but most of all to sap the will of the state to resist by making it increasingly conscious of the falsity of its position, and by shifting the balance of the costs of concession and defence of the status quo until it tipped decisively in favour of retreat, both in the abandonment of efforts to enforce the law and ultimately in acquiescence in its repeal.[63]

The APRTOK model was recycled in the 1860s and 1870s. It became the form of the Travelling Tax Abolition Committee, with its pamphlets, *Gazette*, its attack on the Revenue for its arrogation of the right to interpret the legislation.[64] Through the writings of Holyoake and others it was a presence in radical thinking through to the early twentieth century. What does not seem to have happened is any widespread recognition of the implications of the modes APRTOK employed, of seeking to obtain repeal of laws by attempting to ensure their effective enforcement.[65] The campaigns are more likely to be cited as an inspiration to those advocating civil disobedience, as in the case of Cowen's *Newcastle Chronicle* and its intervention in a conflict over theatrical licences in Newcastle in 1862.[66] Or more simply as evidence that successful parliamentary pressure required a willingness to force the House to division at frequent intervals, even if for years there was a heavy majority against.[67] This said, there are, for example, although the lines of intellectual transmission require teasing out, clear links between the writings of Holyoake, via Indian secularism, to the Gandhi's development of notions of civil disobedience.

Were the campaigns against the taxes on knowledge a success? Without doubt they had a transformative impact on the British newspaper industry, despite the powerful continuities which press historians have recognized across these years. Of course, removal of the newspaper taxes was only one of a number of transformative forces operating on the British newspaper industry in the middle years of the century, including the development of facilities for transport by railways, the exploitation of telegraph for the transmission of news, further mechanical improvements in printing and the slow democratization of reading.[68] Nor was there necessarily an easy correlation between the individual removals and the change in the industry, not least because the reforms of 1855 and 1861 were widely anticipated, and their tendencies blurred by the short-term dislocations which resulted. The underlying trajectories, however, are clear. The removal of the advertising duty in 1853 diminished the capital required to publish a paper and offered greater prospects of profit from newspaper enterprise. William Wood Mitchell's *West Sussex Advertiser* was only one of a surge of new advertising prints launched in1853 and 1854. This may have strengthened the interrelationship of advertisement and commercial success for newspapers, and in doing so created opportunities which working class papers were not well situated to exploit, but in the light of the evidence of the pre-1853 period, it seems perverse to construct this *de facto* into a mechanism of political censorship and capitalist control.[69] As the history of a number of radical papers, among them the well-documented case of Ernest Jones's *People's Paper* shows, repeal of the advertising duty neither solved nor initiated the commercial challenges of the working-class press.[70] Removal also put further pressure on the already cramped columns of many provincial papers, and encouraged the much more widespread use of supplements.[71] In announcing an enlargement to a sheet as large as *The Times* in 1853, the *Scottish Press* noted that with its pages already 'during the advertising season' more than half occupied with advertisements, it needed to respond.[72] Contemporaries noticed a shift: 'what with the war and what with the Reform Bill, politics, literary ability will rise in value', wrote one observer in the autumn of 1853 'I hear of new newspapers setting up every day . . .'.[73]

Mitchell's experience illuminates the significance of the stamp as a barrier to more structural transformation of the press after 1853, and in this sense the repeal of the stamp duty in 1855 has rightly assumed centre-stage a watershed moment in the history of the British press. The partial decay of legal restraints in the face of public demand for news of the Crimean war, coupled with the delays in the spring of 1855 caused by the fall of the Aberdeen coalition, together ensured that the characteristics of the post-repeal frenzy were presaged before repeal. Thereafter, notwithstanding the carnage both of new titles and old, and the initial struggles of the new cheap papers to establish some sort of commercial viability, the transformations of the press were unmistakeable. The result did not produce the political rebalancing that the Manchester radicals had looked for. Despite their sometimes transparently self-reassuring efforts to find signs of change,[74] there was also continued frustration that there seemed little progress towards consistency and a more pacific line in the established metropolitan dailies.[75] Within a year Cobden was conceding to Bright that 'It will be a great measure the repeal of the stamp in its consequences yet, but it will take more time than probably we had calculated on for realizing all its results'.[76]

From the vantage point of the promoters of the *Morning Star*, the benefits of 1855 came rapidly to be seen as dependent on relief from the paper excise; though, as the ultimate fate of the *Star* suggests, the benefits were less easily predictable than the simple arithmetic of taxation and loss implied, and the failure of the *Star* in 1869 would have been a bitter disappointment for Cobden had he still been alive. Undoubtedly, the immediate impact of the removal of the paper duties is much less easily discerned than that of the newspaper stamp. One reason for this is that by October 1861 repeal had been anticipated for almost two years. More generally, once the frenzy of activity associated with repeal itself died away, some form of normality returned. External events played a part here. By the end of 1861 the United States was already set on the road which led to the Civil War and the Lancashire 'Cotton Famine', and a general disruption of the British economy. The demand for cheap papers and magazines in Manchester and Lancashire, which had always been the single most important British market, fell away sharply in early 1862, and conditions did not materially improve until 1864.[77] Perhaps not surprisingly, therefore, the newspaper market, though subject to instability and fierce competitiveness during the 1855–61 period, might thereafter be described as filling out the logics of the removal of advertisement and stamp duties rather than diverging into radically new paths.

The powerful desire to strike a decisive blow against the power of *The Times* went largely unfulfilled. Almost as soon as the paper duties were removed, Cobden was already planning further manoeuvres against the paper, hatching a scheme for launching a national advertising sheet as a way of undermining the advertising revenues on which the hegemony of *The Times* seemed in part to rest.[78] Although this came to nothing, his war of attrition with the paper rumbled on. At the end of 1863 he and Bright became embroiled in a further quarrel with *The Times* over what Cobden took to be the paper's wilful distortion of one of Bright's speeches, which broadened into an assault on the principles of anonymity in journalism, and the irresponsibility and illegitimate influence that this brought papers like *The Times*;[79] and in 1864 Cobden was drawn into a briefer but even less illuminating exchange with Alexander Russel of the *Scotsman* on whether the removal of the taxes had brought the changes he had hoped for. But if there was no dramatic defeat, the situation of the *Times* was nevertheless transformed; although its circulation held up in absolute terms, relatively it had lost ground dramatically by the end of the 1860s, both to the cheap London dailies, and to the provincial press. In the early 1870s, while the daily circulation of *The Times* was 65,000–70,000, the combined daily circulation of the *Daily Telegraph, Daily News* and *Standard* was approaching 500,000, and the larger provincial dailies were probably selling 200,000–300,000 daily, without attempting to estimate the circulation of the weeklies.[80] Musing on the possibility of a reduction in price to 2d 'at some future and not very distant date' in July 1868, John Walter, the senior proprietor recognized that the paper 'must be prepared for an ebb, and the gradual decline in our circulation, which I attribute solely to the Cheap Press'.[81]

Not that the agitation had ever been principally about either *The Times* or the *Morning Star*, even for Cobden and Bright, whose correspondence in the 1850s makes quite clear their underlying commitment to the expansion of newspaper readership to be effected by a penny press. In the longer term, such transformations become more visible. Coupled with the Manchester radicals' disappointment was a recognition that whatever its limitations, the penny press of the 1860s had transformed the conditions within which the established papers operated and placed limits on the politics of conservative possibility: 'any permanent reaction', Cobden told his close associate William Hargreaves

Figure 9.1 'The latest intelligence', *Illustrated London News*, 28 November 1868

in 1860, 'with a quarter of a million of daily penny papers circulating, & weekly penny papers springing up in every little town, is out of the question – It will only lead to a new demarcation of parties, & what may appear the triumph of privilege & exclusiveness will prove its speedy bane & discouragement'.[82]

Later Victorian Liberalism has come to be seen to be predicated on a reconstituted press. As John Vincent observed, 'Before 1855, the press was dominated by, and took its tone from, the traditional holders of power who dominated Parliament. After 1861, the press was chiefly a popular institution, representative of classes with little weight in Parliament'.[83] Collet might have been unconvinced; in the final years of his life he pooh-poohed the dignity of the press as the fourth estate, still fearing the tendency for one title to be allowed a monopoly position whereby it was 'made the means of carrying on conspiracies against the country', promoting the very secrecy that it should be dispelling; that, in Patrick Joyce's formulation, the press might have been more populist than popular (Figure 9.1).[84] But the Liberal anxieties of the 1860s, expressed most trenchantly in the *Culture and Anarchy* essays of Matthew Arnold: the challenge of provincial culture, the new assertiveness of Nonconformity, the erosion of the self-contained middle-class public sphere on which it was supposed that the rationality of progress was predicated, were all coloured to a greater or lesser extent by the changes and challenges wrought by the legacy of repeal, which created a new brand of local press, of the type represented by papers such as the *Ashton Reporter* or the *Rochdale Observer*, which held sway at least until the early 1870s.

In light of this, if it was unduly optimistic, perhaps it was also excusable for John Bright, looking back in 1872 in his letter to William Mitchell of the *West Sussex Gazette,* to allow himself a note of congratulatory complacency, and the judgement that 'I think the great revolution of opinion on many public questions which is now being witnessed in this country is owing mainly to the freedom of the newspaper press. It is silently working a change of the most important and, I hope, of a most beneficial character . . . All that we foretold in or agitation for a free Press has come to pass.'[85]

Notes

Prologue

1 William Woods Mitchell, *The Newspaper Stamp and Its Anomalies Practically Considered: A Letter Addressed to the Rt Hon. the Chancellor of the Exchequer* (1854), 5.

2 J. Timm to Mitchell, 31 October 1853, Add. MS. 13886/28, WSRO.

3 The letter does not survive, but as Cobden's response is dated 18 November, Mitchell must have written within a day or two of the issue of his first stamped edition.

4 Cobden to Mitchell, 18 November 1853, Add. MS. 13886/1, WSRO, *Cobden Letters* II, 551–2; ditto 5 December 1853, Add. MS. 13886/3, WSRO.

5 Cobden to Collet, 18 November 1853, Add. MS. 87371, BL.

6 Cobden to Mitchell, 6 February 1854, Add. MS. 13886/6, WSRO; ditto 22 February 1854 /8.

7 Mitchell, *The Newspaper Stamp*, 7.

8 Ibid., 12.

9 Howard to Mitchell, [nd] Add. MS. 13886/36, WSRO.

10 *Hansard*, 16 May 1854, Vol. 133, cc.453–5.

11 William Woods Mitchell, *The Newspaper Stamp: A Reply to a Letter Written to Lord Stanley By 'A Country Newspaper Proprietor', and a refutation of many statements contained therein* (1854), 8.

12 Mitchell, *The Newspaper Stamp*, 11.

13 Mitchell, *A Reply to a Letter*, 3, which made it clear that Mitchell was not circulating 3,000 copies weekly, but computing the number who would receive a copy at some point in the cycle of sales and shifting free distribution (in effect, that 3,000 was its market penetration).

14 Collet to Mitchell, 27 March 1855, Add. MS. 13886/42, WSRO; suggesting that if Timm seeks to interfere, he should refer him to Ashurst and Co. 'You would be quite safe & would put the last nail in the coffin of the stamp'. For William H. Ashurst, see Holyoake, *Sixty Years*, I, 182–6.

15 *Bury Times*, 3 July 1858.

16 See Cobden to Richard, 18 May 1857, Add. MS. 43658 ff. 332–3: including cutting from *West Sussex Gazette*; Cobden to Joseph Sturge, 3 November 1856, Add. MS. 43722, ff. 167–8, BL.

17 Cobden to John Hilson, 9 February 1858, WSRO CP 52, ff. G34, G35.

18 'Provincial Journalistic Enterprise. The *West Sussex Gazette*', *Printers' Register*, 7 March 1870.

19 See *The Land and the Agricultural Population* (1865).

20 *Sheffield and Rotherham Independent*, 9 October 1880.

21 John Bright to William Mitchell, 23 January 1872, published in *Manchester Evening News*, 22 February 1872, and widely elsewhere.

22 W. H. Smith to W. W. Mitchell, 5 February 1872, printed in F. V. Wright, *A Hundred Years of the West Sussex Gazette, 1853–1953* (1953), 25.

Chapter 1

1 Lucy Brown, *Victorian News and Newspapers* (1985), 4. For Milne, 'The turning point in the history of the provincial press, and a major landmark in metropolitan journalism, was the repeal of the stamp tax in 1855', M. Milne, *Newspapers of Northumberland and Durham* (1971), 15.

2 Joel H. Wiener, *The War of the Unstamped. The Movement to Repeal the British Newspaper Tax, 1830–1836* (1969), xi. Wiener added that 'the series of steps by which these financial restraints were removed has never been studied adequately'. Aled Jones, *Powers of the Press* (1996), cites Sir Hugh Gilzean-Read and P. J. Macdonell, that 1861 (along with the American Civil War) marked the origin of the 'modern press', 15.

3 Presented as one of the fundamental tasks of Stephen Koss, *The Rise and Fall of the Political Press in Britain* (1981), see 69–71 and *passim*. Sense of them as a given, in various references in essays in Michael Harris and Alan Lee, *The Press in English Society from the Seventeenth to Nineteenth Centuries* (1986). For Ieuan Jones, the repeal of the taxes on knowledge was 'the great turning point in Welsh political life', Ieuan Gwynedd Jones, *Explorations and Explanations: Essays in the Social History of Victorian Wales* (1981), 294.

4 Jon Lawrence, 'Popular Radicalism and the Socialist Revival in Britain', *Journal of British Studies*, 31.2 (1992), 168.

5 Main exceptions are 'The Taxes on Knowledge', in Henry R. Foxe Bourne, *English Newspapers, Chapters in the History of* Journalism (1887), II, 209–31; and Henry James Nicholl, 'The Repeal of the Fiscal Restrictions upon Literature and the Press', in his *Great Movements and Those Who Achieved Them* (1882), 291–365 (written with the aid of C. D. Collet). For example, Hannah Barker's, *Newspapers, Politics and English Society, 1695–1855* (1988), despite its terminal point, and Lucy Brown's *Victorian News and Newspapers* (1985), both manage without a mention.

6   No reference in A. C. Howe, *Free Trade and Liberal England 1846–1946* (1997). There is passing attention in David Brown, 'Cobden and the Press' (2006), 86–7, but this is much more interested in Cobden's direct dealings with newspapers.

7   Completely ignored by D. A. Hamer, *The Politics of Electoral Pressure. A Study of the History of Victorian Reform Agitations* (1977); referenced obliquely in P. Hollis, *Pressure from without in Early Victorian England* (1974), but largely as an illustration of general trends.

8   Omitted from E. F. Biagini's *Liberty, Retrenchment and Reform, Popular Liberalism in the Age of Gladstone, 1860–1880* (1992), even in his broad ranging discussion of the 'moral economy of free trade', 93–102; not addressed in Tholfsen, *Working Class Radicalism in Mid-Victorian England* (1976).

9   E. Royle, *Victorian Infidels* (1974), 261–6.

10 Patricia Hollis, *Unstamped Press* (1974), 305.

11 Miles Taylor, *The Decline of British Radicalism* (1995), 106–7 184–5.

12 The treasurer J. Alfred Novello presented himself in correspondence with the Inland Revenue in 1854 as an officer of the 'Active Association for the Repeal of all the Taxes on Knowledge', *Musical Times*, 1 July 1854.

13 APRTOK, *Gazette* (May 1861), 7.

14 Laurel Brake and Marysa Demoor, *Dictionary of Nineteenth Century Journalism* (2009), 126.

15 James Curran, 'The Press as an Agency of Social Control: An Historical Perspective.' *Newspaper History: From the 17th Century to the Present Day* (1978): 51–75.

16 James Curran, 'Press History', in James Curran and Jean Seaton, *Power without Responsibility. The Press and Broadcasting in Britain* (4th edn, 1991; 1981), 28. Curran has continued to plough this line for 30 years see, for example, James Curran, *Media and Money* (2011), 141, 145–8.

17 Curran and Seaton, *Power without Responsibility*, 21.

18 Curran, 'The Press as an Agency of Social Control', 57.

19 Curran and Seaton, *Power without Responsibility*, 28.

20 Collet's account was first published in part in the *Weekly Times and Echo*, and then published in two volumes as a result of a subscription collected by George Jacob Holyoake, his long-time friend and colleague. A one-volume edition was published in the Watts 'Thinkers Library' in 1933.

21 Some of which had been published in E. W. Watkin, *Alderman Cobden of Manchester: Letters and Reminiscences of Richard Cobden* (1891), and much of which now forms the collection of Collet papers in the British Library, Add. MS. 87371–2 (unfoliated).

22 *History of the Times*, II, 193, 193–215.

23 For the following see Hollis *Unstamped Press* and Wiener *The War of the Unstamped, passim*.

24 *Hansard*, 20 June 1836, Vol. 34, c.629.

25 See Wiener, *The War of the Unstamped*, 269–71.

26 See comments of Edwards to the *Select Committee on Public Libraries*.

27 *Gazette*, November 1857, 2.

28 APRTOK *Statement*, 6. Collet, *Taxes*, I, 104, gives figures for 1850 which are of similar order.

29 A. Sinclair, *Fifty Years of Newspaper Life, 1845–1895: Being Chiefly Reminiscences of the Time* (1895), 4–5.

30 Wiener, *The War of the Unstamped*, 11.

31 James Greig to Gladstone, 13 June 1853, Box 34, Miscellaneous Correspondence, GGPGL.

32 APRTOK *Statement*, 6. Collet, *Taxes*, I, 104, gives figures for 1850 which are of similar order.

33 Evidence of Cassell, *Select Committee on Newspaper Stamp*, Q1339.

34 For the basis of much of what follows see D. C. Coleman, *The British Paper Industry, 1495–1860. A Study in Industrial Growth* (1958), 317–36.

35 [John Cassell], 'The Commerce of Literature', *Westminster Review* (1852), 511–54, 512.

36 APRTOK *Statement*, 6.

37 James Robertson, *Fifty Years' Experience in Paper Making* (1897), 40.

38 'The Paper Duty', *Bookseller*, 27 May 1861, 273; see Collet, *Taxes*, II, 34–6. Similar statistics were provided by W. D. Stanwell (Loudwater Mills), 28 April 1858 to Herbert Ingram, in Isobel Bailey, *Herbert Ingram* (1994), 265–6.

39 *Journal of the Society of Arts*, I (1852–3), 401–2; not all agreed, one anonymous manufacturer remarked 'Decidedly not: on the contrary, I think the collection of the duty helps to keep order and regularity in a paper mill.'

40 *Journal of the Society of Arts*, I (1852–3), 402. One case was the proposal to use imported pulp bricks from New Zealand, scuppered when the revenue deemed the bricks to be paper, liable to duty (which would have been charged again had the bricks then been used to make paper), 'Paper Stamp and Emancipation', *Scottish Review* (April 1860), 177–8.

41 *London Journal*, 6 August 1853.

42 *Morning Chronicle*, 17 April 1858.

43 F. T. Fowler to Herbert Ingram, 19 June 1858, quoted by Ingram in his parliamentary speech, 12 June 1858, see Bailey, *Ingram*, 263–4. Ingram himself directed a similar letter to Disraeli in 1852, as quoted by Milner Gibson in his parliamentary speech of 22 April 1852, *Hansard*, 22 April 1852, cc.988–989.

44 *Journal of the Society of Arts*, I (1852–3), 415–16; Liverpool Financial Reform Association, 'Indirect Taxation. Section XXI. Its evils were further exemplified by the taxes on paper, newspapers and advertisements', *Liverpool Mercury*, 20 November 1849.

45 Evidence of Cassell, *SC on Newspaper Stamp*, Q1326.

46 *Gazette*, 12 July 1854, 18–19.

47 'Editorial', *DN*, 12 August 1854; 'How to Get Paper', *Household Words*, 28 October 1854. One newspaper proprietor offered a reward of £100 for a product in plentiful supply which could be used to supply newspapers, *DN*, 18 July 1854.

48 Aileen Fyfe, *Science and Salvation. Evangelical Popular Science Publishing in Victorian Britain* (2004), 155.

49 Chambers to Ireland, 29 May 1854, Dep 342/110, Chambers Papers, ff. 118–20, NLS.

50 Sinclair, *Fifty Years of Newspaper Life*, 28. The *London Journal* claimed 7d per lb in 1848 (which may have been an underestimation, given that the purpose was to point out the heavy percentage burden of the 1½d paper duty, *London Journal*, 23 September 1848.

51 M. Harris, 'London's Local Newspapers: Patterns of Change in the Victorian Period' (1990) 107.

52 'Taxes on Knowledge', *Tait's Edinburgh Magazine* (April 1850), 235; The *Weekly Times* suggested that the paper duties comprised 25% of its revenue; *Weekly Times*, 1 January 1854, cited Andrew King, *The London Journal* (2004), 85; also cites figures for *Family Herald* which suggested in 1849 was paying 13.5% of its trade price on paper duties; the duties were 30% on the cost of production of the *London Journal*, Bailey, *Ingram*, 263.

53 W. and R. Chambers to Ingram, 15 May 1856, Bailey, *Ingram*, 269.

54 See notice, *Sheffield Independent*, 13 November 1858.

55 *Liverpool Mercury*, 14 April 1848.

56 F. H. Wetherall to John [Walter], 12 March 1851, Taxation of Newspapers subject file, Times Newspapers Limited Archive, News UK and Ireland Limited [hereafter TNA].

57 APRTOK 'Address', printed in *Leader*, 1 November 1851; Collet, *Taxes*, I, 123–5.

58 Dennis Griffiths, *Plant Here* The Standard (1996), 91.

59 Cranfield, *The Press and Society from Caxton to Northcliffe* (1978), 198; Koss, *Political Press* suggests 42,000, I, 61.

60 See Andrew King, *The London Journal, 1845–1883* (2004), Louis James, *Fiction for the Working Man, 1830–1850* (1963).

61 Laurence Fenton, *Palmerston and The Times: Foreign Policy, the Press and Public Opinion in Mid-Victorian Britain* (2013); David Brown, 'Morally Transforming the World or Spinning a Line? Politicians and the Newspaper Press in Mid-nineteenth-century Britain', *Historical Research* (2010), 321–42.

62 A. Aspinall, *Politics and the Press, c.1780–1850* (1973), 375–8.

63 See, for example, James Grant, *The Newspaper Press: Its Origin, Progress and Present Position* (1872), Vol. III.

64 'The Blessings of Being a Newspaper Proprietor and Editor', *North Devon Journal*, 28 April 1853.

65 H. Findlater Bussey, *Sixty Years of Journalism* (1906), 61–2, of the *Plymouth Mail*, c.1855, where he 'was practically the entire "staff" of the weekly *Mail*, a paper published once a week. Here, in addition to sub-editorial and reporting duties, I had to write reviews of books, long theatrical notices and occasional leaderettes, as well as to read all the proofs', 61; later resigned as editor of the *Taunton Courier* after five weeks because he refused to 'canvass for advertisements, and perform other duties which I considered derogatory to my position', 72. See 'Country Newspapers and their Editors', [extracted from *Colburn's Magazine*], *Leeds Times*, 13 October 1855.

66 Bright to Hargreaves, 21 June 1855, Add. MS. 62079, ff. 14–15, BL.

67 See 'Taxes on Knowledge', *Tait's Edinburgh Magazine* (April 1850), 234–9; *Nottingham Guardian*, 9 October 1851.

68 See *SC on Newspaper Stamp*, Appendix. Likewise in Newcastle, the *Courant* returns figures implying circulation of around 5,000 per week, with the *Chronicle, Journal* and *Guardian* all between 2,000 and 3,000.

69 'Repeal of the Newspaper Stamp Duty', *Leicester Chronicle*, 16 August 1851.

70 For example, Bradford, where the *Bradford Observer* (BO), a Liberal paper established in 1834 was faced with a series of failed Conservative papers: *Chronicle* (1825–6), *Courier* (1825–8), *Herald* (1842–3), *Gazette* (1847–c.1849), *Times* (1854).

71 See advert in *Mitchell's Newspaper Directory* (1847), 401; although the advertisement claimed Manchester, this ignored the presence of the *Manchester Courier*.

72 *Fife Herald* (Cupar), *Dundee Advertiser* also listed as appearing Tuesday and Thursday.

73 Not always the case; the four Nottingham papers in 1847 all came out on Friday.

74 A London-printed title with little local content, see *Mitchell's Newspaper Directory* (1847), 202. A number of these were relatively short-lived, for example the *Stockport Mercury* (1847–51). A small number of cheaper monthlies, including the 2½d *Midland Gazette*, published in Sutton in Ashfield from January 1846 until ceasing in November 1848, and the 2d (in 1847) *Wisbech Advertiser* (1846–).

75 See evidence of M. J. Whitty, *Select Committee on the Newspaper Stamp*, Q575.

76 Even in 1855 Leigh Hunt engaged to be supplied with *The Times*, each day for 2 hours, delivered at 3pm. Leigh Hunt to Thornton Hunt, 11 July 1855, Leigh Hunt Papers, University of Iowa. For comment on illegality, see 'Taxes on Knowledge', *Tait's Edinburgh Magazine* (April 1850), 234–5.

77 *Sussex Express*, extracted *Morning Post*, 9 September 1851.

78 Leigh Hunt to Marianne Kent, 5 December 1851, MSL H94 Hum 12, f. 93, Leigh Hunt Papers, University of Iowa.

79 See discussion in S. Shuttleworth, *Charlotte Bronte and Victorian Psychology* (1996); and the description of J. C. Atkinson of the *Yorkshire Gazette*, 'passed from one

farmer to another, and its circulation hardly ceasing until it was three or four weeks old', *Forty Years in a Moorland Parish* (1891), 16.

80 See, for example, Letter of 'A Commercial Traveller' dated Bears Paw Inn, News Room, Chowbent, 18 June 1855, complaining that in Chowbent and Tyldesley it was impossible to get the *Times* on the day of publication, Delane Papers, TT/ED/JTD/6/37, *Times* Archive, TNA.

81 H. Whorlow, *The Provincial Newspaper Society, 1836–1886* (1886).

82 Whitty evidence to SC Newspaper Stamps, Q578–9. Later remarks that newspaper proprietors not interested in additional stamping offices: 'they think that they have a monopoly, and they wish to keep it', Q656.

83 See E. F. Collins to Joseph Sturge, 23 December 1854, M20/21, WilsonPMA.

84 *Gazette*, 19 (June 1855), 3.

Chapter 2

1 *Northern Star*, 27 June 1840, 12 June 1841, 19 February 1842; and in contrast the exchange between O'Connor and Hetherington, *The Odd Fellow*, 5 June 1841.

2 Reference to move in February 1847, *Liverpool Mercury*, 12 February 1847; calls for an association, headed by Lord Ellesmere, Monckton Milnes, Edward Bulwer Lytton, Carlyle or Dickens, *DN*, 6 January 1848.

3 *The Era*, 23 January 1848, citing the *Sheffield Times*.

4 See Salford chartists, *Manchester Courier*, 15 March 1848. Along with W. J. Linton, in February 1848 Collet was deputed to carry an address of congratulation from the working men of London to the Provisional Government; both travelled to Paris with Mazzini to the deliver the resolution, W. J. Linton, *Recollections of Three Score Years and Ten* (1894), 103.

5 *Lloyd's Weekly Paper*, 23 January 1848. *Lloyd's* pointed out the more general burdens of the stamps in a leading article, 30 January 1848. See article in *Westminster Review* 49.2 (July 1848), 483–502; positively noted in editorial in *York Herald*, 7 October 1848. See also article in the *Oddfellows Chronicle*, October 1848, cited in *Lincolnshire Chronicle*, 27 October 1848.

6 *Rules of the Peoples Charter Union*, HO45, 24101, ff. 2–10, NA; E. Royle, 'The Cause of the People, the People's Charter Union and 'Moral Force' Chartism in 1848', in Joan Allen and Owen R. Ashton (eds), *Papers for the People. A Study of the Chartist Press* (2005); *Cause of the People*, 10 and 24 June, 1 July 1848 (cited in F. B. Smith, *Radical Artisan. William James Linton, 1812–97* (1973), 87).

7 For further PCU activity see *Reasoner* for 1848 and 1849, also the *Republican*, which contains the PCU Petition of 1848, I (1848), 153–6, and the first half-yearly report of October 1848, II (1849), 38–9.

8   *Manchester Guardian*, 18 May 1848; *Morning Post*, 5 July 1848. There is also an intriguing recollection from Thomas Greenway, in the *South Australian Advertiser*, 27 February 1884, which talks of a meeting at the Reform Club in 1848 [this may have been later], attended by Cobden, Bright, John Cassel, Henry Rawson and others.

9   *Dundee Courier*, 29 March 1848, quoting the *London Mercury*; also *Lancaster Gazette*, 15 April 1848.

10 'The Surplus Revenue', *Preston Guardian*, 26 January 1850.

11 So much so that his audience made little effort to maintain the distinction; see Robertson Gladstone to W. E. Gladstone, 8 January 1849, file 662, Glynne-Gladstone Mss, Gladstone Library, which describes the budget as addressing the wishes of various constituencies, including newspaper stamp which 'will receive the support of the press'.

12 See brief acknowledgement, Cobden to Collet, 22 January 1849. Watkin, *Alderman Cobden*, 141; *Reasoner*, 17 January 1849, 24 January 1849; Collet, *Taxes*, I, 84–7. Of the initial committee only Thomas Cooper, W. J. Linton and two others did not become members of the new Committee.

13 Address of 20 June, *DN*, 8 August 1849.

14 W. E. Adams, *Memoir of a Social Atom* (1903), 186–92 and W. J. Linton, *James Watson. A Memoir* (1879).

15 C. D. Collet, *Life and Career of Richard Moore* (1878).

16 Deborah McDonald, *Clara Collet, 1860–1948. An Educated Working Woman* (Woburn, 2004); Holyoake, *Bygones*, II, 267–71. See reference in Cobden to Charles Rawlins, 13 April 1864, *Liverpool Daily Post*, 5 May 1864. In the early 1850s Collet also attempted to live partly off lecturing on musical topics, with musical illustrations; see *Musical Times* (July 1852), 302; still teaching singing in later 1860s, see *Musical Times*, 1 February 1870; for brief obituary see *Musical Times*, 1 February 1889.

17 'Metropolitan Memoranda', *Preston Chronicle*, 23 April 1853.

18 M. D. Conway, *Autobiography, Memories and Experience* (1904), II, 39; recalls that so far had Collet imbibed Urquhartism that he saw the hand of Russia not only in all the political intrigues of Europe, but even in the American Civil War. South Place Chapel also had James Watson and William Lovett in the congregation.

19 *Free Press* a London title from August 1856; became the *Free Press and Diplomatic Review* and then from 1866 the *Diplomatic Review*. Some details of his relations with the *Free Press* can be found in various letters in the David Urquhart Papers, Balliol College Archives, Oxford, for example, Collet to Mrs Urquhart, 3 May 1856 I.G18 (Sheffield).

20 See T. Frost, *Reminiscences of a Country Journalist* (1886), 125–6.

21 London correspondence, *Yorkshire Gazette*, 17 November 1855; presents Collet as one of the 'agents of mischief'.

22 See *Materials for the True History of Lord Palmerston* (1865), 50.

23 Printed in full, *Reasoner*, 1 August 1849, 67–9 extracted *DN*, 8 August 1849. For Collet's lecturing see, *Reasoner*, 5 December 1849, 367.

24 Other radical supporters at this stage included William Scholefield, MP for Birmingham, W. J. Fox, Charles Lushington, MP for Westminster, Joseph Hume.

25 Noted *Freeman's Journal*, 15 September 1849; annual meeting reported, *DN*, 22 January 1851; moribund when Collet visited in November 1853, see *DN*, 15 November 1853; *Liverpool Mercury*, 21 May 1851.

26 See account of meeting, addressed by Edwards, *Observer*, 27 May 1849. This speech was published as an NSAC handbill, republished *DN*, 2 October 1849 (with a long supporting editorial). See NSAC, 2nd Annual Report, *Leader*, 11 January 1851.

27 *Northern Star*, 22 December 1849, 16 February, 15 June 1850. O'Connor's *National Instructor* was promoted as providing to the poor 'that Political and Social information of which they are at present deprived by the Government "Taxes on Knowledge"'.

28 Noticed *Leicestershire Mercury*, 2 June 1849.

29 Place to Watson, 21 April 1850, Add. MS 87371, BL.

30 Harney estimated start-up costs inflated by £345 paper duty and £1,200 stamp duty; and suggesting costs of daily journal like the *Morning Chronicle* might be £800 weekly.

31 *Northern Star*, 23 February, 9 March 1850. *Democratic Review* I (1850), 284–6, 321–5, 361–6, 401–5, 441–7. Harney had been imprisoned twice during the 1830s unstamped wars, see Adams, *Social Atom*, 218–19.

32 *A Statement of the Injurious Effects of the Excise Tax, the Tax upon Advertisements, and the Stamp Tax upon Newspapers* (1850), [7/8(10), Holyoake Collection, Bishopsgate], 3.

33 [John Wade, 'The Session of 1849]', *Westminster Review* (January 1850), 488.

34 '[The Knowledge Taxes]', *Eclectic Review* (1850), 441.

35 *Blackburn Standard*, 8 November 1848.

36 Editorial, *CM*, 28 January 1850.

37 Bright to Cobden, 29 August 1851, Add. MS 43383, f. 205, BL.

38 *The Christian Socialist*, 17 May 1851, and response of Collet, 5 July 1851.

39 Collet, *Taxes*, I, 86–7.

40 *Weekly Dispatch*, as reprinted in *The Times*, 26 June 1854, 11, and widely noted and extracted.

41 Collet notes that during 1850 the NSAC 'received a great deal of assistance from the *Daily News*, which allowed us occasionally to make use of its columns', *Taxes*, I, 116.

42 Cobden to Hargreaves, 3 April 1852, Add. MS. 43655, ff. 13–14, BL, *Cobden Letters* II, 497; also Cobden to Combe, 15 April 1853, Add. MS. 43661, ff. 72–3, BL. See Bright's account of a meeting with Russell in 1853: 'He did not see why "news" was not an article to be taxed, . . . How puerile for a leading statesman! . . . It were as

well to make all children who go to school pay a tax to the Govt. for liberty to do so, or that every workman hiring a book from a library should pay a tax upon it to the Exchequer!', R. A. J. Walling (ed.), *The Diaries of John Bright* (1930), 141 (entry for 28 April 1853). For Hargreaves, see A. C. Howe and S. Morgan, *The Letters of Richard Cobden* (3 vols, 2007–12), I, 337.

43 By late 1850 he had stopped taking the *Daily News*, see Cobden to Sir Charles Wood, 22 February 1851, BI HALIFAX/A4/170. See his description of the paper as 'the worst of the lot', Cobden to Joseph Parkes, Parkes Papers, UCL, *Cobden Letters* II, 474–5.

44 Cobden to Sturge, 4 February 1853, Add. MS 43656, ff. 327–8, BL. He tells J. B. Smith, 'These foolish cockney scribes – many of them young men fresh from college with no ideas beyond those which tradition, *unquestioned*, has handed down to them – would be quite unable to meet the arguments on the other side if resolutely & pertinaciously brought to book. – But they are not opposed, nor can they be so long as the daily press is confined to 5d sheets', Cobden to Smith, 12 January 1854, J. B. Smith Papers MS 923.2 S345.

45 Brown, 'Cobden and the Press', 92, citing Cobden to Cassell, 24 December 1850, Add. MS ff. 129–30, BL; Cobden to Combe, 15 October 1852, *Cobden Letters*, II, 432–4.

46 Cobden to Bright, 29 January 1852, Add. MS 43649, ff. 249–51, BL. 'The stamp lies at the bottom of the great mound of ignorance and helplessness which bars the path of political and social progress in this country' he told Bright in 1853, Cobden to Bright, 22 November 1853, Add. MS 43650, ff. 39–43, BL, *Cobden Letters*, II, 556–8.

47 'History of the Taxes on Knowledge', *The People's Review* 1 (February 1850), 12–20.

48 Address of 20th June, *DN*, 8 August 1849.

49 Memorial of the Newspaper Stamp Abolition Committee to the Chancellor, 13 November 1850, IR 56/3 NA. See 'The Suffrage and the Newspaper Stamp', *Leader*, 1 March 1851.

50 See Henry Brougham to Cobden, 4 October 1852, Add. MS 43668, ff. 180–1, BL.

51 'Taxes on Knowledge', *Manchester Times*, 4 December 1847.

52 See comment of 'The Newspaper Stamp', *Leeds Times*, 1 July 1854.

53 *DN*, 27 January 1851.

54 See *West Kent Guardian*, 2 July 1853.

55 Russel in *Edinburgh Review*, 493, Whorlow, *Provincial Newspaper Society*, 52–3.

56 Lucy Brown, 'The Growth of a National Press', in Brake et al., *Investigating Victorian Journalism*, 138. Brown offers impatient incomprehension: the response of the press was 'defensive, almost defeatist, in tone', the reaction of the provincial press was 'strange', 'none of the contributors to the debate seem to have delved very far into the economics of an expanding market', and could surely have understood that a reduction in price and general prosperity would continue to expand the market, ibid., 138–9

57 See William Hunt, *Then and Now: Or Fifty Years of Newspaper Work* (1887), 42; remarking that 'it was this narrow trade protection spirit that kept the Society small and comparatively uninfluential'.

58 See editorial recollections 'The Taxes on Knowledge' in the *Leicestershire Mercury*, 11 December 1852.

59 See letter of Robert Marks, *Manchester Examiner and Times*, 23 October 1852.

60 The *Examiner*, reprinted in *The Times*, 13 February 1855, 4.

61 Editorial, *Newcastle Journal*, 20 April 1850: 'it is through these unclean sources that socialism, communism, and principles of the rankest blasphemy and immorality circulate . . .'.

62 'The Coming Budget', *BO*, 10 March 1853; Editorial, *North Devon Journal*, 21 August 1851 expressed similar concerns at the inevitable deterioration of the provincial press which would result from the increase in competition, and the 'lower[ing] of profits to the utmost possible extent', *Leicester Chronicle*, 16 August 1851. For another strong argument of deterioration, of the 'assimilation' of the British press to the American model, see 'The Newspaper Stamp', *Examiner*, reprinted in *Morning Chronicle*, 12 February 1855, in *Freeman's Journal*, 13 February 1855.

63 For example, 'Taxes on Knowledge', *Carlisle Journal*, 22 February 1850. 'Radical Crotchets – the Newspaper Duty', *Lancaster Gazette*, 30 August 1851. One of the most vivid examples of this argument is the letter of 'Anti-Cant', *The Examiner*, 9 August 1851 (which interestingly supports the abolition of the paper duties and the advertisement duty, and argues for a half penny stamp on newspaper supplements), according to the *York Herald*, 30 August 1851, noticed in *Times* and copied into various other papers. See also subsequent letter of Anti-Cant, *Examiner*, 25 October 1851.

64 Collet, *Taxes*, I, 101.

65 For reference to Hill's calculations, see editorial, *Scotsman*, 5 February 1853.

66 William Edwin Baxter, *Notes on the Practical Effects of Repealing the Newspaper Stamp Duty, the Advertising Duty, and the Excise Duty on Paper* (1852) 4, previously in *Sussex Express*, reprinted *Morning Post*, 9 September 1851. It was said that on average each copy of the provincial press was posted at least once, *Universal Postal Stamp*, 9–10.

67 A favourite argument of the *Scotsman*, see editorial, 30 August 1851, and letter of Auchievoulin, Isle of Arran, 25 October 1851.

68 'The Government and the Press', *Examiner*, see reprint, *Hereford Times*, 17 February 1855, and widely reprinted. In fact, this argument had been turned against the supporters of the stamp in the first annual report of the Association, which had noted the statistics of 86M stamped newspapers, 66M postal transmissions, so that even allowing an average of only 2 transmissions for each paper sent through the post, this would allow 33M posted papers, and 53M not posted, APRTOK *First Annual Report* [Holyoake 7/8(11)].

69 *The Coming Budget, or Notes on Several Items of Taxation, the National Defences, the Militia and Volunteer Rifle Corps* (1853) [not located, but extract printed in *BO*, 10 March 1853].

70 'The Newspaper Stamp', *Fife Herald*, 7 December 1854.

71 *Stirling Observer*, 18 September 1851, extracting the *Scotsman*.

72 See Cobden to George Combe, 1 November 1852, *Cobden Letters*, II, 446–7, inc n5 that Cobden advocating this approach at APRTOK annual meeting, 1 December 1852 (see *DN*, 2 December 1852).

73 *Freeman's Journal*, 13 March 1855; similar concessions by other opponents, such as *Bristol Mercury*, 24 March 1855.

74 For approving citations of see editorial, *Scotsman*, 5 February 1853.

75 Baxter, *Notes on the Practical Effects*, 7.

76 See evidence of Bucknall about the *Stroud Free Press*, Select Committee on Newspaper Stamps, Q1244.

77 'I really scarcely see my way through all my liabilities. Today the Advertisement Duty has to be met – a very peremptory affair. And other heavy bills are falling due . . ', E. Piggot to Holyoake, 10 August 1852, #516, Holyoake Papers, CpUL.

78 Evidence of proprietors of *Cheltenham Free Press* and *Devenport Independent*, *Journal of the Society of Arts*, I (1852–3), 475–6.

79 Lucy Brown concluded that for most Victorian newspapers advertising made up about half the revenue, Brown, *Victorian News and Newspapers*, 15–18.

80 See G. Lathom Browne to Disraeli, 'Tuesday Night' 16 [April 1849?], and 27 April [1849], B/XX/A/11,12, Hughenden Mss, Bodleian Library.

81 'New Restrictions on Newspapers', *Era*, 9 March 1848, which reprints correspondence between the *Yorkshireman* and the Stamp Department at Somerset House; *Newcastle Guardian*, 6 October 1849; Circular issued in May 1851 intimating the intention of Somerset House, see *Bristol Mercury*, 17 May 1851. In October, the *Hastings and St Leonard's News* issued a protest at an attempt to charge them four times for a single advert from an insurance agent who was advertising his agency for four firms, see 'The Advertisement Duty', *DN*, reprinted *Manchester Times*, 11 October 1851. Series of articles calling for 'Free Trade in Knowledge' published by the *BO*, 3, 17 January 1850.

82 See *Taxes*, I, 105. William Ewart, President, Francis, Treasurer, John McEnteer, Secretary. For this title see John Francis, *John Francis, Publisher of the Athenaeum: A Literary Chronicle of Half a Century* (2 vols, 1888), I, 15–16; Francis notes that the Committee attracted the support of 100 MPs as vice-presidents. McEnteer, an Irish barrister, was employed in 1852 as lecturer for the League party in Ireland; see *Cobden Letters*, II, 385, n2. For account of early proceedings see *Athenaeum*, 12 January 1850.

83 *Leicestershire Mercury*, 19 January 1850. For the committee see *Athenaeum*,
    12 January 1850 (papers represented on the Committee in 1850 included the
    *Daily News, Morning Advertiser, British Banner, Railway Times, County Chronicle,
    Gardeners' Chronicle, Standard of Freedom, Illustrated London News, Jerrold's
    [Weekly] News, Commercial Daily List*). Subscriptions also from *Worcester
    Chronicle, Suffolk Chronicle* and *Gateshead Observer*.

84 *Leicester Mercury*, 5 May 1849. Some annoyance was expressed in April 1850
    when the Committee sent out engrossed petitions, postage unpaid (subject to
    an 8d charge) to local newspapers, see *Sheffield Independent*, 13 April 1850; note
    in *British Friend* ([February] 1850), 51; advertisement in *Athenaeum*, 23 March
    1850.

85 *Dumfries and Galloway Standard*, 28 April 1852, *Fife Herald*, 29 April 1852. *Fife
    Herald* also prepared to oppose the paper duty, but not the stamp duty, see 22 June
    1854. For another see *Hull Packet*, 14 May 1852, 'Taxes on Knowledge', *Dundee
    Courier*, 19 May 1852.

86 See extract from *Sheffield Times* in *Reynolds's Miscellany*, 26 February 1848, 246.

87 See Editorial, *DN*, 14 February 1850.

88 Editorial, *DN*, 3 May 1850. A standard theme, also the line in review of Mill's
    Principles of Political Economy in *Westminster Review* 49.2 (July 1848), 307–8.

89 See, for example, Editorial, *Morning Chronicle*, 23 April 1852.

90 'Imperial Parliament', *DN*, 8 May 1850.

91 Hence the fear of *Sherbourne Mercury* that repeal would tend to 'multiply immoral
    and scurrilous publications', 2 January 1849.

92 Andrew Moody to Gladstone, 8 June 1853, Box 61, GGPGL.

93 'Taxes on Knowledge', *Scotsman*, 20 April 1850.

94 'The Duty on Paper', *London Journal*, 23 September 1848.

95 '[The Knowledge Taxes]', *Eclectic Review* (1850), 443.

96 Chapman, *Commerce of Literature*, 8.

97 Full reprint *Morning Post*, 8 February 1850, only four days after the dating of the
    text (4 February 1850); widely extracted, for example in '[The Knowledge Taxes]',
    Eclectic Review (1850), 431–43. For one exception see letter of 'An Author', *DN*,
    22 April 1852, which suggested taking the duty off books as a priority.

98 As usual the title was not maintained with any consistency, but this is the title
    printed with the circular from the Association's secretary, George Huggett,
    Morning Post, 23 February 1851.

99 Borthwick MP for Evesham 1831–41, 1847–9; *Morning Post* had been resigned
    to Thomas Crompton, papermaker and mortgagee in 1849, see *History of The
    Times*, II, 147, R. Lucas, *Lord Glenesk and the Morning Post* (1910).

100 *Lloyd's Weekly Newspaper*, 4 February 1849; petition presented by Cowan,
    25 February 1849.

101 *Scotsman*, 26 January 1850; *Morning Post*, 8 February 1850; for suggestion that Wood was favourably disposed see *CM*, 11 February 1850.

102 Lucas, *Lord Glenesk*, 64–5.

103 See accounts of meetings and deputations, for example *DN*, 13 February 1850.

104 For collaboration see dinner of paper makers and publishers to Charles Cowan, MP, in Edinburgh, notice *CM*, 5 December 1850.

105 See *Morning Post*, 30 January 1851. Also John Tallis. See 'The Duty on Paper', *London Journal*, 28 January 1854; *Literary Gazette*, 9 February 1850.

106 Cobden to John Cassell, 24 December 1850, Add. MS 43668, f. 130, BL; Joseph Hume letter of 25 December 1850, printed *DN*, 3 January 1851.

107 Printed in full, *DN*, 26 September 1849 (letter wrongly dated 25 June 1849, but text is the same as the 1848 pamphlet, see version in the British Library).

108 Probably the same as printed in *Morning Post*, 8 April 1850.

109 See notice in the *Yorkshire Gazette*, 28 December 1850, *Newcastle Journal*, 11 January 1851.

110 'The Paper Duties', *Economist*, 1 May 1852, 476–7; Editorial, *DN*, 24 December 1849.

111 'The Paper Duties', *Freeman's Journal*, 7 January 1851.

112 *A Claim for the Repeal of the Paper Duty* (*Exeter Gazette*, 1850), as extracted in *Hertford Mercury*, 20 April 1850, not only in printing and publishing, but also other paper-based manufactures such as papier mache, buttons, ornaments.

113 See 'The Pamphleteer', *Critic*, 15 February 1851.

114 R. C. 'State Burdens on Literature', *CEJ*, 11 January 1851.

115 *Standard of Freedom*, reprinted in *Leicestershire Mercury*, 28 December 1850.

116 'To the Yeomanry and Farmers of East Cornwall', *Royal Cornwall Gazette*, 18 June 1852.

117 Editorial, *The Times*, 23 April 1852.

118 Editorial, *CM*, 28 January 1850; in the same issue the London correspondent of the *Mercury* noted that 'The taxes on knowledge have a paramount claim to consideration'.

119 *Journal of the Society of Arts*, I (1852–3), 475–6.

120 'Taxes on Knowledge', *Tait's Edinburgh Magazine* (April 1850), 239.

121 William Foulkes (Secretary of the LFPRA) to Collet, printed *Taxes*, I, 94.

122 See George Thompson at Northampton, *Northampton Mercury*, 11 August 1849; *Liverpool Mercury*, 14 August 1849; *Scotsman*, 21 November 1849; *Freeman's Journal*, 13 February 1850.

123 Cobden wrote briefly to Francis Place 7 December 1849 suggesting that 'you could do no better than to put the matter in Gibson's hands; his animus is fairly roused upon the question, and I have no doubt he will do you justice', printed in Watkin, *Alderman Cobden*, 141. Joseph Parkes later claimed that it was he who

had introduced Place, who had asked Parkes to 'find him a "sticking" Liberal
Commons member' to lead the agitation in the Commons, Parkes to Rowland Hill
22 June 1864 [copy], Parkes Papers, UCL. It is difficult to get at the full extent of
Gibson's role – he is not the most prolific of correspondents: Bright commented
that he heard 'but rarely' from Gibson, 'he is a bad correspondent', Bright to
Cobden, 19 September 1857, Add. MS 43384, ff. 108–12, BL. But Gibson does
seem to have attempted to mobilize potential allies – see comments of Charles
Cowan, *Scotsman*, 26 January 1850 and Milner Gibson to Bright, 23 January 1850,
Add. MS 43388, f. 43, BL.

124 Dickens to Milner Gibson, 12 February 1850, *Letters of Charles Dickens, Vol. 6
1850–52* (1988), 35.

125 See reference to petitions from Boards of Guardians or town councils of Rochdale,
Manchester Times, 16 February 1850; Sheffield, *Sheffield Independent*, 16 February
1850; Bradford, *BO*, 28 March 1850; Leeds, *Leeds Intelligencer*, 6 April 1850;
letterpress printers of Manchester also sign petition, *Blackburn Standard*, 20
February 1850. Petition circulating in Carlisle, *Carlisle Journal*, 22 February 1850.
J. W. Slater of the Droylsden Mechanics' Institute, urged petitions from mechanics'
institutes, Bible societies and the like, *Manchester Times*, 2 March 1850. For
petition from Novello, 8 April 1850, see Cooper, *Novello*, 117–18.

126 *DN*, 12 March 1850 [printed as handbill, see Holyoake 7/8 (3)]; Collet, *Taxes*,
I, 101–2.

127 Correspondence published in the *DN* and the *Caledonian Mercury*, and largely in
the Second Annual Report of the NSAC, *Leader*, 11 January 1851.

128 See Howe, *Free Trade and Liberal England*, 47–8.

129 Russell to Wood, 24 February 1850, BI HALIFAX/A4/56.

130 Russell to Wood, 26 February 1850, BI HALIFAX/A4/56.

131 *DN*, 21 March 1850. Collet notes that around this time the NSAC 'received a great
deal of assistance from the *Daily News*, which allowed us occasionally to make
use of its columns', *Taxes*, I, 116. Howe comments that it 'offered a prudent fiscal
reform, a measure of progress, although it fell short of the major "experiments"
in tariff revision that the Radicals demanded', *Free Trade and Liberal England*,
48. Contemporaries were less charitable: the *Leicestershire Mercury* talked of
the 'magnificence of the impudence which characterizes the whole whole [*sic*]
proceeding', 23 March 1850.

132 Claiming that the ruse had 'destroyed the Radicals' monopoly of liberal
propos[itio]ns wh:/ they will take care no long to make now that there is a
chance of their being carried', Disraeli to Sarah Disraeli, 18 April 1850 *Disraeli
Letters*, V, 316–17. Correspondence printed in this volume shows that Disraeli
had been in touch with Peter Borthwick and the campaigners from among the
press who were hoping for some relief, see *Disraeli Letters*, V, 317, n4.

133 For a full account of the debate see *DN*, 17 April 1850; letters of Edward Cardwell and T. B. Birch, *Liverpool Mercury*, 21 May 1850; see report in *Leader*, 11 January 1851.

134 See *Leader*, 30 March, 13 April, 8 June 1850, 4, 18, 25 January, 8 February 1851. In January 1851, the NSAC announced that the *Leader* would contain a weekly article 'representing the views of the committee on the taxes on knowledge' NSAC, *Second Annual Report*, 4.

135 London correspondent of the *CM*, 30 September 1850, suggested that this optimism was shared by 'nine tenths of the newspaper press of the metropolis'.

136 Manchester correspondence, *Era*, 5 January 1851; *Leader*, 11 January 1851; *Morning Post*, 13 January 1851.

137 *Freeman's Journal*, 9 January 1851, including subscription list of over £100. *Freeman's Journal*, 17 January 1851, speaks of daily committee meetings and attempts to organize pressure across Ireland; for tracts, 6,000 of which printed for circulation, see *Freeman's Journal*, 23, 31 January 1851. Several thousand signatures collected for petition, *Freeman's Journal*, 5 February 1851.

138 Crompton presides; others include Cassell, Dickens, Knight, S. C. Hall, *London Standard*, 30 January 1851 (noted that £750 had been subscribed).

139 See *Morning Post*, 30 January 1851.

140 'From our Birmingham Correspondent, *Morning Post*, 18 January 1851; *Birmingham Gazette*, 13 January 1851.

141 *Freeman's Journal*, 23 January 1851.

142 *Leader*, 22 March 1851.

143 See account *Observer*, 23 March 1851.

144 Collet, *Taxes*, I, 126.

145 Borthwick to Disraeli, 15 April 1850 (B/XX/A/95), printed in Lucas, *Lord Glenesk*, 65.

146 Holyoake recalls discussions about a deliberate attempt to oppose the separate society, in which Bright was hesitant, but Cobden 'more fearless', *Bygones*, I, 155; Collet, *Taxes*, I, notes that the NSAC invited London radicals from the John Street Institution and the Fraternal Democrats to ensure the meeting was favourable to the general campaign against the taxes on knowledge. For an account of the meeting see also *DN*, 3 January 1851, including reprint of Hume's apology.

147 Crompton noted that he waited on 20 of the leading merchants in Manchester but found that 'not one of them knew anything about this tax'; £65 subscribed, see *Morning Post*, 13 January 1851.

148 *Morning Post*, 18 March 1851.

149 Editorial, *DN*, 20 December 1851. Durham gets Edinburgh Chamber of Commerce to endorse a call for repeal in January 1852, *CM*, 22 January 1852.

150 Collet, *Taxes*, I, 191.

151 For this deputation see *Examiner*, 1 February 1851, and disparaging description, London correspondence, *Manchester Guardian*, 22 March 1851.

152 See 'Taxes on Newspapers', *Liverpool Times*, reprinted *DN*, 6 October 1851, 'The Committee of Inquiry on the Newspaper Stamp Law', *York Herald*, 2 August 1851, noting that of the three it was the advertisement tax for which there could be no extenuation (though arguing that it is the paper duty which 'should be abolished without delay'). Editorial, *Scotsman*, 18 January 1851, ditto 29 January 1851 (tellingly supporters have become 'agitators').

153 See 'Taxes on Knowledge', *Athenaeum*, 18 January 1851.

154 See criticisms of Weston J. Hatfield, in letter to *Leader*, 8 February 1851.

155 'Bradford Freehold Land Society', *DN*, 29 January 1851.

156 Collet headed a deputation to the Executive Committee of the National Charter Association 15 January 1851, obtaining the support of the NCA, *NS*, 18 January 1851. Collet noted, *Taxes*, I, 135, that 'The separate attempt of the paper-makers gave the Chartists something to oppose.'

157 See APRTOK, *First Annual Report* [1851] (Knowsley Collection); *Examiner*, 22 February 1851.

Chapter 3

1 A. J. Lee, *The Origins of the Popular Press in England, 1855–1914* (London: Croom Helm, 1976), 49.

2 'Cheap Paper and Cheap Press', *Scottish Review*, IX (October 1861), 309–23, 310.

3 At meeting on 13 February 1851 at Fendall's Hotel (see APRTOK, *First Annual Report* [1851] (Knowsley Collection); Bright, *Diaries*, notes he was there, 118. For Novello, see Victoria L. Cooper, *The House of Novello. Practice and Policy of a Victorian Music Publisher, 1829–1866* (2003), which gives some superficial notice of Novello's role in APRTOK especially, 114–20.

4 Collet, *Taxes*, I, 137; Collet does argue that although this was 'a new start', the middle-class radicals 'left in the old hands the executive management with which they had associated themselves', and 'The policy adopted was that of the Newspaper Stamp Abolition Committee', ibid., 138. The account of the *Leader* was that the general committee of APRTOK having met on Friday 14 February, and agreed to adopt the policy of the NSAC, the NSAC committee on Wednesday 19 February met for the final time and handed over their books and papers to the new association.

5 Cobden to Collet, 6 March 1851, Add. MS. 87371, BL.

6 Bright to Cobden, 29 August 1851, Add. MS. 43383, f. 205, BL. The suggestion at this stage was Bright was not a longstanding enthusiast (he identifies Collet, rather than assuming his place in Cobden's circle is clear) and remarks 'The more I think of this question, the more I am disposed to think it important.'

7 See Cobden to Collet, 28 August 1853, Add. MS. 87371, BL, printed in *Taxes*, I, 206, which describes Collet as 'a very cool young gentleman' to have sent out a printed circular without approval.

8 Cobden to Collet, 5 December 1853, *Taxes*, I, 207, *Cobden Letters*, II, 561–2: 'cast your eye over the subscription list of the "Association" and you will see how exclusively, almost, we comprise steady, sober middle class reformers . . '. Collet, thought Cobden, was in no position to 'fling saucy phrases at the head of the chancellor of Exchequer'. Tensions between Collet and the parliamentary radicals also surface in a letter from Joseph Hume to Cobden, expressing surprise at a letter from Collet, and urging Cobden to 'state your candid opinion to him as I have done', Hume to Cobden, 12 October 1852, Add. MS. 46338, f. 173, BL.

9 Collet, *Richard Moore*, 11–12.

10 See his 'Where are you?', Cobden to Collet, 18 November 1853, Add. MS. 87371, BL. Holyoake offers a picture which suggests slightly more control in suggesting that 'At every meeting of the committee [Collet] had twenty schemes of action to lay before them, from which Bright, and Cobden and Gibson would select the most practical, and the most mischievous to the enemy', *Sixty Years an Agitator's Life* (1892), I, 280, suggesting that both Bright and Cobden attended committee meetings, and Cobden 'often sent us letters explaining principle or policy', *Bygones*, I, 155.

11 See Cobden to James Grant, 7 October 1852, Add. MS. 65136, ff. 46–8, BL, *Cobden Letters*, II, 431.

12 He presided at the annual business meeting in December 1854. The minute book for 1857–61 has Gibson attending one meeting, and Cobden none, APRTOK, 'Minute Book, 1857–61', Add. MS. 47684, BL. Between January 1857 and June 1857, 6 letters from Milner Gibson are recorded. For 1854, see *Gazette* 17 (January 1855), 4.

13 Bright to Collet, 2 April [1853], Add. MS. 87371, BL.

14 Certainly nothing like the sorts of debates which we can see around the ACLL, or the Liberation Society with its Parliamentary Committee and its Electoral Committee, see Hamer, *Electoral Pressure*, N. McCord, *The Anti-Corn Law League*.

15 See print in *Leeds Times*, 22 November 1851.

16 Collet, *Taxes*, I, 138. See various materials in the Camden collection.

17 Cobden to Joseph Sturge, 11 May 1852, Add. MS. 43656, ff. 277–8, BL, *Cobden Letters*, II, 402 (in reference to a proposed Anti-Militia Society).

18 *Leader*, 8 November 1851; 12 February 1853.

19 Cobden to Collet, 12 June 1854, printed in Watkin, *Alderman Cobden*, 159. Collet had put out a recommendation to vote for Urquhart in opposition to Russell (signed also by Novello and Moore). *Lloyd's* condemned 'the attempt that makes of a just and wise cause the miserable stalking-horse of narrow-minded malice . . . let these taxes be attacked and abolished in a fair and manly way; and let not the cry against their impolicy be turned into an election brawl', 18 June 1854. Milner Gibson wrote to Novello, 22 June 1854, noting that the advertisement was a mistake, and would 'create many enemies'; 'Do stop it. I have written to Collet', Novello-Cowden Clarke Letters, Special Collections, University of Leeds.

20 For sources see J. Ewing Ritchie, 'Rt Hon T. Milner Gibson', *National Magazine*, 8 (1860), 228–30.

21 See Cobden to Edmund Potter, 29 April 1852, MJRL. For an insightful pen portrait, see *Pall Mall Gazette* 12 May 1865.

22 See APRTOK 'Minutes', Add. MS. 47684, *passim*, BL.

23 NSAC flyer dated 19 September 1849, Holyoake 7/8/(1), Bishopsgate, published in *Democratic Review* (January 1850), 286–7. For one, see Weston J. Hatfield to *The Leader*, 8 February 1851, which notes a Cambridge Free Knowledge Society 'composed almost solely of working men'; offers to send a petition and 'a showy placard "Liberty of the Press! The Petition for the Abolition of the Taxes on Knowledge lies here for signature'.

24 Collet, *Taxes*, I, 150–1. This despite Cobden's recognition of the importance of local work, as in his comment to Walmsley that 'To carry the ballot, without which any thing else is mere sham & of doubtful use, will require lectures & an organization in every Town', Cobden to Sir J. Walmsley, 13 January 1853, Add. MS. 37108, f. 8, WSRO.

25 According to Collet, 'The tour, which extended throughout the north of England, showed how enthusiastically this movement which, ostensibly, began in the Metropolis, was received in the centres of industry', *Taxes*, I, 177–8. See *Gazette* (August 1853), 10; *Lincolnshire Chronicle*, 9 December 1853; *Stamford Mercury*, 23 December 1853; *Leamington Spa Courier*, 14 January 1854; *Lincolnshire Chronicle*, 13 January 1854.

26 Circular signed by Cobden, noting that the Association was trying to raise a £500 fund, directed at 'all friends of free trade and to all friends of education', *Sheffield Independent*, 1 May 1852. Collet had also lectured on the Songs of Shakespeare, with vocal illustrations, in aid of APRTOK at the Mechanics' Institution, Southampton Buildings, see advert, *Leader*, 24 May 1851.

27 For example, after Bunting lectured at People's College, Sheffield, efforts were made to establish an 'Anti-Knowledge Tax Society', *Norfolk News*, 10 January 1852.

28 Whereabouts unclear: see cryptic note, 8 May 1852, Holyoake Diary, Holyoake 2/55, Bishopsgate.

29 *Leader*, 4 September 1852.

30 '[A]n association for the repeal of the taxes on knowledge' was formed at Bradford, *Huddersfield Chronicle*, 18 September 1852. For the Leeds association (with support of Baines) and Wakefield (after a lecture on the taxes, see *DN*, 19 October 1852; *Newcastle Courant*, 21 January 1853; *Newcastle Guardian*, 29 January 1853; *Gazette*, 7 (December 1853). *Scotsman* talked of 'paid deputies from the little clique in London. . . . have been going about the English towns for months, seeking to awaken the public to a sense of the wrongs they endure', 5 February 1853.

31 Collet, *Taxes*, I, 178–9. On a few occasions they referred to themselves as 'branches', as in the advert of the 'Huddersfield Branch Association' for Collet's lecture, *Huddersfield Chronicle*, 8 January 1853.

32 See letter of 'A Working Man, Wolverhampton', *Lloyd's London Newspaper*, 12 December 1852.

33 At the end of 1854 the figure was 76, including 7 London districts; for the ACLL see P. A. Pickering and A. Tyrrell, *The People's Bread: A History of the Anti-Corn Law League* (2000), 44–6.

34 See Corbett at Sheffield, *Sheffield Independent*, 16 April 1853, and Taylor at Hanley, *Staffordshire Sentinel*, 28 January 1854.

35 *Carlisle Journal*, 7 January 1853.

36 See S. P. Robinson to Collet, 22 January 1853 noting materials passed on by Watts, Add. MS. 87371, BL.

37 *Blackburn Standard*, 17 March 1852; see letter of Ormerod Kenyon, *Blackburn Standard*, 24 March 1852.

38 *Norfolk News*, 7 June 1851.

39 *MX*, 20 April 1850, and correspondence generated, for example *MX*, 27 April 1850.

40 Cobden to Combe, 15 October 1852, Add. MS. 43661, ff. 38–42, BL, *Cobden Letters*, II, 432–4.

41 *Gazette* (March 1853), 7.

42 See Holyoake, Collet, *Taxes*, I, viii.

43 See *Reynolds's Newspaper*, 27 March 1853: formed on the motion of James Finlen, the Chartist, seconded by Holyoake, at a meeting chaired by Watson and addressed by Collet.

44 Collet, *Taxes*, I, 117 ('we were not in a position in 1850 even to pay all the expenses of our movement').

45 *Reasoner*, 5 December 1849; 2 January 1850.

46 See letter from Collet seeking subscriptions of 6d per member, *Eighth Half-Yearly Report of the Provincial Typographical Association [January–June 1854]*.

47 See 'Financial Report of the Newspaper Stamp Abolition Committee' 26 March 1851, Holyoake 7/8 (5), Bishopsgate. Cobden was down for a guinea, the Bookbinders Trade Society £3, 5/- from many of the committee. Costs including rent £20 and printing just under £40; total expenditure £102.0.9 and so required a

subvention of £46.16.0 to discharge all liabilities. Entries in the *Monthly Circular* of the Provincial Typographical Association, 1852–5 suggest some scattered donation by branches.

48   Cobden to Collet, 14 September 1853, Add. MS. 87371, BL.

49   'In your paper you speak of sixpenny subscriptions from working men. I never knew anything of the kind to pay its expenses. The difficulty is to find honest canvassers. No, if any considerable amount be raised, it must be in good round sums . . '. Cobden to Collet, *Taxes*, I, 206 (notes that Cobden's appeal brought in £108.3s.6d.).

50   See transmission of 5 guinea donation from Charles Buxton, Brewer and another from a Mr Janson, Cobden to J. A. Novello, 4 December 1852, MS. Eng. lett.e.129, f. 45, Bodleian Library. ('Judging by the character of the two voluntary subscriptions I have transmitted to you, it would appear that money might be obtained if it were applied for to a considerable extent – We shall want a good deal before we have finished our task.') APRTOK 'Financial Report from the 13th February 1851 to Michaelmas 1851', noted income of £208.1.6.0, including £100 from E. Lombe [Edward Lombe of Norfolk], £10 from Milner Gibson and Place, and £5 from Baldwin, Cassell, Cobden, Ewart, Le Blond, J. Smith (Bingley), and others, see Holyoake 7/8 (6).

51   Collet, *Taxes*, I, 138.

52   For example at Huddersfield, *Huddersfield Chronicle*, 22, 29 January 1853, a subscription list (mostly quite small sums), which includes 40–50 names, including £2.12.0 from the Journeyman Letterpress Printers. For a picture of Collet lecturing 'wielding his rolled-up copy of the "persecuted" *Potteries Free Press* with all the energy of Costa himself', see 'Metropolitan Memoranda', *Preston Chronicle*, 23 April 1853.

53   Cobden to Collet, 14 September 1853, Add. MS. 87371, BL.

54   Cobden to Ireland, 12 July 1855, Add. MS. 33515, ff. 104–5, BL.

55   By 1854–5 expenses were £700, and income only £300.After another temporary improvement, by the start of 1859 the finances were once again in a parlous state; the accumulated deficit was just over £483, and Collet had not been paid for 21 months and was owed £175: Circular of June 1857, APRTOK Papers, Camden Archives A01223 [unfoliated], noted that a number of gentlemen have contributed or agreed to contribute £20, including with Manchester connections Thomas Bazley, Alexander Ireland, Richard Cobden, Alexander Henry, Sir Elkanah Armitage, E. R. Langworthy, J. G. Holden.

56   Extracted from 'a northern contemporary' by *York Herald*, 17 March 1855.

57   Extensive extract, *DN*, 30 January 1852, 'Repeal of Taxes on Knowledge: Facts for Advertisers', *Norfolk News*, 7 February 1852.

58   See draft of booksellers' petition against paper duties [c.1857], APRTOK Papers, Camden Archives A01223 [unfoliated] (which includes many who are also

publishers); also two draft letters from Collet, dated 12 December 1856; one to booksellers, one to manufacturers of paper, looking at the impact of the duty on manufactures. Summer 1858 Samuel Lucas and Collet were appointed a deputation to obtain subscriptions from booksellers, 'Minutes', 11 August 1858.

59 See flyer of Novello's letter and editorial in response from *Hull Advertiser*, 28 November 1851 (Holyoake 7/8 (8)). Novello had written 'I look forward to the time, when the Duty is removed from Advertisements, to take a certain space by the year; a few lines would best answer my purpose, and if you had a page or a page and a half of such standing matter, it would pay you a good rent, and would save your composition to that extent . . .'. Similar appeal in APRTOK circular to 'the Advertisers of Great Britain' (Holyoake 7/8(9)). The *Hull Advertiser* was a radical title edited by E. F. Collins, who had acted as Joseph Hume's secretary; see reference in Hume to Cobden, 28 September 1850, Add. MS. 46338, f. 168–9, BL.

60 It was symptomatic that George Stiff (of the *London Journal*) was listed as donating £30 in July 1854, but does not appear to have been a regular contributor.

61 *London Standard*, 25 June 1858; Milner Gibson also focusing on support of the cheap press.

62 See Dorothy Thompson, *The Chartists* (1984), chapter 3 and also H. Miller, 'Popular Petitioning and the Corn Laws, 1833–1846', *English Historical Review*, 127 (2012), 882–919.

63 Miller, 'Popular Petitioning', 887–90. There was still a feeling that as elections approached MPs seeking re-election would be unlikely to go against the clearly expressed opinions of their constituencies. See Cobden to Joseph Sturge, 23 and 31 March 1852, Add. MS. 43656, ff. 263–6, 267–8, BL.

64 In the context of his agitation for decimal coinage, 'The Chancellor of the Exchequer is timid and wants public opinion expressed by Petition to justify his making progress', commented William Brown to Wilson, 18 February 1854, M20/21, WilsonPMA.

65 See the instructions for preparing petitions, *Gazette*, 16 (December 1854), 7. Again this was a well-recognized practice, see Miller, 'Popular Petitioning', 915–16, which notes the number of female petitions for the ACLL, not a feature of the taxes on knowledge campaign.

66 NSAC flyer dated 19 September 1849 (Holyoake 7/8/(1)), notes 'From every paper mill, printing office, booksellers' or bookbinders' society, Mechanics' Institution, school, religious or political association, town council and parish vestry, a petition should arise, to demand that the press should no longer be taxed.'

67 *Fifth Half-Yearly Report of the Provincial Typographical Association* [July–December 1851]. For Cobden's recognition of a role for petitioning, see Cobden to Joseph

Sturge, 13 February 1850, Add. MS. 50131, ff. 157–8, BL, *Cobden Letters*, II, 196–7. See Cobden to Joseph Sturge, 8 March 1856, Add. MS. 43722, ff. 107–8, BL.

68 Inevitably, the focus of petitioning shifted depending on the nature of campaigning activity, the political attention to specific components, and the success in achieving repeal of the individual elements of the taxes; hence prior to 1853 in some years there are significant numbers of petitions specifically for the advertisement duty, not repeated once repeal is granted.

69 There is some indication that petitioners were carefully separated into different constituencies to multiply the effect of petitions; hence in March petitions were presented from 'schoolmasters and mistresses' in the borough of Chatham and vicinity, inhabitants of Brompton, nr Chatham, members of the Young Men's Mutual Improvement Society, New Brompton, and of the Chatham, Rochester, Strood and Brompton Mechanics Institution, *Reports of the Select Committee on Public Petitions* (1852), 105.

70 See the call in the annual report of the Nottingham Operatives' Library for exertions of members for repeal of the taxes, *Nottinghamshire Guardian*, 13 February 1851. Plus Joseph Barker successfully calling on Leeds Town Council to petition against taxes, *Leeds Times*, 15 February 1851; ditto Ironside at Sheffield Town Council, *Sheffield Independent*, 15 February 1851.

71 Note evidence of Joseph Cowan having organized petitions in Newcastle, forwarded to John Burgoyne Blackett, MP, for submission, 11 April 1853, see Blackett (Wylam) MSS, ZBK/C/1/B/3/9/39, Northumberland Record Office. (Cowen had also sent Blackett petitions earlier, see Cowen to Blackett, 24 December 1852 and 21 January 1853, ZBK/C/1/B/30 and 36).

72 Fits with Miller, 'Popular Petitions', 900. It is interesting that Manchester's petitioning was dominated by employee petitions (also a majority in Yorkshire), whereas London's were overwhelmingly community petitions, ibid., 905.

73 So donations from the Manchester and Sheffield Printers' Societies in the list of donations in July 1854, *Gazette*, 12 (July 1854), 20.

74 See Figure 2, Miller, 'Popular Petitions', 899.

75 For Bowkett and his later radical career see S. Newens, 'Thomas Edward Bowkett: Nineteenth-Century Pioneer of the Working-Class Movement in East London', *History Workshop* 9 (Spring 1980), 143–8. For Passmore Edwards see P. A. Baynes, *John Passmore Edwards: An Account of His Life and Works* (1994). In 1855 he offered Gladstone a sustained analysis of the distortions of the press, the dominance of the war party and the difficulties that peace advocates had of gaining a hearing for their views. 'We want a daily organ to advocate peace on universal grounds', J. Passmore Edwards to Gladstone, 6 August 1855, Box 24, Miscellaneous Correspondence, GGPGL.

76 *Staffordshire Sentinel*, 3 March 1855, *Oddfellows' Magazine* 3 (April 1862), 65–8. Connections to Holyoake, see W. B. Smith (*Birmingham Mercury*) to Holyoake, 10 February 1849; 18 August 1850, #300, 312, 318, Holyoake Papers, CpUL.

77 *Gazette* 7 (December 1853), 3–4; *Gazette* 6 (August–November 1853), 11–12; *Gazette* 12 (July 1854), 20–1. The Sixth Annual Report of December 1854 shows a smaller subscription list from Manchester, *Gazette* (December 1854), 15–16.

78 Miller makes the point that the average size of the ACLL petitions was much smaller than the Chartist 'monster' petitions.

79 *Newcastle Guardian*, 18 August 1849; see also *Athenaeum*, 11 August 1849, extracted in *Chambers' Edinburgh Journal*, 13 October 1849.

80 Again, a good example is *Universal Postal Stamp*, passim.

81 See comments of Samuel Lucas to R. W. Smiles, 27 April 1851, M136/2/3/2159, Cobden specifically instances the recent taxes on knowledge meeting as an example 'of the interruption to which public meetings are liable in London'. Cobden was not consistent, at times expressing extreme scepticism, as in Cobden to Sturge, 29 October 1856, Add. MS. 43722, ff. 163–4, BL, but at times able, for example, to tell Samuel Morley, 'There is no other way of reaching the public ear but through a large public meeting, for, owing to the state of the newspaper press, the people can have no other unbiassed expression of opinion', Cobden to Morley, 7 March 1857, printed in E. Hodder, *The Life of Samuel Morley* (1887), 142–3.

82 Cobden to Collet, 4 May [1852], Watkin, *Alderman Cobden*, 144. At the same time, Cobden retained this model of radical work which rested explicitly on pressure from without, as he remarked in 1861, 'The middle class have never gained a step in the political scale without long labour and agitation out of doors, and the working people may depend on it they can only rise by similar efforts, and the more plainly they are told the better'. Cobden to Hargreaves, 1 March 1861, Morley, *Cobden*, II, 359.

83 Cobden to Collet, 5 December 1853, printed in Watkin, *Alderman Cobden*, 152–3; viz. his comment to Collet, 2 April 1853, 'with all kinds of agitation choked with the big loaf . . . don't assume too strongly on the part of the public a <sense> of *grievance*, of which there is really but little evidence, & above all don't breathe a syllable of <menace or> defiance', Add. MS. 87371, BL.

84 *Cobden Letters*, II, 553. For pressure on his fellow workers see Bright's thought that he might take the campaign as his 'text' if he speaks to the Bury Athenaeum in late 1853, Bright to Cobden, 5 November 1853, Add. MS. 43383, ff. 278–81, BL; Cobden is encouraging, Cobden to Bright, 9 November 1853, Add. MS. 43650, ff. 31–6, BL.

85 In 1852 the *Morning Chronicle* wrote of 'hundreds unable to obtain admission making a noise outside'.

86 See comment in *Hereford Times*, 29 May 1852, quoting the *Sun*.

87 'Election Intelligence', *DN*, 25 June 1852. At Westminster De Lacy Evans' address stood among other things on his record on the taxes on knowledge, *Morning Chronicle*, 29 June 1852, as did his opponent W. Coningham. Coningham was brought forward by the chartists in a challenge to the 'old reformers' who supported Evans, but was heavily defeated at poll, see Marc Baer, *The Rise and Fall of Radical Westminster, 1780–1890* (2012), 31–2. Cobden's later verdict on Evans was that he was 'a sham radical, & hates us all most cordially', Cobden to Henry Richard, 23 April 1852, Add. MS. 43657, ff. 132–3, BL. These cross-currents offer another instance of the difficulty of categorizing the campaign as simply a 'Manchester School' cry.

88 See collection on 1852 election, Iv/3/173, Lambeth Archives.

89 *Stamford Mercury*, 9 July 1852; *Manchester Times*, 7 July 1852.

90 For example, address 'to the electors of the United Kingdom', issued in March 1857, see APRTOK, Minutes, 11 March 1857, which urges them to reject a system of taxation which 'at once oppresses the industrious classes and starves the revenue'.

91 Noted, for example, *Burnley Advertiser*, 9 April 1859; *Stamford Mercury*, 6 May 1859. The NPPARPD issued an address calling on electors to urge the question of repeal onto candidates and secure pledges, see *WDP*, 21 April 1859.

92 Extracted in *North Wales Chronicle*, 26 November 1852.

93 Alexander Henry to R. W. Smiles, 31 December 1851, M136/2/3/1505, NPSA, Manchester Archives. See Cobden to J. A. Novello, 28 December 1852, Add. MS. 43668, ff. 189–90, BL, *Cobden Letters*, II, 460: ('I doubt the policy of *signing* the address to Lord John by a number of Electors. Send a deputation, or, let the address be signed by a "'chairman on behalf of <the city> Comm^{ee} for repealing the Taxes on knowledge"').

94 Cobden sent Brougham's letter on to Combe for it to be passed, without, Cobden stressed, notice of his involvement, to Russel of the *Scotsman*, in the hope it might sow doubts; Cobden to Combe, 7 November 1852, Add. MS. 43661, ff. 53–4, BL.

95 Cobden to Collet, 18 July 1854, Watkin, *Alderman Cobden*, 161.

96 See Gareth Stedman Jones, *Languages of Class: Studies in English Working Class History* (1984); M. Daunton, *Trusting Leviathan: The Politics of Taxation in Britain, 1793–1914* (2001).

97 See W. Griffith, *Hundred Years: The Board of Revenue, 1848–1949* (1949); Seán Réamonn, *History of the Revenue Commissioners* (1981).

98 See Lewis to Palmerston, 12 October 1856, PP/GC/LE/79, PalPUS.

99 Both Timm and Keogh emerge from the documents as little more than official ciphers, but for a description by Gladstone of Timm as 'square-headed' and with 'one of the best noses for his game (i.e. shooting) I ever knew', Gladstone to Palmerston, 13 February 1860, PP/GC/GL/24, PalPUS.

100 Collet, *Taxes*, II, 46–7.

101 Charles Cowan, *Reminiscences* (1878), 207.

102 Cobden to Collet, 28 April 1851, Collet *Taxes*, I, 145.

103 Cobden to Collet, 20 September 1853; Cobden to Collet, 22 November 1853, Add. MS. 87371, BL.

104 Cobden to Collet, 18 July 1854, Watkin, *Alderman Cobden*, 161.

105 See comments in first issue of the *PFP*, 13 February 1853.

106 William Stewart, 'John Lennox and the 'Greenock Newsclout': A Fight against the Taxes on Knowledge', *Scottish Historical Review* (1918), 322–48.

107 Collet, *Leader*, 17 January 1852.

108 *Gazette*, 12 (July 1854), 11. We can see in this a very early stage of the development of ideas of civil disobedience, a term coined by David Thoreau in America in 1848 to justify his refusal to pay a poll tax; see John Rawls, *A Theory of Justice* (1971).

109 Collet, *Taxes*, I, 115.

110 See William Gallen, memorandum to the Inland Revenue drawing their attention to publication of *Punch* without a stamp, and Thomas Keogh to Gallen, 11 May 1850 declining to enter into discussion of matter of his letter, 'in which you appear to have no personal concern', APRTOK Papers, Camden Archives.

111 Collet, *Taxes*, I, 111.

112 *Leicester Chronicle*, 15 November 1851.

113 *Gazette*, 14 (November 1854), 3–4.

114 Memorial of the NASC to the Chancellor, 13 November 1850, IR 56/9 NA. See Novello to John Wood, Chair of the Inland Revenue, 20 May 1854, *Musical Times*, 5 May, 1 July 1854; and Novello to Sir Alexander J. E. Cockburn, Attorney-General, 9 June 1854, ibid.: Novello complains about 'the present fast and loose method of threatening a prosecution (involving such heavy pecuniary loss whether successful or the contrary), but which in many instances has no other meaning than to frighten the timid out of their property'.

115 See correspondence, *Gazette*, (November 1857), 14–17.

116 These appeared both to define a newspaper as 'any paper containing public news . . . to be dispersed and made public', and also 'any paper containing any public news, intelligence, or occurrences, or any remarks or observations thereon, printed in any part of the United Kingdom for sale, and published periodically, or in parts, or numbers, at intervals not exceeding 26 days between the publication of any two such papers'.

117 Editorial, *DN*, 26 November 1851; also 'What is a Newspaper?', *Glasgow Herald*, 1 December 1851.

118 See *CM*, 26 September 1850. It was noted that return to Commons of 19 February 1850 revealed 51 registered newspapers in habit of issuing some copies without

stamp, and yet this practice is deemed illegal in the case of the *Freeholder* (copy letter of Thomas Keogh to Schofield, MP for Birmingham, 30 May 1850).

119 See notice *Kendal Mercury*, 28 September 1850. Collet, *Taxes*, I, 116–17 notes that APRTOK itself used the strategy of getting additional flyers of material published in the press for circulating as propaganda. Cobden intervened, publishing a letter attacking the prosecution in the *Wakefield Examiner*, 12 October 1850, reprinted in the *Standard of Freedom*, 19 October 1850; see *Cobden Letters*, II, 239. For summary including correspondence see evidence of Collet to SC on Newspaper Stamps, Q865. Part of the Board's justification here is that the mitigated penalty of £10 imposed does little more than recover the stamp duty that should have been paid on the 2,000 sheets issued.

120 Later provides reprints from the *English Churchman* to Sir Charles Wood, suggesting his penalty should be remitted, but without response. Published in, for example, *Newcastle Courant*, 11 April 1851. Largely covered in NSAC, *Second Annual Report* (January 1851), Holyoake7/8(13), Bishopsgate.

121 See full text of the address of 18 December 1850, published in the *Leader*, 1 February 1851. Newspapers cited include the *Protestant Magazine*, *Herald of Peace*, *Evangelical Christendom*, *Punch*, *Builder*, *Medical Times* and *Literary Gazette*. Also instances a number of pamphlets arising out of the Papal Aggression affair, including Russell's own *Letter to the Bishop of Durham*, as unstamped publications which contravene the Newspaper Act.

122 Thomas Keogh to Thornton Hunt, 23 September 1850, reprinted in *DN*, 26 September 1850, and *CM*, 3 October 1850, 2.

123 *Leader*, 18 January 1851.

124 Letter of C. J. Bunting, *Norfolk News*, 25 January 1851, *Manchester Examiner and Times*, 1 February 1851. Bunting was a longstanding supporter, lecturing on the taxes on knowledge; see *Norfolk News*, 13 December 1851.

125 See copies in Camden Archives, A01223 (which show that this was the culmination of an intermittent correspondence stretching back to at least March 1850), and evidence, *Select Committee on Newspaper Stamps*, Q1187–94.

126 Editorial, *DN*, 14 July 1851.

127 See circular, Holyoake Collection 7/8 (7), Bishopsgate.

128 G. Cornewall Lewis to Sir Charles Wood, 28 October 1851, BI HALIFAX/A4/121.

129 See 7 Exchequer Reports 92.

130 Collet, *Taxes*, I, 151–3.

131 *Leader*, 6 December 1851.

132 *Morning Post*, 9 June 1852.

133 APRTOK 1st Annual Report, extracted Collet, *Taxes*, I, 153.

134 Gardiner of the *Wisbech Record* declines, Collet, *Taxes*, I, 154–5.

135 See letters in *Leader*, and long response of Collet, *Leader*, 17 January 1852.

136   Collet, *Taxes*, I, 155–64.

137   See the first issue of *Gazette* 1 (February 1853), reprinted in the *PFP*, 12 March
      1853, and response of Thesiger in the Commons, *Hansard*, 21 May 1852.

138   *Correspondence on Unstamped Publications since 1853*, 4 [August 1853].

139   This tactic had been periodically advocated, as in the letter of W. Stevens,
      Leader, 20 December 1851; although Collet appeared as the publisher, it was
      published by George Turner, 'spirited newsagent of Stoke on Trent', Holyoake,
      Sixty Years, I, 284.

140   Milner Gibson to Collet, 16 February 1853, 'I have much more to say on this
      matter.' Milner Gibson warned Collet. Ultimately the masthead read 'Published in
      conformity with the practice of the Stamp Office, which permits records of current
      events and comments thereon to be published without stamp by the "Athenaeum",
      "Builder", "Punch", "Racing Times", &c.' *PFP*, 13 February 1853.

141   *PFP*, 5 March 1853.

142   *Norfolk Chronicle*, 25 March 1853; for an account of the case see *Worcester
      Chronicle*, 23 March 1853, and *Standard*, 25 March 1853.

143   The British Library file finishes with 10th number, 16 April 1853; Collet,
      Taxes, I, 182, suggests the paper was discontinued without published notice after
      an eleventh issue. Prosecuted and found guilty, though penalties not enforced
      on understanding that the paper was being given up, Collet's later verdict was
      that 'no censure could have been more severe than that of Baron Parke, which
      shattered into atoms the *non ejusdem generis* of the Bow Street magistrate',
      ibid., 187. For an account of the case, see *Morning Chronicle*, 18 March 1853.
      Followed briefly by an unstamped title the *Potteries Weekly Gazette*, see the letter
      in complaint of Thomas Jackson, in *Return of Correspondence relating to the
      Newspaper Stamp since 1853*, 35.

144   See the plea for donations, letter, *Leader*, 27 August 1853 (APRTOK paid Collet's
      legal expenses).

145   See *Return of Correspondence* (1853). In the face of the editor's defiance, the
      Revenue apparently decided that they could not prosecute without also having
      to prosecute the *Athenaeum*, which they were keen to avoid, *Gazette*, 4 (June
      1853), 11.

146   *Morning Post*, 18 March 1853. Similar questions from Ricardo generated a
      'lengthened discussion', see *Aris's Birmingham Gazette*, 21 March 1853.

147   Milner Gibson to Holyoake, 18 April 1853, #568, Holyoake Papers, CpUL.

148   Cobden to Collet, 5 April 1853, Add. MS. 87371, BL.

149   See 'Address', *Gazette*, 10 (April 1854), 4–11.

150   For full details of the speech, see *Morning Chronicle*, 9 February 1854.

151   For details of the case see IR 56/17 NA.

152   Summary of the Shaw case, A Brewster, 8 May 1854, IR 56/17 NA.

153 Letter and comment, *Gazette*, 9 (February 1854), 6.

154 Collet to John Wood, 11 November 1853, printed *Gazette* 9 (February 1854), 7–8. The letter gets a holding acknowledgement from Keogh, but no further or substantive response.

155 Collet, *Taxes*, I, 211.

156 *Gazette* 14 (November 1854), 9–20.

157 See *Appendix to the Thirty-First Report on Public Petitions for 1855*, (1855), 305–6.

158 'False Declarations', *Gazette* 12 (July 1854), 12–13.

159 Trumpeted in *Gazette*, 12 (July 1854), 2–3.

160 Editorial, *The Times*, 17 May 1854.

161 Cobden to Collet, 5 June 1854, Add. MS. 87371, BL.

162 Treasury minute, 4 August 1854, IR 56/19, NA. At the same time, the allowable weight increased to 3oz. New postal regulations of August 1854, *Gazette* 13 (September 1854), 1–2.

163 Holyoake's Engagement Diary, 10 January, 19 February, 5 March, 19 March 1860, Holyoake 2/110, Bishopsgate; (see *MS*, 18 January, 21 February, 30 March 1860).

164 *Gazette*, (February 1857), 5–6.

165 See Cowan, *Reminiscences*, 205–6. The delay noted in *BDP*, 18 April 1859. The 'what is paper' theme taken up by the press in its hostile editorials, see *Bath Chronicle*, 24 June 1858.

166 See APRTOK petition, 6 July 1859, *Gazette* (July 1859), 1–7; and also subsequent petition to Gladstone, 'Minutes', 15 October 1859; 'Since 1846 the Paper Duty has been arbitrarily regulated by the Treasury till it has been brought into confusion.'

167 Editorial, *BDP*, 18 April 1859.

168 Correspondence between John Scott, envelope manufacturer and the Board. January to October 1857, *Gazette* (November 1857), 7–11.

169 See address to Lord Derby, *Gazette* (June 1858), 3. The address takes some glee in rehearsing the inconsistent, arbitrary, and irrational ways in which exemptions to the paper duties were generated, arguing that there should be no restrictions but those absolutely necessary for revenue.

170 See Collet, *Taxes*, II, 46, and correspondence published in 'Eighth Annual Report', *Gazette* (January 1859), 6–9; the petitions strove to extract from the Inland Revenue an indication of what difference in principle there was between waste in envelope manufacture and in writing paper manufacture.

171 *Gazette* (June 1858), 3–5.

172 Quoted *Financial Reformer* (July 1859), 206.

173 'Minutes', 1 June 1859, themselves following up the Board's refusal of Towle, Minutes, 31 August 1859. For Towle's activities see also letter in *MS*, 10 March 1860.

174 *Gazette* (July 1859), 7–8.

175 Cowan, *Reminiscences*, 207.

176 See 'Minutes', 18 January 1860 (in response to request of Gladstone).

177 *Morning Post*, 11 February 1860.

178 Noted at APRTOK committee, 7 March 1860, and subsequent petitions.

179 G. Cornewall Lewis to Sir Charles Wood, 28 October 1851, BI HALIFAX/A4/121: 'The rule however, is a good one and I would propose to extend it to the *entire* newspaper press. . . . I w[oul]d allow all stamped copies to pass free thro' the post office, as at present'. Lewis also proposed that the restriction on the supplement be removed so that the single stamp covers all, deliberately so as to 'prevent any advantage to the local press'.

180 *Stirling Observer*, 29 March 1855; *Bristol Mercury* 24 March 1855; likewise the *Norfolk Chronicle*; extracted in *Morning Chronicle*, 26 March 1855.

Chapter 4

1 See Lansdowne to Russell, n.d. [October 1852], PRO 30/22/10E, NA.

2 See Miles Taylor, *The Decline of British Radicalism* (1995), 137–43.

3 *Leeds Times*, 17 June 1854.

4 Wood to Palmerston, 23 January 1851, PP/GC/WO/26/1–3, PalPUS.

5 One exception is Russell's indication in May 1852 that he was considering proposing a bill 'on the newspaper question – I believe it should be an enacting bill not declaratory', Russell to Wood, 13 May 1852, BI HALIFAX/A4/56.

6 Russell to Wood, 28 December 1850 and Wood to Russell, 2 January 1851, BI HALIFAX/A4/56. Howe suggests that 'despite the unfavourable reception given to Wood's budget, it met most Radical desiderata'. Howe, *Free Trade and Liberal England*, 49.

7 George Grote to Wood, 1 March 1851, BI HALIFAX/A4/181 (part 3).

8 Collet, *Taxes*, I, 146–7.

9 'The Newspaper Stamp Committee', *Blackburn Standard*, 20 August 1851.

10 *Scotsman* quoted *Blackburn Standard*, 20 August 1851; Cobden later recalled that he had invited Russel to breakfast to try to dissuade him from abandoning his free trade principles, without success, Cobden to Edward Alexander, 29 October 1864, Bodl. MS.DON.e.123 ff. 55–6. Russel provided an extended attack on the Committee in an article in the *Edinburgh Review* (October 1853), published as *The Uniform Postal Stamp on Newspapers: Its Cheapness, Fairness and Beneficial Working* [1853].

11   Editorial, *DN*, 14 July 1851. For Rich's draft report see *Morning Post*, 2 August 1851; Milner Gibson to Collet, 11 July 1851, Add. MS. 87871, BL.

12   Lee's verdict was that opponents like Mowbray Morris and Timm 'caused more damage to their own cause than to the other side', *Popular Press*, 47.

13   Milner Gibson to Collet, 17 July 1851, Add. MS. 87871, BL.

14   Hostile coverage in 'Taxes on Knowledge', *John Bull*, 2 August 1851, *Jackson's Oxford Journal*, 16 August 1851 quoting letter of 'Anti-Cant' in the *Examiner* (ditto *Royal Cornwall Gazette*, 29 August 1851), *Morning Post*, 13 August 1851, *Liverpool Courier* (see reprint, *Morning Post*, 14 August 1851).

15   'A Penny for Your Thoughts', *Nonconformist*, reprinted in *Northern Star*, 2 August 1851 ('has placed the whole subject on the basis of solid argument and accurate information'; support of editorial, *Sheffield Independent*, 2 August 1851 (asserting that 'by far the greater proportion' of newspapers were not sent through the post). Cautious agreement in 'The Newspaper Stamp', *Leeds Mercury*, 2 August 1851.

16   Editorial, *CM*, 31 July 1851.

17   'The Newspaper Stamp: Mr Rich's Draft Report', *DN*, 23 September 1851; also *DN*, 7 October 1851 ('The Postage Controversy'). See responses of Anti-Cant, *The Examiner*, 25 October 1851.

18   For example, evidence of Horace Greely, *DN*, 18 September 1851, Rowland Hill, ibid., 24 September 1851.

19   Peter W. Sinnema, *The Wake of Wellington* (2006).

20   Cobden to Robertson Gladstone, 7 February 1852, Bodleian Library, MS.Eng. lett.e.128, ff. 104–5, *Cobden Letters*, II, 374.

21   Russell to Wood, 16 August 1852, BI HALIFAX/A4/56; (see previous Russell to Wood, 13 May 1852 referring to 'A bill I think of proposing on the newspaper question – I believe it should be an enacting bill not declaratory', BI HALIFAX/ A4/56).

22   'I would, after the Manchester dinner and seeing that free trade is now safe, civilly decline all communicat[io]n with Cobden and Co' and try to make a clear line of whig principles between the radicals and Derby, Grey to Wood, 17 November 1852 and Grey to Wood, 21 November 1852, BI HALIFAX/A4/55/1.

23   Hume to Collet, 10 October 1852, published widely, for example, *Morning Chronicle*, 16 October 1852, and partly in Collet, *Taxes*, I, 170 (with italics). 'I quite despond and am disgusted', Graham remarked to Russell, 'Hume's letter makes me indignant' and shows that a cordial union of Liberals is impossible at this time, 21 October 1852, ff. 234–5, Russell Papers, PRO 30/20/10E, NA (also Graham to Ellice, 26 October 1852, ff. 118–22, MS. 15018, Ellice Papers, NLS).

24   For example, Cobden to Combe, 4 September 1852, Add. MS. 43661, ff. 29–34, BL; Cobden to Wilson, 4 October 1852, M20/19, WilsonPMA, *Cobden Letters*, II, 429–30. Hence Russell told Yarborough, 'I entirely concur with Mr Cobden in the opinion that the first thing to be done is to secure & make fast

the free trade policy . . . the object will be rather to continue & strengthen the present commercial policy than to recommend any large measures on that subject', 10 October 1852, PRO 30/22/10E/ ff. 198–9.

25 Cobden to Wilson, 18, 29 September 1852, M20/19, WilsonPMA, *Cobden Letters*, II, 425–6.

26 See 'Scheme for the Readjustment and Extension of the Duty on Advertisements', in the materials on the December 1852 budget in the Hughenden Mss, Box 32/2, B/IV/G/11a, Bodleian Library; the undated document contains calculations based on *The Times* for 9 March 1852, which suggests it was drawn up some time in March. The scheme also included proposals to tax advertisements incorporated into the wrappers of magazines, on placards and posting bills, and displayed in shops, at railway stations, etc.

27 Editorial, *CM*, 30 August 1852; Provincial Typographical Association, *Monthly Circular* (October 1852) noted that the government was reportedly 'somewhat squeezeable' on the question.

28 Angus Hawkins, *The Forgotten Prime Minister: The 14th Earl of Derby* (2 vols; 2007–8), 41–2. Blake cites instructions from Derby, 30 November 1852, B/XX/8/81 Box 109, Hughenden Papers. Stanley noted the following year that repeal of the advertisement duty 'was . . . in the first draft of Disraeli's budget, and he was reluctantly induced to keep the tax on finding the year's expenses exceed by £600,000 the sum at which he had estimated them', Vincent, *Disraeli, Derby and the Conservative Party*, 106 (entry 14 April 1853).

29 For the deputation see *London Standard*, 9 December 1852.

30 An unruly public meeting in Worcester (*Worcester Journal*, 16 December 1852), a resolution of the Manchester Town Council (*Manchester Courier*, 18 December 1852), meeting of electors at Guildhall Coffee House, City of London adopted the petition, printed *DN*, 25 December 1852.

31 Grey to Wood, 5 December 1852, BI HALIFAX/A4/55/1, Robertson Gladstone to Gladstone, 17 December 1853, File 663, Glynne-Gladstone Mss, Gladstone Library.

32 Joseph Parkes to Edward Ellice (Snr), 25 December 1852, MS. 15041, ff. 60–3, Ellice Papers, NLS.

33 '[W]ho have played so shabby a game, and of whom I think so little', Earl Grey to Wood, 22 December 1852, BI HALIFAX/A4/55/1.

34 Editorial, *Exeter and Plymouth Gazette*, 2 April 1853. Alexander Ireland was anticipating the benefits of repeal as early as January. See reference in R. Chambers to Ireland, 21 January 1853, Chambers Papers, Dep342/110, ff. 111–12, NLS.

35 See Collet's explanation of APRTOK strategy, letter, Collet to editor of *Carlisle Journal*, Liverpool, 5 January 1853, *Carlisle Journal*, 7 January 1853. Meetings also in Huddersfield, Bradford, *BO*, 20 January 1853.

36 Support of *Huddersfield Chronicle*, 22 January 1853, *BO*, 27 January 1853; others were prepared now to support repeal of advertisement tax and paper duties, although not yet the stamp, *York Herald*, 15 January 1853. There were still those who are so lukewarm as to be almost opposed, see 'The Advertisement Duty', *Aberdeen Journal*, 20 April 1853, *Derby Mercury*, 20 April 1853.

37 See *Morning Chronicle*, 14 March 1853. Gladstone notes, Add. MS. 44741, f. 122, BL; notes support of Young (*Sun*) for full repeal not to 6d; Gladstone was told that the provincial press was declining absolutely in the face of the pressure of the metropolitan press created by the expansion of the railways.

38 Editorials, *CM*, 28 October 1852; *Dundee Courier*, 24 November 1852.

39 See for example, the opinion of the *Sun* extracted by the *North Wales Chronicle*, 26 November 1852.

40 H. G. C. Matthew, 'Disraeli, Gladstone and the Politics of Mid-Victorian Budgets', *Historical Journal* (1979), 615–43.

41 Russell was apprehensive on income tax proposals (would prefer reduction to 6d), Graham to Aberdeen, 26 March 1853, Add. MS. 44574, ff. 30–1, BL.

42 See Memorandum, [18 April 1853], Add. MS. 44375, f. 67, BL. The reduction of the advertisement duty as a way of making it '(directly or indirectly) more productive' was raised with John Wood at the Treasury in letter of 18 February 1853, Add. MS. 44574, f. 43–4, BL; Wood responded, 6 April 1853, ff. 99–100 that he might repeal the stamp on supplements for little loss (£25,000) which might be recouped through a reduction of advertisement duty.

43 See W. E. Baxter to Gladstone, 7 April 1853, Add. MS. 44374, ff. 210–11, BL (completed at 44574, ff. 107–11); made cheap advertisements would become as much used in Britain as in America. Baxter's plea was for equal benefit for 'influential newspapers' as for 'minor journals'.

44 John D. Cook in an otherwise very fulsome tribute, Cook to Gladstone, 19 April [1853], Add. MS. 44374, ff. 239–40, BL; John Duncan (editor of *Yorkshireman*) to Gladstone, 1 June 1853, GGPGL.

45 Memo of 2 May 1853, Add. MS. 44778, ff. 125–6, BL. Herbert and Newcastle were sceptical that Baxter was at all typical; but there was support from Lansdowne, Wood and Granville, who remarked that 'I do not see why an arrangement becomes more desirable from the fact that it obviates the advantages which the Times has obtained by fair means over other papers', ff. 127–9.

46 *Hansard*, 14 April 1853, vol. 125, c.1129.

47 'Our men frightened when they heard that Disraeli was going to vote with us! – afraid to carry their object, fearing to hurt a Govt. which refuses them this trifle!', Bright, *Diaries*, 141 (entry 14 April 1853); Robertson Gladstone regretted defeat, 'not because I do not wish for the change sought, but defeat, in any shape, is disagreeable', Robertson Gladstone to Gladstone, 18 April 1853,#663, GGPGL.

48   Graham to Aberdeen, 14 April 1853, Add. MS. 43191, ff. 42–3, BL.

49   William Ewart to Gladstone, 15 April 1853, Add. MS. 44374, f. 228, BL.

50   Conacher suggests that the defeat was a jolt, but that 'the cabinet decided to submit, since it was agreed that the tax in question was objectionable and since it had been intended to deal with it anyway', *Aberdeen Coalition*, 63. This is not the tenor of Gladstone's memos on the budget of 11–15 April 1853 (Add. MS. 44778, ff. 84–97, 106–7, 112–13).

51   The upshot being the 1d differential between the custom duty of 1½d per lb, and the excise duty of 1½d per lb.

52   John Prest, *Lord John Russell* (1972), 358.

53   Reported by George Moffatt to Gladstone, 20 April 1853, Add. MS. 44374, ff. 247–8, BL (also reporting that Joshua Walmsley, despite ambivalences among the financial reformers, is determined to support the budget).

54   Bright, *Diaries*, 141 (17 April); 'The Newspaper Taxes', *Leeds Times*, 30 April 1853; shabby is also the word used by Cobden to F. W. Cobden, 21 April 1853, Add. MS. 6011, f. G95, WSRO, *Cobden Letters*, II, 498–9.

55   Bright, *Diaries*, 141–2.

56   Bright to Wilson, 8 May 1853, M20/20, WilsonPMA; later Bright notes a 'long talk' with Sir James Graham, pressing the same object after which Bright thinks he was 'disposed to consider the question again', Bright, *Diaries*, 147 (14 June 1853).

57   Cobden to Joseph Woodhead, 20 April 1853, KC312/17/11, West Yorkshire Archive Service, Kirklees. See Cobden to Collet, 23 April 1853, Add. MS. 87371, BL.

58   Stephen Koss, *The Rise and Fall of the Political Press in Britain* (2 vols; 1981, 1984), 68; see Add. MS. 44577, f. 21 and f. 145, BL. A number of circulars were produced for distribution to MPs and others, supporting removal of the current limitation on the size of newspapers, and so obviating the need of issuing supplements; see copy, Add. MS. 44576, f. 41, BL, including Gladstone's underlining of this point.

59   See Robert Gunn (managing proprietor and editor of the *North British Mail*) to Gladstone, 5 May 1853, Add. MS. 44576, f. 1, BL.

60   Koss, *Political Press*, 67–8, quoting Memorial (May 1853), Add. MS. 44576, f. 16, BL. The papers were *Morning Herald*, *Morning Post*, *Morning Advertiser*, *Morning Chronicle* and *Daily News*.

61   See mss copy of resolutions, Add. MS. 44575, f. 98, BL; similar resolutions were passed at a meeting of Yorkshire newspaper proprietors, see Add. MS. 44575, f. 130, BL. The meeting appointed a deputation led by Jeremiah Garnett of the *Manchester Guardian*, including Baines (*Leeds Mercury*), Livesey (*Preston Guardian*), Jaffray (*Birmingham Journal*). For the fate of this deputation which was unable to meet Gladstone because of his illness, but instead met James Wilson at the Treasury, see Jeremiah Garnett to R. W. Wilbrahim, 5 May 1853, Box 31, Miscellaneous Correspondence, GGPGL.

62 See enclosure in Gedge to R. W. Wilbrahim, 5 May 1853, Box 31, Miscellaneous Correspondence, GGPGL (a return of the opinions recorded by 60 provincial papers represented at the meeting of the Provincial Newspaper Society on 4 May 1853; 52 were in favour of removal of the stamp duty on supplements, 4 against and 4 indifferent; 20 were in favour of priority to entire removal of advertisement duty, 22 more in favour, but subordinate to removal of supplement stamp, 9 favour retention of 6d duty, plus 1 in favour of a graduated duty, 1 (the *Cheltenham Chronicle*) was against any reduction, 1 was indifferent and 6 did not record an opinion).

63 See letter of William Hargrove, 9 May 1855, Box 37, and Jeremiah Garnett to R. W. Wilbrahim, 5 May 1853, Box 31, Miscellaneous Correspondence, GGPGL.

64 *Chester Chronicle*, 17 March 1855.

65 W. E. Baxter to Gladstone, 9 June 1853, Add. MS. 44575, ff. 135–6, BL. Suggests that Christopher Kemplay of the *Leeds Intelligencer*, who chaired the meeting, 'may be actuated by an antagonistic feeling towards Mr Baines of the Leeds Mercury' which does use supplements. See also Charles Anthony of the *Hereford Times* to Gladstone, 8 June 1853, Add. MS. 44575, ff. 128–9, BL, 3 May 1853, Add. MS. 44375, ff. 5–6, BL; G. P. Bacon of the *Sussex Advertiser* to Gladstone, 4 May 1853, Add. MS. 44375, ff. 10–13, BL.

66 See meeting at Nottingham, *Nottinghamshire Guardian*, 21 April 1853, James Greig to Gladstone, 13 June 1853, Box 34, Miscellaneous Correspondence, GGPGL.

67 'We [leathered?] that Puseyite Chancellor of the Exchequer famously yesterday with his ᵈ6 advertisement duty' Cobden rejoiced (in unusually hostile fashion), Cobden to F. W. Cobden, 2 July 1853, Add. MS. 6011, folio G98, WSRO.

68 Collet, *Taxes*, I, 193–6; Bright to Wilson, 5 July 1853, M20/20, WilsonPMA; on 14 July Bright noted that there was 'Nothing yet settled about Advertisement Duty. I have given some members of the Govt. to understand that we shall consider their refusal of our wishes as . . . a declaration of war', Bright, *Diaries*, 150 (14 July 1853); likewise he told Wilson, 13 July 1853, that 'we are doing all we can privately to have the matter settled as we wish it to be', M20/20, WilsonPMA. Conacher, *Aberdeen Coalition*, 77, describes it as 'an annoying, but minor, reversal', and cites PRO 30/20/11/A ff. 132–3, 9 July 1853 showing that Gladstone sought Russell's advice as to the procedure for response.

69 Ironside to Gladstone, 6 July 1853, Add. MS. 44575, ff.195–6, BL.

70 *The Times* objected to Gladstone's failure to remove restrictions on size of newspapers, see editorial, *The Times*, 28 July 1853.

71 'Taxes on Knowledge', *Burnley Advertiser*, 6 August 1853; *Wells Journal*, 13 August 1853. Even opponents inclined to this view, see 'Notes on the Paper Duties, and the Newspaper Stamp', *Liverpool Mail*, reprinted in *Morning Post*, 27 October 1853.

72 Cobden to F. W. Cobden, 20 July 1853, Add. MS. 6011, ff. G102–3, WSRO.

73 Milner Gibson to Holyoake, 18 April 1853, #568, Holyoake Papers, CpUL.

74 Cobden to Collet, 22 November 1853, Add. MS. 87371, BL.

75 22 November 1853, *Cobden Letters*, II, 556–8, 557.

76 Bright to Cobden, 14 December 1853, Add. MS. 43383, f. 288, BL.

77 Cobden to R. W. Smiles, 23 October 1854, M136/2/3/629, NPSA Papers, Manchester Archives; see also Cobden to Combe, 8 May 1854, Add. MS. 43661, ff. 160–3, BL. Milner Gibson of very much the same mind, see Milner Gibson to R. W. Smiles, 11 November 1854, M136/2/3/1204 NPSA Papers, Manchester Archives.

78 *Gazette* 9 (February 1854), 2.

79 Spencer to Collet, 30 May 1854, Add. MS. 87371, BL.

80 Cobden to Kate Cobden, 10. May 1854, CP 80, WSRO, *Cobden Letters* III, 32–3.

81 Aberdeen told Croker in January 1855 that he 'never recollect anything like the current state of the daily press'; 'I should not have the least notion of how to organise a system of counteraction of this kind'. *Croker Papers*, II, 347–8.

82 Croker to Brougham, 21 July 1854, *Croker Papers*, II, 338–9; see also, for example, Granville to Russell, 23 December 1854, Russell Papers, PRO/30/22/11F, ff. 347–50, NA.

83 'Quite dreadful' noted Lady Clarendon, journal, 13 January 1854, *Life and Letters . . . Clarendon*, II, 37. See various references in Sir George Douglas and Sir George Dalhousie (eds), *The Panmure Papers. Being a Selection from the Correspondence of Fox Maule, Second Baron Panmure, afterwards Eleventh Earl of Dalhousie, K.T., G.C.B.* (1908), I, 104, 184, 303, 406.

84 *The Times* 'has become omnipotent and despotic from the consummate ability with which it is conducted'; various copies of this memorandum survive, for example, 15 December 1855, Ellice Papers, MS. 15103, ff. 107–16, NLS.

85 Anderson, *Liberal State at War*, citing *History of the Times*, II, 193–215.

86 Russell to Clarendon, 8 August 1855 [extract], Russell Papers, PRO/30/22/12F, ff. 26–9, NA.

87 Cobden to Mitchell, 19 April 1854, Add. MS. 13886/12, WSRO.

88 'We have seldom had occasion to notice a greater injustice, or a more shameful abandonment of duty on the part of a government', 'The Newspaper Stamp' *The Era*, 6 August 1854; in the meantime, 'impunity for refusing the law is still to be the order of the day'. In June, Milner Gibson tried to nudge Novello and the committee into renewing its encouragement of the sympathetic portion of the press, Milner Gibson to Novello, 22 June 1854, Novello-Cowden Clarke Collection, Special Collections, University of Leeds.

89 Cobden to Collet, 5 June 1854, Add. MS. 87371, BL.

90 *Manchester Examiner and Times*, 7 October 1854.

91 On the Crimean war unstamped papers see Collet, *Taxes*, II, 5–15. Ayerst notes that in response to the Manchester publications, a deputation from the established press had an interview with the government, and Gladstone as Chancellor, and the Attorney-General interviewed the proprietor of the *War Telegraph*; after a few weeks of complying with the stamp the *War Telegraph* went back to 1d, and when the stamp was off appeared at ½d for three days and 2d for the other two. But neither survived the end of 1855, David Ayerst, *Guardian. Biography of a Newspaper* (1971), 116–17.

92 For this circulation, see petition of Thomas Littleton Holt, *Appendix to the Fourth Report on Public Petitions for 1854-5* (1855), 17–19. For alignment see announced intention to form a society in Scotland in aid of APRTOK.

93 *Kendal Mercury*, 9 December 1854.

94 Memorandum of Hugh Tilsley, IR 56/22, NA.

95 Quoted *Gazette* 14 (November 1854), 5.

96 *Gazette*, 16 (December 1854), 17–18: included representatives of 38 papers (though with some dissent expressed by representatives of *Glasgow Sentinel*, *Edinburgh News*).

97 Noted *Leeds Times*, 11 November 1854; 'Stoppage of Unstamped War Publications', *North Wales Chronicle*, 2 December 1855; 'Unstamped Newspapers', *Leeds Times*, 9 December 1855; Holt, petition, *Fourth Report*, 16.

98 *Yorkshire Gazette*, 2 December 1854.

99 *Kendal Mercury*, 9 December 1854.

100 Robert McNair Wilson Cowan, *The Newspaper in Scotland: A Study of Its First Expansion, 1816-60* (1946), 284–5. *War Telegraph*, 22 November 1854, in IR 56/21, NA. Next day notes that 'with the generality of newspapers not merely closed against us, but their conductors actually clamorous for the proceedings referred to', has no choice but to submit to 'proceedings unparalleled in the present day for their arbitrary character', *War Telegraph*, 23 November 1854. Despite its circulation the *War Telegraph* 'eventuated in a fatal pecuniary loss', *Falkirk Herald*, 27 August 1857.

101 See handbill #824, Holyoake Collection, CpUL. First published on 9 December 1854; only four were published. Holyoake took the precaution of obtaining from Collet and the others a letter requesting him to publish their monthly paper for them, *Sixty Years*, I, 285–6.

102 Royle, *Victorian Infidels*, citing Holyoake, *Bygones*, I, 118–23, and Collet, *Taxes*, II, 14–16.

103 *Morning Post*, 23 December 1854. *Hansard*, 22 December 1854, Vol. 136, cc.791–2.

104 'The Newspaper Act – Systematic Violation of the Law and Culpable Negligence of the Government', *The Era*, 17 June 1855.

105   This is the implication of Bright to Wilson, 27 February 1855, M20/22, WilsonPMA; Bright comments that 'It is not possible, I think, for the Attorney General to say anything as to the non-prosecution of papers – there are many now publishing which are liable to the stamp, but I should not think it wise to run the risk with a respectable paper & responsible proprietors.'

106   William Sharman Crawford to Cobden, 25 January 1855, CP 4, 42B, WSRO.

107   Petition of Alexander Ireland, 19 April 1855, Appendix to the *Fifth Report on Public Petitions* (1855), 217.

108   Alexander Campbell to Robert Owen, 19 February 1855, #2348, Owen Papers, CpUL.

109   See notice of the bill by Milner Gibson at the AGM of APRTOK, *The Times*, 22 February 1855. Cobden suggests the bill was introduced on 20 February, although there is no record in Hansard.

110   Quoted in Shannon, *Gladstone*, I, 311.

111   Bright to Wilson, 27 February 1855, M20/22, WilsonPMA; Cobden to Mitchell, 10 March 1855, Add. MS. 13886/20, WSRO, *Cobden Letters*, III, 106. Lewis noted among the various challenges, 'an awkward question about the newspaper stamp which I have had to plunge into', Lewis to Sir Edmund Head, 18 March 1855, reprinted in Head, 'Introduction' to Sir George Cornewall Lewis, *Essays on the Administrations of Great Britain from 1783 to 1830* (1864), xvii–xviii; Cobden to Mitchell, 11 May 1855, Add. MS. 13886/21, WSRO: 'he is not strong of speech and the house is utterly without head', *Cobden Letters*, III, 124.

112   Cobden to Mitchell, 19 February 1855, Add. MS. 13886/19, WSRO; Bright to Duncan Maclaren, 5 March 1855, 1/77/2, Maclaren Papers, University of Nottingham.

113   'An Unrestricted Press', *The Field*, extracted in *Reading Mercury*, 17 March 1854.

114   Editorial, *The Times*, 5 March 1855, disputes that the Post Office can't distribute *The Times* weighing 6oz at a profit for 1d. Looking back in 1858, the *London Standard*, at that point attempting to reposition itself at the forefront of the 'cheap press', wrote of 'a succession of convulsive leading articles, alternately growling and whining, threatening and pleading' 'which denoted the discomposure of the conductors of that journal' at its unpopularity and the threat that the proposed change might bring, 27 May 1858.

115   J. Walter to Dasent, 8 April [1855?], Delane Papers, TT/ED/JTD/6/22, TNA.

116   Arthur I. Dasent, *John Thadeus Delane, Editor of 'The Times'. His Life and Correspondence* (1908), I, 224.

117   See, for example, the contribution of J. F. Maguire (MP for Dungarvon) to the adjourned third reading of the Newspaper Stamp Bill on 11 May 1855, *The Times*, 12 May 1855.

118   For the resolutions of the Scottish newspaper proprietors, 17 March, led by Pagan of the *Glasgow Herald*, supported by Gunn of the *North British Daily Mail*,

and Alexander of the *Glasgow Courier*, see *Aberdeen Journal*, 28 March 1855.
The *Newcastle Guardian* noted a circular 'Objections to the Newspaper Stamp
Act', a 'notable eclecticism of twaddle. . . . [which] vanished on the mere touch,
their fallacies being too flimsy to bear the ordeal of examination, and their fears
too ridiculous to awaken sympathy or even excite compassion', 'Public Opinion
and the Press', 31 March 1855. See petition of the proprietors of the *Leicestershire
Journal, Leicester Advertiser* and *Leicestershire Mercury, Appendix to the Twenty-
fifth Report on Public Petitions* (1855), 217; ditto proprietors of newspapers
printed in county and city of Worcester, ibid., *Twenty-fourth Report*, 204.

119 *Scotsman*, 19 October 1864.

120 'The Newspaper Stamp', *The Times*, 13 March 1855, 12; full set with rebuttal,
Editorial, *Leeds Mercury*, 17 March 1855.

121 See the scathing response in *Manchester Examiner and Times*, 14 March 1855:
claims that the *Times* 'forges a pretext for doing so indirectly out of a gross and
palpable misrepresentation of the bill', quoting the *Times* editorial of 17 May 1854.

122 *Sussex Advertiser*, 20 March 1855.

123 Cornewall Lewis to Palmerston, 10 April 1855, PP/GC/LE/17, PalmerstonPUS;
prepared to proceed on the basis that 'The Exchequer is now, and has been for
some time, inconveniently low', and the government cannot proceed on the
assumption of peace being signed (see also /LE/18, note of 18 April 1855). Lewis
was sufficiently concerned to be musing on the possibilities of raising the paper
duty, and even abandoning the penny post for a 2d postal rate, see letter fragment,
?1855, PP/GC/LE/19, PalmerstonPUS.

124 Gladstone had briefed Lewis carefully on the provisions of the budget, and warned
him specifically 'that the Newspaper Stamp Bill might very probably cause trouble,
not only directly but indirectly and in [unexpected?] forms', memo, 3 March
1855, Add. MS. 44778, ff. 197–8, BL. On 20 March Gladstone told Lewis that he
'regretted' the changes to the Stamp Bill, and predicted that the clauses respecting
registration and securities would not pass, memo, 20 March 1855, Add. MS.
44778, f. 201, BL.

125 See extract in *Morning Chronicle*, 26 March 1855; the *Gazette* also suggested
there would be considerable Conservative opposition, not organized by the
parliamentary leadership, but supported by it. Hostile editorials in, for example,
the *Sunday Times* ('operation about which the public is utterly indifferent, and to
which all whom it affects are strongly opposed'), see reprint in *Morning Chronicle*,
26 March 1855.

126 Sir Edward Bulwer Lytton to Disraeli, [29 March 1855], Hughendon Papers,
B/XX/LY/193, *Disraeli Letters*, VI, 414, n3.

127 See *The Times* circular distributed to MPs, *The Times*, 19 March 1855, along with
a whole series of editorial interventions, including 16, 19, 22 March 1855 and
25 April 1855.

128 Noted and supported, *The Times*, 9 April 1855, *Preston Chronicle*, 7 April 1855, which argues (apparently entirely unconscious of irony), that 'If we are to have, as promised, penny newspapers, a postage charge of a penny will be a tax of a hundred per cent, amounting to an absolute prohibition of their circulation by post'. The memorial of the Yorkshire proprietors argued that the press would actively seek alternative ways of distributing their copies and that the result would be a very substantial drop in the revenue of the Post Office; so the ½d rate was plugged both as a way of encouraging more to take the stamped copy in the first place, and then of reducing the incentive to seek alternative modes of distribution.

129 Speakers at the St Martin's Hall meeting repeatedly attempted to deny that the stamp duty was a tax, while almost in the same breath questioning the wisdom of giving up a large revenue, easily raised, see *Morning Chronicle*, 23 March 1855.

130 *Leader*, 14 April 1855. Similar meeting of newspaper proprietors of Worcestershire, Warwickshire and Staffordshire was noticed, *Worcestershire Chronicle*, 18 April 1855, *Birmingham Gazette*, 16 April 1855: included Smith of the *Birmingham Mercury*, Bray of the *Coventry Herald* and props of the *Worcester Herald*, *Worcester Journal* and *Worcester Chronicle*.

131 London Correspondence, *Manchester Guardian*, 21 March 1855.

132 *Leeds Mercury*, 28 April 1855; there was some anger that Milner Gibson, focusing on his attempt to obtain the same privileges for all printed matter, opposed the 1/2d measure. Reprinted *Sheffield Independent*, 5 May 1855.

133 See 'Stamp Duty on Newspapers', *DN*, 23 March 1855. Edward Truelove was a John Street socialist who became a bookseller and publisher, with offices at 240 Strand, and was involved in related activities to defend the rights to publish radical and rationalist publications, see Royle, *Victorian Infidels*, 254.

134 Bright to Wilson, 21 February 1855, M20/22, WilsonPMA; Bright's verdict was that 'Meeting enthusiastic, and all went off well', Bright, *Diaries*, 187 (entry for 21 February 1855).

135 Bright's diary just has the observation on the second reading in the Commons that 'Our labours on this question have had a great result, and earlier than we at one time expected. Milner Gibson's conduct of the question has been admirable, and Cobden and I have given him throughout our hearty assistance', Bright, *Diaries*, 196 (entry for 11 May 1855).

136 Brougham to Cobden, 2 October 1854, Add. MS. 43668, ff. 180–1, BL. For Cobden's response see Brougham Papers 833, UCL, *Cobden Letters*, II, 445–6.

137 Peter Burke, *The Copyright Law and the Press: An Essay to Show the Necessity of an Immediate Amendment of the Copyright Law upon the Removal of the Stamp Duty on Newspapers* (1855), 4.

138 Editorials, *The Times*, 27 and 28 March 1855. See also *DN*, 5, 20 March 1855, *Morning Post*, 20 March 1855.

139 Joining the game of inventing titles, the *Morning Post* returned with 'The *Finsbury Democrat*, the *Westminster Radical*, the *Whitechapel Republican* [etc.] . . . with some scraps of local news added to the information stolen without acknowledgement . . .', 'Journals whose only capital will be systematic fraud and robbery', *Morning Post*, 24 May 1855.

140 See *The Times*, 20 April 1855, noting that the new clauses would make the process of prosecution for breach of copyright easier; the paper recognized that protection of its rights would not be straightforward, but argued that it should be left to the injured parties to decide if they wished to enforce or abandon their rights.

141 The *North Wales Chronicle* noted that provincial proprietors were petitioning against, not because they wanted to appropriate, but because 'it will be impossible to give their subscribers any early and important news without laying themselves open to information and a fine', 28 April 1855. See editorial, *Hertford Mercury and Reformer*, 21 April 1855. The *Scotsman* carried a hostile editorial, 21 April 1855: news is not invented it is only *carried*.

142 *The Times*, 1 May 1855. Bright noted to Elizabeth Bright that the *Times* had 'rather an amusing discussion on newspaper copyright, which said copyright we rejected without a division', 1 May 1855, 65 Box 3, Ogden Mss, UCL.

143 Little item in *The Times*, 4 May 1855, 12. The *Scotsman* was scathing – Lewis's three new clauses were quite as long and as important as the original bill; then he apparently withdraws them again, or strikes out three and half of the clauses he already had, and the upshot of it all is that Lewis accepts that the bill will not clarify the definition of what is a newspaper, which was ostensibly a key reason for the legislation in the first place, editorial, 9 May 1855.

Chapter 5

1 In June 1854 he had caused consternation by announcing without consultation that the Association was endorsing Urquhart's candidature for the City of London, where he was standing against Russell, and in August his prominent intervention in the London meeting on the Polish problem, which subverted it into a call for the resignation of Palmerston, gained him further notoriety, see comments of *DN*, 10 August 1855. Collet also speaks to form a People's Provision League to campaign for a reduction in the price of bread, *Lloyd's Weekly News*, 11 November 1855 (the PPL seeks revision of the 1838 Turkish tariff, and the treaty of August 1838, see *Yorkshire Gazette*, 17 November 1855, which tars APRTOK retrospectively with association with this sort of nonsense through the Collet connection; *Examiner*, 29 December 1855.

2   See circular, dated 28 February 1856, Camden Archives. Despite Cobden's warnings (23 February 1856, Add. MS. 87371, BL), this meeting seems to have concentrated on liquidating the Association's debt; *London Standard*, 28 October 1856; manuscript circular, June 1857, Camden, suggests the association revived in November.

3   See draft in Camden Archives. This could be the invitation which was refused 'and negotiations were broken off', mentioned in Collet, *Taxes*, II, 30.

4   See editorial, *York Herald*, 22 November 1856. 'The Various Aspects of the Paper Duty', *Leeds Mercury*, 15 November 1856; 'The Duty on Paper', *Blackburn Standard*, 19 November 1856; *York Herald*, 29 November 1856 (which quote directly from the APRTOK circular).

5   *Dundee Advertiser*, 19 December 1856.

6   G. Cornewall Lewis to Palmerston, 31 August 1856, PP/GC/LE/76, PalPUS.

7   *Hull Packet*, 30 January 1857.

8   Circular of June 1857, Camden Archives.

9   Collet, *Taxes*, II, 37–41, *DN*, 5 February 1857.

10 Hawkins, *Forgotten Prime Minister*, 173, *idem, Art of Politics*, 55–6. In *Taxes*, II, 37, Collet notes that he did at one point succeed in carrying a motion at the St Pancras Vestry Hall that the income tax be kept at 10d to allow for repeal of Paper Duty, but generally accepted that 7d was the absolute limit public opinion would accept.

11 Derby to Disraeli, 24 April 1857, Hughenden Mss B/XX/S/148, quoted by Hawkins, *Art of Politics*, 70; Hawkins notes it was not the blanket rout of Radicalism it is sometimes portrayed.

12 Cobden to Samuel Morley, 15 April 1857, Add. MS. 43669, ff. 109–10, BL.

13 J. B. Smith to Cobden, 20 May [1857], Add. MS. 43669, ff. 136–40, BL.

14 Taylor, *Decline of Radicalism*, 275–80.

15 Collet, *Taxes*, II, 42. Radicals waited anxiously for renewal of action: 'Are the men of the Manchester School likely to rally again?' George Thompson asked F. W. Chesson, 21 November 1857, REAS/3/3/1, English Papers, MJRL.

16 Cobden to George Combe, 5 July 1858, Add. MS. 43661, ff. 232–3, BL.

17 *National Reform Record*, No.1. 5, November 1858, 41.

18 See R.E. Ridley to Cowen, 2 March 1858, COW/C/72 TWAS: "Taxation, I will admit, *prevents* the press from being what it ought to become, is a great hindrance to its thorough freedom. But since taxation has become excessive our press had not degenerated in any of its sections'.

19 See account of meeting in Manchester, *Bury Times*, 20 February 1858.

20 Gladstone to Wilson, 20 February 1858, M20/28, WilsonPMA.

21 Prompted considerable press support, see long editorial in *Morning Chronicle*, 17 April 1858, *CM*, 19 April 1858.

22 Hawkins, *Liberal State*, 132–3. Generally well-received, although here was some opposition from Herbert Ingram, Bailey, *Ingram*, 133–4, 261–73.

23 Editorial, *CM*, 23 June 1859. Endorsement from across the spectrum, including praise even from *The Times*, see also 'The Worst Tax', *Liverpool Mercury*, 23 June 1858, London letter of *Manchester Weekly Times*, 26 June 1858, *BDP*, 23 June 1858.

24 See London correspondent of the *Bury Times*, 31 July 1858, 14 August 1858.

25 *Critic* reprinted *Morning Chronicle*, 12 July 1858.

26 See Holyoake in Collet, *Taxes on Knowledge*, I, vii, *Leader*, 17 July 1858; Henry Vizetelly to Collet, 29 July 1858, Add. MS. 87371, BL. A separate association was also formed in Birmingham, *Gazette* (January 1859), 11. Support from the *Daily Telegraph*, *Morning Star* and the *Standard*, see *Standard*, 13 July 1858; dismissed by *Manchester Courier*, 17 July 1858 as merely the cheap press. The London correspondent of the *Bury Times* noted that 'there were not fifty of us there, but wondrous was the power in that little room', 17 July 1858.

27 John Cassell to William Chambers, 6 September 1858, Dep341/86, Chambers Papers, f. 29, NLS; *CM*, 28, 29 October 1858; supporters included John Ritchie (*Scotsman*); also in attendance and apparently in support James Robie (*Caledonian Mercury*), John Stewart (*Edinburgh News*), Greig (*Scottish Press*), C. R. Brown (*Daily Bulletin*). For Dublin see *Freeman's Journal*, 21, 27 October 1858; support from Robinson of the *Daily Express*, James M'Donnell (paper manufacturer), Faulkener, Alexander Thom (Queen's Printer), James Anderson Scott (editor of *Evening Packet*). For Bristol see *WDP*, 10 December 1858. Details of the various committees printed in NPPARPD, *Free Trade in Paper* (1860).

28 *Belfast News-Letter*, 30 October 1858. Cassell also plugged the cause in his temperance lectures, *Leicestershire Mercury*, 8 January 1859.

29 *Freeman's Journal*, 2 November 1858, 14 January and 9 April 1859.

30 The *Western Flying Post*, 16 November 1858; *The Era*, 24 October 1858.

31 Quoted in *North Devon Journal*, 17 February 1859; and later extract from *Magnet* quoted *North Devon Journal*, 28 April 1859.

32 *Leeds Intelligencer*, 26 June 1858.

33 See account of Café Royal Dinner, Edinburgh, *London Standard*, 2 November 1858.

34 Agreed at a meeting in Leeds, 6 April 1858.

35 *London Standard*, 15 February 1859.

36 Response from Belfast, see *Belfast News-Letter*, 16 July 1858. See refusal of Southampton Chamber of Commerce, *Hampshire Telegraph*, 19 March 1859; inconclusive debate in Liverpool Chamber of Commerce in January 1860, *Glasgow Herald*, 31 January 1860.

37 APRTOK was virtually invisible, while the NPPARPD was even inserting adverts noting the iniquity of the tax and seeking subscriptions, see *Newcastle Courant*,

21 January 1859. Some evidence of continued work behind the scenes, for example in getting up 'a good array of petitions', see Collet to Joseph Cowen, 7 December 1858, COW/C/329, TWAS.

38 'The Paper Duty', *Era*, 19 December 1858.

39 *Dumfries Courier*, extracted in the *London Standard*, 5 August 1858. For the delegation to London Society of Compositors, led by Thornton Hunt and Collet, see *Morning Chronicle*, 28 October 1858, *Freeman's Journal*, 29 October 1858. For meeting of Master Printers with Cassell in chair, see *Morning Post*, 19 November 1858. Occasionally referred to as the Association for the Repeal of the Paper Duty, see *Leeds Times*, 23 April 1859; *BDP*, 23 December 1858.

40 Included correspondence with Mr Mead, formerly editor of the *Friend of India*, on supply of a substance made from manila hemp that would make first class paper, *Tax upon Paper*, 21–2.

41 'A Working Man', *BDP*, 18 January 1859, and *idem*, 19 January 1859; comment of R. Charleton, *WDP*, 10 December.

42 See version of Chambers, reported in *CM*, 23 February 1859.

43 See for example, *Nottinghamshire Guardian*, 3 February 1859.

44 Speech at Ashton, *DN*, 9 December 1858.

45 See Ghosh, 'Disraelian Conservatism', 283–4. For the response to Derby's words, see Chambers' report, *CM*, 23 February 1859.

46 The central thrust of his February 1856 'Memorandum on Finance', Shannon, *Gladstone*, I, 400.

47 Editorial, *London Standard*, 28 June 1859. Similar observation in the *Scientific Englishman*, quoted in *Hereford Times*, 2 July 1859, ditto *Kentish Chronicle*, 9 July 1859, 'The Paper Duty', *North British Daily Mail*, reprinted, *Freeman's Journal*, 12 July 1859.

48 See W. L. Humphrey [?] (Sheffield) to Gladstone, 19 July 1859, Add. MS. 44392, ff. 64–5, BL.

49 Gladstone to Palmerston, 25 November 1859, PP/GC/GL/20, PalPUS. On income tax see correspondence with Charles Pressley, Add. MS. 44392, passim, BL.

50 Gladstone to Robertson Gladstone, 2 August 1859, Add. MS. 44530, f. 57, BL.

51 Bright to Cobden, 6 October 1859, f. 21 and 12 December 1859, CP 20, f. 40, WSRO.

52 Editorial, *Leeds Times*, 24 December 1859.

53 'Repeal of the Paper Duty', *DN*, 17 December 1859.

54 Coningham at Brighton, *Reynolds's Newspaper*, 22 January 1860.

55 *Bright Diaries*, 244 (entry for 25 January 1860), including Sir James Graham, 'strong for repeal of Paper Duty', 247 (entry for 1 February 1860).

56 Gladstone to Ayrton, 25 January 1860, Add. MS. 87371, BL. Cobden confided in Bright that 'I am receiving the most urgent <indeed most annoying> letters from Gladstone, begging me to get *something* into the ~~tariff~~ Treaty binding the French

government to some measures of *immediate* reduction of duties, & telling me that less importance is attached to a low maximum <for everything> in Oct 1861 than to *something* being done *now!*', 16 January 1860, Add. MS. 43651, ff. 60–7, BL.

57 Maxwell, *Life and Letters of . . . Clarendon*, II, 208.

58 Gladstone to Palmerston, 7 February 1860, PP/GC/GL/22 PalPUS.

59 See Gladstone to Lord Cowley [copy], 25 January 1860, Add. MS. 44393 ff. 64–5, BL; Gladstone to Palmerston, 8 February 1860, PP/GC/GL/23/1, PalPUS. Palmerston had made it clear in a letter to Sir Charles Wood 14 January 1860, that he was concerned that Gladstone's proposals would be used as a basis to oppose expenditure on the naval and military establishment and fortifications, BI HALIFAX/A4/63/125.

60 See *Memoirs of Adam Black* (1885), 196–7.

61 Jenkins (ed.), *Trelawny Diaries*, 98; Samuel Laing to Gladstone, 11 February [1860], Add. MS. 44393, ff. 99–100, BL.

62 Frederic Hill described it as 'so great a trouble to us, and so fertile a source of error, abuse and complaint', that he was determined to remove it, without disadvantaging newspaper proprietors. Frederic Hill to Edward Baines, 14 March 1860, quoted *Belfast News-Letter*, 24 March 1860. Gladstone had been in correspondence with Rowland Hill about the impact of a revised postal arrangement which covered papers of up to 4oz (which Hill argued would include almost all papers bar *The Times* and the *Illustrated London News*), see Rowland Hill to Gladstone, 31 January 1860, ff. 77–8; Hill to Gladstone, 10 February 1860, Add. MS. 44393, ff. 88–9, BL.

63 'Private Correspondence', *BDP*, 13 February 1860. By the next day Argyll was reporting that 'Already I hear of members saying they would prefer to keep the paper duty and get off the penny income tax', Ian Campbell, Duchess of Argyll, *Autobiography and Memoirs of George Douglas Campbell, Duke of Argyll* (1906), II, 155. In contrast, Chesson recorded it in his diary as 'great economical reforms which have not been equalled since the adoption of free trade', noting in particular the 'great boon to the cheap press' offered by the repeal of the paper duties, 10 February 1860, Chesson Diaries, REAS/11/7, English Papers, MJRL.

64 Cobden to Julie Salis Schwabe, 15 February 1860, Yale University Library. See also Bright to Cobden, 13 and 26 February 1860, Add. MS. 43383, ff. 185–6, ff. 187–90, BL.

65 See for example debates in the Liverpool Chamber of Commerce, with some opposition from the paper and shipping interests, but ultimately a majority in favour, *The Times*, 20 February 1860.

66 Bright to Cobden, 5 February 1860, Add. MS. 43383, ff. 179–81, BL; see petitions and addresses, CP, 1010–22, WSRO.

67 See extract of W. J. R. Jeffery to Robertson Gladstone, 12 February 1860, file 665, GGPGL.

68 'The Budget and the Country', *BDP*, 13 February 1860.

69 Editorial, *Sheffield Independent*, 11 February 1860; Maxwell, *Life and Letters of . . . Clarendon*, II, 208.

70 Robert Cecil [Lord Salisbury], 'The Budget and the Reform Bill', *Quarterly Review* (April 1860), 523, quoted in Stewart, 'Conservative Reaction', 104.

71 Not even the *Standard* was propitiated by the paper duty repeal, railing against an incoherent filigree scheme, *London Standard*, 13 February 1860; London correspondence, *Yorkshire Gazette*, 10 March 1860.

72 See Cowan, *Reminiscences*, 210–11. Thomas Wrigley of Bury contributed two letters to the *The Times*, and *The Times* further endorsed the position with several editorials; for a summary see Thomas Wrigley, *The Case of the Paper Makers* (1864). At the end of February Gladstone had predicted 'a strong and perhaps formidable' campaign to limit the free entry of paper goods to those countries allowing the export of rags, and that the government 'might be pressed – and even beaten – through the combination of *party* interests with those of *Class*' on this question. Gladstone to Lord Cowley [copy], 28 and 29 February 1860, Add. MS. 44574, ff. 179–80, ff. 182–3, BL; Gladstone pressed Cowley to try to get 'some expression of willingness to allow the Export of Rags', f. 180.

73 Nicholl, *Great Movements*, 344–5, *The Times*, 20 February 1860; A. Kintrea to Gladstone (with memorial from paper manufacturers), 15 February 1860, Box 49, GGPGL. Various responses, including letter of Moy Thomas in *Morning Star*. Milner Gibson assured Gladstone that the paper-makers cry was unjustified and simply protectionist, Milner Gibson to Gladstone, Add. MS. 44574, ff. 254–5, BL.

74 Cobden to Michel Chevalier, 26 February 1860, W. S. Lindsay, *Incidents in the Life of Richard Cobden Esq.* (privately printed, 1869).

75 *The Times*, 15 March 1860.

76 Joan Evans, *The Endless Web: John Dickenson and Co, Ltd, 1804–1954* (1955), 104.

77 First in two letters published in the *Morning Advertiser*, 27 and 28 February 1860, then as Henry G. Bohn, *The paper duty considered in reference to its action on the literature and trade of Great Britain: showing that its abolition on the terms now proposed in Parliament would be prejudicial to both* (1860).

78 Editorial, *The Times*, 11 February 1860. It was certainly believed at Printing House Square that *The Times* 'shall come out of this matter without loss, perhaps even with an increase, as heretofore on similar occasions', Mowbray Morris told Thomas Wrigley, 15 March 1860, Managers Letterbooks (first series), 10/47, TNA.

79 E. J. Stanley to Henrietta Maria Stanley, 11 February 1860, DSA 99/8, Stanley Papers, CRO.

80 Editorial, *The Times*, 13 February 1860. Coleman notes that Delane was on close terms with the families who owned the Dickenson paper company, as well as having his own direct interest in Delane, Magnay and Co., *British Paper*, 330.

81 Editorials, *The Times*, 13, 14, 21, 24 and 27 March 1860; letters of Thomas Wrigley, *The Times*, 9, 21 and 26 March 1860. Supported by Richard Herring, author of *Paper and Paper Making, Ancient and Modern* who argues that the paper produced by Routledge, was serviceable perhaps for 'the commonest description of the penny newspapers, . . . [but] for the great bulk of printing paper is utterly useless', *The Times*, 12 March 1860, and by A PAPERMAKER, ibid., and A Country Papermaker, ibid., 19 March 1860.

82 Bright to Cobden, 20 May 1860, Add. MS. 43384, ff. 197–202, BL. Cobden told Rawson that 'the opposition . . . is so clearly dishonest . . . that a majority of the House will hardly be likely to lend itself to such merely piecemeal and sinister objects', 4 April 1860, CP 83, ff. 56–7, WSRO.

83 See full text, *MS*, 18 February 1860; a meeting of newspaper proprietors of Lancashire and Cheshire petitioned in support, see note in *MS*, 22 February 1860. Further address of the NPPARPD dated 6 March, opposing item by item the arguments in against repeal, see *MS*, 8 March 1860; for an account of the meeting, see *Cheltenham Chronicle*, 6 March.

84 *MS*, 1 March 1860. *Staffordshire Sentinel*, 25 February 1860. Editorial, *York Herald*, 25 February 1860, 'Newspaper Stamp', *Carlisle Journal*, 20 March 1860.

85 *MS*, 2 March 1860.

86 Collet, *Taxes*, II, 89–95.

87 See entries for 19 and 24 February, 4, 5 and 6 March 1860, Holyoake Engagement Diary, Holyoake Papers 2/110, Bishopsgate.

88 Minutes, 22 March 1860; published in full in *MS*, 17 March 1860 and *MS*, 29 March 1860. For account of the paper-makers' meeting, which included interventions of Baldwin noting that many who were now supporting protection, including Wrigley, had until very recently held the position that with the repeal of the excise duty should go the import duty on paper, see *MS*, 22 March 1860, *The Times*, 22 March 1860. Wrigley asserted that 'Those who would be benefitted were the proprietors of newspapers and the publishers of books; the readers of penny newspapers and books would not get a fraction of the remitted duty into their pockets.' Several speakers dismissed Baldwin as having atypical interests because he only made cheaper sorts of paper; see also 'The Paper Makers' Demand on the Public Purse Examined', APRTOK Minutes, 16 May 1860.

89 W. E. Gladstone, 'Free-trade, Railways and Commerce', *Nineteenth Century* VII (1880), 374.

90 Denis Le Marchant to Brougham, 14 March 1860, Brougham Papers, 43159, UCL. On 4 April Cobden noted 'I have seen Gibson to day, he seems pretty sure that paper will pass, and yet he says there are tremendous efforts made to prevent it', Cobden to Rawson, CP 83, ff. 56–7, WSRO.

91 Sir G. C. Lewis to Clarendon, 13 April 1860, Maxwell, *Life and Letters of . . . Clarendon*, II, 213. For William Cory 'The vice of the Budget is this: that it looks like "log-rolling" or coalition bargaining'; Palmerstonians spending millions more than needed on defence to trump Pakington etc., while 'the non-Whig member of the Cabinet, Mr Gibson, drawing with him the support of Bright, is to be allowed his million for paper duties', Cory to W. H. Gladstone, 12 April 1860, *Letters and Journals of William Cory*, 71–4.

92 Gladstone to Palmerston, 29 March 1860, PP/GC/GL/29, PalPUS, as well as correspondence in Guadella, 133–4.

93 See Hawkins, *Forgotten Prime Minister*, 245–6 (quoting Greville, *Journal*, viii, 315, Malmesbury to Derby, 23 April 1860, Derby Mss, 144/2a), Shannon, *Gladstone*, I, 423, citing *Letters of Queen Victoria*, III, 429. Through Spring 1860 Disraeli and Derby were kept informed of cabinet discussions by C. P. Villiers, see *Disraeli Letters*, VIII, 5 n1.

94 At this point, there were efforts behind the scenes to try to obtain some concession from the French in the form of a duty rather than absolute prohibition of the export of rags, see Cobden to Lord Cowley, 9 May 1860, FO519/300, NA, Cobden to Gladstone, 11 May 1860, Add. MS. 44135, ff. 295–6, BL.

95 G. Cornewall Lewis to Palmerston, 4 May [1860], PP/GC/LE/127, PalPUS.

96 J. R. Jeffery to Robertson Gladstone, copy in RG to Gladstone, 16 May 1860, File 665, GGPGL.

97 Robertson Gladstone to Gladstone, 15 May 1860, File 665, GGPGL.

98 It was suggested by an editorial in the *Bath Chronicle* that this was a scheme which had been urged by the Post Office, 'where newspapers are regarded with especial dislike', but Gladstone pleaded the impossibility of effecting the change in the absence of Rowland Hill, Editorial, *Scotsman*, 16 May 1860.

99 See comments of Le Marchant to Brougham, [Mon before Lords debate] 16716, Clarendon to Brougham, 17 May 1860, Brougham Papers, UCL; Granville urged Palmerston to contact Liberal peers to warn them not to let the House of Lords take an imprudent step, Granville to Palmerston, 17 May 1860, PP/GC/GR, PalPUS.

100 Henry Slack to Cowen, 31 May 1860, COW/C/1405, TWAS. At a number of points Cobden suggested to correspondents that if only the government would indicate its determination to resign if defeated, the Lords would not dare persist; see for example, Cobden to Hargreaves, 21 May 1860, Add. MS. 43655, ff. 122–3, BL.

101 See account of debate at Wylde's Reading Rooms, *MS*, 15 May 1860.

102 Published in *MS*, 14 May 1860. See 'Memo on the relations of the two Houses of Parliament on matters of supply and taxation' (Confidential: Printed Solely for the use of the Cabinet), May 15, 1860, Ne c.12677, Newcastle Papers, University of

Nottingham. See also the printed sheet 'Lord Lyndhurst, the Peers and the Paper Duty', taken from *Manchester Examiner and Times*, 16 May 1860, Ne c 12696, Newcastle Papers.

103 *MS*, 16 May 1860. Followed by a working-class meeting in the same hall, Richard Moore in the chair, and Wilks, Holyoake, Lucraft among the speakers. Letter of J. H. and R. C. Rawlings, *MS*, 24 May 1860; for deputation see, 19 May 1860, Chesson Diaries, REAS/11/8, English Papers, MJRL.

104 APRTOK Minutes, 20 May 1860. The petition of the St Martin's Hall meeting was presented only after Lord Eversley had required the expunging of paragraphs describing the rejection as 'a usurpation of the privileges of the of House of Commons and of the rights of the people' and 'an act of unprovoked disrespect to the Crown', ibid., 23 May 1860.

105 Evans, *The Endless Web*, 105. Bright told Cobden that Bulwer Lytton was 'bullied' into silence by the Tories, 20 May 1860, Add. MS. 43384, ff. 197–202, BL.

106 Quoted Robert Stewart, '"The Conservative Reaction": Lord Robert Cecil and Party Politics', in R. Blake and H. Cecil (eds), *Salisbury, the Man and His Policies* (1987), 91.

107 Clarendon to Brougham, 23 May 1860, 30180, Brougham Papers, UCL. 'Ellice is gouty, but rejoices over the Paper Duty, and the Reform Bill; so does Lowe, and so, with decorous reticence, do I' Delane told Sir J. Rose on 12 June, cited Dasent, *Delane*, II, 9.

108 London Correspondence, *New York Times*, 18 June 1860.

109 Shannon, *Gladstone*, I, 416–17. The *Morning Star* dismissed it as 'a conspiracy for the concoction of a case in support of a foregone conclusion'. Bright reported to Cobden that Walpole, the chair of the committee, was earnest in his opposition to the Lords' action, but did not seem disposed to urge any action, 17 June 1860, Add. MS. 43384, ff. 203–6, BL.

110 Palmerston to Gladstone, 1 June 1860, see Guadella, 135.

111 Gladstone to Charles Pressley [copy], 29 June 1860, Add. MS. 44393, ff. 376–7, BL.

112 *MS*, 26 May 1860.

113 Richard B. Reed to Holyoake, 22 May 1860, #1218, Holyoake Papers, CpUL; Reed hoped that the rejection 'will affect the agitation for reform better than any other thing'. See later comment of Reed to Holyoake, 9 July 1860, #1229, Holyoake Papers, CpUL: willing to 'co-operate heartily with the movement for bringing down the Lords a peg'. 'I hereby turn over Pam to David Urquhart to be beheaded on Tower Hill or elsewhere. I am quite satisfied he is a Russian or a native of some other foreign clime.'

114 On the grounds that it 'extended through a wider circle than ours'; confining himself to APRTOK activities which show that 'it led us neither to a slavish submission nor to a revolutionary or pedantic excess', Collet, *Taxes*, II, 106.

115 See Cobden to Healey, 4 June 1860, *Leeds Mercury*, 7 June 1860.

116 APRTOK Minutes, 16 May 1860. The Committee questioned Ayrton's caution, worried at lack of Commons resistance, and arguing that it would be appropriate for the public to vindicate the right that is ultimately their own.

117 See copy COW/C/1384, TWAS; Collet to R. B. Reed, 12 and 16 May 1860, COW/C/1390–91, in which he urged Reed not to 'set the Lords the example of going beyond what is sanctioned by Constitutional Law'.

118 See examples of three different rubrics in the Cowen papers, COW/C/1393–94, Cowen.

119 The NPPARPD called a meeting on 6 July to explore the propriety of a joint conference with the representatives of the provincial press, see circular Holyoake Diary, Holyoake 2/10, Bishopsgate Institute. Further meeting in August, see circular, ibid.

120 APRTOK Minutes, 4 July 1860.

121 See *Morning Chronicle*, 26 May 1860. Meeting chaired by James White, late MP for Plymouth. For Hargreaves' support for the taxes on knowledge campaign, see Cobden to Hargreaves, 14 February 1853, Add. MS. 43655, ff. 23–4, BL.

122 Alex Ireland and Co to Cowen, 11 May 1860 COW/C/1386, TWAS. Argues that it is a question 'far beyond the scope of Newspaper Proprietorship[;] it will in numberless ways effect the public life of England'; also Wilson to Cowen, 11 May 1860, COW/C/1387; and E. Hutchings to Cowen, 26 May 1860; and 5 June 1860, COW/C/1400 and /1413, TWAS.

123 Printed, *MS*, 30 May 1860; St Pancras, City, *Lloyd's Weekly London News*, 10 June 1860. See petitions in Cowen Papers, C1393, 1393b, 1394, TWAS; London correspondence, *Trewman's Exeter Flying Post*, 20 June 1860.

124 See evidence of collectors for various wards, *DN*, 21 September 1860; *Manchester Courier*, 9 June 1860, *Leeds Mercury*, 7 June 1860, which prints Cobden's letter to Alderman Healey, *Newcastle Guardian*, 9 June 1860; *Worcestershire Chronicle*, 18 July 1860; meetings at Bury, 11 June (including William Stokes, *WDP*, 15 June 1860), Hanley, Brighton; *Birmingham Post*, 5 July 1860.

125 See account, *MS*, 6 June 1860; including Watkin attempting to reignite hostility to paper duty as a tax on knowledge and education, 'the food of the mind'.

126 *BO*, 26 July 1860.

127 *Leeds Mercury*, 14 June 1860; *Leeds Intelligencer*, 16 June 1860.

128 Collet, *Taxes*, II, 107.

129 *Lloyd's Weekly London News*, 10 June 1860.

130 See handbill from the Defence Committee: an anti-aristocratic squib: the Lords not only 'extort from the people more than £70,000,000 a year' 'a large portion . . . infamously wasted', but have now 'entered into a conspiracy to overthrow the constitution' and ensure an additional tax burden of

one-and-a-half million, 27D, CP 6, WSRO. For one echo, see letter of 'ONE OF THE "FARQUHAR FRANKHEART FAMILY"', *Leeds Mercury*, 3 July 1860.

131 As in Henry Vincent's well-established lecture on Oliver Cromwell, which was extended to include 'a sly hit at the rejection of the Paper Duties Bill by the House of Lords', *Ipswich Journal,* 4 August 1860; see also Whalley at the Peterborough Freehold Land Society, *Lincolnshire Chronicle*, 14 December 1860; *Dumfries and Galloway Standard*, 11 July 1860. In contrast, Ernest Jones publicly disavowed any connection with the movement in a letter to the *Morning Star.*

132 Editorial of *Glasgow Herald*, 3 July 1860. For links see editorial, *Morning Chronicle*, 9 July 1860. Opposition to the duty as a tax on knowledge was not entirely lost sight of; see editorial *Wrexham Advertiser*, 7 July 1860 and E. W. Watkin at Stalybridge, *Manchester Courier*, 14 July 1860.

133 Henry Slack to Cowen, 6 July 1860, C/COW/1438, TWAS. For handbill see C/COW/1439.

134 Letters of James Taylor, Jnr, and 'Hampden', *Birmingham Journal*, 9 June 1860.

135 *Liverpool Mercury*, 10 July 1860.

136 *Liverpool Daily Post*, 17 July 1860.

137 See circular of Thomas B. Potter (chairman), 26 June 1860, M20/30, WilsonPMA.

138 *WDP*, 17 July 1860.

139 Henry Slack to Cowen, 31 May 1860, COW/C/1405, TWAS.

140 Hargreaves to Cobden, 5 June 1860, 24D, CP 6, WSRO.

141 Clarendon to Brougham, 27 May 1860, 30181, Brougham Papers, UCL; see *Leamington Spa Courier*, 14 July 1860.

142 Granville note, n.d. [early July 1860], CAB/124, PalPUS.

143 Hargreaves to Cobden, 24 June 1860 25D, CP 6, WSRO.

144 Cobden to Lucas, 9 August 1860 [copy]. Cobden 134, WSRO.

145 Editorials, *London Standard*, 2 July 1860; *CM*, 3 July 1860.

146 Papers which asserted their opposition included *Liverpool Mercury* (see 1 August 1860).

147 Toulmin Smith to Holyoake, 24 June 1860, #1225, Holyoake Papers, CpUL.

148 Resolutions of the Constitutional Defence Committee, *DN*, 6 July 1860.

149 For a vivid account see London Correspondence of the *Exeter Flying Post*, 11 July 1860; also *Newcastle Journal*, 7 July 1860.

150 Clarendon to Lewis, 19 July 1860, Maxwell, *Life and Letters of . . . Clarendon*, II, 217.

151 Bright to Cobden, 3 July 1860, Add. MS. 43384, ff. 207–10, BL. Slack to Cowen, 27 June 1860, COW/C/1428, TWAS.

152 Robert Mills to Gladstone, 10 July 1860, Box 60, Miscellaneous Correspondence, GGPGL; handbill in Holyoake Diary, Holyoake 10/2, Bishopsgate. The committee obtained private interview with Chancellor; see account of Chesson, focusing on

the speech of Lord Teynham's, which 'placed the people above the Lords and the Crown', 11 July 1860, Chesson Diaries, REAS/11/8, English Papers, MJRL.

153 Teynham to Reed, 1 July 1860, COW/C/1432, TWAS. Letter printed in *MS*, 1 June 1860. For example, Magnus C. Rendall in the *CM*, Box 75, Miscellaneous Correspondence, GGPGL.

154 *Kentish Chronicle*, 9 June 1860; even *Lloyds'* expressed doubts at the violence of the rhetoric, 'Lord's Aggression', *Lloyd's Weekly Newspaper*, 24 June 1860.

155 See comments of Milner Gibson to Gladstone, 12 January 1861, Gladstone Papers Add. MS. 44395, ff. 52–3, BL: 'We have got a House of Commons, I believe, that is more afraid of dissolution than anything else.'

156 Gladstone to Palmerston, 1 July 1860, PP/GC/GL/34, PalPUS.

157 J. E. Denison, *Notes from My Journal When Speaker of the House of Commons* (1899), 70–1; Frank Crossley (Manchester School MP for Halifax) to the Bradford Working Men's Financial and Parliamentary Reform Association, *Lancaster Gazette*, 28 July 1860; voting list 2 July 1860, CAB/129, PalPUS.

158 Bright to Cobden, 15 July 1860 [copy], Add. MS. 43384, ff. 211–15, BL; though see his less optimistic comment to Charles Sturge, 14 July 1860, Add. MS. 64130, ff. 104–5, BL.

159 See London correspondent of the *Staffordshire Sentinel*, who accepted that 'the enthusiasm which greeted the Right Hon. Gentleman at the commencement of the session has very considerably declined, and . . . his financial policy is now regarded in many quarters with grave distrust', 21 July 1860.

160 Milner Gibson to Wilson, 22 November 1861, M20/30, WilsonPMA. See also tribute to Gladstone's 'able and manly defence of the rights and privileges of the House of Commons', J. A. Readwin to Gladstone, 11 July 1860, Add. MS. 44394, ff. 18–19, BL.

161 'Private Correspondence', *Birmingham Journal*, 7 July 1860; viz London correspondent of the *Freeman's Journal*, 10 July 1860.

162 See various letters of Teynham for August 1860 in the Cowen Papers, TWAS; Reed and Cowen refused to take sides, sending a resolution of gratitude to Bright (see Bright to Reed, 16 August 1860).

163 Editorial, *Newcastle Journal*, 18 August 1860.

164 Hargreaves to Cobden, 12 July 1860, 28D, CP 6, WSRO.

165 Slack to Cowen, 7 July 1860, COW/C/1443, TWAS; similarly the Manchester CDC passed a resolution condemning those Liberal MPs unwilling to take action to oppose the Lords, COW/C/1449.

166 *Newcastle Guardian*, 21 July 1860. White's return was aided by local secularists and radicals, see his letter of thanks to Holyoake, 18 July 1860, #1231, Holyoake Papers, CpUL.

167 London letter, *Manchester Weekly Times*, 14 July 1860, noting the offer of Mr Towle of Oxford to refuse payment. (Towle was a longstanding associate

of APRTOK, see Minutes, 13 April 1858, 12 May 1858, etc. for notice of correspondence.) See also letter of Magnus C. Rendall, *CM* 14 July 1860, advocating a general refusal to pay the duty.

168 *Sheffield Independent*, 14 July 1860. Slack to Cowen, 6 July 1860, including handbill of the Constitutional Defence Committee, C/COW/1438–9, TWAS.

169 Hargreaves to Cobden, 18 July 1860, 29D, CP 6, WSRO; H. Brookes to Holyoake, 18 July 1860, #1240, Holyoake Papers, CpUL.

170 At same time *Reynolds's* contributed to the anti-Lords pressure, see GRACCHUS, 'The Strife between the Peers and the People', *Reynolds's News*, 15 July 1860; also features in speeches at the annual gathering for the newspaper, ibid.

171 *Liverpool Mercury*, 2 August 1860 (see letter of INQUIRER, *Liverpool Daily Post*, 6 August 1860, which suggests that the opposition was orchestrated by church leaders and encouraged from the pulpit). In contrast, the non-electors' candidate at the Stafford election attacked Palmerston and Russell, urging a stopping of the supplies until the Lords' measure was reversed, *DN*, 3 August 1860.

172 Hargreaves to Cobden, 23 September 1860, 39D, CP 6, WSRO.

173 Brookes letter published, *DN*, 11 August 1860; it is clear that Bright's conduct had alienated many radicals; see Slack to Cowen, 13 August 1860, COW/ C/1483, TWAS. The Conservative press continued to make capital of Brookes's letter, see editorial, *The Standard*, 15 August 1860. The Liberal press rallied round against, for example, describing Brookes as 'merely a salaried clerk', editorial, BDP, 14 August 1860. Brookes was more than just a 'clerk', and had been active within London radicalism for a number of years, see his letter to Wilson, 16 November 1858, M20/28, Wilson Papers, and his pamphlet, *The Peers and the People, and the Coming Reform* (1857), and had been a member of the Political Reform League Committee, see Brookes to Cowen, 28 September 1858, COW/C/188, TWAS.

174 Chesson's account of the meeting was that 'Brookes did not show & he was quietly shelved', 16 August 1860, Chesson Diaries, REAS/11/8, English Papers, MJRL. The London Committee continued to meet, *DN*, 17 August 1860.

175 Noted in *Royal Cornwall Gazette*, 10 August 1860.

176 For a rare contribution outside the *Star* see Rhys Ap Howell, *Hereford Times*, 18 August 1860.

177 'Summary', *Wells Journal*, 14 July 1860.

178 *BDP*, 18 July 1860.

179 Gladstone to Cowley, 28 and 29 February 1860, and 28 April 1860, Add. MS. 44393, ff. 179–80, 182–3, 287, BL; Milner Gibson to Gladstone, 11 April 1860, Add. MS. 44393, f. 254–5, BL.

180 [H. Bruce and D. Chalmers], *Gladstone and the Paper Duties by Two Midlothian Paper Makers* (1885). We get a sense of modest sympathy in the

balanced editorial of *Carlisle Journal*, 4 September 1860; *Bury and Norwich Post*, 14 August 1860.

181 For notices see, for example, Editorial, *Huddersfield Chronicle*, 4 August 1860. See also letter of Wrigley in *DN*, 6 August 1860. It is clear that the overwhelming majority of paper-makers endorsed Wrigley's position, See 'Case', dated London, July 1860, signed by over 164 paper-makers, *Standard*, 6 August 1860.

182 C. E. Rawlins, Jnr to J. C. Ewart, 3 August 1860, published *Liverpool Mercury*, 4 August 1860. At the monthly meeting of the council of the Liverpool Chamber of Commerce on 6 August, a resolution seeking equal bonding privileges to imported paper was endorsed, *Liverpool Daily Post*, 7 August 1860. See 'Fair Play for British Paper Mills' signed J. H. & R. C. Rawlins, Hope Mills, Wrexham, July 1860, Box 73, GGPGL.

183 London Correspondence, *Leeds Mercury*, 10 July 1860. Evans, *Endless Web*, 106. Later in the month Bright informed Cobden that 'the import duty on Paper is said to be in great peril' but Government after vacillation have agreed to propose it, 25 July 1860, Add. MS. 43384, ff. 215–17, BL.

184 Cobden to Lord Cowley, 2 August [1860], FO 519/300, NA.

185 Palmerston Memorandum, 3 August 1860, PP/CAB/141, PalPUS; Gladstone's response of the same date, PP/CAB/142, was to note that the Cabinet had expressly agreed '*not* to make any application respecting the Paper Duties to the Government of France'; in this he was supported by several other cabinet members, including Russell, Argyle and Gibson, PP/CAB/143–147.

186 'Metropolitan Gossip', *Aris's Birmingham Gazette*, 4 August 1860; London correspondence, *Yorkshire Gazette*, 4 August 1860.

187 For an unsympathetic account of the meeting, see London correspondence, *Yorkshire Gazette*, 11 August 1860; Stanley, noting the large cabinet majority in favour of the planned expenditure on fortifications, commented 'Gladstone swallowed them as well as I believe he will swallow everything else rather than resign', E. J. Stanley to Henrietta Maria Stanley, 3 August 1860, Stanley Papers, DSA 99/8, CRO.

188 Gladstone to Lord Elgin, 5 September 1860 [copy], Add. MS. 44394, ff. 96–9, BL.

189 See reference to letter to Argyll, in *Autobiography and Memoirs*, II, but the response of the Duke on 8 September is the obstacles of the China War and the fortifications were temporary, and the principle of the budget has been tested and is being proved 'remunerative', II, 166. He had previously told Graham that 'Never at any time of my life have I had such a sense of mental and moral exhaustion', C. S. Parker, *Life of Sir James Graham*, 2 vols (1907), II, 399.

190 Editorial, *Carlisle Journal*, 7 August 1860.

191 See Cobden correspondence in Foreign Office files, NA; especially in late September when it seems murmurings were made that the Board of Trade should

review and revise the whole of the tariff that Cobden had negotiated in Paris, Gibson was drawn into this, see Cobden to E. Hammond, 23 September 1860, PRO FO97/207, NA.

192 Graham to Aberdeen, 15 August 1860, Add. MS. 43192, ff. 318–21, BL.

193 Milner Gibson to Cobden, 1, 2, and 3 October 1860, Add. MS. 43662, ff. 151–3, 154, 155–6, BL; Cobden, 8 October 1860, ff. 157–8; also Gibson to Palmerston, 7 October 1860, PP/GC/GI/7, PalPUS; Milner Gibson to Bright, 29 October 1859, Add. MS. 43388, f. 87, BL; for his glee see Hargreaves to Cobden, 27 December 1860, 48D, CP 6, WSRO.

194 Bright to Cobden, 13 August 1860, Add. MS. 43384, ff. 218–21, BL; of his speech on 10 August he noted 'Gladstone and Gibson sat there, in a pitiable submission to their master'. Cobden perhaps even more scathing, see letter to Hargreaves, 4 August 1860, Add. MS. 43655, ff. 162–6, BL.

195 *Dunfermline Press*, 16 August 1860, letter in *Carlisle Journal*, 4 September 1860; Bright to Cobden, 19 September 1860 and 26 October 1860, Add. MS. 43384, ff. 222–3, ff. 228–9, BL.

196 See Hargreaves to Cobden, 26 November 1860, 44D, CP 6, WSRO.

197 Bright to Cobden, 10 November 1860, Add. MS. 43384, ff. 232–3, BL.

198 Hargrcaves to Cobden, 9 November 1860, 40–1D, CP 6, WSRO.

199 Disraeli to Lord Malmesbury, 21 December 1860, *Disraeli Letters*, VIII, 82. By mid-January Disraeli was reporting that Gladstone had a large deficit in his plans, and Stanley imagining that the paper duties repeal will have to be abandoned, ibid., 87–8. In contrast, Bright was telling Cobden (2 December 1860, ff. 238–9) that Gibson had felt there was a turn in the tide, and that 'people begin to think our expenditure is too great, and may now be reduced'.

200 Bright to Wilson, 21 January 1861, M20/30, WilsonPMA: talks of a 'capital letter' from Cobden which he has sent on to Gibson.

201 Gladstone noted, 'the battle in parliament was hard, but was as nothing to the internal fighting', quoted Hawkins, *The Forgotten Prime Minister*, 257; for Paget's effusive but unhelpful sympathy, see Lord Charles Paget to Gladstone, 16 January 1861, ff. 60–5, and Gladstone to Paget, 26 January 1861 [copy], also second note, and ditto 28 January 1861 [copy], Gladstone Papers Add. MS. 44395, f. 105, f. 106, f. 125, BL.

202 Palmerston to Sir Charles Wood, 25 January 1861, BI HALIFAX/A4/63/129; Palmerston to Herbert, 26 January 1861, in Lord Stanmore, *Sidney Herbert . . . A Memoir*, II, 420–1.

203 Palmerston cabinet note, 25 February 1861, PP/CAB/153, and note on possible adjustments, PP/CAB/155, PalmerstonPUS. In responding, given that, as he put it, he was 'obliged to put in a strong paper of objection, amounting at one point nearly to a complaint', Gladstone took the unusual step of sending the memo and

his response back to Palmerston, rather than just sending it on round the cabinet, Gladstone to Palmerston, 25 February 1861, PP/GC/GL/48.

204 Gladstone memorandum, 25 February 1861, PP/GC/GL/48/enc. 1; further resistance in Gladstone to Palmerston, 20 March 1861, PP/GC/GL/50, which noted that even in the last four weeks the Board of the inland Revenue had added £250,000 to their projection of the excise deficiency for 1860–1.

205 According to Wilson, *Memories*, 134.

206 Including Baines, Ewart, James White and Francis Crossley, memo to Palmerston expressing the 'anxious concern with which we view the present state of the public expenditure', and pressing for a considerable reduction in expenditure; Memorandum, 21 January 1861, PP/GC/CR/68 enc.1, PalPUS.

207 Collins to Collet, 16 February 1861, Add. MS. 87371, BL.

208 The modest venue was indicative of lack of interest, Collet, *Taxes*, II, 110.

209 See *Manchester Examiner and Times*, 4 May 1861, *Morning Chronicle*, 2 May 1861, and widely reported. Issued a handbill, the text of which is printed in *BDP*, 2 May 1861.

210 Bright to Cobden, 28 March 1861, Add. MS. 43384, ff. 250–1, BL.

211 John Brooke and Mary Sorensen (eds), *Autobiographica* (1971), 88.

212 Note on the cabinet vote on repeal of paper duty, 12 April 1861, PP/CAB/156, Gladstone to Herbert, 3 April 1861, Stanmore, *Sidney Herbert*, 425–6. Bright reported that Milner Gibson was 'in great anxiety about the cause of the gov[ernmen]t in reference to Paper Duties', Bright to Elizabeth Bright, 13 April 1861, Ogden Mss 65, Box 3, UCL.

213 Noted in the Morley, *Gladstone*, II, 39; for Palmerston's obstructionism, see Memorandum, 12 April 1861, Add. MS. 44778, ff. 265–6, BL; again only Gladstone and Gibson were decisively in favour. See Lord Granville to Lord Canning, 9 April 1861, in Edmund Fitzmaurice, *Life of Granville George Leveson Gower, Second Earl Granville* (1905), I, 395.

214 Granville to Palmerston, 14 April 1861, PP/GC/GR/1881, PalPUS.

215 Palmerston to Gladstone, 14 April 1861 [copy], PP/GC/GL/194, PalPUS. Wood notes he agrees with Palmerston and was not in favour, but 'But we were all committed more or less', Wood to Palmerston, 15 April 1861, PP/GC/WO/156, PalPUS. For an account of these debates which presents Gladstone as largely outmanoeuvred, see Steele, *Palmerston and Liberalism*, 104–6.

216 Henry Lennox to Gladstone, 9 May [1861], Gladstone Papers, Add. MS. 44396, ff. 73–4, BL.

217 Richard Potter to Cornewall Lewis, 19 May 1861, C2232, Harpton Court Mss 4, NLW. In contrast, Benjamin Jowett's verdict on the budget was 'right in its proposals, viz. a penny less of Income Tax and no Paper Duties, which means, I believe, the *Times* for two pence . . .', Jowett to Miss Elliot, 16 April 1861, *Letters of Benjamin Jowett*, 56.

218 Northcote to Lady Northcote, 19 April 1861, quoted in Andrew Lang, *Life, Letters and Diaries of Sir Stafford Northcote, First Earl of Iddlesleigh* (1891), 104.

219 'Lord D[erby]. much put out . . . he would undoubtedly have liked to defeat ministers, and especially Gladstone, of whom he speaks in very angry terms', Vincent, *Derby, Disraeli and the Conservative Party*, 171 (entry for 31 May 1861); for Disraeli's efforts, see *Disraeli Letters*, VIII, 113–21.

220 Palmerston to Granville, 15 April 1861, Bell, *Palmerston*, ii, 283. London correspondence, *Yorkshire Gazette*, 4 August 1860, talked about the agitation being created by 'Mr Bright's organs, and the provincial journals that emanate from the London newspaper manufactories'; *Hull Packet*, 6 July 1860; for tory jibes that the CDC was an association of 'cheap publishers and cheap printers', see London correspondence, *Bury and Norwich Post*, 5 June 1860.

221 *BDP*, 11 April 1860.

222 Letters to *Standard*, 18 May and 4 August 1860.

223 For continued anti-*Times* sentiment, see for example, Henry Slack to Cowen, ?20 May 1860, COW/C/1395 ('The row got up by Horsman will also be good, as it tends to open people's eyes to the character of the *Times*' and its influences.) Cobden was forthright in his hostility, suggesting to Edward Baines that 'The Times seems bent on goading the two countries into war. Its conduct is so false, *so wilfully false* on the subject of the Treaty', 5 June 1860 and ditto 13 July 1860, CP 115, ff. 36–7, ff. 40–50, WSRO. Opinion at *The Times* was more optimistic: Mowbray Morris was happy with outcome of the Walter-Horsman controversy; and the good speeches of Walter, Palmerston and Disraeli – 'Altogether the result was satisfactory and must tend to increase our reputation', Morris to T. W. Bowlby, 10 May 1860, 10/165, TT/MRG/MM/1, Mowbray Morris Correspondence, Times Archive.

224 'Taxes on Knowledge and Indecency', *Saturday Review*, 27 April 1861, 419.

225 *Aris's Birmingham Gazette*, 4 August 1860. The Union's annual report included thanks to the cheap press, identifying especially the *Morning Star*, *Telegraph*, *Reynolds's*, *Lloyd's*, *Weekly Times*, and the *Ballot*, for reporting their activities, *Reynolds's Newspaper*, 5 August 1860.

226 'Extraordinary Scene in Hyde Park', *Herts Guardian*, 8 September 1860.

227 *Dublin University Magazine* extracted in *Manchester Courier*, 14 July 1860. See also the *Scotsman* railing against 'a knot of newspaper proprietors, who from the first have agitated the whole question of the Paper-duty on motives of self-interest . . . calculat[ing] on putting the whole of it into their own pockets', quoted *Saturday Press* [Dunfermline], 4 August 1860.

228 D. C. Coleman, *The British Paper Industry, 1495–1860* (1958), 338–9. The situation was eased by increasing use of cotton and flax waste, and by straw, but above all by the spread of the use of esparto grass. Coleman describes early developments from mid-1850s, especially the progress of Thomas Routledge at Eynsham. Coleman

notes that in the discussions much less attention had been given to wood pulp, and developments in the production of wood-based paper were largely pursued on continent and in America.

229 Scott Bennett, 'The Golden Stain of Time: Preserving Victorian Periodicals', in Laurel Brake, Aled Jones and Lionel Madden (eds), *Investigating Victorian Journalism* (1990), 171.

230 *WDP*, 3 October 1861.

231 A. Sinclair, *Fifty Years of Newspaper Life, 1845–1895: Being Chiefly Reminiscences of the Time* [1895], 30–1. Lucy Brown, *Victorian News and Newspapers* (1985), 4. By removing the requirement that newsprint was produced in sheets, it made possible the introduction of rotary printing presses, ibid., 8.

232 *The Era*, 19 October 1862.

Chapter 6

1 Cobden to Catherine Cobden [copy], 3 March 1856, CP 81, WSRO.

2 'Cheap Literature', *London Review*, quoted in *Westmorland Gazette*, 12 October 1861.

3 Taylor, *Decline of Radicalism*, 256–7; Taylor notes that in 1855–65 36% of new suburban London newspapers failed within their first year and over half within 5 years.

4 Cowan, *Newspaper in Scotland*, 275. The figures that he gives are 74 in 1852, 85 in 1854 and 105 in 1856, with proportionally more of the increase in Edinburgh and Glasgow than elsewhere.

5 J. R. R. Adams, *Northern Ireland Newspapers: Checklist with Locations* (1979).

6 Twelve Irish papers failed 1862–5, M.-L. Legg, *Newspapers and Nationalism: The Irish Provincial Press, 1850–1892* (1999), 49.

7 See Koss, *Political Press*; Dennis Griffiths, *Plant Here the Standard* (1996); A. J. Lee, *The Origins of the Popular Press in England, 1855–1914* (1976).

8 Aled Jones, *Powers of the Press. Newspapers, Power and Public in Nineteenth Century England* (1996), 23, figures from Saunders, Otley and Co., *Newspaper Press Census for 1861* (1861).

9 Aled Jones, *Press, Politics and Society. A History of Journalism in Wales* (1993), 2.

10 Mowbray Morris to J. T. Pitt (*Sanders' News Letter*), 25 October 1855, Manager's Letter Books (1st series) 5/589, TNA.

11 For the *Illustrated Weekly Times* and its competition with the *Illustrated London News* see C. N. Williamson, 'Illustrated Journalism in England: Its Development – II', *Magazine of Art.* (1890), 334–40.

12 'Literature of the People', *London Review* (October 1859), 11.

13 M. Harris, 'London's Local Newspapers: Patterns of Change in the Victorian Period', in Laurel Brake, Aled Jones and Lionel Madden (eds), *Investigating Victorian Journalism* (1990), 111.

14 For Doncaster, see, *Twelfth Half-Yearly Report of the Provincial Typographical Association [January–June 1856]*.

15 See details provided by a libel case against the *Sheffield Telegraph*, *Sheffield Independent*, 24 December 1858. By December 1858, the *News* was a halfpenny paper. Harrison notes he acquired the *Sheffield Times* in mid-1853 for £4,200, plus various other costs amounting to in effect a further £3,000.

16 Abergavenny, Ashton-under-Lyne, Beverley, Bicester, Bridgnorth, Burton, Chatham, Dartford, Faversham, Filey, Folkstone, Frome, Godalming, Gravesend, Hartlepool, Heywood, Kettering, Luton, Malvern, Matlock, Newbury, Newport, Peter borough, Rochdale, Ross, Sevenoaks, Sheerness, Staines, Sudbury, Tredegar, Tunbridge, Tunbridge Wells (2), Uttoxeter, see *Era*, 23 December 1855.

17 *Leicester Journal*, 31 August 1860.

18 Cowan, *Newspaper in Scotland*, 276.

19 Also the penny *Wednesbury Observer* (–1858); the *Aldershot Military Gazette*, which had two pages of metropolitan news printed in London.

20 *Critic* quoted in *Bury Times*, 24 May 1862. For this sort of sheet, see Jones, *Press, Politics and* Society, 27–9. For *Mercury*, see M. Milne, *The Newspapers of Northumberland and Durham. A Study of Their Progress During the 'Golden Age' of the Provincial Press* (1971), 59, half sheets were initially provided by Cassells and later by the General Press, 59.

21 See figures in 'The Newspaper Press at the Close of 1855', *Era*, 23 December 1855.

22 Cobden to Cassell, 25 September 1850, Add. MS. 46338, ff. 106–7, BL. 'The middle & working classes can have no *daily* organ whilst the penny stamp exists, & and it is the daily press constitutes public opinion in the eyes of the world. Hence we are misrepresented by the *Times, Chronicle, Post*, & *Herald*.' 'You must crown your publishing triumphs by having one day a daily *penny* paper with a circulation of over 60,000.'

23 Bright to Hargreaves, 21 June 1855, Add. MS. 62079, ff. 14–15, BL.

24 John Hamilton to Gladstone, 21 September 1855, Box 36, Miscellaneous Correspondence, GGPGL.

25 *Geelong Advertiser*, 2 January 1856.

26 *Leicestershire Mercury*, 14 August 1858. See Andrew McCulloch, *The Feeneys of the Birmingham Post* (2004).

27 See Lee, *Popular Press*, 274–5.

28 *The Times*, 17 May 1856; the *Grantham Journal* noticing the *Times*'s coverage, provides the rest of the valedictory, which suggests the editor was making a conscious decision to close a still profitable paper, rather than being forced to close an unprofitable one, 24 May 1856.

29 *WDP*, 23 March 1860.

30 Congratulating itself for having stood aside from the 'revolutionary agitation in the press' caused by the 1855 stamp act, convinced that 'the period has arrived when the position of a daily paper can be fully developed without risk to its conductors', *Nottinghamshire Guardian*, 20 June 1861; by October it was publishing the daily and a bi-weekly 2d paper.

31 Taylor, *Decline of Radicalism*, 363.

32 Then the *Ulster Examiner* (1870) and the *Belfast Morning News* (1872). Although the *Belfast Mercury* (established in 1851) seems to have survived as a daily from 1854 to 1861, its initial proprietor (previously a sub-editor and journalist for the *Northern Whig*) apparently was bankrupted and committed to a lunatic asylum, *York Herald*, 11 December 1858, quoting *North British Mail*.

33 'To Our Patrons and Readers – the Newspaper Stamp Returns', *Newcastle Journal*, 2 October 1858.

34 Andrew Hobbs, 'Reading the Local Paper: Social and Cultural Functions of the Local Press in Preston, Lancashire, 1855–1900', University of Central Lancashire, DPhil thesis (2010), 209.

35 Hobbs, 'Reading the Local Paper', 201–2; see 'The Modern Newspaper', *Quarterly Review* (1872).

36 'Press Reform in Chester on "Our Chapel" Principles', *Chester Chronicle*, 20 August 1859.

37 Brown, *Victorian News*, 41.

38 Bright remarked that the *Daily Telegraph*'s reduction of its price to 1d was a 'desperate bid not to die', Bright to Cobden, 21 September 1855, Add. MS. 43384, f. 12, BL. For a retrospective of the early career of the *Daily Telegraph*, which does not stint as to its limitations, see *The Busy Hives around Us* (1861), 239.

39 See report in *The Star* (Ballarat, Australia), 19 July 1856; *Luton Times*, 17 May 1856.

40 For the *Standard*'s claims of success in penetrating local markets, see *Standard*, 16 February 1858. This perhaps helps to explain its success in these years, which Lucy Brown found so puzzling.

41 *Bury Times*, 17 July 1858.

42 Bright to Cobden, 29 November 1855, Add. MS. 43384, f. 31, BL; Robert Chambers congratulated Alexander Ireland on the news of the paper's progress in June 1856: 'These recent sales have been quite unexampled in the British newspaper press (excepting only in the Times) and they do great credit to your sagacity in coming down at once to the penny', Chambers to Ireland, 3 June 1856, W. & R. Chambers Papers, Dep341/112, ff. 139–40, NLS; in January 1857 Chambers commented that Ireland's figures present 'an enormous circulation for a provincial district', ditto, 17 January 1857, NLS.

43 According to its own figures, reported *Shoreditch Observer*, 28 January 1860.

44 *CM*, 9 October 1857.

45 Alexander Ireland to Cowen, 8 March 1858, COW/C/78, TWAS.

46 *Salisbury and Winchester Journal*, 7 September 1861. It was suggested that this was merely a device to undermine a halfpenny journal started just previously, *Leeds Times*, 14 September 1861.

47 See advert, for example in *Bucks Herald*, 7 July 1860.

48 *Leeds Mercury*, 21 March 1862.

49 *Lancaster Gazette*, 5 October 1861. *Leeds Intelligencer* reduced price from 3d to 2d (eventually ceased publication in 1866, replaced by the *Yorkshire Post and Leeds Intelligencer*, a penny daily).

50 'Our New Year', *Hertford Mercury*, 4 January 1862.

51 London Correspondence, *Luton Times*, 8 March 1856.

52 Letter of 'Enquirer', *CM*, 11 December 1857.

53 *MS*, quoted by *Dunfermline Press*, 19 July 1860.

54 Cobden to Parkes, 22 October 1856, Add. MS. 43664, ff. 48–9, BL.

55 According to the London correspondent of the *Manchester Guardian*, see *Huddersfield Chronicle*, 2 August 1856. It was suggested in May 1856 that the circulations of the metropolitan dailies were 6,000 for the *Morning Advertiser*, 5,500 for the *Daily News*, 4,500 for *Morning Herald*, 3,000 *Morning Chronicle* and *Morning Post*, *Elgin Courier*, 9 May 1856.

56 It was suggested that when Glover took over the *Chronicle* it was losing £12,000 a year, and that Glover by a programme of swingeing economies was able to make it break even on a circulation of 2,000 with an average of six columns of advertising at £9 per column, see W. W. Clarke to Dean of Bristol, 12 October 1855, Russell Papers, PRO 30/22/12F, ff. 194–5, NA.

57 Letter to the *Geelong Chronicle*, 12 May 1863, quoted in the Melbourne *Argus*, 15 May 1863.

58 Andrew Wynter, 'Our Modern Mercury', *Once a Week* (February 1861), 160–3.

59 Joseph Hatton, *Journalistic London: Being a Series of Sketches of Famous Pens and Papers of the Day* (1882), 193.

60 Virginia Berridge, 'Content Analysis and Historical Research on Newspapers', in M. Harris and A. Lee (eds), *The Press in English Society from the Seventeenth to the Nineteenth Century* (1986)', 208. Even so, after a jump, it did not maintain same level of advertising as *Lloyd's* (only 14–15% in the 1860s, viz. 25–8% for *Lloyd's*), ibid., 209.

61 'A Glance at the London Newspaper Press', *Western Mail*, 19 June 1869.

62 'The Literature of Crime', [extracted from *DN*], *Lincolnshire Chronicle*, 16 May 1868. See Linda Stratmann, *Cruel Deeds and Dreadful Calamities. The Illustrated Police News, 1864–1938*, (2011).

63 An 'example of the progress made by the newspaper press during the last twenty-five years, as seen in the direct representation of every important, class, trade or calling, by its own special journal', *Hereford Journal*, 10 May 1862.

64 Bearnard Palmer, *Gadfly for God. A History of the Church Times* (1991), 30; for 1863 circulation averaged just under 4,000; 1864 just under 6,000; 1866, 9,174.

65 Extract *WDP*, 20 August 1860.

66 See advert, *The Times*, 10 May 1856, 3.

67 'The Newspaper Press at the Close of 1855', *Era*, 23 December 1855.

68 Legg, *Newspapers and Nationalism*, 36.

69 *Leicester Journal*, 31 August 1860.

70 For these figures from *Newspaper Press in 1860*, see *CM*, 18 September 1860, quoting *MS*.

71 Expanding from a sheet and half a week to two sheets, *Hereford Times*, 3 January 1861.

72 *Bristol Mercury*, 29 September 1860; *WDP* observes that the *Mercury*, the one-time advocate of the dear press, has been forced to capitulate. A year later, the *Mercury* was able to boast at a circulation of 10,000 every Saturday, and claim the *Bristol Daily Post* as the 'most popular and widely circulated daily journal in the West of England', *Bristol Mercury*, 31 August 1861. At the end of 1862 it enlarged to 56 columns, and reduced to 2d, *Bristol Mercury*, 27 December 1862.

73 Noted in *CM*, 15 February 1861.

74 *Leicestershire Mercury*, 28 September 1861.

75 'The Newspaper Press', *Lancaster Gazette*, 4 April 1863, quoting *Dublin University Magazine*.

76 Jones, *Press, Politics and Society*, 63.

77 Editorial, *Brighton Daily News*, 17 June 1869.

78 *Greenock Advertiser* reprinted in *Dundee Courier*, 5 July 1855.

79 *Carlisle Journal*, 9 November 1855.

80 *Scotsman*, quoted by *Liverpool Mercury*, 22 March 1856.

81 Quoted *Leicester Journal*, 2 January 1857.

82 Gibb and Beckwith, *Yorkshire Post*, 23; a similar experiment was abandoned by the *Carlisle Examiner* after three months in November 1855.

83 The conclusion of the *West Sussex Gazette* was that 'it has not a sufficient number of subscribers in one locality to pay a parcel of unstamped newspapers to agents', reprinted by the *Luton Times*, 30 May 1857.

84 Sinclair, *Fifty Years of Newspaper Life*, 39–40.

85 William Shepherdson, *Reminiscences in the Career of a Newspaper. Starting a Daily in the Provinces* (1876), 16–17.

86 *CM*, 1 June 1861.

87 'The Prosperity! of Cheap (?) Newspapers', *Liverpool Courier*, 20 February 1856.

88 'The Kilkenny Cats at Liverpool', *Leeds Times*, 22 December 1855.

89 *Manchester Courier*, 7 July 1855.

90 *Leeds Times*, 22 December 1855. *Manchester Courier*, 16 February 1856; the paper had become a thrice weekly 1½d print.

91 And partly, apparently, on account of bankruptcy proceedings against its former proprietors, see *Cheshire Observer*, 26 January 1856. Editorial comment noted that the *Liverpool Mercury* had also recently changed hands, 'and with its change has adopted a wiser policy, suited to the times', *Manchester Courier*, 16 February 1856.

92 *Leinster Express*, extracted in the *Belfast News-Letter*, 8 May 1856.

93 'Career of Samuel Robinson, the Forger', *Dundee Advertiser*, 22 April 1862.

94 'The Press and the Public', *Newcastle Guardian*, 5 January 1856.

95 'To Our Readers', *BO*, 3 January 1861.

96 'The Press and the Public', *Newcastle Guardian*, 5 January 1856.

97 The call of the *Newcastle Daily Chronicle* picked up via the *Scotsman* by papers such as the *Dundee, Perth and Cupar Advertiser*, 31 August 1858, *WDP*, 6 September 1858; see also *Richmond and Ripon Chronicle*, quoted in *Wrexham Advertiser*, 25 September 1858.

98 *York Herald*, 11 December 1858, quoting *North British Mail*.

99 Collet to Mrs Harriet Urquhart, 3 May 1856, I.G18 (Sheffield), Urquhart Papers, Balliol College.

100 One estimate was that the costs of the *Daily News* excluding paper and taxes were £400–500 per week; Hamilton to Wilson, 30 December 1855, M20/23, WilsonPMA.

101 Griffiths, *Plant Here the Standard*, 92. By contrast, a three-quarter share of the *Era* newspaper was sold to its proprietor Strutt for £2,250, sometime before his insolvency in 1854, *Morning Chronicle*, 25 March 1854. It was reported that the *Morning Chronicle* was sold later in the year for £3,000, Joseph Parkes to Edward Ellice (Jnr), 2 December 1854, MS. 15043, Ellice Papers, ff. 31–4, NLS. In 1855 Glover was touting the paper for £16,500, although those negotiating for its sale were only prepared to offer around £5,000, see W. W. Clarke to Dean of Bristol, 12 October 1855, Russell Papers, f. 194–5, PRO 30/22/12F, NA.

102 *Sheffield and Rotherham Independent*, 27 January 1855.

103 Harris, 'London's Local Newspapers', 111. The *Bristol Advertiser* was launched in 1855 with £800 for plant, machinery, etc. (along with further loans of about £4,000 before the paper failed), *Bristol Mercury*, 25 December 1858.

104 See quote for *Rochdale Observer*, 11 February 1857, f. 42, A. H. Burgess Letter Book, Misc/740, Manchester Archives.

105 'The New Year', *North and South Shields Gazette*, 27 December 1855. In comparison, it was suggested that when Samuel Robinson paid £1,400 for the *Fifeshire Journal* around 1855, he paid over the odds; see 'Career of Samuel Robinson, the Forger', *Dundee Advertiser*, 22 April 1862.

106 W. W. Clarke to Dean of Bristol, 13 October 1855, Russell Papers, ff. 200–1, PRO 30/22/12F, NA; for the context, see Koss, *Political Press*, I, 115–20.

107 See *Disraeli Letters*, VI, 495 n1, which references a letter from the Duke of
     Manchester (B/XXI/M/120) which indicated Disraeli was trying to raise £1,000
     for the paper.

108 Shepherdson, *Starting a Daily in the Provinces*, 19.

109 The paper continued under various titles.

110 London Correspondence, *Bury Times*, 7 December 1861.

111 *Leeds Times*, 22 December 1855.

112 *Birmingham Journal*, quoted *Newcastle Courant*, 28 August 1857.

113 'A Newspaper Nuisance', *BO*, 23 December 1858, quoting *Glasgow Daily Mail*.

114 *London Standard*, 11 February 1856; Shepherdson, *Starting a Daily in the
     Provinces*, 19–20.

115 'Local Newspaper Press of London', *Saturday Review*, 27 March 1858.

116 Robert Chambers to Alexander Ireland, 13 January 1857, W. & R. Chambers
     Papers, Dep341/112, ff. 147–8, NLS.

117 Berridge, 'Content Analysis', 204–5.

118 *Sydney Herald*, quoted in *The Colonist* (New Zealand), 16 November 1858.

119 Sinclair, *Fifty Years of Newspaper Life*, 40–2.

120 See J. Baxter Langley to Cowen, 6 February 1859, COW/C/481, TWAS.

121 S. J. Reid, *Memoirs of Sir Wemyss Reid*, (1905), 39–40, the sub-editor doubling at
     times as a reporter and responsible for 'particularly the selection and adjustment
     of the news taken from the papers or derived from other sources', 'Death of
     Mr Stirling Mitchell', *Glasgow Herald*, 15 May 1862.

122 See account of Proudfoot vs Crowther, *Norfolk Chronicle*, 11 June 1859.

123 Hobbs, 'Reading the Local Paper' 79, 85.

124 Reid, *Memoirs*, 37.

125 *Sheffield Independent*, 27 January 1855.

126 Beresford Hope in *Cambridge Essays*, quoted in 'Newspaper Press Reporters',
     Belfast News-Letter, 4 January 1859. For a similar account of the transformation
     traced above all to 'the emancipation of newspapers during the last few years
     from the advertisement duty and the compulsory stamp', see editorial, *Dundee
     Advertiser*, 18 January 1864. Contemporaries expressed a variety of often-
     contradictory opinions; see Lee, *Origins*, 104–8.

127 'Honour to the Press', *Carlisle Journal*, 10 February 1860.

128 See John Hamilton to Wilson, 30 December 1855, M20/23, WilsonPMA.

129 It was suggested that this would allow printing of 17,500 copies an hour, Cobden
     to Joseph Sturge, 8 January 1857, Add. MS. 43722, ff. 200–1, BL.

130 *Bury Times*, 3 July 1858.

131 Milne, *Newspapers of Northumberland and Durham*, 26; *Morning Post*, 2 February
     1861; *Freeman's Journal* received delivery in September 1859, see notice in *WDP*,
     14 September 1859. *Standard* announced in May 1859 an 8-sheet feeder capable of
     printing 16,000 to 20,000 copies an hour, Griffiths, *Plant Here the Standard*, 97.

132 'A New Invention in Printing Machinery', *Scotsman*, reprinted, *Dundee Courier*, 14 January 1864.

133 *North and South Shields Gazette*, 27 December 1855; *Sheffield Daily Telegraph*, 1 January 1856; Peters, 'Wrexham Newspapers', 66–7; *Falkirk Herald*, 8 October 1857.

134 'The *Hereford Times* to the Public', *Hereford Times*, 3 January 1861. At the start of 1863, the paper announced that the arrangement of one four-feeder capable of producing 5,000 copies an hour, alongside a two-feeder producing 2,000 an hour was not sufficient for its needs (a circulation claimed to be 7,000), and that it was adding a second four-feeder and second steam engine, 'To our Readers', 3 January 1863. At the start of 1862 the *Dundee Advertiser* was advertising its old two-sheet feeder, with an output of 1,800 copies an hour for £120, *Dundee Advertiser*, 1 January 1862.

135 *Chambers' Journal* cited in *Hertford Mercury*, 18 August 1855.

136 *Glasgow Herald*, 13 September 1858.

137 *Freeman's Journal*, 9 June 1855. There was some controversy at high charges of some companies. South-Eastern Railway 3d for 6 lbs etc., South-Western 3d for 4 lbs etc., *Lloyd's Weekly News*, 8 July 1855.

138 Memorandum of Mowbray Morris, 30 October 1856, Managers Letter Books (1st series) 6/257, TNA.

139 *Carlisle Journal*, 18 March 1864.

140 *Sun*, quoted by *Reading Mercury*, 8 September 1860.

141 London Correspondence, *Yorkshire Gazette*, 5 October 1861.

142 *Yorkshire Gazette*, 28 September 1861.

143 A fight that was ultimately successful, see Todd, *Democracy Militant*, 56.

144 For example, *Shoreditch Observer*, 16 May 1867; see letters *Glasgow Daily Herald*, 1 January 1868.

145 For the range of shops which sold papers, see Hobbs, 'Reading the Local Paper', 175–8, which notes that shops devoted mainly to selling papers and magazines was a rarity in working-class districts. Hobbs notes that while the population of Preston doubled from mid-century to 1901, the numbers of newsagents increased from 7 in 1853 (all of these also classed as booksellers) to 76 in 1901.

146 'A would-be Customer', *Grantham Journal*, 16 December 1865.

147 *Publishers' Circular*, 15 June 1870.

148 *Hertford Mercury and Reformer*, 15 September 1855.

149 *Kentish Gazette*, 20 January 1857. (Compare the *Elgin Courier*, 22 January 1855 which had suggested a break-even of around 10,000.)

150 London Correspondence, *Luton Times*, 7 February 1857.

151 'To our Readers', *Hereford Times*, 3 January 1861.

152 Koss, *Political Press*, *passim*.

153 For example, the *Empire*, see Chapter 8.

154 Griffiths, *Plant Here the Standard*, 103–5. Saved in part by the American Civil War: lively reporting from North and South enabled circulation to reach 100,000 copies some days.

155 Cowan, *Newspaper in Scotland*, 282.

156 See printed handbills of letters from Robie 'To Andrew Fyfe, Esq.', and 'Reply, by Mr Duncan M'Laren, to the Misstatements of Mr James Robie', in MS. 2782, NLS.

157 *Leicester Chronicle*, 12 April 1856.

158 *Leicester Journal*, 15 November 1861; London Correspondence, *Hereford Times*, 16 October 1861.

159 *Yorkshire Gazette*, 3 May 1862.

160 *Leicestershire Mercury*, 12 April 1862.

161 Frost, *Country Journalist*, 119.

162 Joseph Parkes to Edward Ellice (Jnr), 2 November 1858, MS. 15043, ff. 89–90, Ellice Papers, NLS.

163 Lee, *Origins*, 77–78.

164 Ayerst, *Guardian*, 141.

165 'A Glance at the London Newspaper Press', *Western Mail*, 12 June 1869.

166 *Printers' Register*, 6 April 1870.

167 See discussion in Taylor, *Decline of Radicalism*, 356–62.

168 Apparently claimed by *The Times*, quoting 'a northern paper'; disputed by the *WDP*, 28 December 1859.

169 *Dundee Courier*, 18 July 1855.

170 'It appears neither necessary nor desirable' it noted in its last number, 'to continue its publication, now that the news has ceased to be of momentous interest', quoted *Leamington Spa Courier*, 24 November 1855.

171 *Newcastle Guardian*, 5 July 1856.

172 *Lyceum* (weekly), *Scottish Thistle* (weekly), *Edinburgh Advertiser* (biweekly), *Express* (daily) (previously the *Edinburgh Guardian*, bought in 1855 for £3,400, see *Scotsman*, 31 July 1858), *Chronicle* (weekly), *Edinburgh Evening Post* (biweekly), *Week*, *Weekly Review*, *Scottish Railway Gazette* (weekly), *Scottish Press* (biweekly) (mostly newer papers absorbed by the older titles) and *Edinburgh News* (described as the oldest of the Edinburgh weeklies) amalgamated with the *Weekly Herald and Mercury*, *Sheffield Independent*, 3 February 1863.

173 Other slower Conservative casualties included the *Glasgow Courier* which lasted until the mid-1860s, Cowan, *Newspaper in Scotland*, 287.

174 *WDP*, 2 November 1858.

175 Lee, *Origins*, 90.

176 Arthur Miall to Wilson, 22 June 1866, M20/34, WilsonPMA, notes in all he needs £2,000, £400 to buy the copyright and connexion from the shareholders, and £1,600 for 'new blood', which would be enough to keep going for 2 years.

177 *Newspaper Press*, 1 January 1867.

178 Editorial, *Dundee Advertiser*, 18 January 1864.

179 'English Country Newspapers', *Temple Bar* 10 (1864), 128–41. Notes that the provinces thus far had been unable to sustain weeklies on the lines of the *Spectator* or the *Examiner*.

180 Harris, 'London's Local Newspapers', 107.

181 Lee, *Origins*, 91–3.

182 *Printers Register*, 6 January 1868.

183 *York Herald*, 11 December 1858, quoting *North British Mail*.

184 Peters, 'Wrexham Newspapers', 82–4.

185 'Paper and Stamp Emancipation', *Scottish Review* (April 1860), 182.

186 *Liverpool Daily Post*, 15 February 1862.

187 *Dundee Advertiser*, 22 September 1862; *Rochdale Observer*, 4 August 1866.

188 *Sussex Advertiser*, 29 April 1865. Compare with accounts from 1854 about Crimean victories, which do talk about additional editions, but give more of a picture of crowds round the newspaper offices to see news posted up.

189 *Hereford Times*, 4 January 1862, *Norfolk Chronicle*, 23 April 1859.

190 *MS*, quoted by *Dunfermline Press*, 19 July 1860; estimates another approximately 20,000 high price dailies, but about 260,000 of the penny daily press.

191 Brown, *Victorian News*, 31.

192 James Baldwin in *Gazette* (February 1857), 9.

193 Estimate of Guest of Birmingham, as reported by Edward Baines, see *Leeds Mercury*, 12 May 1864. For discussion see Brown, *Victorian News*, 32–6, though Brown offers little hard data on circulations before 1870, see table, 52–3.

194 *Leicester Chronicle*, 12 April 1856.

195 Editorial, *Daily Telegraph*, 6 October 1855.

196 Charles Wilson, *First with the News: A History of W. H. Smith, 1792–1972* (1985), 98–101. Between 1852 and 1867 Smith's expenditure on bookstall rents and advertising increased from about £10,000 to about £34,000.

197 Editorial, *The Times*, 30 March 1860.

198 *Standard*, 24 August 1859, quoting the *London Daily Guide*.

199 'Literature, the Press, etc.', *Chester Chronicle*, 14 July 1855.

200 *Wells Journal*, 28 March 1857; just as much in the provinces, see 'The Newspaper Stamp Returns', *Newcastle Journal*, 2 October 1858. By contrast, in 1852 use of large placards by the London dailies was novel and limited, see Lucas, *Lord Glenesk*, 113–14.

201 See account in Richard Whiteing, *My Harvest* (1915), 56–8; compare Joel H. Wiener, *The Americanization of the British Press, 1830s–1914. Speed in the Age of Transatlantic Journalism* (2011), 43, 112.

202 See comment in the notice of impending merger of *Dial* and *Star*, *Morning Post*, 8 September 1860.

203 'Cheapest News', *Leisure Hour* 7 (1858), 477–9. Interestingly the *Sheffield Daily Telegraph* asserted that it didn't use newsboys to sell its papers, *Sheffield Daily Telegraph*, 1 August 1855.

204 'Cheapest News', *Leisure Hour* 7. "'Standard!" gentlemen, here you are! forty-eight columns for one penny – all the news of the day – arrival of the Bombay mail, storming of Lucknow, slaughter and flight of the bloody-minded Sepoys – hextrornary trial – horrid murder at Portsmouth! – Coroner's inquest and verdict – Debates in Parliament, gentlemen, and all the foreign news – Only a penny – forty-eight columns for a penny'.

205 'Metropolitan Gossip', *Sheffield Independent*, 21 September 1861.

206 See the evidence of W. Astwood (newsagent), William Hodgson, shoemaker and newsvendor, George Downing, razor smith, *Sheffield Independent*, 24 December 1858.

207 *Aris's Birmingham Gazette*, 25 August 1860. The *Belfast News-Letter* described the city's *Morning News* as 'avowedly established on the street-hawking principle, and for the supply of' 'our servants, our street-sweepers, our pedlars and our pot-boys', 16 August 1856.

208 *Western Morning News*, extracted in *WDP*, 11 July 1860; *Western Times*, 27 March 1863.

209 Quoted in *Westmorland Gazette*, 2 January 1858.

210 *WDP*, 26 August 1859.

211 Eason to G. E. Ilherry, Great Southern and Western Railway, 14 January 1864, in Legg, *Newspapers and Nationalism*, 37.

212 'Advantages of the Cheap News Paper Press', *Grantham Journal*, 1 September 1855.

213 *Quarterly Review*, quoted in *WDP*, 15 April 1859; *Newton's Newspaper Gazetteer* (1860), quoted by *Newcastle Journal*, 1 September 1860.

214 Rev. W. F. Tregarthen, 'Newspapers and Nightschools', *Dorset Chronicle*, 5 March 1863.

215 'The Effects of Cheap Paper', *Kentish Gazette*, 26 April 1864.

216 *Leeds Mercury*, 12 May 1864.

217 This was certainly the common construction, both of supporters and opponents: see *Saturday Review*, 12 November 1859.

218 A point made in 'Penny Literature', *Literary Gazette*, 15 October 1859, 377. Of course not entirely, Hobbs notes that diary of Ward records him walking a mile into Clitheroe each Saturday evening to read the press in the pub, for the period 1856–61.

219 *Leamington Spa Courier*, 4 September 1858. Similar comments at a special meeting of the Bristol Library, *WDP*, 22 February 1860. In contrast, Lee, *Origins*, suggests that 'The repeal of the taxes on knowledge, and the appearance of the cheap penny and halfpenny press did not do any detectable harm to the newsrooms', 37.

220 *Manchester Guardian*, 30 December 1856.

221 Quoted in *CM*, 11 December 1863. For a discussion of railway reading (though focusing largely on fiction), see Mary Hammond, *Reading, Publishing and the Formation of Literary Taste in England, 1880–1914* (2006), 51–84.

222 Quoted in *WDP*, 15 April 1859.

223 Tregarthen, 'Newspapers and Nightschools'. Similar increases in the weekly light reading papers such as the *Family Herald*, the *London Journal, Cassell's Paper*, and the halfpenny journals said to have sprung up since the repeal of the paper duties, whose weekly sale had increased from around 50 copies (15 years ago) to about 600, readers 'mostly young girls of from 12 years and upwards'.

224 *Kendal Mercury*, 26 March 1861.

225 Letter of 'A Conservative', *London Standard*, 24 August 1858; 'In many large and influential districts Whig organs hold undivided sway.'

226 Jones, *Powers of the Press*, 166.

227 Legg, *Newspapers and Nationalism*, 33.

228 Ibid., 41.

229 Cowan, *Newspaper in Scotland*, 286.

230 See 'Newspaper Sewage', *Saturday Review*, 5 December 1868.

231 Shepherdson, *Starting a Daily in the Provinces*, 70–2.

232 *Publishers' Circular*, 15 February 1870.

233 *Printers' Register* 6 April 1870; Milne, *Newspapers of Northumberland and Durham*, 23; generally rejected by the provincial press.

234 'Notes on Social Questions', 28 October 1864.

235 Ayerst, *Guardian*, 151.

236 *Printers' Register*, 6 July 1870.

237 'Mr Bright, MP on Political Changes', *Standard*, 30 January 1864.

238 *Falkirk Herald*, 21 February 1867.

239 Lee, *Origins*, 83, but Lee notes that no company actually had this amount of subscribed capital, and purchase prices tended to be much lower.

240 Lee, *Origins*, 89.

241 *Huddersfield Chronicle*, 15 October 1870.

242 *Manchester Courier*, 15 October 1859. For similar comments see Wynter, 'Our Modern Mercury'.

243 See, for example, letter of R. M., 'in a love of fair play and justice to all classes, in a hatred of jobbery, corruption, and patronage, in advocating a cheap press and a liberal unsectarian education, the modern Conservative contrasts favourably not only with the old Tory, but also, in many of these respects, even with the modern Whig', *London Standard*, 9 June 1858. *Standard* made a habit of publishing letters lauding the 'cheap press', see 'A Conservative', 6 July 1858, 'A Liberal Conservative', *Standard*, 24 June 1858.

244 See, for example, the boosterism of *The Busy Hive around Us*.

245 *Glasgow Morning Journal*, extracted in *WDP*, 2 July 1858.

Chapter 7

1   For example, Thomas Archer, *Gladstone and his contemporaries* (1883), 231.

2   Cobden to Joseph Sturge, 14 December 1853, Add. MS. 50131, ff. 320–1, BL, *Cobden Letters*, II, 568. There is extensive correspondence on the 'newspaper project' in the various papers of Cobden, Bright, Sturge, Wilson and Gladstone in 1855–6, which offers a much fuller week-by-week picture of the discussions over the *Star* than space allows for here. A fuller but still only partial account is contained in S. Frick, 'Joseph Sturge and the Crimean War, ii: The Founding of the *Morning Star*', *Journal of the Friends' Historical Society*, 53 (1975), 335–58.

3   Cobden to Bright, 22 July 1856, Add. MS. 43650, BL, *Cobden Letters*, III, 224.

4   See Chesson to George Wilson, 28 April 1855, M20/22, WilsonPMA; Koss, *Political Press*, I, 88. For letters from Elton which Koss had not located, see Box 25, MCGP.

5   See letters of Hamilton and Elton in the Wilson papers, including extracts from letter of Sir Arthur Elton to Hamilton, 25 November 1855, M20/23, A. H. Elton to Wilson, 2 January 1856, MS.20/24, WilsonPMA. Elton noted that Sleigh of the *Daily Telegraph* was confident that he could easily get the subscribers he needed for 5,000 £10 shares; a letter of 5 January 1856 notes that although Sleigh speaks as though it is all sorted, he has also indicated to Elton in a letter received that morning that if the *Star* party would take all the shares, he would place the *Daily Telegraph* in their hands. ('I fear your paper will be swamped at the present juncture if launched in *opposition* to the *Daily Telegraph* (at the same time Elton affirmed that he believed Hamilton's misfortunes 'are not due to any moral fault, but to circumstances over which he had no control').

6   For the history of the *Empire*, into which it was claimed that £6,000–7,000 had been sunk without ever achieving profitability, in part because of its unpopular stance against the Crimean War, see entries for 17 and 23 November 1854, Chesson Diary, 1854–5, REAS/11/3, English Papers, MJRL Chesson notes a meeting of *Empire* supporters at Newall's Building, Diary, 20 January 1855; Hamilton to Wilson, 20 July 1855, M20/23, Joseph Sturge to Wilson, 6 September 1855, Hamilton to [Joseph Sturge], 24 November 1855, M20/23, WilsonPMA; Hamilton to Gladstone, 13 September 1855, Box 36, MCGP. The travails of winding up the *Empire* pursued Thomson to India in autumn 1857, when he was still trying to find the £100 needed to satisfy the paper's creditors and enable him finally to put aside the 'vexation, labour, anxiety and loss' associated with the enterprise, Thompson to Chesson, 21 November 1857, REAS/3/3/1, English Papers, MJRL.

7   Bright to Joseph Sturge, 12 September 1855, Add. MS. 43723, ff. 45–6, BL.

8   Joseph Sturge to Wilson, 7 July 1855, M20/23, WilsonPMA.

9   Cobden to Wilson, 27 August 1856, M20/25 WilsonPMA.

10 Bright to Wilson, 4 August and 24 August 1855, M20/23, WilsonPMA; for further complaints, see Bright to Wilson, 12 September 1855.

11 Cobden initially had reservations, but Bright was adamant that Rawson was necessary for oversight and for mobilizing support in Manchester, Bright to Charles Sturge, 9 December 1855, Add. MS. 64130, ff. 55–6, BL.

12 Milner Gibson to Wilson, 5 December 1855, M20/23, WilsonPMA.

13 Bright to Cobden, 3 October 1855, Add. MS. 43384, f. 16, BL.

14 Bright to Cobden, 16 October 1855, Add. MS. 43384, f. 21, BL; ten days later Manchester supporters were even cooler, 'frightened at the rate of interest', Bright to Cobden, 26 October 1855, Add. MS. 43384, f. 22, BL; Sturge to Wilson, 6 September, 27 October and 5 November 1855, M20/23, WilsonPMA.

15 Bright to Wilson, 4, 23 August 1855, M20/23, WilsonPMA. At this stage the plan seems to have been to invest the contributions in Wilson's name, with Cobden and Bright as sort of trustees, see Bright to Joseph Sturge, 16 November 1855, Add. MS. 43723, ff. 51–2, BL; Bright was anxious that things not be complicated by Haly having an investment as well as being editor, Bright to Charles Sturge, 7 December 1855, Add. MS. 43723, ff. 56–8, BL.

16 Bright to Wilson, 5 December 1855, M20/23, WilsonPMA; Bright to Sturge, 14 January 1856, Add. MS. 43723, ff. 73–4, BL. 'I did not know that Robt Charlton expected any interest for any money advanced', Bright confessed to Charles Sturge in 1859, 30 November 1859, Add. MS. 64130, ff. 88–9, BL.

17 Sturge was seeking detail as to Bright's views, Sturge to Wilson, 22 August 1855, M20/23, WilsonPMA.

18 Cobden to Joseph Sturge, 1 May 1856, Add. MS. 43722, ff. 114–15, BL.

19 Hamilton to Wilson, 30 December 1855, WilsonPMA: 'The *Daily Telegraph* is in reality an evening paper – it is a day late in everything save police intelligence . . . and a cheap evening paper would beat it by giving the same news twelve or fourteen hours earlier.'

20 Editorial, *MS*, 17 March 1856.

21 Bright to Sturge, 28 February 1855, Add. MS. 43723, ff. 65–6, BL; Haly to Wilson, 12 May 1856, also account in Bright to Wilson, 13 May 1856, WilsonPMA. Bright had been looking since September 1855 when he had visited Applegath about a press, *Diaries*, 7 September 1855.

22 Bright to Wilson, 27 March 1856, M20/24, WilsonPMA.

23 Cobden had earlier been optimistic that, 'The "Star" as I get it the Evening Edition is a really marvellous penny-worth, & cannot fail to sell very largely', Cobden to Bright, 21 March 1856, Add. MS. 43650, ff. 194–7, BL. Joseph Sturge to Wilson, 19 March 1856, M20/24, WilsonPMA; 'the wrong man is at the head and unless he is changed quickly, the paper is lost', Joseph Sturge to Wilson, 28 April 1856, M20/24, WilsonPMA.

24 31 March 1856, f. 59. There were even anonymous complaints: 'Scrutator' advised that 'if the blunders and mistakes, such as those of *orthography*, omissions, transposition, which have occurred in almost every number continue much longer,

they will soon *destroy* the character of your paper (annotated 'Another example of the sort of complaint which reaches me daily . . .'), 8 April 1856, M20/24, WilsonPMA.

25   Cobden to Bright, 7 April 1856, Add. MS. 43650, ff. 205–6, BL; Cobden to Joseph Sturge, 19 March 1856, *Cobden Letters*, III, 197–8.

26   Joseph Sturge to Wilson 12 January 1856 M20/22 [out of sequence]; Cobden to Wilson, 20 March 1856, M20/24, WilsonPMA.

27   Cobden to Wilson, 20 March 1856, M20/24, WilsonPMA. 'Rawson' he told Bright, 'will be disappointed if he reckons too much on the newsmen. They get a profit now by lending out the Times &c at 1^d an hour & afterwards sending them to the Country. Naturally they will feel a repugnance to a class of papers which will put an end to this trade – It is all very well to say they may have the new trade in 1^d papers. But you know men don't eagerly adopt new machines of any kind when it puts old out of use', Cobden to Bright, [10 February 1856], CP4, f. 88, WSRO.

28   See Cobden to Bright, 23 February 1856, Add. MS. 43650, ff. 178–9, BL. Cobden later noted that 'Haly had a New York plan of selling them. Rawson was for relying upon the old machinery', 'Cobden to Joseph Sturge, 1 May 1856, Add. MS. 43722, ff. 114–15, BL.

29   Milner Gibson to Bright, 24 March 1856, Add. MS. 43388, ff. 60–1, BL. 'I hear it well spoken of in the London clubs'; Joseph Sturge to Wilson, 2 May 1856, M20/24, WilsonPMA; repeated in a letter of the 7th, 'There are large districts in which the Star is unknown'; Sturge thought circulation could be doubled or trebled. In June he was again urging the division of the country into districts and the appointment of people to promote the circulation, Joseph Sturge to Wilson, 3 June 1856, WilsonPMA. See also 16 June 1856, noting that friends in Northumberland and Durham 'hear nothing of it'.

30   J. B. Smith to Cobden, 27 March 1856, 98B, CP, WSRO. Or, in the less sympathetic version of the *Manchester Guardian*, 'thrust their penny trash into the faces of the bystanders with incessant vociferations, and an importunity that entitles them to the speedy notice of the police', 18 March 1856.

31   Cobden to Joseph Sturge, 19 March 1856, Add. MS. 43722, ff. 111–12, BL; Wilson to Cobden, 18 March 1856, Add. MS. 43663, f. 182, BL; 'newspaper reading has so fallen off since the war has closed, and there seems to be such apathy in the public mind on every question that it is difficult to get them to read anything less exciting than horrible murders', commented J. B. Smith to Bright, 20 April 1856, Add. MS. 43388, ff. 160–1, BL.

32   Cobden to Richard, 18 August 1856, Add. MS. 43658, ff. 119–22, BL; Cobden to Joseph Parkes, Wednesday, May 1856 [*sic*], CP30, f. 245, WSRO.

33   *Elgin Courier*, 9 May 1856, suggesting that at this level its circulation was greater than all the high-priced London dailies, excepting the *Times*, combined.

34   Cobden to Joseph Sturge, 30 August 1856, Add. MS. 43722, ff. 154–6, BL. 'From this 10 per Ct must be deducted for returns leaving net sale 153,000. The *morning*

paper has less than 12,000 <net> circulation, & of this a ~~small~~ considerable portion goes to the Country. So that we have really a poor hold on the ~~Country~~ Metropolis.'

35 According to Cobden to Sturge, 26 December 1856, Add. MS. 43722, ff. 195–6, BL.

36 Hamilton to Sturge, 27 November 1855, M20/23, WilsonPMA; a similar figure was identified in discussions between Bright, Wilson, Rawson and Ireland in Manchester, Bright, *Diaries*, 16 August 1855; Cobden to Bright, 23 February 1856, Add. MS. 43650, ff. 178–9, BL.

37 Cobden to Haly, 15 June 1856, CP30, f. 641, WSRO.

38 Cobden to Joseph Parkes, 11 June 1856, Add. MS. 43664, ff. 44–6, BL; Bright to Cobden, 8 August 1856, ff. 69–70; Bright thought a little money spent bringing its circulation up to 25,000 would make it pay very satisfactorily although it was said solvency was still a couple of years away.

39 Cobden to G. P. Bacon, 17 June 1856, Add. MS. 48590, ff. 35–6; Cobden to Bright, 11 August 1856, Add. MS. 43650, ff. 215–20; *Cobden Letters*, III, 224–5, Cobden to Richard, [21 August 1856], Add. MS. 43658, ff. 125–31, BL.

40 Cobden to Joseph Sturge, 5 June 1856, Add. MS. 43722, ff. 120–1, BL. By the end of the year, though he could see that advertising was increasing, Cobden was not convinced they were all genuine or paid for, Cobden to Richard, 7 December 1856, Add. MS. 43658, ff. 205–12, BL.

41 Perhaps not until 1858–9, see Bright to Joseph Sturge, 12 May 1859, Add. MS. 43723, ff. 136–7, BL. Even so, the paper used for the first number was described as 'so bad, that when damp, it has little more adhesion than pulp, and when dry, conspires with the type and printing to ruin the eye of the reader', *Manchester Guardian*, 18 March 1856.

42 Rawson to Bright, 5 April 1856, 99B, CP, WSRO.

43 Rawson to Wilson, 6 April 1856, M20/24, WilsonPMA.

44 Wilson and Rawson to Haly, 9 May 1856, Add. MS. 43663, ff. 186–7, BL; Rawson to Cobden, 9 July 1856, 121B, CP, WRSO.

45 Cobden to Richard, 15 July 1856, Add. MS. 43658, f. 87, BL.

46 *Punch*, 2 August 1856; see Cobden to Richard, 3 August 1856, Add. MS. 43658, ff. 105–6, BL; see also Bright to Wilson, 28 August 1856, M20/25, WilsonPMA.

47 Cobden to Wilson, 16 June 1856, M20/25, WilsonPMA.; see also Joseph Sturge to Richard 7 July 1856 #264a, Mss 14023D, NLW : 'The great fault of Rawson appears to be dilatoriness and procrastination'.

48 Cobden to Joseph Sturge, 9 June 1856, Add. MS. 43722, ff. 125–6, BL; Cobden to Paulton, 30 June 1856, Add. MS. 43662, ff. 177–9, BL; Cobden to Richard, 31 May 1856, Add. MS. 43658, ff. 33–7, BL; ditto, 5 June 1856, Add. MS. 43658, ff. 41–3, BL; Cobden to Sturge, 18 July 1856, Add. MS. 43722, ff. 139–40, BL. Cobden was concerned that Richard should have 'a real power at the Office'.

49 17 July 1856, Chesson Diary, REAS/11/4, English Papers, MJRL, notes Hamilton's report of being offered the editorship by Cobden, Wilson and Rawson. Clear from

Cobden to Richard, 31 July 1856, that Hamilton was in charge, though Cobden is still hoping Richard will come in and Hamilton will go back to being second in command. In September Hamilton tells Gladstone that he has 'had all the responsibility of editorial management', 19 September 1856, Box 36, MCGP.

50 16 August 1856, Chesson Diary, REAS/11/4, English Papers, MJRL.

51 Cobden to Bright, [11 August 1856], Add. MS. 43650, ff. 215–20, BL, *Cobden Letters*, III, 225–6; Joseph Sturge to Richard, 7 July 1856 #264a, Richard Papers, Mss 14023D, NLW. Richard claimed a de facto position as joint editor with Hamilton, with responsibility for 'general supervision of the affairs of the paper', as per a signed agreement drawn up to embody Rawson's wishes, Charles S. Miall, *Henry Richard, M.P.: A Biography* (1889), 113–14; Hamilton to Wilson, 2 August 1856, M20/25 WilsonPMA; Bright to Joseph Sturge, 17 September 1857, Add. MS. 43723, ff. 81–2, BL.

52 25 October1856, Chesson Diary, REAS/11/4, English Papers, MJRL; quote in Cobden to Bright, [11 August 1856], Add. MS. 43650, ff. 215–20, BL.

53 See Hamilton to Wilson, 12 February 1857: For Richard's illness see Cobden to Sturge, 3 October 1857, Add. MS. 43722, ff. 275–6, BL.

54 Paulton to Cobden, 4 July 1856 [copy], CP99, WSRO.

55 Cobden to Joseph Sturge, 29 October 1856, Add. MS. 43722, ff. 163–4, BL. 'I can say no more than I have done to Rawson & Co about the newspaper. It will end in some spirited people getting up a penny daily that will beat you to nothing in circulation. I have told them this again & again. Nobody deserves success who does not look after his own concerns', Cobden to Richard, 21 December 1856, Add. MS. 43658, ff. 220–1, BL.

56 See Cobden to Joseph Sturge, 27 June 1856, Add. MS. 43722, f. 134, BL.

57 Hamilton to Gladstone, 1 January 1856, Box 36, MCGP.

58 Bright to Wilson, 11 June 1856, M20/25, WilsonPMA.

59 Joseph Sturge to Wilson, 7 July 1856, M20/25, WilsonPMA.

60 7 April 1856, f. 61 (enclosing note from Rawson); Bright to Wilson, 5 April 1856, M20/24, Sturge to Wilson 23 April and 25 July 1857, M20/27, WilsonPMA.

61 Bright to Joseph Sturge, 3 May 1859, Add. MS. 43723, ff. 134–5, BL; Bright was sanguine that the value will have risen, especially if the paper duty is removed.

62 This is the implication of the complex arrangements under which the amalgamation with the *Dial* was arranged in 1860, see Lucas to Wilson, 7 November 1860, M20/30, WilsonPMA; Joseph Sturge to Wilson, 3 June 1856, M20/25, WilsonPMA. Bright confessed that further capital had been raised in a letter to Charles Sturge, 30 November 1859, Sturge Papers, Add. MS. 64130, f. 88–9, BL, and noted that he had raised a further £4,000 in £500 contributions over the previous few weeks, which he expected to increase to £5,000; for Hargreaves, see Bright to Mrs Hargreaves, 7 December 1860, Add. MS. 62079, ff. 38–9, BL.

63 Bright to Wilson, 19 April 1857, M20/27, WilsonPMA; see report of conversation in W. W. Clarke to Dean of Bristol, 16 November 1855, Russell Papers, PRO 30/22/12G, f. 80–1, NA.

64 Parkes to Bright, 1 July 1857, Add. MS. 43388, ff.240–3 BL.

65 Bright to Cobden, [17 September 1857], f. 110; also noting *Examiner* at 25,000 daily and good ad revenue; Bright to Cobden, 24 November 1857, Add. MS. 43384, ff. 115–18, BL. For animadversions about Rawson's lack of vigour in pursuing advertisements, see Baxter Langley to Wilson, 24 June 1857, M20/27, WilsonPMA. Lucas was slightly more energetic, approaching Cobden to drum up business from Liberal organizations such as the Freehold Land Society, Cobden to Samuel Lucas, 5 July 1858, CP 134, WSRO.

66 *Manchester Courier*, 28 February 1857, quoting *Leeds Times* summary of a lecture by Merriman (for which see J. J. Merriman, 'The English Newspaper', *Popular Lecturer*, II (1857)).

67 Bright to Wilson, 30 December 1857, M20/27, WilsonPMA.

68 See recollections of Ralph Harrison, *Printers' Register*, 6 September 1870.

69 See comments of Bright to Joseph Sturge, 23 April 1858, Add. MS. 43723, ff. 97–8, BL; Villiers to Bright, [25 December 1859], Add. MS. 43386, ff. 279–98 [f. 285], BL.

70 Recollections of Ralph Harrison, *Printers' Register*, 6 September 1870.

71 Cobden to Richard, 27 March 1858, Add. MS. 43659, ff. 19–20, BL. Cobden urged that if there is any chance of a paying circulation for a 1d double sheet, and 'if capital can be found'; Bright to Joseph Sturge, 14 February 1858, Add. MS. 43723, ff. 90–1, BL.

72 Bright to Joseph Sturge, 8 January 1858, Add. MS. 43723, ff. 87–8, BL; for cost (including steam engine, etc. and the move to Fleet Street (£3,000, to include a £2,000 mortgage) see ditto, 14 February 1858, ff. 90–1; ditto, 23 August 1858, ff. 111–12; 21 September 1858, 43723, ff. 113–14; the plans were still for an enlargement and also a 2d weekly, but 'more capital will be wanted to create a really useful newspaper establishment'.

73 'When I last came down here I was speaking to the man who sells newspapers at the Waterloo station & he told me he sold 6 Telegraphs to 1 Morning Star', Cobden to Richard, 12 August 1858, Add. MS. 43659, ff. 24–5, BL; see also *Maitland Mercury* (Australia), 5 February 1859.

74 Lucas to Cowen, 16 February 1859, COW/C/526, TWAS.

75 'The effects of cheap paper', *Kentish Gazette*, 26 April 1864.

76 Cobden to Joseph Sturge, 6 August 1858, Add. MS. 43722, ff. 149–50, BL.

77 Cobden to Richard, 10 January 1858, Add. MS. 43659, ff. 6–7, BL.

78 Bright to Joseph Sturge, 3 May 1859, Add. MS. 43723, ff. 134–5, BL.

79 Bright to Joseph Sturge, 12 May 1859, Add. MS. 43723, ff. 136–7, BL.

80 Bright to Cobden, 9 April 1858, Add. MS. 43384, ff. 124–7, BL.

81 See *People's Paper*, 26 June 1858.

82 Bright to Joseph Sturge, 14 February 1858, Add. MS. 43723, ff. 90–1, BL. Lucas was on the committee of the NPPARPD.

83 Lucas to Holyoake, 14 February 1859, included in Holyoake to Cowen, 5 February 1859, COW/C/478, TWAS where it is described as 'this infernal missive'. By this point Bright was more understanding about the pressures of newspaper production, and the occasional slips that could result, see Bright to Charles Sturge, 11 June 1859, Add. MS. 64130, ff. 80–1, BL.

84 Miall, *Henry Richard*, 114–15, Charles Sturge to Richard, 13 June 1859, #259, Richard Letters, Mss 14023D, NLW. This was news to Bright in mid-June, telling Sturge that Richard had 'not intimated anything of the kind to S. Lucas, nor . . . made any *serious* complaint of his articles being altered', 15 June 1859, Add. MS. 64130, ff. 82–3, BL.

85 Cobden to Richard, 10 August 1860, Add. MS. 43659, ff. 55–8, BL. Bright had suggested to Charles Sturge, 30 November 1859, Sturge Papers, Add. MS. 64130, ff. 88–9, BL, that the morning edition was now 'clearing itself', and the evening paper making a surplus of £25–30 a week, but this seems to have been before expenses (excluding paper) which were running at £300–330 per week. There might be a small profit through the winter as the high point for advertisements.

86 *Herts Guardian*, 15 September 1860; Bright to Cobden, 13 August 1860, CP20, f. 120 [copy], WSRO.

87 See London Letter, *New York Times*, 18 June 1860. This was certainly a consideration: as Bright noted to Sturge, the paper duty cost the paper £150 per week, and without its removal, the prospect of profit was distant, 30 November 1859, Sturge Papers, Add. MS. 64130, ff. 88–9, BL; 'had I known all the difficulties I would not have undertaken it without having helpers or partners of more means'.

88 Thomas Wrigley, *Mr Milner Gibson and the Paper Trade: Being a Reply to a Speech Delivered by That Gentleman to His Constituents at Ashton-under-Lyne* (1860), 5.

89 See Slack to Cowen, 13 August 1860, COW/C/1483, TWAS.

90 According to a reported conversation with London correspondent of *Trewman's Exeter Flying Post*, 13 June 1860; Clarendon to G. C. Lewis, [May or June 1860], MS. Clar Dep c.533 [not foliated], Bodleian Library: report of conversation Bright had with friend of Lady Clarendon; Lewis to Clarendon, 13 April [1861], MS. Clar Dep c.531, Bodleian Library.

91 Noted in Bright, *Diaries*, 1 April 1860.

92 See 'Memorial Address of the Members of the National Newspaper League to the Chairman of Their Association', *The Homilist* (1870), 251. See Rev D. Thomas, *Journalism and the Pulpit* (1857).

93 See BT 41/270/1554, NA. See also papers for Evans vs National Newspapers League Company, C 16/489/E72, NA; London Correspondent of the *Witness*, extracted in the *Elgin Courier*, 11 July 1856.

94 See *Wrexham Advertiser*, 13 June 1857; it was noted that 34 towns already visited and subscriptions good; 22 shares subscribed for at Oswestry (later noted 22 Rhyl, 20 Abergele, 21 Llandudno, 16 Conway, 26 Holyhead, *North Wales Chronicle*, 19 September 1857). There was some concern at the way that the *Dial* company was being promoted; the London correspondent of the *Monmouth Beacon* speaking of promotion meetings being set up under the guise of a 'lecture' on the newspaper press, with supporters 'accidentally' in the room appearing to support the scheme and take up a subscription, as a way of encouraging others, noted, *North Wales Chronicle*, 20 June 1857. The scheme limited shareholders to no more than 20 shares; claimed 149 shareholders in Derby, *Derbyshire Times*, 23 January 1858. It was suggested by the *Standard*, 15 February 1858, that £100,000 had been raised, but that divisions over religious scruples had prevented the newspaper from being launched. By September 1858 figures are 6,000 shareholders and £115,000 subscribed capital, *Bury Times*, 18 September 1858.

95 Bright to Charles Sturge, 5 October 1860, Add. MS. 64130, ff. 106–7, BL.

96 Arrangement because they agreed to have only four shareholders on each side, see Lucas to Wilson, 7 November 1860, M20/30, WilsonPMA. It would seem that after Lucas's death Bright also administered his shares on behalf of his sister, Lucas's widow, see Reid, *William Black*, 49; Bright was able to keep his direct interest obscure, even, apparently from Justin McCarthy, who suggested in his *Reminiscences* that Bright 'looked after some shares which belonged to a relative', I, 162.

97 Bright to Cobden, 10 October 1860, Add. MS. 43384, ff. 224–7, BL.

98 See letter of Dymond, *Derby Mercury*, 4 June 1862. The editor, Peter Bayne, resigned, blaming the *Dial*'s lack of success on the prejudice attracted by its connection with the *Star*, *Elgin Courant*, 25 April 1862.

99 Arnold to Mary Penrose Arnold, 5 November 1863, *Letters of Matthew Arnold. II. 1860–65*, edited Cecil Y. Lang (1997), 237.

100 'The Ethics of Editing', *Edinburgh Evening News*, 1 September 1885.

101 Charles A. Cooper, *An Editor's Retrospect. Fifty Years of Newspaper Work* (1896), 112–13.

102 See 'Memorial Address', 252; Thomas later attacked the *Star*'s 'un-national spirit, literary inferiority, and miserable management'. There are scattered indications of resistance to what Bright at one point described as 'the "Thomas" influence', in which Edmond Beales, one of the *Dial* directors, apparently joined, see Bright to Hargreaves, 23 April 1865, Add. MS. 62079, ff. 79–80, BL.

103 *Reading Mercury*, 8 September 1860, quoting the *Patriot*.

104 'Memorial Address', 251. There seems to have been a substantial investment in new machinery before the juncture, because Bright was suggesting that the accession of capital would allow the repayment of loans advanced for 'the new machine', Bright to Charles Sturge, 5 October 1860, Sturge Papers, Add. MS. 64130, ff. 106–7, BL.

105 'Report of the London Press Co. Ltd, for the *Star* and *Dial* Newspapers',
      18 November 1863, M20/32, WilsonPMA.

106 21 October 1860, Chesson Diary, REAS/11/8, English Papers, MJRL; in December
      1860 Hargreaves noted the *Star* thriving, with adverts now more than two pages.
      'Cheaper paper alone is wanted to make the property secure', Hargreaves to
      Cobden, 27 December 1860, 48D, CP6, WSRO.

107 See resale figures, *Newcastle Journal*, 21 January and 22 April 1863, *Morpeth
      Herald*, 23 July 1864.

108 *Ipswich Journal*, 9 August 1862.

109 Bright to Charles Sturge, 8 November 1864, ff. 157–8.

110 A comparison of advertisements for 21 March 1856 found that while the *Times*
      had 1865 adverts, and the *Standard* 516, the *Morning Star* had only 416, *London,
      Provincial and Colonial Press News*, 15 August 1867, cited Lee, *Origins*, 86–7.

111 Bright complaining to Hargreaves, 17 August 1861, Add. MS. 62079, ff. 43–4, BL.

112 Bright, *Diaries*, 15 March 1864.

113 See 'The "Morning Star" – a retrospect', McCarthy, *Reminiscences*, I, 142–65.

114 Cobden to Lucas, 20 November 1864, CP 126, WSRO.

115 Bright to Hargreaves, 23 October 1865, Add. MS. 62079, ff. 83–4, BL.

116 Justin McCarthy, *Portraits of the Sixties* (1903), 111; see Miall, *Henry Richard*, 115;
      see fragmentary correspondence, including with Milner Gibson, James Stansfeld,
      William Ewart, W. E. Forster, etc., in U DX/163/1, Thomasson Papers, Hull
      Archive Centre.

117 Hargreaves to Cobden, 27 December 1860, 48D, CP6, WSRO. Lucas was absent
      for several months in the summer of 1864, see Bright to Charles Sturge, 1 July
      1864, Add. MS. 64130, ff. 155–6, BL. In February 1864, Lucas's appearance at the
      office was sufficiently unusual to be noted in Chesson's diary, and even then he
      was 'still, however, very unwell', Chesson Diary, 15 February 1864.

118 Cooper, *An Editor's Retrospect*, 100, though accepting that Lucas generally
      presided over an afternoon meeting to discuss editorials, etc.

119 David Thomas favoured Mason Jones, who was very keen, but whom Bright
      considered 'earnest and able' but 'fear[ed] his Irish impulse'; mention was also
      made of John Gorrie, Bright to Hargreaves, 23 April 1865, Add. MS. 62079, ff.
      77–8, BL. The appointment of McCarthy as editor (or 'literary editor' as Bright
      put it in letter to Elizabeth, 13 June 1865, Ogden Mss 65, Box 3, UCL), noted in
      Diaries, 13 June 1865; salary £500, and 5 per cent of profits shared with Dymond.

120 Cobden to Paulton, [5 July 1856], Add. MS. 43662, ff. 181–2, BL.

121 Cobden to Joseph Sturge, 31 October 1856, Add. MS. 43722, ff. 165–6, BL;
      Cobden to Joseph Parkes, 3 November 1856, Add. MS. 43664 ff. 54–7, BL; Cobden
      to Richard, 5 November 1856, Browning Settlement, Peace Society Papers,
      Swarthmore College.

122 Cobden to Sturge, 23 December 1856, Add. MS. 43722, ff. 193–4, BL.

123 Cobden to Sturge, 6 December 1856, Add. MS. 43722, ff. 187–8, BL; Cobden
to Bright, 20 February 1858, Add. MS. 43650, ff. 277–9, BL. Apparently Sturge
suggests no immediate prospect of raising the finances, so by mid-December
Cobden agreeing that it must stand over, Cobden to Sturge, 15 December 1856,
Add. MS. 43722, ff. 191–2, BL. An *Edinburgh Star* was apparently briefly published
in March 1858, on 'democratic' principles, but did not survive the month, see
Cowan, *Newspaper in Scotland*, 286; it is not clear if it had any direct connection
with the *Morning Star*.

124 Cobden to Richard, 4 November 1856, Add. MS. 43658, ff. 174–5, BL. In 1860 he
urged William Hargreaves to get Lucas to talk to John Bigelow, joint proprietor
of the *New York Evening Post*, with a view to some understanding of how it was
possible to make a significant number of New York cheap papers pay: Cobden to
Hargreaves, 1 February 1860, Add. MS. 43655, ff. 84–6, BL.

125 Cobden to Richard, 7 November 1856, Add. MS. 43658, ff. 182–3, BL. Compare
later advice to 'Look at the New York cheap Press see how they sparkle with full
or short leaders on the living & moving drama of public life', Cobden to Richard,
27 December 1856, Add. MS. 43658, ff. 225–8, BL; Cobden to Henry Richard,
8 June 1856, Add. MS. 43658, ff. 46–7, BL.

126 Rawson to Bright, 5 April 1856, 99B, CP, WSRO.

127 Cobden's continued recommendation of short 'original paragraphs' along the lines
of Jerrold's in *Lloyd's Weekly News*, Cobden to Richard, 18 May 1857, Add. MS.
43658, ff. 332–3, BL: 'With this sort of sharpshooting an incessant fire may be kept
up at a policy or a premier without wearying or boring people. If I were <going>
to start a penny paper, I should take the New York Herald & Tribune as my models
for the plan <of> catering for the public both in the leaders & news'.

128 See his comment to Joseph Sturge on the *DN*, 22 March 1850, Add. MS. 50131,
ff. 167–9, BL: 'a daily paper is obliged to put nonsense of this kind in its columns
to please all parties, & classes of readers, just as it gives sporting news & police
reports for the same reason – We must content ourselves with being able to find
a *part* of a paper which is written for us'. Even so, by 1857 Bright at least was
convinced that 'With regard to *Racing*, there is no need whatever for the quantity
of matter on that subject that is inserted', Bright to Joseph Sturge, 17 September
1857, Add MS. 43723, ff. 81–2, BL.

129 Wiener, *Americanization*, 122–4.

130 See Cobden to Hargreaves, 14 October 1863, Add. MS. 43655, ff. 337–40, BL.

131 'Political Mediocrity', *Saturday Review*, 12 November 1859. Wiener's use of
Whiteing's description of McCarthy's journalism as 'all picture, suggestion, felicity
of phrase', potentially conflates McCarthy's later writings with the *Star* era, Wiener,
Americanization, 121–2.

132 See Barbara Black, *A Room of His Own: A Literary-Cultural Study of Victorian Clubland* (2012), 140–1. Yates also contributed leading articles and reviews, Edmund Hodgson Yates, *Edmund Yates: His Recollections and Experiences* (1885), 295; Wiener, *Americanization*, 140–1.

133 See 'Memories of an Old Fleet Street Journalist' in *T.P.'s Weekly* (1905), reprinted in *Otago Witness*, 11 Whiringa-ā-nuku (1905).

134 See Bridget Brereton, *Law, Justice and Empire. The Colonial Career of John Gorrie, 1829–1892* (1997), 23.

135 See Thomas Wemyss Reid, *William Black, Novelist* (1902), 39–59.

136 Reid, *William Black*, 49. See commendation of the improved writing in the *Star* (and offer to assist McCarthy when he can) in Milner Gibson to Bright, 2 November 1865, Add. MS. 43388, ff.107–8, BL.

137 McCarthy, *Reminiscences*, I, 235 (Butt); Reid, *William Black*, 49–51, Cobden to Joseph Sturge, 28 April 1857, Add. MS. 43722, ff. 236–7, BL, including staff of the *Star* and foreign radicals such as Blanc, Kinkel.

138 Whiteing, *My Harvest*, 59.

139 McCarthy, *Reminiscences*, I, 86.

140 Joseph Parkes to Edward Ellice (Snr), 29 August 1860, Add. MS. 15042, ff. 143–6, Ellice Papers, NLS.

141 Second Duke Wellington to Delane, 14 August 1859, Delane Papers, TT/ED/JTD/9/118, TNA, playing back to Delane a conversation they had had.

142 Joseph Sturge to Richard, 21 November 1856 #266, Richard Papers, Mss 14023D, NLW.

143 Bright to Joseph Sturge, 8 January 1858, Add. MS. 43723, ff. 87–8, BL.

144 Cobden to [William Fisher], 9 April 1857, Yale University Library. The virulence and unchecked nature of the *Morning Star's* attacks on Palmerston and the government attracted widespread condemnation as entirely partisan and unrepresentative of even radical opinion, see *Aris's Birmingham Gazette*, 28 July 1860.

145 'Admirers', *Saturday Review*, 12 April 1862.

146 Bright to Joseph Sturge, 23 August 1855, Add. MS. 43723, ff. 41–2, BL.

147 A numerous and representative selection of Cobden's letters to Richard are printed in J. A. Hobson, *Richard Cobden, The International Man* (1918). It would seem that similar flow of advice was directed to Hamilton, though fewer letters survive. Hamilton noted a barrage of advice about how to make the journal decent and respectable, Hamilton to Gladstone, 19 September 1856, Box 36, MCGP; see Cobden to Hamilton, Add. MS. 43669, ff. 124–5, BL. For Lucas, see Cobden to Samuel Lucas, 15 September 1859, Cobden Papers 134, WSRO; followed up by editorial, *MS*, 17 September 1859; ditto 17 September 1859, ibid. Compare Cobden to Lucas, [10 October 1859], ditto, 11 October [1859], WSRO Cobden 136. Cobden continues occasional instructions re editorial topics and approaches

through 1860, Cobden to Lucas, 25 July 1860, Hull University Archives DX/163/1/5. Viz. the rather peremptory tone of the request/instruction in Cobden to Lucas, 16 August 1860 [copy], WSRO Cobden 134. Also Cobden to Lucas, 26 November and 1 December 1862; 27 July and 18 October 1863; 9 January and 2 February 1864, CP 135, WSRO; Cobden to Hargreaves, 22 January 1863, Mallet Papers. Still it is hardly convincing to argue, as David Brown does, that he was the 'de facto editor' at any point, David Brown, 'Morally Transforming the World or Spinning a Line? Politicians and the Newspaper Press in Mid-Nineteenth-Century Britain', *Historical Research* (May 2010), 335.

148 Charles Sturge to Richard, 19 January 1857 #255, Richard Letters, Mss 14023D, NLW.

149 Cobden to Richard, 27 May 1856, Add. MS. 43658, ff. 30–2, BL. Joseph Sturge to Richard, 24 November 1856 #265; Jos Sturge to Richard, 27 November 1856 #267a; Richard Papers, Mss 14023D, NLW; Joseph Sturge to Wilson, 8 September 1856, M20/25, WilsonPMA.

150 Cobden to Richard, 26 April 1858, Add. MS. 43659, ff. 85–6, BL; 14 July 1856, Add. MS. 43658, ff. 21–2, BL; Cobden to Richard, 15 May 1857, Add. MS. 43658 ff. 326–8. While later objecting that 'I consider the Star is too diplomatic – too mealy mouthed in fact', Cobden to Joseph Sturge, Add. MS. 43722, ff. 243–4, BL.

151 See London correspondence of the *Empire* (Sydney, Australia), 20 May 1857.

152 Quoted in *Glasgow Daily Herald*, 16 August 1860. *Scotsman* argued that the Manchester clique of Radicalism was particularly inclined to the use of kept papers, and had for a decade or more showed 'extraordinary antipathy' to a genuinely independent press.

153 Bright to Edward Ellice (Snr), 16 December 1859, Add. MS. 15006, ff. 78–83, Ellice Papers, NLS; Cobden was similarly keen to protest his distance, telling T. B. Potter, 'it is entirely independent. I never had a shilling of money in it, & I really think I know more about the proprietary of the Daily News, Times, & Telegraph, than of the Star', 9 January 1864, Add. MS. WSRO 2761, f. B63.

154 *Nottinghamshire Guardian*, 17 January 1861.

155 Bright to Cobden, 9 April 1858, Add. MS. 43384, ff. 124–7, BL. For the notion that Bright frequently wrote editorials, see T. H. S. Escott, *Personal Forces of the Period* (1898), 25, 'A visit to the London Newspaper Offices', *New Zealand Herald*, 10 June 1867; and contradiction of Edward Russell, *That Reminds Me* (1900), 84–5. Bright noted writing a short article, *Diaries*, 3 and 14 June 1859. He had in the early 1850s written reasonably regularly for the *Manchester Examiner and Times*, see for example, Bright to Elizabeth Bright, 21 and 27 February 1851, Ogden Mss 65, Box 3, UCL.

156 McCarthy, *Reminiscences*, I, 64. Corresponded with suggestions, ibid., 77–8. Meetings with Lucas to discuss contemporary affairs were regularly reported in his letters to his wife, Ogden Mss Box 3, UCL.

157   See his plea to Joseph Parkes to intervene in a libel case, 16 June 1857, Parkes
      Papers, UCL.

158   See George Thompson to F. W. Chesson [copy], 7 January 1856, M20/24, Wilson
      Papers, Manchester Archives; F. W. Chesson to Wilson, 12 January 1856, ibid.,
      seeks such an arrangement. After the *Morning Star* he worked for the *Scotsman*
      and the *Daily News*, and at his death he was described rather unkindly by *York
      Herald* as 'not a journalist of the highest type' but 'nevertheless a plodding
      persevering, conscientious man', *York Herald*, 1 May 1888.

159   See Cobden to Sturge, 17 March 1857, Add. MS. 43722, ff. 218–19, BL.

160   For brief biographies of Mead (or Meade) and Faucher see Howe, *Letters of
      Richard Cobden, III, 1854–59*, 150, 346.

161   See *Letters of J. E. Thorold Rogers and Mr Henry Tupper on the History and
      Working of the Laws of Primogeniture* (1864); correspondence with Bright in
      Thorold Roger Papers, Bodleian Library, Oxford.

162   McCarthy, *Reminiscences*, I, 102–41.

163   D. Home, *D. D. Home. His Life and Mission* (1888), 216–17; see J. S. Mill to
      J. M. Ludlow, 21 July 1867, *Later Letters of John Stuart Mill [Collected Works
      XIII]* (1972), 1112A; for Conservative opponents it became the mouthpiece of
      'Brightism and Bealism', *Bath Chronicle*, 1 November 1866.

164   Holyoake to editor of the *Morning Star*, [December 1864, various fragments],
      #1572 and 1572/1, Holyoake Papers, CpUL.

165   Lucas to Holyoake, 10 January 1865, #1577, Holyoake Papers, CpUL. (This did
      not prevent numerous other contributions from Holyoake, see letter, *MS*, 6 May
      1867.

166   Gladstone, *Diaries*, 24 January 1861, printed 25 January 1861; 4 October 1865,
      printed 5 October 1855, 16 February 1867, printed 18 February 1867; it is clear
      from McCarthy to Gladstone, 16 February 1867, Add. MS. 44412, ff. 72–3, BL, that
      McCarthy had had no dealings in person or on paper with Gladstone while at the
      Star, although see exception of exchange of letters printed in the *MS*, McCarthy
      to Lucas 'Thursday Night' [April 1865], Gladstone to[McCarthy], 6 April 1865 U
      DX/163/1/14,15, Thomasson Papers, Hull Archive Centre.

167   See comments of Hargreaves to Cobden, 12 October 1861, 107D, CP6, WSRO.
      In 1864 Cobden complained to Paulton that the *Star* seemed no more consistent
      than the rest of the press in its treatment of Palmerston, Cobden to Paulton, 6 June
      1864, Add. MS. 43662, ff. 306–8, BL.

168   See Kossuth to Lucas, 11 March 1860, Louis Blanc to [Lucas], 14 September
      and 17 October 1864, U DX/163/1/13, 43, 44, Thomasson Papers, Hull Archive
      Centre.

169   See Goldwin Smith, *Britain and America* (1865), 22. For the almost universal
      anti-Northern flavour of the British press, see Michael de Nie, 'The London

Press and the American Civil War', in Joel H. Wiener and Mark Hampton, (eds), *Anglo-American Media Interactions, 1850–2000* (2007), 129–54, though it makes no attempt to discuss the place of either the *Star* or the *Daily News*.

170 See letters sent on cotton supply and American affairs to *Star* by Bright, extracted in other papers, for example *Manchester Courier*, 24 April 1865. Bright pushed for the strengthening of the paper's representation in the States from the start of 1861, see Bright to Hargreaves, 11 January 1861, Add. MS. 62079, ff. 41–2, BL, which recommended a weekly contribution from William Bigelow.

171 'It would be a great advantage to the *Morning Star* to be able to publish any interesting dispatches in advance of its competitor, & its honest dealing with the American question, is rendered all the more effective when it can show itself possessed of accurate information on subjects on which the public take a deep interest', Bright to Charles Sumner, 6 November 1863, Rush Rhees Library, University of Rochester.

172 Charles Sumner to Lincoln, 7 August 1863, *Selected Letters of Charles Sumner, 1859–1874*, (1990), 186.

173 D. Leighton, *The Greenian Moment. T. H. Green, Religion and Political Argument in Victorian Britain* (2004), 13; Lady Grogan, *Reginald Bosworth Smith* (1909), 51–2. See also the remark of Baptist Noel that, 'I have often been cheered while writing it by your able articles on the American war, and by the views of your correspondent', Noel to [Lucas], 29 October [1863?], U DX/163/1/28, Thomasson Papers, Hull Archive Centre.

174 *New York Times*, 11 August 1862.

175 See Francis W. Hirst, *Early Life and Letters of John Morley*, I, (1927), 39–40; James Grant, *Newspaper Press: Its Origin, Progress and Present Position* (1870–2), I, 378.

176 See correspondence between Bright and McCarthy reprinted in McCarthy, *Reminiscences*, I, 79–84; Editorial, *Hampshire Advertiser*, 16 October 1869.

177 Cobden to Richard, 31 January 1859, Add. MS. 43659, ff. 12–13, BL. Bright also urged caution in 1866, see Bright to McCarthy, 19 January 1866, printed McCarthy, *Reminiscences*, I, 83–4.

178 'The "Interview" with Muller', *Sheffield Independent*, 20 September 1864.

179 Lists included various associates of *The Times*, including Delane himself, and was generally denied; for the response see 'A Scandal of Journalism', *Westmorland Gazette*, 14 October 1865.

180 Bright to Hargreaves, 12 August 1865, Add. MS. 62079, ff. 79–80, BL.

181 Bright to Charles Sturge, 1 July 1864, Add. MS. 64130, ff. 155–6, BL; this was still an issue in November, see ditto, 8 November 1864, ff. 157–8.

182 Bright to Hargreaves, 19 April 1865, ff. 75–6, 12 August 1865, ff. 79–80, Add. MS. 62079, BL. Evans was 'a good man of business, is well off, and is thoroughly of our

views', ditto 3 April 1865, ff. 77–8; he showed some interest, see Chesson Diary, 17 June 1865.

183 By September 1866, as the commercial crisis bites, he 'say[s] nothing about the *Star* as I have nothing to recommend', Bright to Hargreaves, 29 September 1866, Add. MS. 62079, ff. 99–100, BL.

184 Cooper, *An Editor's Retrospect*, 143–4. Dymond, supporter of the abolition of capital punishment, was on the staff from 1857 until the paper ceased publication in 1869, when he emigrated to Canada, see *Dictionary of Canadian Biography* XIII (1994), www.biographi.ca/en/bio/dymond_alfred_hutchinson_13E.html.

185 William Tinsley, *Random Recollections*, (1900), I, 78, 305. This perhaps explains the entry about discussing the editorship of the *Star* with Edward Dicey, in Bright, *Diaries*, 1 July 1868.

186 *Newspaper Press*, (July 1867).

187 Little note in *WDP*, 22 October 1867.

188 Bright to Hargreaves, 2 October 1867, Add. MS. 62079, ff. 113–6, BL.

189 'National Newspaper League Company Ltd', *BO*, 2 September 1869.

190 Bright to Hargreaves, 5 August 1867 and 17 April 1868, Add. MS. 62079, ff. 107–10, 117–18, BL.

191 'Memorial Address of the Members of the National Newspaper League to the Chairman of their Association', *The Homilist* (1870), 252. Thereafter the company was wound up, with about a third of the £30,000 capital raised returned to shareholders. Not without, at least according to Thomas, having contributed to the repeal of the 'taxes on journalistic literature' and the establishment of the cheap press.

192 Part of the arrangement was that Rawson 'should influence all who had been associated with the *Star* as contributors or readers to transfer their support in favour of the *Daily News*'.

193 Being presaged, with new machines, in February 1868, see *Printers Register*, 6 February 1868; also extended proprietary, including Henry Labouchere, Samuel Morley, J. W. Probyn; 'A Glance at the London Newspaper Press', *Western Mail*, 12 June 1869, whose damning verdict on the *Star* was that it 'has been unfortunate from the commencement. There has been a cheese-paring policy united to ultra-democratic opinions which have not found favour with the multitude. The constant cry of "Wolf" on its placards has alienated many of its supporters'.

194 'Credo' in *Sydney Morning Herald*, 17 January 1868.

195 The suggestion of *True Witness and Catholic Chronicle*, 19 December 1888.

196 Bright to J. E. T. Rogers, 28 August 1875, quoted in Koss, *Political Press*, I, 204; see Bright to Hargreaves, 23 October 1865, Add. MS. 62079, ff. 83–4, BL.

197 *Morning Post*, quoted by *Liverpool Daily Post*, 11 October 1869.

198 This figure was suggested by Fox Bourne, *English Newspapers*, II, 272 and has been widely repeated.

199 Suggestion of McCarthy, *Reminiscences*, I, 163.

200 Whiteing, *My Harvest*, 93.

201 Chesson Diary, 5 and 9 October 1869, REAS/11/16, English Papers, MJRL.

202 Editorial, *MS*, 13 October 1869.

203 Grant, *Newspaper Press*, I, 379. Impressionistically, such figures were often bandied about; it was suggested in 1876, for example, that the *Daily News* accumulated losses of as much as £100,000 before finally becoming a paying concern at the start of the 1870s, as a result in part of its coverage of the Franco-Prussian war, see 'London Newspapers during 1876', *Warwick Examiner* (Queensland), 14 April 1877.

204 Noted *Dundee Courier*, 9 January 1871; see William Tinsley, *Random Recollections*, I, 306. The plant was apparently put up for sale in 1871, see *Manchester Evening News*, 1 April 1871, but only eventually sold in 1880, see *Printing Times*, (1880), 139.

205 *Daily Telegraph*, 16 October 1869; a communicated correction appeared in the *Morning Herald*, 15 October 1869.

206 Editorial, *Exeter and Plymouth Gazette*, 15 October 1869.

207 Whiteing, *My Harvest*, 93.

Chapter 8

1 Robert Chambers to Alexander Ireland, 25 June 1861, Dep 342/110, Chambers Papers, ff. 192–3, NLS.

2 'Minute Book and Subscriptions for Testimonial to John Francis', Dep 342/425, Chambers Papers, NLS, which indicates two main rounds of activity in February–June 1862, and then November–December 1860, with a few further contributions, totalling £136.3.6, including a number of individuals with publishing connections, including Holyoake, but predominantly drawn from publishing houses and the newspaper press.

3 The testimonial Committee was chaired by William Ewart, with John Francis as Hon. Sec., *Morning Chronicle*, 5 February 1862. For the support of William Chambers, see Chambers to Holyoake, 8 October 1861, 1358, Holyoake Papers, CpUL. See Collet, *Taxes*, II, 140–3. A deputation offering thanks to Milner Gibson and Ewart had previously met them at the end of July 1861, *WDP*, 3 August 1861.

4 For Thornton Hunt's early initiative see Holyoake to Hunt, 24 April 1862, Brewer Leigh-Hunt Collection, University of Iowa.

5 'But it is useless to now to talk of his merits to the general public which has
   forgotten the subject', Cobden to Mitchell, 29 October 1863, Add. MS. 13886/25,
   WSRO. Mitchell sends £5; Cobden indicates that he thinks he should approach
   Lawson of the *Telegraph*, 'as the Leviathan of the penny press' to make up whatever
   deficiency remains. Cobden to Mitchell, 1 November 1863, Add. MS. 13886/26,
   WSRO. See also F. W. Newman to Holyoake, 22 February 1862, #1405, Holyoake
   Papers, CpUL, willing to offer support, 'If you have reason to believe that it will be
   taken up vigorously enough to make Mr Collet not ashamed to receive it'; Newman
   recalls that 'I had backed out myself from the agitation for the abolition of the duty,
   because I thought the destruction of the beer & spirit retail trade far more urgent,
   & I could not press for both at once. But I recognise and rejoice in the free trade
   of paper as a high benefit'. In 1864 Cobden attempted to drum up support from
   provincial supporters of the association, such as Charles Rawlins in Liverpool,
   Cobden to Rawlins, 13 April 1864; *Liverpool Daily Post*, 5 May 1864; Cobden to
   Edward Alexander, 13 April 1864; CP 105, H24 WSRO.
6 See Cobden to Moore, 24 October 1864, Add. MS. 46345, f. 17, BL.
7 *Sheffield Independent*, 27 July 1861.
8 John Watts continued as sub-treasurer, see letter of Watts, 27 July 1861.
9 Collet, *Taxes*, II, 148.
10 Joel H. Wiener, *The War of the Unstamped. The Movement to Repeal the British
   Newspaper Tax, 1830–1836* (1969), 266.
11 See Wiener, *The War of the Unstamped*, 269–71, citing W. J. Fox, 'Mr Spring Rice
   and the Newspaper Press', *Monthly Repository* X (1836), 278–80; Thomas Wakley,
   A Letter to the People of England, on the New Project for Gagging the Press (1836),
   11–20.
12 A point made in the 1868 debate, repeated in editorial of *MS*, 5 February 1869.
13 See the petition of the National Political Union against the dispensing powers of the
   Stamp Commissioners, in Place Mss, Add. MS. 27796, f. 56, cited Wiener, *The War
   of the Unstamped*, 6.
14 Collet, *Taxes*, I, 93.
15 *DN*, 2 December 1852. For stratagem see Collet, *Taxes*, I, 171–5. Collet noted in
   a brief letter to the *Leader* that any impression that APRTOK 'intended to burk
   the Security Question' was misleading and that Cobden was ready to support the
   amendment had not Milner Gibson done so first, *Leader*, 11 December 1852. There
   was concern in radical circles that more was not made of the system of requiring
   heavy libel sureties from newspaper publishers, see editorial, *Reynolds's Weekly
   News*, 5 December 1852.
16 Attacked by Milner Gibson at the APRTOK soiree of February 1857 as 'absurd,
   anomalous and impracticable', *Morning Chronicle*, 9 February 1854. It was much
   less part of Cobden's preoccupation, though at the same meeting he notes that, 'he
   utterly abominated it'.

17 See J. B. Whitehead at a Rawtenstall reform meeting, both urging removal of the security regulations and remaining duties, but also raising the spectre of a law which makes reading a newspaper without a magistrate's permission an offence, *Bury Times*, 26 February 1859.

18 *Preston Chronicle*, 6 March 1858.

19 *Morning Post*, 17 May 1854.

20 For this see Lee, *Origins*, especially 21–41; for example James F. Stephens, 'Journalism', *Cornhill Magazine*, VI (1862), 57–8.

21 'Scientific Censorship of the English Press', *Leader*, 18 January 1851; 'The will of the Board is felt to be so precarious, that no one dares to embark a large capital in an unstamped political paper.'

22 'Taxes on Knowledge', *Tait's Edinburgh Magazine* (April 1850), 234–9.

23 A brief campaign which resulted in acquittals, see Royle, *Victorian Infidels*, 234.

24 Thomas Jackson to Commissioners of the Inland Revenue, 9 May 1853, printed in *Correspondence relating to the Newspaper Stamp since 1853*, 33. Abolition of the securities 'would only tend to facilitate defamation by the pauper agents of wealthy knaves, or by men who aim at converting slander into hard cash', *Freeman's Journal*, 13 March 1855.

25 *Morning Post*, 17 May 1854.

26 One instance of a paper pursued for registration, but not for stamp, is the *Ratepayer* in 1851, see Collet, Q835, *Report of the Select Committee on the Newspaper Stamp*.

27 *Report of the Select Committee of the House of Lords Appointed to Consider the Law of Defamation and Libel* (1843).

28 *Morning Post*, 17 May 1854.

29 As instanced by papers sent reminders about the need to register even though they already were. For example, J. R. Kelly (*Uttoxeter New Era*) to Keogh, 24 April 1857, *Return of all Correspondence, PP* (1857–8), 19.

30 See the complaint of John Pollard, editor of the *Wigan Examiner*, 14 July 1857, *Return of all Correspondence, PP* (1857–8), 30.

31 As reported in *Hansard*, 17 July 1862, cc.404–13.

32 See the complaints of William Pressey of the *Luton Weekly Recorder*, 22 November [1858] in IR 56/45, NA. There were similar problems with a previous *Dunstable Reformer* published by the same, see memo dated 5 January 1858.

33 See, for example, Timm to J. T. Jones (editor of the *Gwytony Cymraeg*), 13 August 1853, MS.3366F, NLW; apparently Jones's first nominee gave notice to Timm that he refused to act as surety and Timm had to chase Jones for a substitute, Timm to J. T. Jones, 6 September 1853, ibid.

34 See correspondence of the editor of the *Nelson and Colne Guardian* ('I can assure you there is much difficulty in getting sureties to that amount, otherwise the matter would have been attended to sooner', Pickles Sunderland to Stamp Office, 14 November 1868, IR83/163, NA). Sunderland offers one example of a proprietor

let down by his nominated guarantor when it comes to executing the legal commitment, see ibid., 20 February 1869.

35 Sunderland to IR, 22 February 1869; finally confirms compliance, ibid., 17 March 1868, IR83/163, NA.

36 As reported in *Hansard*, 17 July 1862, cc.404–13.

37 Editorial, *Newcastle Journal*, 14 April 1855.

38 See circular on 'Newspaper Reform' produced and circulated by the proprietor of the *CM*, reprinted *Dundee Courier*, 18 April 1855.

39 A. H. Keane to Inland Revenue, 7 April 1865, IR 56/45, NA, although the paper appears to have been deposited with the British Library from the first issue.

40 John T. Walters (Newmarket) to Cobden, 19 March 1855, CP 54B, WSRO.

41 See *Gazette* (March 1859), 8–11.

42 'The New Newspaper Code', *Freeman's Journal*, 13 February 1855: 'Under the new law any nameless, houseless, "vagrant" may be set up as a newspaper publisher and proprietor by a Minister or a Lord of the Treasurer, or any such personage who desires to demoralise public opinion . . . and every man who is not a tool of the "starters" will be brought under his scurrilous pen.'

43 'The Newspaper Stamp', *The Times*, 13 March 1855.

44 *DN*, Editorial, 5 March 1855; Bright had discounted prospects of opposition in the Commons, but had noted that talk is that Lord Campbell will oppose repeal of securities measures in the Lords; '"What an imposter is this Lord Chief Justice!" 'There is hardly a man I despise more in public life . . . this dread of a free press . . '', Bright to McLaren, 5 March 1855, 1/77/2, McLaren Papers, University of Nottingham.

45 For a while it seemed Cornewall Lewis's measure would require sureties for stamped papers, but not for entirely unstamped ones, which the *Chelmsford Chronicle* noted was 'to deliberately establish a free trade in libel for the very class that is most likely to abuse the privilege', 23 March 1855.

46 *Gazette*, 19 (June 1855), 14.

47 See the various enquiries printed in the *Return of All Correspondence, PP* (1857–8).

48 William St Leger Babington, letter to Comptroller of Stamps, 1 September 1856, *Return of All Correspondence, PP* (1857–8), 8.

49 *Return of All Correspondence, PP* (1857–8), 9–10 (21 April 1857). The circular reinforced both the registration regulations and the requirement to lodge with the Commissioners a signed copy of each issue, which was required to be produced in evidence in the case of any proceedings. Again report in the *Gazette* pointed out the unevenness of the implementation of the statutes, in that pamphlets are still not to be proceeded against, so that the law is in effect being determined by the Attorney-General, who instructs Somerset House to act (yet Brown was not averse to conjuring the effects of the cheap press in fitting the working classes for the franchise); see hustings speech reported in *DN*, 8 March 1859.

50 Ayrton ascribed renewed efforts at imposition to Brown's intervention, see *Hansard*, 17 February 1859, cc.484–91. The prosecution was prompted by a complaint in a letter to Board of Inland Revenue, 16 August 1856, printed in *Return of All Correspondence, PP* (1857–8), 6.

51 *North Wales Chronicle*, 13 June 1857.

52 *Return of All Correspondence, PP* (1857–8), 24.

53 *Morpeth Herald*, 27 June 1857.

54 23 May 1857; though also London correspondence considered it 'strange . . . that proprietors do not see the advisability of submitting to the law', ibid., 20 December 1857.

55 See annotations to letter of Pressey and Crew, 16 July 1857, IR 56/45, NA. Timm's later comment (18 August 1857) is that the repeal of the previous act (6&7 WmIV c76) that expressly included 'remarks or observations' on the news, he believes the sample copies of the *Free Press* he has looked at, 'would not be deemed by a court and jury to be newspapers'.

56 Editorial, *Morning Post*, 2 July 1857.

57 Circular, 16 May 1857, Camden Archives. See APRTOK, Minutes, 20 May 1857, which listed large numbers of papers who had been required to register but not yet done so, and also more than a dozen who had not been contacted by the Board (both established papers like the *Bradford Observer* and newer papers like *Dunstable Reformer*, the *South Bucks Free Press*); ditto 27 May 1857, which noted a number of papers who had received but disregarded the notice, and ibid., 24 June 1857 (though thereafter the activity of the committee seems to have waned rapidly).

58 [APRTOK] to Joseph Timm, 17 June 1857, Camden Archives.

59 *Gazette* (November 1857), 17–19, 21. Collet in *Taxes*, II, 57–60, explains the background of this. Correspondence on the case was published in the *Free Press* 'with a scathing article by Mr. Urquhart', 60.

60 The *Dunstable Reformer* was one paper which took up the suggestion to use the non-prosecution of the *Free Press* as a justification for not prosecuting them either, see *Return of All Correspondence, PP* (1857–8), 31. Less sympathetically, so did the *North Wales Chronicle*, 13 June 1857.

61 Court of Exchequer, 28 November 1857; 'Annual Report for 1858', in *Gazette* (January 1859), 2.

62 See the telling correspondence in *Return of All Correspondence, PP* (1857–8), 32–4; also Camden Archives.

63 *Gazette* (June 1858), 6. In February 1859 the Association wrote a long memorial to the Solicitor General noting that in publishing a pamphlet of 630 square inches printing Sir H. Cairns's speech on the government of India, without providing security under 60 Geo III s.9, the government's printer, Taylor, has broken the law, noticed in *Falkirk Herald*, 24 February 1859.

64 *Gazette* (March 1859), 11–13. For correspondence APRTOK conducted with
    Stanley and Lytton on this issue, see *Gazette* (March 1859), 14–15.

65 See the account in APRTOK memorial, *Gazette* (April 1859), 1–4.

66 Noted by the *MS*, extracted by the *Derby Mercury*, 13 April 1859.

67 *Hansard*, 17 February 1859, cc.490. Later Sir Hugh Cairns (Solicitor General) notes
    that the government would like to keep registration of props of newspapers under
    6&7 Wm IV, and 2&3 Vict, *Hansard*, 18 March 1859, c.383.

68 *Hansard*, 7 April 1859, cc.1523–26.

69 *MS*, 7 February 1860. The *Kentish Chronicle*, 25 February 1860, also rejoiced
    prematurely at the 'great success' in the 'repeal of another vexatious restriction – the
    security system'.

70 APRTOK 'Minutes', 16 June and 11 July 1860, BL. It is not clear what sort of
    governmental support this bill had; but it was included by the (hostile) *Derby
    Mercury* in the defeats of the administration in 1860, 1 August 1860; for 1861,
    Hansard, 2 August 1861, cc.1840–2; 1862, *Hansard*, 17 July 1862, cc.404–13.

71 Collet, *Taxes*, II, 162–3.

72 Collet, *Taxes*, II, 165, noting no entries in the Association's minute book from July
    1862 to June 1868. This Minute book does not seem to be extant.

73 Harris, 'London's Local Newspapers', Brake et al., *Investigating Victorian Journalism*,
    107. For this case see *Lloyd's Weekly Newspaper*, 5 July 1868.

74 *Newspaper Press* (July 1868), 157, quoted in Harris, 'London's Local
    Newspapers', 107.

75 See the confession of ignorance of P. Sunderland of the *Nelson and Colne Guardian*,
    letter to IR, 9 February 1869, IR83/163, NA; Editorial, *Sherbourne Mercury*,
    11 December 1866.

76 Vincent to Keogh, 28 April [1857], *Return of All Correspondence, PP* (1857–8), 18.

77 London: 64, England 232, Wales 21, Scotland 30, Ireland 14: J. Fisher to the Board
    of Inland Revenue, 8 September 1866 [copy], IR 56/41, NA.

78 Memorandum (signed WHC) in IR 56/41, NA.

79 Material in IR 56/43; account based on Legg, *Newspapers and Nationalism*, 35.

80 Mss Return of all correspondence with the Board of IR on newspaper registration
    1865–8, IR 56/45, NA.

81 W. Castle to IR, 10 June 1867 and 1 July 1867, Sargent to Castle, 24 June,
    IR 56/45, NA.

82 Fisher to the Board of Inland Revenue, 8 September 1866, IR 56/41, NA.

83 Fisher to the Board of Inland Revenue, 8 September 1866, IR 56/41, NA (quoted
    Legg, *Newspapers and Nationalism*, 34).

84 Fisher to IR, 16 January 1867, IR 56/41, NA. Significantly Fisher was himself
    subject of proceedings in April 1866 in respect of invalid securities, see Fisher to
    IR, 10 April 1866, IR 56/45, NA.

85 See *Newspaper Press* (June 1867), 128.

86 C. Mitchell and Co, to [S. Sargent?], 26 April 1867, IR 56/41, NA.

87 See Royle, *Victorian Infidels*, 266; the registration question was further complicated in April 1867 by the decision of Baxter vs Freeman at Southwark County Court that unregistered papers could not recover debts in court, see *Hertfordshire Guardian*, 27 April 1867.

88 Copy of memorandum of Stephen Dowell, [Assistant Solicitor to the Inland Revenue], 1 November 1866, IR 56/41.

89 *The Owl: A Wednesday Journal of Politics and Society*, established in 1866.

90 Letter of F. Algar to *Newspaper Press*, 1 April 1867, 88. Responded to by 'The Proprietor of two Registered Papers' portraying the action as a response to a quite proper request from the Provincial Newspaper Society, *Newspaper Press*, 1 May 1867, 108.

91 Collet, *Taxes*, II, 168 (italics in original).

92 Brockman and Harrison to Commissioners of the Inland Revenue, 26 December 1867, and ditto, 26 March 1868, and associated correspondence which indicated a close investigation into the standing of the sureties of the paper, IR 83/163, NA. In October 1868 Brockman and Harrison alleged further libels; see letter 26 October 1868; the Board is urged to obtain '*substantial sureties*'.

93 Memorandum, 24 June 1868, IR 56/45, NA.

94 Letter from Messrs Tucker and Bird, 21 April 1868, IR 56/45, NA. Similar case of *Cleckheaton Guardian*, where apparently sureties are deemed insufficient; letter from Edgar Barker, proprietor, 2 May 1868 confesses that he has 'tried his utmost' to get sureties but has failed; wonders if fact that his is 'a very unpretending little sheet, published solely for the object of recording local events' really makes it appropriate for such action.

95 H. G. Reid [to IR], 26 February 1869, IR83/163, NA. Reid noted that the fact of this 'ugly law-suit' did not make getting sureties any easier, ditto 4 February 1869.

96 Editorial, *Camden and Kentish Town Gazette*, 11 July 1868.

97 *Law Times*, 18 July 1868, 226. Noted at this point that the *Owl* was still only in the course of registering.

98 Letter of 'Fair Play', *Camden and Kentish Towns Gazette*, 18 July 1868; an editorial of 25 July spoke of other letters of support, but none were printed and the matter was allowed to drop.

99 Hansard, 24 May 1867, cc.1076–87; *Examiner*, 25 May 1867. Support from *Newspaper Press*, editorial June 1867, 125.

100 Quoted by *MS*, 5 February 1869.

101 Editorial, *DN*, 4 July 1868; speaks of 'harassing proceedings'; *Manchester Guardian*, quoted in *Newspaper Press* (July 1868), 157.

102 For a summary of this case see Hypatia Bonner-Bradlaugh, *Charles Bradlaugh. A Record of His Life and Work* (1895), I, 137–51.

103 Attendance included Ayrton, Milner Gibson, J. S. Mill, Moore, Collet, E. Truelove, A. Holyoake; the petition was put into the hands of Ayrton; see *National Reformer*, 21 June 1868.

104 This is the claim of Bradlaugh in his account of the termination of the proceedings, *National Reformer*, 2 May 1869.

105 For full case, see *National Reformer*, 25 April 1869.

106 See 'County Newspapers – Reregistrations', IR 83/163, NA. A further 27 papers were identified as requiring registration; see 'Country Newspapers Requiring Re-Registration' (n.d.).

107 Achilles Page to S. Dowell, 23 January 1869, IR83/163, NA (Page pointed out that his solicitor had told him that 'the entire thing is obsolete, that hundreds of newspapers have not given bonds', ditto 16 January 1869).

108 Special Edition of the *National Reformer*, 7 February 1869. Bradlaugh also picks on the Attorney General's mistaken comment that provisions re pamphlets have been repealed, showing, Bradlaugh points out, the Attorney-General's ignorance of the act.

109 See letter of Bradlaugh, *Morning Post*, 5 February 1869.

110 Quoted in *National Reformer*, 21 February 1869. Further dismissal of Bradlaugh's case in the new Conservative paper, the *Blue Budget*, quoted *National Reformer*, 21 March 1869.

111 See *National Reformer*, 21 March 1869, noting that the accounts in the mainstream press had suppressed reference to Bradlaugh.

112 See *National Reformer*, 25 April 1869.

113 *Hansard*, 8 April 1869, c.450.

114 The sense is that it is hurried through without debate: first intimations that it is on the cards towards middle of April, see *BDP*, citing the *Echo*, 12 April 1869. *National Reformer* notes final indignity of lack of debate and the comment of Lansdowne in moving the second reading of the bill, of the statute as never having been enforced lately except to gratify a grudge against some particular journal, *National Reformer*, 6 June 1869.

115 At this point the regulations were that a copy of every newspaper published in the United Kingdom should be deposited in the British Library.

116 *Printers' Register*, 6 January 1870.

117 'Newspaper Copyright', *Printers' Register*, 6 September 1869, also 7 June 1869.

Chapter 9

1 Efforts were made from the later 1870s: see bill of Samuel Waddy, Sir Charles Russell and Henry Cole in April 1877.

2   Harris suggests rather the impact of suburbanization, 'London's Local Newspapers', 111.

3   See Wiener, *Americanization*, 67–9.

4   Lee, *Origins*, 80–2.

5   'Provincial Journalistic Enterprise: Mackie's Series of Newspapers', *Printers' Register*, 6 July 1870; Brown, *Victorian Newspapers*, 117–18.

6   *Printers' Register*, 6 July 1869.

7   *Brighton Daily News*, 17 June 1869.

8   See Hobbs, 'Reading the Local Paper'.

9   Hobbs notes evidence that the value of second-hand papers increased in 1870, and a club expenditure on newspapers increased by 40%, 'Reading the Local Paper'.

10 Ayherst, *Guardian*, 157.

11 Meeting mentioned by Julius West, *History of Chartism* (1920), 259; for petition see *Appendix to the Twenty-Fourth Report of the Select Committee on Petitions* (1870), 302. This had been an element of the APRTOK position earlier; see exchange of letters between Collet and Alfred Bishop (London newsagent), *Morning Star*, 14 February 1860. For presentation of this as a culmination of 20-year's agitation against the taxes on knowledge, see Editorial, *English Mechanic*, 14 October 1870, XII, 73. (Notes that the reform comes somewhat spontaneously, and without any public pressure.) The editor (J. Passmore Edwards) noted his own role 'from the first, intensely interested in this movement – having wrought on committees, attended public meetings, and done our best through the press to awaken and direct public attention to the great advantages of distributing knowledge cheaply and expeditiously.'

12 Collet to Holyoake, 19 October 1887, Holyoake 1/4, Bishopsgate; see materials in the Urquhart Collection, Balliol College Archives. See also Taylor, 'Collet', *Oxford Dictionary of National Biography*.

13 See G. J. Holyoake, *Bygones Worth Remembering* (1905), I, 42–4; minutes of the Committee, Holyoake Papers, Bishopsgate.

14 George Newnes to Holyoake, 15 April 1899, Holyoake/1/5, Bishopsgate.

15 See references supra, Chapter 1, n.5.

16 Holyoake, *Bygones*, I, 154–5.

17 For just a few citations see Joseph Howes, *Twenty-five Years' Fight with the Tories* (1907), 36, quoting a letter from the *Leeds Express* in 1880.

18 See Bright at Blackburn, *Scotsman*, 1 December 1865. For David Johnstone at Glasgow in 1866, the abolition of the taxes on knowledge stood with the removal of slavery and corn laws as the three great works of the middle classes since 1832, *Scotsman*, 26 January 1866; Gladstone at Liverpool, *Scotsman*, 7 April 1866. For the 1870s, see for example, the letter of 'Another East Cornwall Elector', *Royal Cornwall Gazette*, 31 January 1874; Bright at Birmingham, *York Herald*, 2 February 1874, Godwin at Bradford, 2 February 1874.

19 Editorials, *Reynolds's Newspaper*, 12 July 1868; 25 July 1869; 7 August 1881; 27 April 1884; GRACCHUS, 15 September 1858; contribution of 'Mr Jarman, a Working Man', *Leicester Chronicle*, 14 February 1874, and the retrospect of Sir Harry Verney, *Liverpool Mercury*, 25 February 1874.

20 Suggested by *Perthshire Constitutional*, in 1877, in face of Bright's claims for his role in the Taxes on Knowledge that 'Lord Stanley (the present Lord Derby) was the leading spirit of that movement', quoted *Lancaster Gazette*, 20 January 1877.

21 *BDP*, 24 March 1870. And so taken by republican rhetoric as one of the good things that the post-1832 parliament produced, albeit it is by 1872 exhausted, *Reynolds's Newspaper*, 15 September 1872; for later examples *Reynolds's Newspaper*, 23 June 1889.

22 Wilson, *Memories*, 135; cites the construction of Justin McCarthy, which presented the taxes as remnants of an 'ancient system of finance . . . originally imposed with the object of checking the growth of seditious newspapers'. For Wilson it was simply a matter of the poor being denied cheap literature and so education. It is notable that this was one of a number of studies which was, like Collet's *Taxes* volume itself, published by Thomas Fisher Unwin, whose Cobdenite pedigree, having married Cobden's daughter, was unassailable; see comments in A. C. Howe, *Free Trade and Liberal England* (1997), 264.

23 See speech at Bolton, *Liverpool Daily Post*, 12 October 1864.

24 Though not entirely unacknowledged, see for example, W. E. Williams, *The Rise of Gladstone* (1934).

25 It is very clear from Bright's correspondence with Cobden that right up to the repeal in 1861, Bright was unable to get rid of the fear that Gladstone would betray the cause at the last moment; even in March 1861 he was telling Cobden that he would have no part in getting Gladstone returned for South Lancashire, 'for his return would tend to show an approval for the course of the government which I do not entertain', Add. MS. 43384, f. 250–1, BL.

26 *Greville Memoirs*, VIII, 300.

27 See E. D. Steele, *Palmerston and Liberalism, 1855–1865* (1991), 15.

28 Point briefly made by E. F. Biagini, *Liberty, Retrenchment and Reform, Popular Liberalism in the Age of Gladstone, 1860–1880* (1992), 105, citing Wilson, *Memories*, 133–7, and *Gladstone the Friend of the People, by George Potter – Leaflets for the New Electors – Price One Penny* [1885], in 'Collection of Electoral Propaganda Material', Nuffield College, Oxford. This was an identification pushed by Holyoake, see his 'The Liberal Situation, or the Parliamentary Treatment of the People, *Newcastle Weekly Chronicle*, 18 March 1865, cited by Biagini, *Liberty, Retrenchment and Reform*, 106. For later panegyrics to Gladstone's single-handed routing of the Lords' pretensions to usurp the authority of the Commons, see Harry Jones, *Liberalism and the House of Lords. The Story of the Veto Battle, 1832–1911* (1912), 30–40. The account was often garbled, as in C. H. Jones, *A Short Life of William*

Ewart Gladstone (1880); according to *The Passing of Gladstone: His Life, Death and Burial* (1898), 'Among all Mr Gladstone's wonderful achievements probably none had been more productive of wonderful and widespread results than the repeal of the paper duties', 134. Occluded for Bright, see William Robertson, *Life and Times of John Bright* (or 1877; 1912).

29   Quoted *Scotsman*, 24 February 1860.

30   Cobden to Richard, 27 January 1857, Add. MS. 43658, ff. 251–4, BL; 'I am afraid he is not even yet committed to any broad & intelligible principles, & if so he may be only invested with powers of mystification by the praise you lavish on him – Lord Grey is the only man of the Cabinet Minister stamp whose conduct can be honestly indorsed by us.'

31   For discussions with Derby, see Shannon, *Gladstone*, 329–31.

32   E. J. Stanley to Henrietta Maria Stanley, 6 February 1860, DSA, 99/8, Stanley Papers, CRO.

33   Editorial, *Leeds Mercury*, 9 August 1860.

34   Quoted in *Hereford Times*, 14 July 1860; 'It is daily more and more evident', noted the *Hull Packet*, 6 July 1860, 'that Mr Gladstone, who, not long since was too Conservative for a Whig administration, has become too democratic for any government save an one [sic] as Mr BRIGHT might form.'

35   See Gladstone to Milner Gibson, 29 December 1859 [copy], Add. MS. 44392, f. 355, BL.

36   See Cobden to Bright, 30 January 1860: 'Gladstone has shown much heart in this business . . . Gladstone has a strong aversion to the waste of money on our armaments – He has no class feeling with the "services" – He has much more of our sympathies – It is a pity you cannot avoid hurting his convictions by such sallies as your "adulterous connexion" &c. – He has more in common with you & me than any other man of his power in Britain.'

37   Cobden to Bright, 25 August 1860, Add. MS. 43651, ff. 173–5, BL: 'the democracy of the Chancellor <of the Exchequer,–> – for the latter (I mean in his desire to serve the interests of the million & not of a class.) is at heart a democrat of the purest type!' Cobden recognized that, as he told him, that 'if you had not been in the Cabinet the Treaty would never have been made', 23 September 1860, Add. MS. 44136, ff. 33–4, BL.

38   John Pearson to Gladstone, 1 August 1860, Box 68, GGPGL; for similar sentiments of support see James Todd to Gladstone, 6 July 1860, Box 91, GGPGL.

39   'What changes there are in this world. Gladstone going to Bradford with Bright & Cobden & Milner Gibson . . .' commented Philip Rose to Disraeli, 13 December 1860, R/1/B/72a,b, *Disraeli Letters*, VIII, 79n3.

40   Cowen to Holyoake, 13 August 1862, #1437, Holyoake Papers, CpUL. At the time of the Milner Gibson testimonial in 1861 the claims of Gladstone for recognition alongside had been frequently urged; see [unnamed correspondent? John Laney?]

to Holyoake, 10 October 1861 #1360, Holyoake Papers. For later variations on this theme, see Justin McCarthy, 'The Useless House of Lords', *North American Review* (August 1893), 215–24 (which neatly conflates the paper duty repeal and the appearance of the penny press). See the address of the workingmen of York to Gladstone, *Reynolds's Newspaper*, 19 June 1864.

41 See the jaundiced comments of Teynham to R.B. Reed, 17 July 1860, COW/C/1455, TWAS.

42 This was noted in 1860, as in an editorial of *Dunfermline Press*, 5 July 1860, 'His affinities are more with the Manchester School, represented by Cobden and Bright, than with . . . Palmerston'.

43 'It is useless for him to disassociate himself from the Constitutional Defence Committee, from the orators of St Martin's Hall . . . He is theirs, body and soul', *London Standard*, 11 August 1860; 'His unfortunate union with JOHN BRIGHT has entirely destroyed the fair fame the right hon. Gentleman once possessed', 'Private Correspondence', *North Wales Chronicle*, 4 August 1860.

44 Robert Cecil, 'The Conservative Reaction', *Quarterly Review* (July 1860), 280.

45 Roberts notes that prior to 1860 Cecil had generally spoken only three or four times a year; but in 1860 he spoke 13 times, and thereafter kept this rate up for the rest of his Commons career, A. Roberts, *Salisbury. Victorian Titan* (1999), 73–4. Included in this is his notorious stab that Gladstone's 1861 manoeuvre was 'more worthy of an attorney than a statesman', 74.

46 'My idea of angelic behaviour consists of supporting Palmerston and opposing Bright on all possible occasions – at all events the latter', as Cecil wrote to Lord Carnarvon, 31 March 1861, quoted C. C. Westock, *The House of Lords and Ideological Politics: Lord Salisbury's Referendal Theory and the Conservative Party, 1846–1922* (1995), 45, [Salisbury Papers, D/30/3]. See also 'Democracy on Its Trial', *Quarterly Review* (July 1861).

47 See Editorial, *Reynolds's Newspaper*, 18 March 1855.

48 See Ironside to Palmerston, 28 December 1851, PP/GC/IR/1, PalPUS.

49 For Cowen's contribution to the agitation, see Joan Allen, '"Resurrecting Jerusalem": The Late Chartist Press in the North-east of England, 1852–1859', in Allen and Ashton, *Papers for the People*, 168–89. Allen suggests the *Northern Tribune* was part of a deliberate policy 'to educate the people of the north of England and to publicise the renewed campaign to remove the Stamp Duty on newspapers', 173. Allen argues that Cowen's tactic of drip feeding petitions on the question to local MP J. F. B. Blackett, indicates 'determined campaigning [which] runs counter to the claim that during this period extra parliamentary groups "failed to exert sufficient pressure for reform"', 173, referencing Hugh Cunningham, *The Challenge of Democracy*. The *Northern Tribune* was sold on to Holyoake after the removal of the stamp, and incorporated into *The Reasoner*.

50 For a good example, see 'Repeal of the Paper Duty', *Dundalk Democrat*, extracted in *Freeman's Journal*, 26 July 1859.

51 Editorial, *Reynolds's Newspaper*, 28 January 1855.

52 For example, GRACCHUS, *Reynolds's Newspaper*, 21 December 1851; 1 April 1855; 25 March 1860.

53 See Benjamin Wilson's *Struggles of an Old Chartist*, in Vincent, *Testaments of Radicalism*, 216, 228.

54 The one-sidedness of the surviving correspondence perhaps exaggerates this impression, but the lack of any sense of input from Collet and others is marked.

55 London correspondence, *Dumfries and Galloway Standard*, 24 April 1850.

56 Cobden to F. W. Cobden, 20 July 1853, Add. MS. 6011, ff. G102, G103, WSRO.

57 G. J. Holyoake, *Sixty Years of an Agitator's Life* (1892), I, 280.

58 *MS*, 2 March 1860.

59 'But it is useless to now to talk of his merits to the general public which has forgotten the subject', Cobden to Mitchell, 29 October 1863, Add. Mss 13886/25, WSRO.

60 *CM*, 25 November 1856; notes success 'arose in a great measure from their incessant persecution of the Board of the Inland Revenue, the Lords of the Treasury, and all the other branches of the circumlocution office.'

61 But what is the use of mere words – 'What can we *do*?', as Cobden asked Bright, 16 October 1852, Add. MS. 43649, ff. 283–8, BL.

62 Collet, *Taxes*, I, 134. Cobden carries on throughout the period demonstrating his underlying suspicion if not antipathy to the platform; for example, his comment to Bright at the end of 1859 that 'Your greatest power is in the House, In quiet times, there is no influence to be had from without, & if we fell into evil days of turbulence, & suffering & agitation, less scrupulous leaders would carry off the masses', 29 December 1859, Add. MS. 43651, ff. 48–55, BL.

63 As Cobden told J[oseph] Woodhead of the stamp law (4 August 1854, KC312/17/11,West Yorkshire Archive Service, Kirklees), 'in the meantime the Law Officers of the Crown admit that the Law cannot be properly defined & I don't think any further attempt will be made either to define or enforce it.'

64 See Collet, *The Tax on Travelling: The Laws as to Its Assessment Set Aside By the Inland Revenue* (1879).

65 One exception was the letter of Holyoake to *The Examiner*, 12 June 1875, in his comments on the way to attack the Sunday acts: 'If every Sabbatarian Act in the Statute Book was enforced, as it might and ought to be, vexation, confusion and resentment would be stirred up, in every town in the empire, and the working people of England would live no longer under the indignity and humiliation of [its restrictions]'. Compare with the letter of William Tebb, an anti-Vaccinator, justifying resistance to the legal provision for vaccination on the grounds that

the taxes on knowledge agitation, along with the repeal of the Corn Laws, the exemption of Quakers from oaths, were obtained by 'persistent resistance to the law', *The Times*, 26 November 1877.

66 Nigel Todd, *The Militant Democracy. Joseph Cowen and Mid-Victorian Radicalism* (1991), 62.

67 'Political Apostacy [sic]', *Reynolds's Newspaper*, 16 August 1874.

68 Hunt, *Then and Now*, 91 ('It may confidently be asserted that no branch of our national industry was subjected to such substantial changes during the ten years between 1854 and 1864 as newspapers'). For a later example see the comment of the first issue of the *Yorkshire Post*: the railway and telegraph meant 'the old line of demarcation between town and country had been broken through. Railways and the electric telegraph have established a frequency of locomotion and a circulation of ideas which rob country society of all that inertness and incuriousness which were once its peculiar characteristics . . ', quoted Gibb and Beckwith, *Yorkshire Post*, 33. Note Jones's comment that the railway was 'the single most important contribution to the growth of a mass newspaper market', *Press, Politics and Society*, 106. For the introduction of esparto grass, and the changing technologies of paper making more generally, see Bennett, 'The Golden Stain of Time', 166–83.

69 See Mark Hampton, *Visions of the Press, 1850–1950* (2004), 34–5, citing James Curran, 'Press History', 22–7.

70 See Miles Taylor, *Ernest Jones, Chartism and the Romance of Politics, 1819–69* (2003), 137–94.

71 *Eighth Half-Yearly Report of the Provincial Typographical Association [January–June 1854]*.

72 See handbill enclosed in James Greig to Gladstone, 13 June 1853, Box 34, Miscellaneous Correspondence, GGPGL.

73 J. B. Blackett to Congreve (tps), 26 October 1853, MS. Eng. Lett. c.185, f. 159, Bodleian Library.

74 'The removal of the Stamp has so enlarged the basis of the newspaper press that it can never again be *monopolised* by clique, club, or party', Cobden to Richard, [c.22 October 1856], Add. MS. 43658, ff. 168–9, BL; Cobden to Joseph Sturge, 31 October 1856, Add. MS. 43722, ff. 165–6, BL.

75 Cobden to Richard, 7 November 1856, Add. MS. 43658, ff. 179–81, BL.

76 Cobden to Bright, 3 April 1856, Add. MS. 43650, ff. 200–3, BL.

77 *Leicester Chronicle*, 3 May 1862.

78 See Duncan McLaren to Cobden, 8 January 1862, 6–8E, CP 7, WSRO. It may well be that Cobden was dissuaded by McLaren's observation that the scheme 'would not for many years affect the Times injuriously' and would rather 'affect the weaker papers much more'.

79 See *Mr Cobden and the Times* (1863), and *Cobden-Delane Correspondence: Opinions of the Liberal Press on the Correspondence between Mr. Cobden, MP, and Mr. Delane*,

Editor of the 'The Times' (1864), and William Hargreaves, *Is the Anonymous System a Security for the Purity and Independence of the Press* (1864), which detailed the various government offices which family connections of the *Times* held; see support of Hargreaves' position in 'An Impersonal Press', *Rochdale Observer*, 18 June 1864.

80 For some figures, see Brown, *Victorian Newspapers*, 52–3.

81 *History of the Times*, II, 497.

82 Cobden to William Hargreaves, 6 July 1860, Add. MS. 43655, ff. 147–51, BL.

83 J. Vincent, *The Formation of the Liberal Party, 1857–1868* (1966). 'The effect of the repeal of the stamp and paper duties was to raise to first position a quite new class of newspaper, democratic, but not Radical, cheap but respectable'; see also J. P. Parry, *The Rise and Fall of Liberal Government* (1993), 169.

84 Collet to Holyoake, 4 August 1895, #3520, Holyoake Papers, CpUL; see Patrick Joyce, *Visions of the People. Industrial England and the Question of Class, 1848–1914* (1991).

85 John Bright to William Mitchell, 23 January 1872, published in *Manchester Evening News*, 22 February 1872, and widely elsewhere.

Bibliography

Primary printed

A Claim for the Repeal of the Paper Duty (Exeter: *Exeter Gazette*, 1850).

A Selection from the Correspondence of Abraham Hayward, Q.C. (London: John Murray, 1886), ed. Henry E. Carlisle.

A Sketch of the Political History of the Past Three Years, in Connexion with the Press Newspaper, and the Part It Has Taken in the Leading Questions of the Time (London: Press Office, 1856).

Amphlett, J., *The Newspaper Press* (London: Whittaker, 1860).

Aspden, H., *Fifty Years a Journalist. Reflections and Recollections of an Old Clitheroean* (Clitheroe: Advertiser and Times, [1930]).

Association for the Promotion of the Repeal of the Taxes on Knowledge, *A Statement of the Case for the Repeal of the Taxes on Knowledge* (London: APRTOK, 1852).

Baldwin, J., *A Letter Addressed to the Right Hon. Lord John Russell Showing the Evil Effects and Injustice of the Excise Laws* (Birmingham: M Billing, 1848).

Baxter, W. E., *Notes on the Practical Effects of Repealing the Newspaper Stamp Duty, the Advertising Duty, and the Excise Duty on Paper* (London: Simpkin, Marshall and Co., 1852).

[Birmingham Association for the Abolition of the Taxes on Knowledge], *A Statement of the Injurious Effects of the Excise Tax, the Tax upon Advertisements, and the Stamp Tax upon Newspapers* (Birmingham: 1850).

Brodrick, G. C., 'What are Liberal Principles', *Fortnightly Review*, 25 (1 February 1876), 174–93.

Brooke, J. and Sorensen, M. (eds), *Autobiographica* (London, H. M. S. O., 1971).

Brougham, H., *Cheap Literature for the People* (London: Partridge and Co., [1858]).

[Bruce, H. and Chalmers, D.], *Gladstone and the Paper Duties by Two Midlothian Paper Makers* (1885).

Burke, P., *The Copyright Law and the Press: An Essay to Show the Necessity of an Immediate Amendment of the Copyright Law upon the Removal of the Stamp Duty on Newspapers* (London: 1855).

Burley, F. [pseud.], *England Subsists by Miracle* (London: James Blackwood, 1859).

Bussey, H. F., *Sixty Years of Journalism* (Bristol: J. W. Arrowsmith, 1906).

Buxton, S., *Finance and Politics* (London: J. Murray, 1888).

Campbell, I., Duchess of Argyll, *Autobiography and Memoirs of George Douglas Campbell, Duke of Argyll* (2 vols; London: J. Murray, 1906).

Carrington, F., 'Country Newspapers and Their Editors', *New Monthly Magazine* (October 1855), 142–52.

Cecil, R. [Lord Salisbury], 'The Budget and the Reform Bill', *Quarterly Review* 107, (April 1860), 514–54.

—, 'The Conservative Reaction', *Quarterly Review* 108, (July 1860), 265–302.

Chapman, J., *Cheap Books and How to Get Them* (London: John Chapman, 1852).

'Cheap Newspapers', *London University Magazine* I (August 1856), 240–2.

'Cheap Paper and Cheap Press', *Scottish Review* (October 1861), 309–23.

'Cheapest News', *Leisure Hour* 7 (1858), 477–9.

Cobden, R., 'The National Budget for 1849' (National Expenditure No. 4), Cowen Tracts.

Collet, C. D., *Life and Career of Richard Moore* (London: John Watts, 1878).

—, *History of the Taxes on Knowledge* (London: T. Fisher Unwin, 1899).

'Conservative Journalism', *New Quarterly Review* 9, (September 1860), 385–96.

Cooper, C. A., *An Editor's Retrospect. Fifty Years of Newspaper Work* (London: Macmillan, 1896).

Cowan, C. A., *Reminiscences* ([Edinburgh]: privately printed, 1878).

Croal, D., *Early Recollections of a Journalist, 1832–1859* (Edinburgh: Haddington, 1898).

Crompton, T. B., *Excise Duty on Paper, Considered as Affecting the Employment of the Poor, the Grievances of the Manufacturer, and the Injury to the Consumer* (Farnworth, 1851).

Dallas, E. S., 'Popular Literature – The Periodical Press', *Blackwood's Edinburgh Magazine* 85 (January 1859), 96–112.

Dasent, A. I., *John Thadeus Delane, Editor of 'The Times'. His Life and Correspondence* (2 vols; London: J. Murray, 1908).

Diaries of W. E. Gladstone, ed. M. R. D. Foot and H. G. C. Matthew (Oxford: Clarendon Press: 1968-).

Dicey, E., 'Provincial Journalism', *Saint Paul's Magazine* 3 (1868), 61–73.

—, 'Journalism Old and New', *Fortnightly Review* 83 (1905), 904–18.

'English Country Newspapers', *Temple Bar*, 10 (1864), 128–41.

Escott, T. H. S., *Platform, Press, Politics and Play* (Bristol: J. W. Arrowsmith, [1895]).

Excise Duty on Paper: Letter to the Right Hon. Lord John Russell, M.P., from a Papermaker (Edinburgh, 1850).

Financial Surplus: A Claim for the Repeal of the Paper Duty (London: 1850).

Foxe Bourne, H. R., *English Newspapers, Chapters in the History of Journalism* (London: Chatto and Windus, 1887).

Frost, T., *Forty Year's Recollections: Literary and Political* (London: Low, Marston Searle and Rivington, 1880).

—, *Reminiscences of a Country Journalist* (London: Ward and Downey, 1886).

Gladstone and Palmerston: Being the Correspondence of Lord Palmerston and Mr Gladstone, 1851–1865, ed. Philip Guadella (London: Gollzanc, 1928).

Grant, J., *The Newspaper Press: Its Origin, Progress and Present Position* (3 vols; London: Tinsley Brothers, 1870–2).

Greg, W. R., 'The Newspaper Press', *Edinburgh Review* 102, (October 1855), 470–98.

Guest, J., 'A Free Press and How it Became Free', in W. Hutton, *The History of Birmingham* (1861).

Hargreaves, W., *Is the Anonymous System a Security for the Purity and Independence of the Press?* (London: William Ridgeway, 1864).

Harvey, W., *The Busy Hives around Us* (London: James Hogg and Sons, [1861]).

Hilson, J., *The Newspaper Press, in Nine Papers* (Kelso: Murray, 1858).

'History of the Taxes on Knowledge', *The People's Review* 1 (February 1850), 12–20.

Hitchman, F., 'The Penny Press', *Macmillan's Magazine* 43 (April 1881), 385–98.

[Hoare, C. J.], 'The Penny Press', *Englishwoman's Magazine and Christian Mother's Miscellany* ns V (1850), 721–3.

Holyoake, G. J., *The Government and the Working Man's Press, Two Letters to the Rt Hon Thomas Milner Gibson* (London: Free Press Union, 1853).

—, *Sixty Years of an Agitator's Life* (2 vols; London: T. Fisher Unwin, 1892).

—, *Bygones Worth Remembering* (2 vols; London: T. Fisher Unwin, 1905).

'How to Get Paper', *Household Words*, 28 October 1854.

Jenkins, T. A., *The Parliamentary Diaries of Sir John Trelawny, 1858–1865* (London: Royal Historical Society, 1990).

Jennings, L. J. (ed.), *The Croker Papers: The Correspondence and Diaries of the Late Right Honourable John Wilson Croker* (3 vols; London: J. Murray, 1885).

Knight, C., *The Struggles of a Book against Excessive Taxation* (London: 1850).

—, *The Case of the Authors against the Paper Duty* (London: 1851).

—, *Passages from a Working Life* (London: Knight & Co., 1865).

Laughton, J. K., *Memoirs of the Life and Correspondence of Henry Reeve* (2 vols; London: Longmans Green and Co., 1898).

'Literature of the People', *London Review* 13, (October 1859), 1–31.

Marx-Engels Collected Works (London: Lawrence and Wishart, 1975–2005), XC.

Maxwell, Sir H., *Life and Times of . . . W. H. Smith* (Edinburgh: W. Blackwood and Sons, 1893).

—, *Life and Letters of the Fourth Earl of Clarendon* (2 vols; London: Edward Arnold, 1913).

Mayne, F., *The Perilous Nature of the Penny Periodical Press* (London: Oxford Printing Press, [1852]).

Memoirs of Adam Black, ed. A. Nicholson (Edinburgh: Adam and Charles Black, 1885).

Memories of a Labour Leader: The Autobiography of John Wilson (London: T. Fisher Unwin, 1910).

Miall, C. S., *Henry Richard, M.P.* (London: Cassell, 1889).

Mitchell, W. W., *The Newspaper Stamp and Its Anomalies Practically Considered: A Letter Addressed to the Right Hon. the Chancellor of the Exchequer* (Arundel: 1854).

—, *The Newspaper Stamp: A Reply to a Letter to Lord Stanley by a 'County Newspaper Proprietor'* (Arundel: 1854).

Mitchell's Newspaper Press Directory (London: 1846–1963).

Mr Cobden and the Times: Correspondence between Mr Cobden and Mr Delane, Editor of The Times (Manchester: Ireland, 1863).

Newspaper and Periodical Press Association for Obtaining the Repeal of the Paper Duty, *Free Trade in Paper* (London: 1860).

Newspaper Press Census for 1861 (London: Arthur Hall and Co, 1861).

Nicoll, Sir W. R., *James MacDonell, Journalist* (London: Hodder and Stoughton, 1890).

'Paper', *Cornhill Magazine*, 4, (November 1861), 609–23.

Paterson, A., 'Provincial Newspapers', in *Progress of British Newspapers in the Nineteenth Century* (London: Simpkin, Marshall, 1901).

Petter, G. W., *Objections to the Repeal of the Paper Duty Considered* (London: Cassell, Petter and Galpin, 1860).

Reid, S. J., *Memoirs of Sir Wemyss Reid* (London, Cassell, 1905).

Report of the Proceedings of a Meeting (Consisting Chiefly of Authors) Held May 4th at the House of Mr John Chapman, 142, Strand, for the Purpose of Hastening the Removal of the Trade Restrictions on the Commerce of Literature (London: John Chapman, 1852).

[Russel, A.], 'The Newspaper Stamp', *Edinburgh Review*, IIC (1853), 488–518.

—, *The Newspaper Stamp. A Reply to Lord Stanley's Letter. The Government Plan. Reprinted from the Scotsman, 10 February* (Edinburgh: Scotsman Office, 1855).

Shepherdson, W., *Reminiscences in the Career of a Newspaper. Starting a Daily in the Provinces* (London: William Reeves, 1876).

Sinclair, A., *Fifty Years of Newspaper Life, 1845–1895: Being Chiefly Reminiscences of the Time* (Glasgow: Private Circulation, [1895]).

Society for the Diffusion of Pure Literature, *Periodicals for the People* (London: Robert K. Burt, 1856).

Stanmore, L., *Sidney Herbert, Lord Herbert of Lea: A Memoir* (2 vols; London: J. Murray, 1906).

Stephens, J. F., 'Journalism', *Cornhill Magazine* 6, (July 1862), 52–63.

'The British Newspaper: the penny theory and its solution', *Dublin University Magazine* 61, (March 1863), 359–76.

The Diaries of John Bright, ed. R. A. J. Walling (London: Cassell, 1930).

'[The Knowledge Taxes]', *Eclectic Review* 28, (1850), 431–43.

The Law of Libel, as Affecting the Newspaper Press, with Proposed Amendments (London: 1867).

'The Modern Newspaper', *British Quarterly Review* 55, (April 1872), 348–80.

The Newspaper Press of the Present Day: Its Birth and Growth throughout the United Kingdom and British Islands, from 1665: Including the Young Cheap Press and the

Metropolitan and Suburban District Papers, 1860 (London: Saunders Otley and Co, 1860).

The Newspaper Press Reviewed. By a Quarterly Reviewer (London: C. Dolman, 1857).

'The Newspaper Press, Its Origin, Progress and Present Position', *London Quarterly Review* 38, (April 1872), 87–123.

'The Newspaper Press', *New Quarterly Review* 10, (January 1861), 81–109.

The Paper and Rag Duties Considered, in a Letter Addressed to the Right Hon. W. E. Gladstone, M.P., Chancellor of the Exchequer, by a Free Trader (London: Reynolds, 1860).

The Rag Tax. The Paper Makers' Grievance and How to Redress It (London: Blades, East and Blades, 1863).

'The Rise and Fall of the *Daily Flambeau*', *Chambers Edinburgh Journal*, 7 June 1862.

The Tax upon Paper: The Case Stated for Its Immediate Repeal (London: Petter and Galpin, 1858).

Tilsley, H., *Treatise on the Stamp Laws* (London: Stevens and Norton, 1854, etc.).

Vincent, J. R. (ed.), *Disraeli, Derby and the Conservative Party. Journals and Memoirs of Edward Henry, Lord Stanley, 1849–69* (Hassocks: Harvester Press, 1978).

Watkin, E. W., *Alderman Cobden of Manchester: Letters and Reminiscences of Richard Cobden* (London: Ward Lock, 1891).

Watson, A., *A Newspaper Man's Memories* (London: Hutchinson and Co., 1925).

Watson, J., 'Reminiscences', in David Vincent (ed.), *Testaments of Radicalism* (London: Europa, 1977).

'What Will Be the Effect of the Abolition of the Newspaper Stamp', *Scottish Review* 3, (July 1855), 193–205.

[Whitty, E. M.], *An Argument for Cheap Morning Papers* (London: B. D. Cousins, 1853).

Whorlow, H., *The Provincial Newspaper Society, 1836–1886* (London: Page, Pratt and Co., 1886).

Wiebe, M. G., Conacher, J. B., Matthews, J. and Robson, A. P. (eds), *Benjamin Disraeli Letters* (London: University of Toronto Press, 1982–).

Wrigley, T., *Mr Milner Gibson and the Paper Trade: Being a Reply to a Speech Delivered by That Gentleman to His Constituents at Ashton-under-Lyne* (Bury: Bury Times, 1860).

—, *The Paper Trade: Its Position as Affected by British Legislation Contrasted with the True Principles of Free Trade* (Edinburgh: Murray and Gibb, 1863).

—, *The Case of the Paper Makers* (Bury: 1864).

Secondary

Adams, J. R. R., *The Printed Word and the Common Man: Popular Culture in Ulster, 1700–1900* (Belfast: Institute of Irish Studies, 1987).

Anderson, O., 'The Janus Face of Mid-Nineteenth Century English Radicalism: The Administrative Reform Association', *Victorian Studies* VIII (1965), 232–42.

Ayerst, D., *Guardian. Biography of a Newspaper* (London: Collins, 1971).

Bailey, I., *Herbert Ingram* (Boston: Richard Kay, 1996).

Berridge, V., 'Content Analysis and Historical Research on Newspapers', in M. Harris and A. Lee (eds), *The Press in English Society from the Seventeenth to the Nineteenth Century* (Rutherford, N. J.: Farleigh Dickinson University Press, 1986).

Biagini, E. F., *Liberty, Retrenchment and Reform, Popular Liberalism in the Age of Gladstone, 1860–1880* (Cambridge: Cambridge University Press, 1992).

Black, J., *The English Press, 1621–1861* (Stroud: Sutton, 2001).

Brake, L. and Demoor, M. (eds), *Dictionary of Nineteenth Century Journalism in Great Britain and Ireland* (London: Academia Press, 2009).

Brock, P., 'Joseph Cowen and the Polish Exiles', *Slavonic and East European Review* 32 (1953), 52–69.

Brown, D., '"Compelling but Not Controlling?": Palmerston and the Press, 1846–1855', *History* 86 (2001), 41–61.

—, 'Cobden and the Press', in A. C. Howe and S. Morgan (eds), *Rethinking Nineteenth Century Liberalism. Richard Cobden Bicentenary Essays* (Aldershot: Asghate, 2006), 80–98.

—, 'Morally Transforming the World or Spinning a Line? Politicians and the Newspaper Press in Mid-Nineteenth-Century Britain', *Historical Research* (May 2010), 321–42.

Brown, L., *Victorian News and Newspapers* (Oxford: Oxford University Press, 1985).

Burnham, L., Peterborough Court. *The Story of the Daily Telegraph* (London: Cassell, 1955).

Ceadel, M., *The Origins of War Prevention* (Oxford: Clarendon Press, 1996).

—, *Semi-Detached Idealists: The British Peace Movement and International Relations, 1854–1945* (Oxford: Oxford University Press, 2000).

Chalaby, J., *The Invention of Journalism* (Basingstoke: Macmillan, 1998).

Colclough, S., '"Purifying the Sources of Amusement and Information?": The Railway Bookstalls of W. H. Smith & Son, 1855–1860', *Publishing History* 56 (2004), 27–51.

—, '"Station to Station": The LNWR and the Emergence of the Railway Bookstall, 1848–1875', in J. Hinks and C. Armstrong (eds), *Printing Places: Locations of Book Production and Distribution since 1500* (London: British Library, 2005), 169–184.

Coleman, D. C., *The British Paper Industry, 1495–1860* (Oxford: Clarendon Press, 1958).

Coltham, S., 'English Working-class Newspapers in 1867', *Victorian Studies* XIII (1969), 159–80.

Cowan, R. W. McNair, *The Newspaper in Scotland: A Study of Its First Expansion, 1816–60* (Glasgow: G. Outram and Co., 1946).

Curran, J., 'The Press as an Agency of Social Control: An Historical Perspective', in Boyce, G., Curran, J. and Wingate, P., (eds) *Newspaper History: From the 17th Century to the Present Day* (Newton Abbott: David and Charles, 1978), 51–75.

—, 'Press History', in James Curran and Jean Seaton, *Power without Responsibility. The Press and Broadcasting in Britain* (London: Routledge, 4th edn, 1991; 1981).

Dagnall, H., *The Taxation of Paper in Great Britain, 1643–1861* (Edgware: British Association of Paper Historians, 1998).

—, 'The Taxes on Knowledge: The Excise Duty on Paper', *The Library* 20, (1998), 347–63.

Daunton, M., *Trusting Leviathan: The Politics of Taxation in Britain, 1793–1914* (Cambridge: Cambridge University Press, 2001).

don Vann, J., 'The *Times*, the *Morning Chronicle* and the *Newspaper Stamp Tax*', *Victorian Periodicals Review* 18 (1972), 36–41.

Evans, J., *The Endless Web: John Dickenson and Co, Ltd, 1804–1954* (London: Jonathan Cape, 1955).

Fenton, L., *Palmerston and The Times: Foreign Policy, the Press and Public Opinion in Mid-Victorian Britain* (London: I. B. Tauris, 2013).

Flett, K., *Chartism after 1848. The Working-class and the Politics of Radical Education* (London: Merlin Press, 2006).

Frick, S., 'Joseph Sturge and the CrimeanWar, II: The Founding of the *Morning Star*', *Journal Friends' Historical Society* 53 (1975), 335–58.

Fyfe, A., *Steam-Powered Knowledge: William Chambers and the Business of Publishing, 1820–1860* (Chicago: University of Chicago Press, 2012).

Gibb, M. A. and Beckwith, F., *Yorkshire Post* ([Leeds]; Yorkshire Conservative Paper Co., 1954).

Grant, A., *American Civil War and the British Press* (Harlow: Longman, 2000).

Griffiths, D., *Plant Here* The Standard (Basingstoke: Macmillan, 1996).

Hamer, D. A., *The Politics of Electoral Pressure: A Study in the History of Victorian Reform Agitations* (Hassocks: Harvester, 1977).

Hammond, M., *Reading, Publishing and the Formation of Literary Taste in England, 1880–1914* (Aldershot: Ashgate, 2006).

Hampton, M., 'Liberalism, the Press and the Construction of the Public Sphere: Theories of the Press in Britain 1830–1914', *Victorian Periodicals Review* 37, (2004), 72–92.

—, *Visions of the Press, 1850–1950* (Urbana: University of Illinois Press, 2004).

Harris, M., 'London's Local Newspapers: Patterns of Change in the Victorian Period', in Laurel Brake, Aled Jones and Lionel Madden (eds), *Investigating Victorian Journalism* (London: Macmillan, 1990), 104–19.

Harrison, S., *Poor Men's Guardians: A Record of the Struggles for a Democratic Newspaper Press, 1763–1973* (London: Lawrence and Wishart, 1974).

Hawkins, A., *The Forgotten Prime Minister: The 14th Earl of Derby* (2 vols; Oxford: Oxford University Press, 2007–8).

Haywood, I., *The Revolution in Popular Literature: Print, Politics and the People, 1790–1860* (Cambridge: Cambridge University Press, 2004).

Hobbs, A., 'Reading the Local Paper: Social and Cultural Functions of the Local Press in Preston, Lancashire, 1855–1900', University of Central Lancashire, DPhil thesis, 2010.

Hollis, P., *Pressure from without in Early Victorian England* (London: Edward Arnold, 1974).

Howe, A. C., *Free Trade and Liberal England* (Oxford: Clarendon Press, 1997).

Howe, A. C. and Morgan, S., *The Letters of Richard Cobden* (3 vols; Oxford: Oxford University Press, 2007–12).

Howe, E., *The London Society of Compositors* (London: Cassell, 1948).

Huch, R. K. and Ziegler, P. R., *Joseph Hume. The People's M.P.* (Philadelphia: American Philosophical Society, 1985).

Huett, L., 'Among the Unknown Public: *Household Words, All the Year Round* and the Mass-market Weekly Periodical in the Mid-nineteenth Century', in *Victorian Periodicals Review*, 38.1 (2005), 61–82.

Humphreys, A. and James, L., *G. M. W. Reynolds: Nineteenth-century Fiction, Politics and the Press* (Aldershot: Ashgate, 2008).

Jones, A., *Press, Politics and Society. A History of Journalism in Wales* (Cardiff: University of Wales Press, 1993).

—, *Powers of the Press. Newspapers, Power and Public in Nineteenth Century England* (Aldershot: Scolar, 1996).

Jordan, H. D., 'Richard Cobden and the Penny Postage: A Note on the Processes of Reform', *Victorian Studies* 8.4 (1965), 355–60.

King, A., *The London Journal* (Aldershot: Ashgate, 2004).

Kinzer, B. L., *The Ballot Question in 19th Century English Politics* (New York: Garland, 1982).

Koss, S., *The Rise and Fall of the Political Press in Britain* (2 vols; London: Hamilton, 1981, 1984).

Law, G., *Serializing Fiction in the Victorian Press* (Basingstoke: Palgrave Macmillan, 2000).

Lee, A. J., *The Origins of the Popular Press in England, 1855–1914* (London: Croom Helm, 1976).

Legg, M.-L., *Newspapers and Nationalism: The Irish Provincial Press, 1850–1892* (Dublin: Four Courts Press, 1999).

Lucas, P. J., 'Furness Newspapers in Mid-Victorian England', in Peter Bell (ed.), *Victorian Lancashire* (Newton Abbot: David and Charles, 1974), 83–102.

Lucas, R., *Lord Glenesk and the* Morning Post (London: Alston Rivers, 1910).

Matthew, H. G. C., 'Disraeli, Gladstone and the Politics of Mid-Victorian Budgets', *Historical Journal* 22.3 (1979), 615–43.

McCulloch, A., *The Feeneys of the Birmingham Post* (Birmingham: University of Birmingham Press, 2004).

McDonald, D., *Clara Collet, 1860–1948. An Educated Working Woman* (London: Woburn Press, 2004).

McIntire, M., 'Odds, Intelligence and Prophecies: Racing News in the Penny Press', *Victorian Periodicals Review* 41.4 (2008), 352–73.

Miller, H., 'Popular Petitioning and the Corn Laws, 1833–1846', *English Historical Review* 127 (2012), 882–919.

Milne, M., *The Newspapers of Northumberland and Durham. A Study of Their Progress during the 'Golden Age' of the Provincial Press* (Newcastle upon Tyne: Frank Graham, 1971).

Mitchell, S., 'The Forgotten Woman of the Period: Penny Weekly Family Magazines of the 1840s and 1850s', in M. Vicinus (ed.), *A Widening Sphere: Changing Roles of Victorian Women* (Bloomington: Indiana University Press, 1977), 29–51.

Morley, T., '"The Arcana of that Great Machine": Politicians and *The Times* in the Late 1840s', *History* lxxiii (1988).

Morison, S., *The English Newspaper, 1622–1932. An Account of the Physical Development of Journals Published in London* (Cambridge: Cambridge University Press, 1932).

Mussell, J., *The Nineteenth-Century Press in the Digital Age* (Aldershot: Ashgate, 2012).

Musson, A. E., 'The First Daily Newspapers in Lancashire', *Transactions of the Lancashire and Cheshire Antiquarian Society* 65 (1955), 104–31.

Nowell-Smith, S., *The House of Cassell* (London: Cassell, 1958).

O'Malley, P., 'Capital Accumulation and Press Freedom, 1800–1850', *Media, Culture and Society* 3 (1981), 71–83.

O'Malley, T. and Soley, C., *Regulating the Press* (London: Pluto Press, 2000).

Oats, L. and Sadler, P., 'Securing the Repeal of a Tax on "The Raw Material of Thought"', *Accounting, Business and Financial History* 17.3 (2007), 355–73.

Onslow, B., *Women of the Press in Nineteenth Century Britain* (Basingstoke: Macmillan, 2000).

Palmegiano, E. M., *Perceptions of the Press in Nineteenth-Century British Periodicals: A Bibliography* (New York: Anthem Press, 2012).

Peters, L., *Politics, Publishing and Personalities: Wrexham Newspapers, 1848–1914* (2011).

Powell, M. and Wyke, T., 'Manchester Men and Manchester Magazines: Publishing Periodicals in the Provinces in the Nineteenth Century', in John Hinks, Catherine Armstrong and Matthew Day, *Periodicals and Publishers* (2009), 161–84.

Prest, J., *Lord John Russell* (London: Macmillan, 1972).

Réamonn, S., *History of the Revenue Commissioners* (Dublin: Institute of Public Administration, 1981).

Roberts, F. D., 'Early Victorian Newspaper Editors', *Victorian Periodicals Newsletter* 14 (1972), 1–13.

—, 'More Early Victorian Newspaper Editors', *Victorian Periodicals Newsletter* 16 (1972), 15–28.

Royle, E., *Victorian Infidels* (Manchester: Manchester University Press, 1974).

—, 'The Cause of the People, the People's Charter Union and 'Moral Force' Chartism in 1848', in Joan Allen and Owen R. Ashton (eds), *Papers for the People. A Study of the Chartist Press* (London: Merlin Press, 2005), 146–67.

Rubery, M., *The Novelty of Newspaper. Victorian Fiction after the Invention of the News* (Oxford: Oxford University Press, 2009).

Saab, A. P., 'Foreign Affairs and New Tories: Disraeli, "The Press", and the Crimean War', *International History Review* 19.2 (May 1997), 286–311.

Seville, C., *Literary Copyright Reform in Early Victorian England* (Cambridge: Cambridge University Press, 1999).

Spicer, A. D., *The Paper Trade* (London: Methuen, 1907).

Splichal, S., *Principles of Publicity and Press Freedom* (Oxford: Rowman and Littlefield, 2002).

Springhall, J., 'The "Penny Dreadful" Publishing Business since 1860', *Economic History Review* 47.3 (1994), 567–84.

Steel, J., 'The "Radical" Narrative, Political Thought and Praxis', *Media History* 15.2 (2009), 221–37.

Steele, E. D., *Palmerston and Liberalism, 1855–1865* (Cambridge: Cambridge University Press, 1991).

Stratmann, L., *Cruel Deeds and Dreadful Calamities. The* Illustrated Police News, *1864–1938* (London: British Library, 2011).

Sumpter, C., 'The Cheap Press and the "Reading Crowd": Visualizing Mass Culture and Modernity, 1838–1910', *Media History* 12.3 (2006), 233–52.

Symon, J. D., *The Press and Its Story: An Account of the Birth and Development of Journalism up to the Present Day* (London: Seeley, Service and Co., 1914).

Taylor, A. D., 'Palmerston and Radicalism, 1847–1865', *Journal of British Studies* 33.2 (1994), 157–79.

Taylor, M., *The Decline of British Radicalism, 1847–1860* (Oxford: Oxford University Press, 1995).

—, *Ernest Jones, Chartism and the Romance of Politics, 1819–69* (Oxford: Oxford University Press, 2003).

Thomson, A. G., *The Paper Industry in Scotland, 1590–1861* (Edinburgh, Scottish Academic Press, 1974).

Todd, N., *The Militant Democracy. Joseph Cowen and Mid-Victorian Radicalism* (Whitley Bay: Bewick Press, 1991).

Trevelyan, G. M., *The Life of John Bright* (London: Constable, 1913).

Turner, M. J., *Independent Radicalism in Early Victorian Britain* (Westport: Praeger, 2004).

Wadsworth, A. P., *Newspaper Circulations, 1800–1954. Transactions of the Manchester Statistical Society* 4 (1954–5), 1–41.

Wasson, E. A., 'The Whigs and the Press, 1800–1850', *Parliamentary History* 25.1 (2006), 68–87.

Wiener, J. H., *The War of the Unstamped. The Movement to Repeal the British Newspaper Tax, 1830–1836* (Ithaca: Cornell University Press, 1969).

—, *The Americanization of the British Press, 1830s–1914. Speed in the Age of Transatlantic Journalism* (Basingstoke: Palgrave Macmillan, 2011).

—(ed.), *Papers for the Millions: The New Journalism in Britain, 1850s to 1914* (London: Greenwood, 1988).

Williams, F., *Dangerous Estate: The Anatomy of Newspapers* (London: Longmans Green, 1957).

Wilson, C., *First with the News: A History of W. H. Smith, 1792–1972* (London: Jonathan Cape, 1985).

Parliamentary papers

Appendices to the Reports of the Select Committee of the House of Commons on Petitions 1854–5 LIV, 1861 L. 1865 XLIV.

Copies of Correspondence since April 1853 to the Present Time, between the Solicitor and Secretary of the Board of Inland Revenue and the Publishers of Unstamped Publications, with Cases of Proceedings, &c. . . . . 1854 XXXIV (426).

Report of the Commissioners of Inland Revenue to the Treasury upon the Repeal of the Duty upon Paper (March 1860), 1860 XL (122).

Report of the Select Committee on Inland Revenue and Customs Establishments 1862 XII (370–1), 1863, VI (424).

Report of the Select Committee on Newspaper Stamps 1851 XVII (558).

Report of the Select Committee on Paper (Export Duty on Rags) 1861 XI (467).

Reports of the Commissioners of the Inland Revenue (1858–61).

Reports of the Select Committee of the House of Commons on Public Petitions (1848–61).

Return of All Correspondence on the Subject of the Registration of Newspapers and of Securities on the Publication of Newspapers and Pamphlets since June 1855, 1857–8 XXXIV (186).

Return of All Correspondence with the Solicitor of Inland Revenue Respecting the 'Stockport Free Press and Monthly Advertiser', 1854 XXXIX (504).

Return on the Paper Duty 1857–8 XXXIV (507).

Newspapers/Periodicals

Camden and Kentish Town Gazette (1866)

Financial Reformer (1858–60)

Morning Star (1856–69)

National Reformer (1868–70)

Newspaper Press (1866–70)

Parochial Critic (1867)

Printers' Register (1868–70)

Publishers' Circular (1870)

Reasoner (1846–1862)

Research for this volume also involved extensive use of a number of digital newspaper and periodical collections:

British Library Nineteenth-Century Newspapers Collection

British Newspaper Archive (extended Brightsolid collection of Nineteenth-Century Newspapers)

Manchester Guardian and *Observer* archive

New York Times Archive

Newspaper Archive (www.newspaperarchive.com)

Nineteenth-Century Serials Edition (especially *Northern Star* and *Leader*)

Past Times (Australia)

The Times Archive

Trove (New Zealand)

A significant proportion of the primary printed material comes from the Nineteenth-Century Pamphlets Collection, accessed via the JSTOR platform, or via the Internet Archive platform.

No attempt has been made in endnotes to distinguish between hardcopy, microform or digital versions.

Manuscript collections

Balliol College, University of Oxford
David Urquhart Papers

Bishopsgate Institute
Holyoake Papers

Bodleian Library Oxford
Disraeli Papers (Hughenden deposit)
Clarendon Deposit
Bradbury and Evans Correspondence

British Library
Aberdeen Papers
Bright Papers
Cobden Papers
Collet Papers
Association for the Repeal of the Taxes on Knowledge, Minute Book 1857–61
Gladstone Papers

Hargreaves Papers
Sturge Papers

Camden Archives
Association for Promoting the Repeal of the Taxes on Knowledge, Papers

Cheshire Record Office
Stanley Papers

Co-operative Union Library
Holyoake Collection

Durham University Library
Grey Papers

Hertfordshire Archives and Local Studies
John Dickinson and Co Papers

Manchester Central Library
A. H. Burgess Letter-book.
National Public Schools Association Papers
J. B. Smith Papers
George Wilson Papers

Modern Records Centre, Warwick
Provincial Typographical Society Minutes, Circulars, etc.

National Archives
Inland Revenue Papers
Lord John Russell Papers

National Library of Scotland
W. & R. Chambers Papers
Edward Ellice Papers

F. S. Oliver Papers
George Combe Papers

National Library of Wales
George Cornewall Lewis Papers
Henry Richards Papers

News UK and Ireland Limited Archive
The Times Archive

St Deiniols Library
Glynne-Gladstone Papers, including Miscellaneous Correspondence

Tyne and Wear Archives Service
Cowen Papers

University College, London
John Bright Papers
Henry Brougham Papers
Joseph Parkes Papers

University of East Anglia
Cobden Letters Transcripts

University of Hull
Thomasson Papers

University of Leeds: Brotherton Library
Glenesk–Bathurst Papers
Novello-Cowden Clarke Papers

University of Manchester: John Rylands Library
George Thompson/F. W. Chesson Papers

University of Nottingham
Newcastle Papers
Priscilla Maclaren Papers

University of Reading Special Collections
W. H. Smith Archive

University of Southampton Special Collections
Palmerston Papers

West Sussex Record Office
Cobden Papers
W. W. Mitchell Papers

York University: Borthwick Institute for Archives
Halifax Papers

Cobden Letters: A note

Extensive use has been made in this study of the letters of Richard Cobden. Most of these have been accessed via the full set of transcripts prepared by the Richard Cobden Letters Project directed by Professor Anthony Howe at the University of East Anglia. Where used, references are given to the relevant archival location. Where letters are published in the three currently available printed volumes of the *Correspondence of Richard Cobden*, reference is also given to the printed version. The full corpus of extant Cobden letters will eventually be published online via the Cobden Letters Project. I am very grateful to Professor Howe for allowing me access to his transcripts, which as well as saving considerable time and providing important links to other relevant material, made available to me letters from repositories it would have been impossible for me to visit.

Index